Seizing

the **Future**

How the Coming Revolution in Science, Technology, and Industry Will Expand the Frontiers of Human Potential and Reshape the Planet

Michael G. Zey, Ph.D.

Simon & Schuster

New York London
Toronto Sydney
Tokyo Singapore

SIMON & SCHUSTER
Rockefeller Center
1230 Avenue of the Americas
New York, New York 10020

Designed by Karolina Harris
Manufactured in the United States of America

10 9 8 7 6 5 4 3 2 1

Library of Congress Cataloging in Publication Data
Zey, Michael G.
  Seizing the future : how the coming revolution in science, technology,
and industry will expand the frontiers of human potential and reshape
the planet / Michael G. Zey.
    p. cm.
  Includes bibliographical references and index.
  1. Social prediction. 2. Economic forecasting. I. Title.
HN17.5.Z49 1994
303.49—dc20   93-31199
                                                                CIP
ISBN: 0-671-74948-X

Acknowledgments

One cannot complete a book of this size and complexity without the aid and comfort of friends, researchers, and well-wishers.

I would first like to thank the members of my research staff. Since 1991, Sheri White has spent long hours, many during two hot New Jersey summers, researching the various topics covered in this book. A former student, Sheri contributed not only her time, but her knowledge and expertise to this project. I only hope that Ms. White, herself a budding writer, remembers the joy of this project and not the arduous nature of the enterprise. I also hope that for her first book she picks a simpler topic than this one.

Samuel Proctor has worked with me on various projects since 1989. I am eternally grateful that he could find the time to help in the research. His insights into various aspects of technology and the economy were of great assistance during the writing of the book.

Nancy Witte contributed greatly to this enterprise. Her research on the family helped tremendously. I also benefitted from the conversations we had about the future of the family in America and the art and science of childrearing.

In addition, I would like to thank other researchers, including Judy Forgione and Janet Casey, who provided invaluable and time-saving assistance, including library research and summarizations. I am grateful to the other numerous researchers who gave of their time and energy to contribute to this enterprise.

I would like to thank especially Cindy Zey for her emotional support, patience, and encouragement during this project. She also provided invaluable insights into the book's structure and content and gave the book several critical readings during its evolution over the years. I truly could not have completed this project without her.

I would also like to thank Michael Aloisi for his intellectual assistance in this and other projects. Also, thanks to family and friends for their nurturance and support throughout the writing of this book and in particular F. Zey, for his constant prodding to "get back to work."

Special accolades to those who made the publishing of this book possible: Robert Asahina, the senior editor at Simon & Schuster who made the original decision to take on this project in the first place and made numerous contributions to its completion; Sarah Pinckney, whose editing, advice, and "gentle suggestions" have helped bring this project to fruition; and agents Bob Tabian and ICM's Gordon Kato.

To Jacqueline

and her generation

Contents

When mankind has once realized that its first function is to penetrate, intellectually unify, and harness the energies which surround it, in order still further to understand and master them, there will no longer be any danger of running into an upper level of its florescence.

—Teilhard de Chardin,
The Phenomenon of Man

Part One

The Promise of
a Better World

1: The Imperative of Growth

The human species is about to burst the boundaries of nature and unleash the power of its technology and human ingenuity, hurtling itself to the next stage of its evolution. In doing so, it will fulfill its destiny to expand its own capabilities and enhance the planet and the universe. Humanity is programmed, genetically perhaps, for growth and progress. Unlike other species, humanity cannot and will not stand still.

Consider for a moment just some of the changes wrought by human effort. The United States, Japan, and Europe are making plans to establish a Moon base by the year 2000 and a Mars colony by the year 2019. To compensate for the tight, crowded conditions in Tokyo and other major cities, Japan is constructing underground housing complexes and, along with Monaco, developing huge offshore artificial islands that can house up to a million people. Soon the species will construct new skyscrapers that will extend over a mile or more into the sky.

Genetic engineering will revolutionize agriculture, initiating a new era of abundance and eliminating starvation. Some of that same technology will lead to medical breakthroughs that will increase the human life span on average to 110 years. And what medicine cannot cure, the individual will: Experiments show that through biofeedback humans are learning to control their own heartbeats, brain waves, and the autonomic nervous system.

Scientists at several locations worldwide work toward perfecting cold fusion, an energy source that should extend cheap energy and national prosperity to all countries, even nations we currently consider under-developed.

These changes are unfolding at a lightning-fast rate. At first glance, these intriguing phenomena appear to be fragmentary, random events. In actuality, they form a unified trend of advancements on the technological, artistic, intellectual, and physical levels that signals a singular movement of the human species into the next stage of societal development.

In this book, we will look at the incredible positive transformation that our world is about to experience, the exponential growth anticipated by only a few but sure to be welcomed by all. We will not only discuss these incipient changes, but will explore those actions we all must take in order to ensure a smooth transition into the next era.

As we take a more in-depth look at the emerging new era, one thing will become ever so clear. The future is not what what we thought it would be. It will be much, much better!

The Macroindustrial Era: Society's Next Stage

Often people living during an era of cataclysmic change in their government, technology, or even their style of living do not comprehend that they are experiencing one of the defining moments of history. After all, how many people at the time genuinely realized that they were living through the Renaissance or the Industrial Revolution? However, the people who did suspect that their particular epoch represented something magnificent, something extraordinary, were able to not only enjoy the benefits of that period more, but contribute to and enhance that era.

We are living through one of those defining moments of human history, the onset of the Macroindustrial Era, an exciting new stage of societal development that will afford us a greater ability to control our destiny, our environment, and even our own evolution. The Macroindustrial Era has already begun in a number of areas, including the fields of manufacturing, space, medicine, and human potential.

The term *macro* refers to anything that exists on a large scale. This certainly seems an appropriate label for an era in which humanity will be involved with a wide range of activities in which it will be extending, enlarging, expanding, and enhancing not only its productive capabilities, but its presence in the universe. The second part of the term, *industrial,* refers to the fact that production of tangible objects of value will be the species' central activity in this emerging era.

A few general characteristics separate this nascent era from all previous human experience. First, this era will witness humanity extending its domination in six separate dimensions. This evolutionary change will simultaneously occur in the dimensions of time, space, quantity, quality, size, and scope (Table 1.1).

The Dimensions of the Macroindustrial Era

SPACE   The exploration and colonization of the planets; the extension of the species under the Earth's surface; penetration of inner space of matter, including molecules and cells

TIME   Expansion of the human life span through genetic engineering and nanotechnology; high-speed transportation and communication breakthroughs in robotics and time-saving technologies and devices

QUANTITY   Large-scale production, macromanufacturing, computer-integrated manufacturing; breakthroughs in new energy sources, e.g., cold and hot fusion; application of biotechnology to agriculture

QUALITY   Better foods genetically produced; advanced material revolution; enhanced standard of living and quality of life; overall improvement of physical condition through bioremediation and nanotechnology; extension of earthlike conditions to other planets through terraformation

SCOPE   Increased participation of world population in the production and consumption of goods; true global economy and the raising of global standard of living

SIZE   Enormous buildings/skyscrapers, global transportation system, macroengineering projects, such as artificial islands, man-made lakes, megairrigation projects, and space colonies

Second, in anticipating this era, we can for the first time meaningfully append the label *global* to the achievements of humankind. The successful transition to the Macroindustrial Era will require total involvement of every nation and race on the planet.

Third, and possibly most important, the fundamental relationship between humanity and environment will be permanently transformed. This Era will witness the species finally gaining control over the forces that have relentlessly buffeted it for the entire span of human existence. This enhanced ability to control and direct nature and ourselves will be a defining characteristic of the Macroindustrial Era.

During the Macroindustrial Era, we will live better, longer lives. More importantly, the very definition of "the good life" will itself be expanded.

Space

Nothing typifies the changes wrought in the Macroindustrial Era more than humanity's extension into and domination of both the inner and outer reaches of physical space.

In its quest to improve both the species and the universe, humanity has begun to challenge and conquer outer space. Even now countries are planning joint missions to Mars and the Moon to establish permanent space colonies. Robotic spacecraft missions are probing deeper into the outer regions of the Solar System and beyond.

This penetration of outer space, the increased liberation of humanity from its home planet, will be a major landmark of the emerging Macroindustrial Era. However, the extension of humankind's spatial influence is not exclusively relegated to interplanetary travel. This process includes exploring and eventually controlling the inner reaches of space.

In an effort to extend human existence to the subterranean level, humanity is beginning to burrow underneath the Earth's surface. For instance, Japan has already broken ground to construct large urban centers a hundred feet below the Earth's surface, replete with shopping centers, offices, homes, and power plants. Such macroprojects represent a total reconstitution of the concept of real estate.

The species has continued its penetration and control of the inner space of matter itself. The bright new fields such as molecular technology (dubbed nanotechnology) have enabled the human species to begin to construct materials from the bottom up, as it were. Through new techniques, we can now foresee a time when we will build materials, houses, and even new skin and body parts one atom at a time.

The new field of biotechnology has made the inner space of the human body accessible to exploration and modification. Genetic engineering enables us to enter the inner sanctum of the cell and restructure its genetic code.

In the Macroindustrial Era, there will be no region that lies beyond humanity's grasp.

Time

We have always considered time a fixed resource that we could not expand. If time is measured by the passing of certain immutable natural events, such as the changing of the seasons or the position of the sun in the sky, then this concept of time as a fixed resource is valid. However, as humans, we define time in terms of how we choose to use it. To that extent, in the Macroindustrial Era, the human species will transform this seemingly intractable dimension.

This transmutation of the time dimension can be observed in the radical expansion of the human life span. Due to breakthroughs in medicine, surgery, and biotechnology, we can now envision a human life span of over one hundred years. Although such a development does not change absolute time, it does radically increase the amount of time each individual possesses to make his or her unique contribution to society.

The species will expand time in other ways. The introduction of superfast transport will enable individuals to expend less time traveling and devote more time to accomplishing goals. The supertrain, operating at speeds of 300 miles per hour, will eliminate the concept of commuting time, allowing more time to be spent at work and leisure. NASA has on its drawing board hypersonic aircraft that will reconstitute our perception of global travel time.

We also measure time in terms of how long it takes us to accomplish tasks. To that extent, the Macroindustrial Era's technological developments will transform the dimension of time by empowering individuals and groups to achieve their objectives more quickly and with less effort. Thus they can apportion their time to other tasks. For instance, researchers are already designing robots that will be able to perform household chores, freeing up humanity's time for more important activities. In the occupational sphere, robots will perform such jobs as hamburger flipper and hospital orderly, again liberating humans from such drudge tasks so that they can use their time more productively.

Breakthroughs in communication will also liberate humanity further from the constraints of time. Through advances in fiber optics, soon employees will be able to substitute video conferencing for face-to-face meetings, saving themselves many days of travel each year. As we shall see, digitized universities and schools will eliminate the need for students to travel to the classroom, because instruction will be transmitted from classroom to the home.

Quantity

In the Macroindustrial Era, we will witness the miracle of the species finally eliminating the scarcity that has plagued it since time immemorial. A variety of sophisticated and advanced technologies will create food, resources, and products in such quantities that we will move into a new age of abundance. In the next era, overproduction may be the only problem facing businesses.

Humanity will introduce new methods of large-scale production. This macromanufacturing will be possible due to a number of mind-boggling innovations. One of these, the cybernetic factory, combines computers and robotics that turn out high quantities of goods from radios to surgical equipment. Another, magnetic machinery, involves machines whose parts never touch as they float in electromagnetic fields. This lack of friction allows them to operate at ultrahigh speeds with almost no wear.

The production of a higher quantity of goods depends on a powerful and reliable energy source. The macromanufacturing machines will have available to them energy systems that will dwarf in output current oil- and coal-generating plants. Safer and more efficient nuclear power plants will provide the power during the transition to fusion power. Both of these will exist during the Macroindustrial Era. As we shall see, countries like France and Japan have staked their futures on the improvement of nuclear fission, and others are racing to develop fusion power.

Food will also be produced in abundance. Biotechnology and genetic engineering will enable the species to produce massive amounts of food, very often in climates and soil that would have been considered totally inhospitable to the growing of any crop. Through these technologies, we will have the power to mass-produce almost any food we so desire anywhere, both vegetable and livestock.

We cannot overstate the humanitarian effect of this increase in the quantity of goods. Such advances will create a world whose population is well fed, well clothed, and comfortably housed for the first time in human history.

Quality

The very same technologies that will make possible the breakthroughs in quantity will also deliver a higher state of quality. Biotechnology will enable researchers to develop more nutritious and appetizing foods, and macroengineering will be capable of producing customized, high-quality goods with little retooling.

This enhancement of quality will come about also because of the breakthroughs in material science. Using nanotechnology, the science of rearranging atoms, scientists are now able to develop completely new materials that are more durable, resilient, and adaptable. Many people have already benefitted from early innovations in materials science applied to such products as tennis rackets, golf clubs, and clothing.

The next step may be the development of what some label "smart materials" that can actually adapt autonomously to environmental conditions. Researchers are attempting to impart to material a crude sort of intelligence by infusing artificial nerves and muscles into this inorganic material. The air force is sponsoring work on one such material, an adaptive helicopter rotor that can sense and stiffen in response to turbulence. There is also talk of developing a "stealthy" material for submarine hulls that would flex to change shape and reduce underwater turbulence.

In the Macroindustrial Era, the enhancement of the quality dimension will be facilitated by the development of a highly educated population. As we shall discover, the time draws near when science will not be the exclusive domain of academics or degreed biologists and physicists. Rather, innovations in computer and information technology will enable the nonspecialist to experiment with concepts and designs that may eventually be incorporated into the scientific knowledge base. We may all become experimenters and creators.

Scope

One of the defining characteristics of the Macroindustrial Era will be the expansion of the scope of both production and consumption to global proportions. The benefits of the Macroindustrial Era will not be limited to the West or the North, but will expand to all regions, making terms like the *Third World* or the *industrialized sector* obsolete. These countries will be equal contributors to the progress of the species.

This will occur not because sentiments of benevolence overwhelm the current group of "haves," but because the current Third World countries will become part of the global economic group as producers, workers, and consumers. The developing countries realize that in order to participate permanently in the emerging prosperity they must develop the skills that this Era requires. They can then exchange these skills on the world market for money and goods, thereby building their own base of wealth.

They are well on their way to accomplishing this goal. In terms of sheer numbers, the developing countries now have the work force that can contribute to the development of the human species. Although the worldwide work force is growing dramatically, from 1.5 billion people in 1970 to an estimated 2.7 billion by the year 2000, the lion's share of that increase is accounted for by growth in countries like China, India, Indonesia, Brazil, Pakistan, Thailand, Mexico, and South Korea. The workers in the developing countries will be far younger than those in the United States, Japan, Germany, and the United Kingdom.

These new workers from the developing regions are skilled and educated. Now, the developing countries such as Singapore, Hong Kong, and Eastern bloc countries like Hungary and Poland are scoring well ahead of the United States and Canada on biology, chemistry, and physics standardized tests. In other words, the developing countries are quickly mastering the skills needed in the Macroindustrial Era.

In fact, many of these countries' citizens are already fueling the economic engine of the West. Companies like Bell Laboratories and Schering-Plough are as likely to recruit physicists or computer specialists from India or Taiwan as from the United States, and New York hospitals must advertise in Ireland and the Philippines to recruit desperately needed skilled nurses.

There has been a change from the Industrial Era, when the Third World and developing regions solely provided low-skilled agricultural and factory labor, to the current era in which they contribute to the creation of knowledge. As an example, today India graduates more than 400,000 engineers a year, a higher number than any other English-speaking country.

One other factor that will help enlarge the scope of production and consumption is the increasing worldwide expectations about the good life, which is translating into global pressure to increase the standard of living. Emerging nations, having caught "progress fever," will no longer be denied what they perceive as their piece of an ever-growing pie. In other words, the demand for consumer goods has spread throughout the globe. All that is needed is a more prosperous Third World with the purchasing power to buy Western goods. American and European manufacturers would benefit tremendously from a truly global consumer market that includes Asia, South America, and Africa. The automobile industry, for one, would experience exponential growth. Currently, car ownership worldwide is no larger than 400 million, at most one-tenth of the world's population. Over half of these owners live in the United States, and the rest, in the industrialized countries.

As the emerging era expands the scope of production, that is, as these emerging countries reach prosperity, the faster they will enter the car-buying market. Ford, General Motors, and Toyota would quintuple sales in a very short time.

In truth, as we enlarge the scope of prosperity, production, and consumption in the Macroindustrial Era, we can for the first time in history meaningfully speak of the global economy.

Size

Nothing stands as a trademark of the Macroindustrial Era more than the redefinition of the concept of size. Many of the projects humanity will embark on in the Macroindustrial Era will inspire awe if for no other reason than their sheer size.

Enlarging the size of objects, including buildings, bridges, and cities, has often symbolized the onset of new eras. The skyscrapers of the early twentieth century signaled the emergence of a new era of technological proficiency. Skyscrapers have an incredible symbolic value: They symbolize humankind's, or a specific nation's, dominance over the laws of nature, as they seemingly point to heaven and bring us that much closer to the cosmos.

As if to confirm the fact that the torch of progress has been passed to the Macroindustrial generation, we continue to build larger skyscrapers. In the offing is the Houston Tower, 1.3 miles high, and the 2500-foot World Trade Center in Chicago, standing proud at 210 stories high. They incorporate wholly new architectural principles that make them wind and earthquake resistant.

While skyscrapers are paeans to an earlier era, other projects will define the new one. On the drawing board are irrigation projects that move bodies of water so large that their translocation will lead to the creation of new lakes. Also, the species is creating new land masses where none existed before. Countries like Japan and Monaco are extending their limited geography by building artificial islands in the middle of oceans and lakes that can accommodate up to 1 million inhabitants.

The Macroindustrial obsession with size is galvanizing architects to develop structures that are part building, part city. In fact, several Japanese corporations are developing what some term "city-buildings" in many different shapes and forms. One example of these new structures is a volcano-shaped city inspired by Japan's Mount Fuji. The one-building city would stretch 2.5 miles high, accommodate up to 700,000 people, and feature nature and space observatories, energy plants, and a resort. The inhabitants on the top levels would be looking down at the clouds below.

Such city-buildings are meant to be totally self-sufficient, serving both residential and business needs. These cities can be located anywhere—on land, artificially created islands, and in one case on a boat. The United States-based World City Corporation has instituted a project to construct what it calls the *Phoenix World City*, a cruise ship housing more than 5000 passengers, several medium-rise apartment units, and businesses. Construction will begin on this floating city in 1994 and will be completed around 1997. Takena, a Japanese construction firm, has proposed to build Sky City 1000 in Tokyo. Despite its location, Sky City will truly be a city in itself, towering 3300 feet, or 300 stories high, sitting on a 2000-acre base, and housing 10,000 residences. The interior view of Sky City 1000 reveals that the superbuilding has fourteen shelflike sections, each with its own transportation, water supply, schools, stores, offices, and a central park. The design brings fresh air and sunshine to all sections, even those in the middle of the building.

Possibly nothing will more characterize the redefinition of size in this new era than the projects planned as part of the nascent international space program. Obviously, building space stations the size of football fields and establishing space cities on the Moon and Mars will establish new standards for the dimension of size.

As we will discover, these pale by comparison to the process of terraformation. This novel concept is one in which the species attempts to transform the atmosphere and living environment of planets and spheres so that they closely approximate Earth. By doing so we can establish permanent colonies throughout the Solar System and eventually the galaxy.

The Macroindustrial redefinition of size will occur in a second direction. It is perhaps indicative of the evolving consciousness of the human species that we feel compelled to test the frontiers not only of the colossal, but also the minuscule. As part of the nanotechnology revolution referred to previously, the species will develop computers, assemblers, and machine parts the size of atoms and molecules. They will be used in construction of everything from spaceships to body parts, and may even play a role in cleaning toxic wastes and polluted oceans.

One fact will become increasingly obvious as we explore this exciting new epoch of human development: In the Macroindustrial Era, the primary emphasis will be on the production of material goods and the accomplishment of tangible projects and goals. The enhancement of the quality of human life will occur as a direct effect of the increase in the quantity and quality of goods, the enlargement of the scope of these goods' production and distribution, and the expansion of humanity into inner and outer space.

The onset of the Macroindustrial Era rings the deathknell for the theory, popular since the 1970s, that we will soon be living in a "postindustrial society" or an information-based economy. The postindustrial myth languished in academic circles until Alvin Toffler's book *The Third Wave* was published in the late 1970s. When John Naisbitt's book *Megatrends* became the runaway best-seller of the early to middle 1980s, the myth received the official imprimatur of both government policymakers and corporate leaders.

Toffler proclaimed that we were moving out of what he labeled the "second wave" of production, industrialization. He also claimed that we should recognize that the human species no longer must produce "coal, rail, textiles, steel, autos, rubber, machine tool manufacturing." We must overcome our second wave obsession with bigness and growth, all part of what Toffler labeled *maximization*, and work toward a world in which large-scale production and energy systems are eliminated. The home will be the new worksite, and centralized energy grids will become a remnant of a bygone era.

John Naisbitt extended the postindustrial myth to its logical limits. He decided that because so many people were employed in information work, we must be moving into a society whose major function is the production of information. To prove his thesis, Naisbitt quite creatively reinterpreted every occupation, regardless of whether it involved production of goods or services, as primarily an information job. By his criteria, bankers, engineers, and robotics designers could be lumped with bona fide information specialists like teachers and librarians.

Information society mythologists even interpreted the space program as essentially an information endeavor. In discussing the space shuttle program, Naisbitt wrote that this mission has "a lot more to do with the globalized information economy than it ever will have to do with space exploration." The conceptualization is so circumscribed that instead of picturing satellites as bridges to the heavens, as launching pads to expansion and exploration, he portrays them as a solid ring of metal further entrapping us on our planet, a belt around the Earth that supresses human endeavor and locks us in. As Naisbitt said, "Satellites have turned the earth inward, upon itself."

It is true that ideas and information play a key role in the creation and production of goods. However, that does not imply that we have become an information society whose raison d'être is the production and transmission of information.

Western society is now paying for this critical intellectual mistake, for we now see that the acceptance of the concept of the "age of information" by business, government, and the general public tragically impacted real growth.

Lester Thurow, in his recent book on international economic competition—*Head to Head: Japan, Europe, America—Who Will Prevail?* —illustrates this point. He demonstrates that the United States has fallen into a weakened economic position due to the fact that it permitted the demise of such industries as commercial aircraft, textiles, steel, automobiles, and machine tools, the very sectors Toffler deemed obsolete. Its productivity growth, which had hurtled forward at a 3 percent rate for 150 years, grew only 1.2 percent per year in the 1980s.

Although naming the usual culprits such as lagging investments in plant, equipment, research and development, and education, he places most blame on the growth of white-collar bureaucracies. As Thurow points out, the United States made more investments in office technology than any country in the 1980s, but instead of higher productivity, the country got more information and huge bureaucracies to produce and disseminate it.

He paints a bleak picture of information bureaucracies endlessly generating data—quarterly accounting reports become daily reports, and on-line information is the rule of the day. And although there is no evidence that our new information wizards are increasing productivity, white-collar employment continues to grow faster than output.

In the United States and elsewhere, this services/information revolution has had a pernicious economic impact on individual citizens. Between 1979 and 1992, America has seen a dramatic increase in jobs in the services, finance, retail, and governmental sectors and has experienced a simultaneous decrease in jobs such as construction, manufacturing, and mining. The sectors upon which nations' fortunes depend, namely, those involved in real physical production of goods, are slowly being replaced by services that support the truly productive sectors. The comparative wage rates of each sector reflect its ultimate importance to society: In 1992, the average wage earner in manufacturing industries made $455 per week; the average retail worker made $200 per week; the average mining job paid $630 dollars per week; real estate and bank jobs paid $373 per week.

Can we deduce from these statistics that the market economy has judged manufacturing and mining activity to be twice as valuable as services jobs? We have only to look at how incomes have stalled in the United States since 1973 to realize the impact of the services revolution on the average worker. In the period 1948 to 1973, in a U.S. economy based on the production of goods such as automobiles, machinery, and houses, the average worker's salary doubled. That is, the average worker in 1973 could buy twice as much as a 1948 worker. Since 1973, however, wages have flattened—the worker today can buy no more than could the worker in 1973. Sadly, the average household has been able to maintain its standard of living only by working more hours. Family buying power has remained stable since 1973 only because millions of wives and mothers have entered the work force and added their salaries to the net family wage.

This economic stagnation occurred as the economy followed the false god of information and services. Because the market for jobs related to these sectors is just not as strong as the market for steel, timber, automobiles, and houses, workers in these fields will see their standard of living fall.

Fortunately, signs abound of a growing awareness that only by returning to an enhanced manufacturing base can the United States achieve real economic growth. Throughout the 1980s, the Berkeley Roundtable on the International Economy, through its research and conferences, became a major proponent of the view that the United

States must recover its manufacturing base or become a second-rate nation. It produced a major statement summarizing its position, entitled simply *Manufacturing Matters*. By 1992, even *Business Week* agreed that "it ain't a recovery until the factories hum."

The coming era is not postindustrial, geared toward the production of services and information. These sectors will exist but as supports for the main mission of the Macroindustrial Era—production of goods, advances in medicine, the physical extension of the human species in time and space. Any other path leads to economic and social decline.

As we shall see, the rules of the game have not really changed for the last 500 years.

Why Civilizations Succeed

Although the Macroindustrial Era represents a major leap of the human species in terms of its control over time, space, and the other dimensions discussed, it is also a continuation of a trend that started several centuries ago.

The roots of this trend are decidedly Western. Six hundred years ago, any observer would be hard put to predict that of all societies, western Europe's would be the one to lead the world into the future. China, India, and the Islamic world were more advanced than Europe. Why, then, did France, England, Spain, and eventually America come to dominate the globe and shape its future?

Although many analysts have attempted to explain the West's success in terms of its technology, science, natural resources, or geographic location, the ultimate answer lies in its culture and belief system.

The West succeeded because it envisioned the world as one in which improvement is possible and growth inevitable. In other words, the West evolved a cultural system based around the concept of progress. When the West embraced the concept of progress and made it the core value of its culture, it established the conditions for its domination of the globe and of nature itself.

Progress can be understood as an advancement, from inferior to superior, on several different levels. First, it is a gradual and cumulative improvement in knowledge—new information, data, theory, and facts —that helps the species cope with problems presented by nature or by the species itself. Second, it is the improvement in humanity's moral or spiritual condition on Earth. Third, the material condition advances—

we become richer, live longer, have greater access to more sophisticated goods and services.

To believe in progress is to assume that mankind has advanced in the past from some lesser state and will continue to advance in the foreseeable future.

Robert Nisbet, a leading theorist in this area, claims that progress is a way of looking at the world that represents a clear break from earlier ways of thinking. According to Nisbet, a society that believes in progress accepts the worth of economic and technological growth, has faith in reason and in the kind of scientific and scholarly knowledge that can come from reason alone and believes in the inherent value of life on this earth.

In his insightful monumental tome *The History of the Idea of Progress,* Nisbet traces the many roots of the Western idea of progress as far back as Greco-Roman culture. Its first modern articulation appears in the writings of St. Augustine, who applied the Christian concept of the perfectibility of people to the whole of human history.

The concept of progress permeates Western thought, reflected in the writings of such giants as Isaac Newton, Hegel, Karl Marx, Thomas Jefferson, Benjamin Franklin, Charles Darwin, and every major thinker and leader in the United States from the Founding Fathers on. Nisbet locates the more advanced thinking on progress and growth in the twentieth century Jesuit visionary Teilhard de Chardin, who synthesized his insights into anthropology, technology, and evolution into a unique theory of human progress.

In the 1400s, the West began to pull ahead of the rest of humanity in several areas, including science, technology, weaponry, and exploration. Just as the West's advancement was precipitated by its belief in the inevitability of progress, other societies declined because of the shackles placed on them by their own world views, which either did not predispose them toward accepting the idea of progress or simply did not include the concept at all.

China was the world's most advanced civilization in the fifteenth century, but the increasingly influential Confucian philosophy eventually sabotaged China's dominant world influence. Up to that time, China had a thriving maritime culture whose ships had sailed to Africa and through the Persian Gulf and Indian Ocean. However, Confucianism scorned both military and commercial activities. As Confucianism tightened its hold on China's culture and government, this nation's bureaucratic state passed laws prohibiting the building of ocean-going ships. From the fifteenth century onward, China insulated itself, thereby missing the entire era of global modernization and entering into a five-century decline.

India's culture scorned individual achievement and discouraged the very values the West promoted as part of its progress ethos—science, personal gain, national ambition, and the quest for glory. India's cultural biases made it exceedingly vulnerable to the imperial tendencies of the British.

The story of Islam and the gradual deterioration of the Arab world's position vis-à-vis the West is the most revealing portrayal of the effect of culture on a nation's material fortunes. Islam certainly had the spirit for expansion—its conquests included the Middle East, North Africa, and Spain. Certainly through the twelfth century, Islamic countries were far ahead of the West in manufacturing, commerce, weaponry, and shipbuilding.

However, the West's ethos of progress encouraged it to acquire a cultural trait that escaped the Moslems, the love of science. Kurt Mendelssohn, in his book *The Secret of Western Domination*, speaks of how the Western countries used the scientific method to dominate the world eventually. Science, of course, spawned among other things the technology used in exploration and war. It is no mere coincidence that just at the time that Spain's shipbuilding technology led to its discovery of the New World, she also developed the weaponry to expel the Moslems from her shores.

One other idea helped the West advance over other civilizations. That concept, the idea of irreversible time, changed the way the West thought about history, development, growth, and the human condition in general.

To understand how revolutionary this change was, we must understand the way most civilizations envisioned the flow of time. Most societies saw time as essentially cyclical—events, lives, and human history itself have a beginning, end, and then a return to the beginning again. Some picture this process in terms of birth, growth, disease, death, and rebirth. Various cultures and religions, including the Hindus, Buddhists, and some Greek mythologies maintained this picture of reality.

It is understandable that cyclical thinking would be the most natural way for early people to conceptualize time. After all, such a concept reflects the logic of everyday life. Day turns to night and then back to day. The seasons have a marked regularity, and human life itself is composed of birth, adulthood, old age, and then death. Some cultures even superimposed the concept of the endless cycle onto human life, claiming that humans can become reincarnated through successive lifetimes.

Although cyclical thinking comforts the human species with the illusion of regularity and predictability, it became a prime obstacle to the species' growth and advancement. Societies endowed human history itself with the same cyclical property, so that they spoke of every society, including their own, as having a beginning and end. Absent from this concept is the idea of continual improvement over time.

Many such societies became obsessed with the idea of a long-lost "golden age," which they continuously referred to in their writing and were forever trying to regain. Ironically, such golden ages themselves were perceived as stages in a cycle, which even if attained would by necessity deteriorate, marking the beginning of a new cycle.

Shackled with mind-sets that precluded the notion of continuous human advancement, most ancient societies could not progress beyond a certain point. A culture that induces all individuals to conceptualize the flow of time in terms of recurring cycles will prevent those individuals from thinking in terms of eternal, continuous linear progress.

To Augustine, a cyclical theory of history was abhorrent. Writing in the early fifth century, Augustine proclaimed the cyclical theory of astrologers as lies; these men taught that the pattern of events was repetitive, determined by the returning cycles of celestial arrangement. In his classic *The City of God*, Augustine fired a succession of broadsides at the pagan theory of cycles, boldly proclaiming that Christianity's concept of the individual striving for perfection, an omega point, was the true picture of reality.

Today, the idea of progress is so ingrained in the Western psychological and ideological framework that most Westerners would find it difficult to envision the world operating along any other principle. They inherently believe that each successive era surpasses the achievements of the last and that this process will continue indefinitely into the future.

Before we can achieve true success, we must believe that progress is inevitable. Such a belief is as powerful a determinant of success as any physical ability or intellectual aptitude. As we have seen, history attests to the fact that any society that maintains the belief in progress will have a better chance of achieving its goals than a society without it.

As other nation's have come to understand the effect of such a concept on the West's success, they, too, have internalized the concept of progress and made it their own!

The Imperative of Growth

Having reached its current lofty point of development, the species will not choose to regress. The fact that the species is forging its way en masse into the Macroindustrial Era proves that our need to grow is almost a genetically based predisposition. The species innately understands there can be no turning back on the road of progress.

However, no outside force guarantees the continued progress of the human species, nor does anything mandate that the human species must even continue to exist. In fact, history is littered with races and civilizations that have disappeared without a trace. So, too, could the human species. There is no guarantee that the human species will survive even if we posit, as many have, a special purpose to the species' existence.

Therefore, the species innately comprehends that it must engage in purposive actions in order to maintain its level of growth and progress. Humanity's future is conditioned by what I call the Imperative of Growth, a principle I will herewith describe along with its several corollaries.

The Imperative of Growth states that in order to survive, any nation, indeed, the human race, must grow, both materially and intellectually. The Macroindustrial Era represents growth in the areas of both technology and human development, a natural stage in the evolution of the species' continued extension of its control over itself and its environment. Although 5 billion strong, our continued existence depends on our ability to continue the progress we have been making at higher and higher levels.

Systems, whether organizations, societies, or cells, have three basic directions in which to move. They can grow, decline, or temporarily reside in a state of equilibrium. These are the choices. Choosing any alternative to growth, for instance, stabilization of production/consumption through zero-growth policies, could have alarmingly pernicious side effects, including extinction.

This imperative, based on certain immutable tendencies of systems and organisms, becomes immediately apparent once articulated. It will become ever clearer as we now explore the corollaries of the Imperative of Growth (Table 1.2).

The Imperative of Growth

PRINCIPLE

In order to survive, all nations, societies, and groups must continue to grow and progress, both materially and intellectually.

COROLLARY 1

Each successive level of progress contains the seeds for greater growth.

COROLLARY 2

When a system pursues growth, not only will it progress along the lines it intended, but it will expand the very concept of its progress and growth.

COROLLARY 3

Growth contains the solutions to the problems it produces.

COROLLARY 4

Each member either contributes, or has the potential to contribute, more to the system than he or she consumes.

COROLLARY 5

A society remains in a state of equilibrium only temporarily, from which point it eithers grows or declines.

COROLLARY 6

If the society chooses not to grow, it will decline and possibly disappear either through internal disintegration or absorption by other nations or groups.

First, each successive level of progress contains seeds for greater growth. As society builds machines and automated systems to do the grunt work of production, people can spend more time to study, research, and improve their minds. Technology thus liberates human beings so they can pursue the scientific and experimental cogitation necessary for the discoveries and inventions that lead to higher levels of societal progress.

The building of wealth allows the society to divert some of its workers into nonmarket but equally productive endeavors, such as family-centered activity. A society like Japan that has reached the stage of development in which it can afford to maintain a stable family unit, with its members having the time to nurture and educate their children, has established a necessary condition for moving into the next level of progress.

The second corollary of this principle states that when the system pursues growth, not only will it progress along the lines that it intended, but the very concept of progress and growth becomes expanded. Our concept of "maximal growth" in one era becomes replaced by a more expansive concept in the next. At the turn of the century, even social observers familiar with state-of-the-art technology could not predict that we would eventually visit the Moon, develop resistance to diseases through vaccines, or communicate through radio waves. By pursuing their visions of growth at the time, though, those people helped propel the species into the world we see today.

So, too, in the Macroindustrial Era, will human control over nature and itself reach an unprecedented level, but those of us living through this era will have only a hint of how the advances of this new era will affect human progress in the future.

This explains the difficulty in planning for growth—we never know where growth will take us. Once we discover new capacities, both technological and human, we are set off in novel directions, crossing boundaries and exploring frontiers we never thought existed. The Spanish explored the New World in order to extract natural resources such as gold from the Earth and spread Christianity. Many English settlements were established by people simply trying to escape religious intolerance. None could have guessed that their expression of progress circa 1600 would lead to the birth of an independent nation that became the crucible for personal liberation and technological innovation.

The fact that progress itself leads to new definitions of human growth also explains the West's faith in progress. Our accomplishments consistently exceed our wildest dreams. Regardless of the stated purpose of a technology, the applications usually exceed such purposes. The automobile became important as a means of redistributing the population from cities to the suburbs; the discovery of the steam engine revolutionized industry and the very concept of abundance.

Third, growth itself contains the solutions to the problems it produces. Supporting this principle is the World Bank's 1992 report "Development and the Environment," which blatantly states that growth is a powerful antidote to a number of ills plaguing Third World countries, including the pollution that growth supposedly generates. The report thus contends that eliminating poverty should remain the top goal of world policymakers.

Although economic growth can initially lead to such problems as pollution and waste, the resulting prosperity also facilitates the developments of technologies that lead to cleaner air and water. In fact, once a nation's per capita income rises to about $4000 in 1993 dollars, it produces less of some pollutants per capita, mainly due to the fact that it can afford technology like catalytic converters and sewage systems that treat a variety of wastes.

According to Norio Yamamoto, research director of the Mitsubishi Research Institute, "We consider any kind of environmental damage to result from mismanagement of the economy." He claims that the pollution problems of poorer regions such as Eastern Europe can be traced to their economic woes. Hence, he concludes that in order to ensure environmental safety "we need a sound economy on a global basis."

So the answer to pollution, the supposed outgrowth of progress, ought to be more economic growth. The World Bank estimated that every dollar invested in developing countries will grow to $100 in fifty years. As that happens, these countries can take all the necessary steps to invest in pollution-free cars, catalytic converters, and other pollution-free technologies, such as the cleanest of all energy sources, nuclear power.

Japan has become a leading proponent of the practice of utilizing sophisticated technology to cure the ills of industrialization. In 1970, Japan enacted tough antipollution laws that induced Japanese industry to invest in smokestack scrubbers and water purification devices. Japan now has become an exporter of such technologies. It showed up at the June 1992 Earth Summit in Rio di Janeiro, Brazil, pledging to fill international coffers with $7.7 billion over the next five years for a variety of environmental projects. Not surprisingly, Japan's championing of the technological solution to industrialization's problems made it the star of the summit.

Third-corollary reasoning has led Japan to embark on an ambitious program of nuclear power plant construction. Because nuclear power generates no carbon dioxide, the leading greenhouse gas, the Japanese contend that they are pursuing the most environmentally sound energy policy by constructing forty nuclear power plants, including the fast breeder reactor, in their country over the next twenty-five years.

One of the clearest examples of the third corollary of the Imperative of Growth is the employment of advanced biotechnology to eliminate toxic waste. Advanced technology has led to the development of what is referred to as bioremediation to combat wastes and impurities that poison water supplies. Bioremediation utilizes living organisms to clean up waste, even entire contaminated sites—such microorganisms literally eat hazardous materials.

Companies now use such bacteria to "eat" oil spills, and other contaminants in the air, in the sea, or on land. In the United States, demand for bioremediation products and services will increase 16 percent each year, reaching $230 million in 1995. In the near future, biotechnology and genetic splicing will produce a "superbug" with a ravenous appetite for the most hazardous and poisonous chemicals that pollute our air, soil, and water.

According to the American Academy of Microbiology, the types and classes of synthetic chemicals that can be neutralized by bioremediation will increase dramatically. For instance, until recently, hydrochlorofluorocarbons, or HCFCs, one of the chemical classes that supposedly destroy the ozone layer, were considered to be nonbiodegradable. However, scientists at Envirogen, a New Jersey-based biotechnology firm, have discovered microbes that render HCFCs harmless. Therefore, such organisms can be used to treat HCFC waste and by-products before they are released into the atmosphere.

The human imagination knows no bounds when it applies itself to the problems of pollution and industrial waste. In fact, a whole new field, geoengineering, has evolved to tackle these environmental conundrums. On the drawing board sit imaginative plans such as that of Melvin Prueitt, a researcher at Los Alamos National Laboratory. His scheme involves cleaning the air of Los Angeles with ninety-five towers that utilize a complex technology to suck in L.A.'s impure air, "scrubbing" it, and releasing clean air back into the city's atmosphere. He claims that this method alone could clean and recycle half of L.A.'s air daily.

Princeton University professor Thomas H. Stix possesses an even bolder plan. He suggests that laser beams strung across mountain passes could "process" the Earth's atmosphere: The beams would break up chlorofluorocarbons before they reach the stratosphere. Other proposals suggest "injecting" 50,000 tons of propane into the stratosphere to reduce ozone loss.

These examples demonstrate that even if growth does initially cause society some environmental problems, the solution must be more, not less, growth. Technology and research, both elements of progress, become the solutions to the negative byproducts of progress. As some environmentalists and biologists stated in a recent *Harper's* magazine article, "humanity is the only savior of the environment."

The fourth corollary states that each unit or actor either contributes or has the potential to contribute to the system more than it consumes. This actually leads to an exponential contribution of each member of the system. This property differentiates human systems from other group structures. In human society, the whole is greater than the sum of its parts.

Each individual with a productive idea can communicate his or her ideas not just to one other person, but to millions at a time. With the growth of modern electronics, including computer networking, each individual's power to contribute beyond his or her immediate environment grows.

It is a historical truism that the denser the population, the greater the exchanges of ideas, goods, and services; hence the importance of cities and large universities in the development of civilization. They stimulated the mind and fostered the creativity of their inhabitants by increasing the total amount of human interface.

This corollary also reveals the importance of the enhancement of *scope* in the Macroindustrial Era. The dimension of scope refers to the increased inclusion of more individuals into the global production/consumption network. By including in the international scientific and academic dialogue Indians, Africans, and Third Worlders, we increase the chance of key contributions by people whose ideas and inventions may never have reached the rest of the world.

Conversely, each individual upon withdrawing from the system, through migration, death, or other means, implies a loss greater than one. The exodus of German Jewish physicists from Germany in the 1930s cost that country more than the total number of such exiles would suggest. When they left, so did the entire country's potential for developing a superweapon such as the atomic bomb. Hence, each reduction in individual contributors must be seen as a system loss.

The fifth corollary of the Imperative of Growth claims that a society can remain in a state of equilibrium only temporarily. In reality, a society seemingly in a phase where it neither improves nor regresses is actually in a transition to either growth or decline.

Such periods easily seduce their contemporaries into a false sense of security, that their institutions will last forever, they have all the science they need, and there are no more challenges. In fact, during such periods some imagine that they have reached their "golden age," perhaps even the "end of history." During such periods of supposed equilibrium, the population ceases to prepare itself for new challenges and becomes risk averse. Importantly, they reject the idea that growth and progress are necessary for their survival.

The sixth corollary evolves from the fifth. If the system chooses not to grow, it will decline and eventually disappear, either because other organisms or systems overtake it or because it is impossible to maintain itself even at static levels without in some way deteriorating. This is the Law of Spiraling Regression.

It is indeed a curiosity of the late-twentieth-century culture that this truism has been ignored. In the morass of claims about the risks of technological growth and its impact on the ecosystem, the mainstream media and orthodox academics have decided not to consider what harm the full pursuance of zero growth or non growth might inflict on the sociotechnical system, which includes our technological infrastructure, culture, and standard of living.

In fact, during the 1980s and 1990s, legislation and mandates prohibiting growth have become so pervasive that some countries may experience a validation of this sixth corollary of the principle of the Imperative of Growth.

Some examples will suffice. Most nations have become unwilling to further drill for oil off their shores, effectively mandating a reduction in the amount of oil available to a growing Macroindustrial Era society. The global warming furor, although increasingly discredited in scientific circles, is tempting nations to reduce energy output and throughput and thereby cut back their standard of living. In the United States, the Clean Air Act of 1990 has an enormous potential to demonstrate how tampering with the sociotechnical system can force that system to disassemble.

The Clean Air Act of 1990 requires states to adopt strict clean air policies over the next several years. Although everyone supports the concept of clean air (as well as motherhood or apple pie, for that matter), the way that this particular bill is worded provides a splendid example of the potential for sociotechnical disaster.

The 1990 Clean Air Act was supposed to close loopholes in the 1970 Clean Air Act and increase enforcement and penalties for noncompliance severely. The act specifically mandates a 15 percent reduction in pollution in the areas now classified as suffering from "severe" pollution. It also calls for strict limitations on emissions of pollutants from stationary sources like factories and power plants. It also requires the use of cleaner-burning fuels and low-emission automobiles.

The bill gives the federal government enormous power, so much so that some fear it could someday transform the government into an omnipotent Leviathan. In this case the U.S. government can withhold hundreds of millions of dollars in federal transportation aid from states not meeting the above standards.

According to Walter Rand, a Democratic state senator from New Jersey, where federal law has designated eighteen of the state's twenty-one counties as "severe" ozone pollution areas, "we are going to be changing the habits of a culture."

The act requires employers with more than one hundred employees at a given physical location to increase the average occupancy of vehicles arriving at the work site by 25 percent. As Nancy Wittenberg, the director of the Office of Energy in New Jersey, admits, "it puts the employer in a position of having to start meddling with the way his employees get to work. Right now, the issue of where you live or how you get there doesn't even come up. But all of a sudden, the employer has to be concerned."

Car traffic in general will be reduced. Autonomous automobile travel has been one of the building blocks of industrial growth and will be needed in the Macroindustrial Era. The automobile has allowed companies to move closer to markets, water supplies, and needed natural resources, and has facilitated the diffusion of the population across the country and the globe. Trucking has made the national and international dispersal of goods possible. Cities can receive goods from any part of the country. The car has afforded individuals the freedom to experience the new, to learn, to expand.

All of these factors make the automobile key to human progress. The Clean Air Act of 1990 offers no suggestions on how to replace the automobile or its benefits.

In so doing, society will feel the full brunt of spiraling regression. By restricting truck traffic the act will lead to a reduction in quantity and quality of food delivered to the cities and probably eliminate the servicing of many outlying areas. Some people will be pressured to bicycle to work so that the employer can meet the national clean air standards. In Los Angeles, they already envision people riding to their jobs huffing and puffing on their bicycles, arriving fatigued and overstressed.

Their offices may not be an oasis of comfort. Since the Clean Air Act mandates that states reduce the use of chlorofluorocarbons, the use of office air-conditioning will be restricted. In normal times, when air-conditioning malfunctions, the workers are sent home. In the world of the Clean Air Act, the warm office will be seen as a normal working condition.

These workers' productivity will decline, and their companies output will suffer. If this scenario is replicated in offices and factories throughout the nation, spiraling regression will ensue. As its productivity sharply declines, the United States will become vulnerable to economic domination by countries who adhere to the Imperative of Growth.

Countries must heed the Imperative of Growth when passing legislation and engaging in activities that can influence their future. Quite clearly the Macroindustrial Era represents a progressive step for the human species. In this era, the species moves into ever higher forms of complexity in its technological, sociological, and intellectual achievements. According to the Imperative of Growth, any country heeding this imperative will most definitely thrive over the next decades, but any society haphazardly passing antigrowth legislation does so at its own peril.

The Siren Call of Sustainable Development

A theory that has been posited as a more balanced approach to species growth and progress is that of sustainable development. A core organizing principle at the 1992 United Nations Conference on Environment and Development held in Rio de Janeiro, the theory is usually presented as a middle-ground theory that seeks to support material growth while duly recognizing environmental requirements.

However, a closer look at the underlying philosophy behind this new logo reveals why this new model of the global future is an overwhelming favorite among proponents of zero growth. At its core, this model pits the growth of humankind against the environment, directly blaming human prosperity for the problem of enviromental degradation.

Much of the sustainable development theory is based on the work of Donella and Dennis Meadows. It was their 1972 computer model that became the basis for their best-selling book *Limits to Growth* and provided the "facts" for the policy group the Club of Rome's famous dicta concerning the depletion of the world's resources. Using data on population growth and resource utilization, the Meadowses predicted that the world would experience several major catastrophes throughout the 1970s. The world would choke on its own pollution, run out of petroleum and other materials, and suffer mass starvation. Although practically every one of their predictions was subsequently proven incorrect, policymakers, academics, and many scientists swallowed their projections whole.

Although they incorrectly predicted the first catastrophe of the 1970s, the Meadowses have somehow become emboldened to predict our next environmental crisis in their 1992 book, *Beyond the Limits: Confronting Global Collapse, Envisioning a Sustainable Future.* Published right before the Rio de Janeiro global environmental summit, the book was widely quoted by government leaders and activists attending the conference. Importantly, it provided the mass media a conceptual theme on which to focus, the idea of sustainable development.

The Meadowses claim that the fact that over the last twenty years the global population has leaped 66 percent should alert us to impending disaster. They recite a litany of problems caused by the human species, including the greenhouse effect, mass starvation, and "global warming." Not once do they cite the scientific debates surrounding such issues, nor do they mention the political and economic conditions that might lead to shortages of food and other resources. They also conveniently ignore the fact that during the period in question world economic output nearly doubled.

Their solution to these problems is the adoption of the sustainable development model by all governments. This would involve stabilizing population, preferably through government-induced population control methods, and restraining consumption. The latter would be accomplished by reducing the number of gas-guzzling cars, promoting an information-based economy, and encouraging green consumption.

The way such a concept is introduced to the public serves as a testimony to modern marketing techniques. We as a society have to "develop" instead of grow, much like a library that retains the same number of volumes but improves itself by replacing worn-out books. The sustainable development economy would concentrate on an improved quality of life and educational and health system. Although such a system seems benign, a deeper examination of the production and consumption aspects of such a system reveals a bone-chilling austerity.

According to this model, in order to eradicate the harmful effects of human activity, the species would have to reduce its total use of resources by 80 percent. Importantly, world output of consumer goods per capita would be stabilized at a level comparable to that of Western Europe in 1990 and below that of the U.S. 1990 consumption level. In other words, the sustainable development requires that the world forever live below the standards of 1990 America.

Some even see this 1990 cutoff date for our standard of living as a smoke screeen. The Meadowses and other proponents of zero growth quietly wish that the public would seriously consider preindustrial society a valid model for the future. Unfortunately, few members of the public know that promulgators of sustainable growth admire such primitive models of living.

Terms like *austerity* are verboten in the sustainable development vocabulary to describe this new life-style. Acceptable substitutes include phrases like "sophisticated modesty," a direct descendent of the 1970s concept "voluntary simplicity" spawned by the earlier "limits to growth" scare.

Perhaps we should consider ourselves lucky that the sustainable development proponents will stop at preindustrial society. Clive Ponting, another purveyor of this new cosmology, thinks that the species ought to look to preagricultural societies, not merely the preindustrial one, for a model of nondestructive human behavior. Ponting claims that great civilizations collapse because they overwhelm their environment with their own needs and throughput. The problem, from Ponting's point of view, started when Adam and Eve began tampering with Mother Nature. The history of the species since then can be seen as a vicious cycle of environmental decay that leaves both society and the land exhausted.

Regardless of the protestations of its supporters, the sustainable development concept is a model of dedevelopment. According to Brazil's José Lutzenburger, an eco guru and the recently fired head of Brazil's Environmental Ministry, the Third World and developing countries ought to assume a new model for growth—from the current economy based on dam and road projects, ranch mining, and commodity agriculture to a sustainable one emphasizing small farming, forestry, and wildlife management.

In other words, Lutzenburger suggests that the less developed countries remove themselves from the developmental loop of the Macroindustrial Era, which includes mega-agriculture, biotechnology, large-scale irrigation, macromanufacturing, and space exploration. India, Brazil, and other developing regions would thus abandon technologies that might propel them into the forefront of world economic leadership.

The species will summarily reject such a theory, however. In the final analysis, humanity does not have to choose between progress and the health of the environment. Not only are these two not in conflict, they are very much interdependent. As the Macroindustrial Era evolves, society will simultaneously tap the potential of its own inventions and utilize technology to improve the environment.

At that point fantasies such as sustainable development will find themselves safely sequestered out of harm's way in libraries and university social science departments.

Humanity Will Control Its Destiny

The breakthroughs that will enable humanity to control its destiny are already on the drawing board. In fact, many are already in operation. Humanity is about to overcome scarcity, biological restrictions, and nature itself. As we shall see, this is an exciting time to be alive. Ours and the generations to come will have more to celebrate than any generation in human history!

The journey through this next era will also be a demanding one. As further chapters reveal, if our nations and the species as a whole are to make a smooth transition into the next era, each of us must work harder, become smarter, and contribute more. To change the world, we may have to transform ourselves.

Other factors must coalesce to facilitate this transition. Our culture must encourage risk taking, our artists must provide us with a vision, and our leaders must inspire. Such a major leap in human evolution requires a total societal effort. I will cover in great detail the actions that individuals, government, corporations, and society itself must take in order to maximize the benefits of this emerging era.

Globally, the Macroindustrial Era has already begun. We see Japan, Europe, and Far Eastern countries like Hong Kong moving toward technologies that expand the species' mastery over the six dimensions mentioned earlier. The Third World countries are clamoring to be included in this global effort. Ironically, although the United States has all the basic skills and resources to commandeer the helm of the Macroindustrial world, its culture is rife with sentiments for concepts such as zero growth and "living in balance with nature." As we will learn later, however, America may yet guide the world in this new adventure.

Although the jury is still out on who will assume the mantle of moral and economic leadership in the Macroindustrial Era, we do know for certain that the initial stages of this exciting new Era have already begun.

Welcome to the Macroindustrial Era!

2: Hyperprogress

Humanity Takes Control in the

Macroindustrial Era

We can no longer consider the outburst of creative thought and activity of the late twentieth century within the realm of ordinary human advancement. The rapid acceleration of the rate of invention, the enhanced application of these innovations, and the substantive superiority of current technological breakthroughs over past accomplishments require a new label: hyperprogress.

The species is shaping the planet by extending land mass outward and under the ground, augmenting nature's own ability to produce energy through nuclear and fusion generation, and literally reversing the flow of gravity. As the Macroindustrial Era unfolds, the species will redefine time and space, rewriting both global history and natural law in its own hand, signing it in the name of humanity.

Reshaping the Earth

No set of activities better characterizes hyperprogress in the Macroindustrial Era than the species' endeavors to reshape the Earth. This reshaping is the product of gargantuan macroengineering projects in which humanity creates artificial islands, transatlantic tunnels, and underground cities, as well as mammoth irrigation projects whose size dwarfs previous efforts.

Although only part of the entire Macroindustrial surge, they capture perfectly the overall character and spirit of this emerging era.

There have been other periods in human history in which the species achieved major engineering feats that seem impossible by earlier standards. The Pyramids of ancient Egypt come to mind, as do the Romans' aqueducts and continental roadway system.

Although the year 1914 is usually remembered chiefly for the commencement of World War I, chroniclers of human development view it as a watershed for the development of major engineering projects. In that year, pressure from automobile owners forced the U.S. federal and state authorities to construct a transcontinental road, the Lincoln Highway stretching from New York to San Francisco. A major bridge-building campaign was underway throughout the United States, which led to the construction of spans like New York's Hell Gate Bridge, the world's largest steel structure. A series of large buildings, the first real skyscrapers, were also constructed. The just-completed Woolworth Building was outstripped in terms of sheer mass by the Equitable Building, which covered a full square block.

This year also saw the completion of the Panama Canal, which linked the Atlantic and Pacific oceans. This canal, started by the French but completed by the Americans, triumphantly crowned a century of American canal building. A young America had built her nascent economy with canals and dams. Now the Panama Canal solidified a mature America's position as a world-class superpower.

Fans of social history will be interested to know that in the midst of the species' massive imposition of its will on nature in 1914, the best-selling book of the day was Edgar Rice Burroughs' *Tarzan of the Apes*. This work glorified humankind living in a natural state, unsullied by the trappings of civilization. The general public also displayed a keen interest in spiritualism and séances. During periods of rapid technological change, some segments of the species seem to find comfort in such regressive fantasies. We can only hope that the engineering projects of the Macroindustrial Era do not elicit a similar escapism. In order to succeed, the citizenry must enthusiastically offer these projects both financial and moral support. In fact, the general population must provide input into the planning and implementation of such projects.

Underground Cities

There is no greater evidence of the species' veritable mastering of space, both inner and outer, than the macroengineering project being planned in Japan. Taisei Corporation of Tokyo is planning a network of underground cities, which it dubs Alice Cities, a name doubtlessly suggested by Lewis Carroll's heroine who found herself chasing rabbits and mad hatters in a subterranean wonderland.

Taisei's subterranean cities have several major advantages. They will help solve Japan's infamous paucity of available real estate—Japan's 120 million people are squeezed into an area the size of Montana. Second, such cities are less vulnerable to the destruction from the earthquakes that periodically plague Japan. Because during an earthquake the ground is more stable below the surface than above, Japan's new underground cities are considered safer than those on the surface. Third, since the near-constant natural underground temperature makes underground living more energy efficient, such structures will help alleviate that country's dependence on foreign energy supplies.

It is proposed that each Alice City be divided into three sectors. The town space will include underground boulevards and open-air and atrium-style plazas, all of which will include shopping malls and entertainment complexes. The office space will house the business operations, shops, hotels, and parking lots. The infrastructure grid, which will be isolated from the town and office sectors, will contain facilities for power generation, heating and air-conditioning, sewage treatment, and so on. Part of the Alice City might be covered with a transparent dome that would allow the residents to have a full view of sky and stars.

Another plan was developed by the Shimizu Corporation. Its Urban Geo Grid is essentially a vast network of subterranean city spaces linked by tunnels. Each *grid station*—a complex of shopping malls, hotels, and offices—would be connected to several grid points providing services such as convenience stores and spas. In the Shimizu model, several such grid stations would be in turn connected to other such complexes by tunnels. Shimizu planners believe that a half million people could be accommodated by such complexes.

Such macroengineering miracles allay concerns about overpopulation and overcrowding.

The Chunnel

Anyone who doubts the ability of the species to achieve the superhuman need only consider the Chunnel, a nearly completed undersea link between Great Britain and France. Such a tunnel will improve transportation between these two countries dramatically. Water travel by ferry and boat has historically suffered from the vagaries of weather and other unpredictable factors. The new Eurotunnel system will be impervious to weather conditions.

Businesspeople and visionaries for centuries dreamed of such a tunnel. Some claim the original idea for the Chunnel was conceived by a

French farmer desiring a cheaper way to transport his crops to England. In 1802, Napoleon himself had approved such a connection. Finally, in 1975, this privately financed effort began in earnest.

In the summer of 1991, workers tunneling from both sides of the Channel joined forces midway and celebrated the occasion with French champagne and English biscuits. The major ground excavation was complete. Connecting Folkstone, England, and Coquelles, France (near Calais), the Chunnel will be comprised of a pair of parallel rail tunnels, thirty-two miles long, plus a third service tunnel. Three types of trains will use the tunnel, freight, high-speed passenger, and shuttles that will operate every twenty minutes. The tunnel, which will accommodate both cars and trucks, is expected to open some time in 1994.

Although principally meant to facilitate trade in the spirit of the "borderless" European Community, the Chunnel is expected to prove a boon to tourism. According to Arre Benard, chairman of the Eurotunnel Authority, "When the two new rail tunnels under the English Channel begin operating between Great Britain and the European continent next year, North American tourists will enjoy faster, more frequent, and more predictable travel than has ever before been possible."

Other macrotunnels will suddenly seem more feasible because of the Chunnel's success. Certainly, a cross-Atlantic supertunnel first detailed thirty years ago will attract more backers and supporters.

Artificial Islands

The Chunnel is indeed a marvel of the Macroindustrial Era. However, humanity's quest to reshape the Earth is not limited to digging underground. There exist nascent plans to expand the very land base upon which the species lives.

As we have seen, in order to overcome the natural limits of land and space, Japan has begun to dig underground to enlarge its geographic possibilities. Its other response to the density problem, however, the construction of artificial islands, exemplifies the very essence of the macroindustrial spirit.

Japan has budgeted $200 billion for a project known as Ocean Communications City. The country's first city on an artificial island, Ocean City has daunting ambitions and dimensions. It will stand in 670 feet of water out at sea, seventy-five miles from Tokyo. The city itself will stretch nine square miles on a platform rising 260 feet above water's surface.

Ocean City's formulator, Kiyohide Terai, a professor at the University of Electronic Communications in Tokyo, envisions this city containing homes, a business and financial center, a shopping district, and various entertainment facilities. Most importantly, this island will serve as a home for over 1 million people. His city will rest atop 10,000 hefty columns anchored to the bottom of the sea with multimillion-ton concrete blocks.

Although the stuff of science fiction, the conceptualization is architecturally feasible. Many consider this plan superior to that suggested in 1988 by another architect, Kisho Kurokawa, who suggested that the island could be built from the sea floor up, using sand and recycled waste as the base. Kurokawa envisioned this artificial island sitting in the middle of Tokyo Bay.

Access to Ocean City will be provided by plane and hovercraft riding at 115 miles per hour. The cost of constructing an artificial island and providing its inhabitants continual transportation is expensive but not prohibitive. Regardless of its cost, however, most analysts agree that it may be cheaper for the Japanese to build a whole new island than enlarge existing structures in Tokyo.

This idea has quickly spread to other countries, such as Monaco. Although incredibly wealthy, this tiny country suffers from a major land shortage problem. Hemmed in by the foothills of the French Alps and the Mediterranean, this kingdom occupies a total of 480 acres. The principality now intends to expand on its limited real estate.

In its quest, it has developed and patented a revolutionary method of constructing a protective dike without resorting to massive landfills. The sea that confronts Monaco would be controlled by a system of submerged "containers" that would be linked together and supported by pylons. This technique will allow the installation of the dike at depths up to 260 feet.

Then, prefabricated pontoons containing apartments, carparks, and mooring bays will be towed out to sea and assembled. This floating structure, named *Fontvieille II*, would create living space for nearly 2000 persons.

Regardless of their architecture, these new cities built at sea will have profound sociological effects on global relations. Certainly, such wonders reduce the chances of war. History provides countless examples of small, isolated, land-locked countries that employ such tactics as forced migration, invasion, or war to expand their borders. Structures such as artificial islands and underground cities help such countries to satisfy their population and resource needs by physically expanding their own territory instead of invading and annexing others.

Also, the building of artificial islands pulverizes the orthodox economic contentions that we live in a world of limited or scarce resources. Although economists love to use the example of finite land mass as a proof of such zero-growth concepts as "matter can be neither created nor destroyed," we see that matter, in this case, land mass, can be manipulated in such a way that for all practical purposes matter does grow and expand. By constructing such islands, Japan and Monaco have effectively created more real estate.

Large-Scale Water Projects

Canals and irrigation have always been among the most grandiose of humanity's schemes. In the Macroindustrial Era, large-scale movement of water will accomplish a host of goals, including the expansion of the water supply of urban areas and the creation of new forests in desert areas to replace, among other things, the wilting Amazonian rain forest.

One such technology to accomplish large-scale irrigation is that devised by Professor Joseph Debanne of the University of Ottawa. His planned submarine aqueduct would involve water pumped through plastic tubes laid on sea floors. He wanted to employ this technology to carry the water of the Rhône River under the Mediterranean Sea and over the Atlas Mountains to the North African region. Such a project could double the irrigated acreage of North Africa, thereby facilitating the maintenance of protective tree belts and making possible the establishment of new garden communities.

Dozens of communities could benefit from an enhanced ability to manipulate water flow and supply. The southern California region could use irrigation projects to solve its seemingly interminable insecurities spawned by lengthy droughts. As we shall see in Chapter 5, India's Gandhi Canal has already transformed this country into a potential net exporter of food.

The midcontinent of North America, dependent on water for its agricultural economy, could benefit from a number of water technologies. One such suggestion envisions transporting massive amounts of water from Alaska down to the Great Lakes region, which would then serve as a reservoir for the Midwest. Another scheme daringly calls for the damming of James Bay in Canada to produce an artificial freshwater lake at the base of Hudson Bay. This would provide a continuous flow of high-quality water to the Great Lakes and a continuous flow of high-quality capital back to Canada.

The Russians have their own plans for using water transference to improve the quality of life. The Ob and Yenisei rivers daily discharge hundreds of billions of gallons of fresh water into the Arctic Ocean. The idea has arisen to reverse these north-flowing rivers and create a lake the size of Italy to irrigate the central Soviet steppes. According to engineers, one problem is that such a translocation of water might shift so much weight toward the equator that the planet would begin to wobble. An alternative may be to dam the Bering Strait between Alaska and Siberia to create such a water reservoir.

The Japanese will not be excluded from this new human adventure. One of the most advanced schemes, Greening the Sahara Desert, involves myriad macroengineering plans contributed by several construction companies. In one such scheme, colossal aqueducts that stretch from the Mediterranean Sea and Atlantic Ocean would be connected to huge desalting plants. Other plans have the Japanese building huge underground reservoirs and injecting the desert with substances that will help the desert retain water. They also want to build enormous dams in the Himalayas to prevent flooding in Bangladesh. The Japanese government has been quite supportive of such ideas.

Visionaries are also suggesting that coastal deserts be partially irrigated by icebergs transported from their ocean origins to a more southern destination. The icebergs would be captured and towed while still frozen and then unfrozen at their destination. Such melted icy water may also be used to cool nuclear reactors.

All of these projects not only require an expenditure of human energy, they also need creativity and ingenuity. Only by thinking in often counterlinear and unexpected ways do we begin to envision artificial islands and underground cities. Only by thinking big, in expansionary terms, can society even begin to conceive of reversing the flow of rivers. To achieve such Brobdingnagian projects the species must also possess the willingness and courage to take risks.

The Bold New World of Transportation

In order to achieve economic growth and compete on the international scene, countries must attain a high degree of internal organization. One cornerstone of internal societal integration is an advanced transportation system. Societies need such systems to distribute food and other commodities throughout the nation, send personnel to areas that require their services, and in general enhance the quality of life of all involved.

In the Macroindustrial Era, there will be no greater example of hyperprogress than our ability to comfortably and safely move people and goods at greater and greater speeds.

The Advent of the Supertrain

Over the years, America and other countries have increasingly depended on aviation and the highway to transport people. The railway, which for a century or more had been the transportation mode of choice, quickly became relegated to the roles of freight and commuter service.

That is all changing. The supertrain will become the quintessential mode of ground mass transit of the Macroindustrial Era. Currently, the fastest train in regular commercial use is the French TGV Express, which zips around France at a lightning speed of 186 miles per hour. Compare this to America's fastest train, Amtrak's Metroliner, which travels from New York to Washington at 125 miles per hour, with most American trains traveling at far slower speeds. Amtrak has imported the Swedish X-2000, which should eventually run the New York–Boston route at about 150 miles per hour. It is projected that the ride from Los Angeles to Las Vegas on such a supertrain would take 75 minutes.

The next stage of development in train technology will truly revolutionize travel. This new development is known as the *maglev*, a hybrid term from the words *magnetic* and *levitation*. This supertrain is currently under development in Germany and Japan. Predictions about its ultimate top speed vary, but in experimental runs, the Japanese maglev was clocked at 321 miles per hour. Some project that top speeds of newer models will exceed 400 miles per hour. At that speed, this mode of transportation will challenge current aviation technology for crosscontinental and regional travel and freight transportation.

The maglev concept operates along revolutionary physical principles. For one thing, the train will come equipped with powerful superconducting magnets. It will glide along a U-shaped guideway that has copper coils placed along its two walls and its floor.

As anyone who has ever experimented with small magnets knows, magnets attract metal but repel each other. The train will be motored by such a principle. Electromagnetic forces between the superconducting magnets on the train and the copper coils on the guideway propel the train along the guideway. The magnet on the train is attracted by a guideway coil of opposite polarity immediately ahead of it and repelled by a coil of the same polarity immediately behind it. The operating system rapidly alternates the polarity of the guideway coils, and this alternation propels the train forward.

An additionally intriguing aspect of this train is that the repulsive forces of the magnets raises the train about four inches above the bottom of the guideway. The train seems to glide on air miraculously, requiring no wheels and creating no friction. The absence of such friction allows the train to travel faster than it would if it rode directly on tracks.

Also, the fact that the train itself contains no engine makes it lighter and thus faster. The electromagnetic currents between the magnets and coils in the train and the guideways are produced by centralized generators located in power plants. Its main weight, then, is its own body and the magnets. However, superconductors, which reduce the amount of energy needed to power the trains, may allow us to utilize lighter, smaller magnets on the train. Incredibly, the next generation of maglevs may be faster than our present ones.

The lack of friction makes these trains remarkably unobtrusive. In Germany, where maglev systems have been under research since 1983, test models of the maglev sweep through the countryside at ultrahigh speeds on overhead guideway structures. These trains glide so quietly that cattle grazing directly below the "tracks" do not even lift their heads when the maglev model passes directly overhead. One German farmer asked about his community's attitude toward the new train remarked, "We don't even know it's there."

Two of the major train systems proposed are the German Transrapid and the Japanese MLU002, both designed for top speeds of between 250 and 300 miles per hour. However, some engineers believe that in the future the combination of reduced train bulk weight and emerging improvements in aerodynamic technology could increase the speeds of such trains to an incredible 1700 miles per hour.

The United States may build its first maglev ultrahigh-speed system in Florida, connecting Orlando International Airport with Disney World. With construction set to begin in 1993, we can expect the first passengers to embark in 1997.

Pittsburgh's regional planners have expressed a desire to Americanize the German Transrapid maglev system. They plan to manufacture the train under license from Germany, test it and perfect it regionally, and then sell it elsewhere in the United States. Public agencies and private companies have formed Maglev, Inc., to oversee the fulfillment of this grand scheme.

Still, the United States has a long way to go to compete in this vital area of the Macroindustrial Era. Even though U.S. scientists developed much of the fundamental technology for maglev and the application of superconducting materials to the propulsion system, Washington foolishly killed the country's advanced train program in 1975. Now the United States has fallen as much as twenty years behind such countries as Japan, which ironically uses American technology for their maglev system.

American companies still seem unsold on the feasibility of such systems. However, this vacuum will be filled by foreign manufacturers, such as Siemans, A.G., of West Germany, who are offering to build maglev train systems in such areas as Nevada, between the Las Vegas Airport and the downtown area, as a means of penetrating the American market.

In America, opposition to the supertrains predictably often emanates from companies representing competing transportation modalities. As plans materialize for a high-speed train system linking Houston and Dallas, a panic-stricken Southwest Airlines in Dallas increasingly lobbies against the train system's construction. They realize that a 400-mile-an-hour train connecting the downtowns of regional cities would attract current customers of local airlines. Southwest cleverly employs environmental, not economic, arguments in its efforts to preemptively derail high-speed train transport in the region. It claims that the rail system would be unsightly, unsafe, and noisy. Because Southwest based its opposition to the supertrain on such ecological arguments, a host of hardcore environmental groups are now lobbying with it against the supertrain.

Unfortunately, this may be a harbinger of the formation of future political alliances between antitechnology environmentalists and businesses fearing competition from new competitive technologies. The environmental argument against the train is inherently weak. It echoes the assumption voiced by some ecologists that as technology becomes more advanced—faster, bigger, more powerful—it also becomes more damaging to the environment. In fact, maglev trains offer proof that high technology actually helps the environment. The trains produce less noise and emit no gases or pollutants. This is another example of the Imperative of Growth's third corollary, that the solution to the problems of progress is more sophisticated science and technology.

We can easily intuit how the supertrain, a prototypical Macroindustrial mastery of time and space, will trigger a veritable cultural explosion. For one thing, the supertrain will make possible the liberation of American society from the grip of living and working in central cities. They can live in new entities, such as those planner Joel Garreau labels "edge cities." These communities, located on what used to be considered the outskirts of major urban centers, suburbs, are themselves becoming major cultural, occupational, and business units.

California leads the United States in total edge citification. New Jersey is second with twenty-six such centers, including Morristown, the Newark airport area, the Bridgewater mall area, and the Amtrak area, all of which have developed their own self-integrated identity independent of Philadelphia or New York City.

The supertrain will play a significant role in the development of such cities in the twenty-first century. High-speed transport will facilitate the transportation of new residents, workers, goods, and culture into these areas. The location of supertrain depots in central areas of the new edge cities will help such new entities develop a downtown that should quickly imbue each edge city with a unique identity, character, and flavor.

Supertrain development will impact the employment picture positively. Although not explicitly a public works project, any region planning and implementing such a transportation system should expect a massive influx of jobs. There will emerge a tremendous need for engineers, designers, construction workers, and materials designers. The revived downtown area surrounding the supertrain depot will require shops, restaurants, and hotels, all of which hire in a variety of skill areas.

As these supertrains become a viable alternative to other forms of travel, the world will construct train systems serving international travel needs. Engineer J. Vincent Harrington has devised plans for a supersonic railway service across the North Atlantic. It would stretch from the northern tip of Scotland to the northern coast of Labrador, cutting a path through the North Atlantic Ocean, Iceland, and Greenland. The ocean portions of the system would involve tunnels under waters whose depths would not exceed 3000 feet.

Most developed countries are planning to either build their own supertrain link or connect with other countries' systems. Belgium proposes to connect their system with the French TGV at the border and extend it via Brussels to Amsterdam; Russia has a plan for building a high-speed link between St. Petersburg and Moscow; and Australia, South Korea, Italy, and Switzerland are planning long high-speed supertrain routes. When Africa, Latin America, and Asia develop such systems, they will truly be joining the Macroindustrial Era.

As progressive as the maglev and other high-speed concepts seem, they may as yet be outdistanced by the *hypersonic* train, which travels at supersonic speeds. The principle behind this astrotrain is simple—it is propelled by a vacuum created by the pumping of air out from a long-distance transit tube. The technology was first demonstrated in 1985 at a Massachusetts Institute of Technology (MIT) athletic field, and some claim a prototype could be built for a mere $100 million. For high-speed train transport, the future is now!

Superflight

Perhaps one of the truly colossal transportation feats of the Macroindustrial Era will be the attainment of superfast global flight. As the species continues its reconstitution of the very concept of time, high-speed jets will make global transportation available to everyone.

NASA (emphasizing its A for *aeronautics*) has sunk over $205 million into research that will allow supersonic vehicles such as the Concorde to extend its flight radius. Currently, fuel restrictions make it impossible for the Concorde to fly distances farther than that of its current New York–Paris route. However, NASA is looking into ways that will enable Concorde-style aircraft to double or triple its fuel efficiency in order to fly long distances, making a Paris–Pacific Ocean region flight possible. Such a breakthrough will put the United States in the forefront of long-distance supersonic flight, NASA's engineers believe.

NASA's National Aero-Space Plane project embodies a totally new concept for speedy long-distance flight, the combination of orbital aeronautics with more conventional methods of flying. In this scenario, a shuttle-type vehicle would blast off from Earth from a conventional runway, roar into space at twenty-five times the speed of sound, establish a short Earth orbit, and return to Earth and land at an airport at its destination city. A flight from New York to Japan could conceivably be cut to a few hours from the current fourteen- to twenty-hour range without the need to refuel. The problem right now is the unreliability of shuttle travel relative to conventional jet transportation and the incredibly prohibitive cost of such a flight. However, this type of travel at least requires no major scientific discoveries to reach fruition, only improvements in the technology already at our disposal.

In the Macroindustrial Era, we may also see the return of the dirigible. Blimps now grace the Superbowl and other sports events, often serving as mere oversized ads. At one time, however, the dirigible was the airship of choice. At the time that the famous *Graf Zeppelin* was withdrawn from service in June 1937, it had flown over 1 million miles in ten years without an accident, carrying over 13,000 passengers and over 100,000 tons of mail.

Dirigibles, though slower than other forms of transportation, have the ability to carry rather heavy pieces of equipment in one piece. At present, ships can perform this function, but in countries such as the United States cross-country shipping involves sailing through the Panama Canal and traveling the full lengths of the eastern and western American coasts.

It would be an ironic twist indeed if hyperprogress suddenly emerged dressed in a technology from a bygone era. After all, ballooning predates even the first Industrial Revolution!

Smart Highways

In the Macroindustrial Era, the very way that we drive will change dramatically. The millions of car accident deaths have led many planners to rethink the issue of automobile transportation. David Gordon of MIT developed what he calls the Palleted Automated Transportation (PAT) system, in which cars travel bumper to bumper on electronically driven pallets. This would allow cars not only to travel faster, but more economically, because they would not be using gas or wearing down tires and other parts as quickly as they do now. Also, the problem of road congestion would be almost eliminated.

Conceivably this PAT system could be combined with the more autonomous form of car driving. A driver would have the choice of using this publicly funded form of transportation or pursuing more independent driving with the knowledge that the latter would put miles on the car, increase the probability of having an accident, increase car insurance, and add to the fuel bill. The PAT system would then be a voluntary alternative to independent automobile transport. It has been predicted that most people would utilize the PAT system in conjunction with autonomous, self-drive local travel.

Driving will be made smarter by virtue of other technological breakthroughs. For instance, electronic tolls and traffic management will make it possible for cars to speed through unmanned toll booths equipped with lasers that read a bar code sticker on the vehicle. The driver, instead of paying tolls, buys a sticker valid for a certain amount of trips. Another innovation will be an onboard navigation system mounted on a car's dashboard that can inform the driver of his or her geographic location and also warn of weather and traffic conditions.

The Electric Car: Help or Hindrance?

In the Macroindustrial Era, pressure will mount for the development of energy that will deliver more power but at the same time be safer and less polluting. Public sentiment will lead to a variety of diverse inventions, including the often-heralded electric car.

Unfortunately, these cars at present have two major drawbacks, both linked to the state of battery technology. First, because the batteries must be frequently recharged, the cars have a limited range of about 120 miles. For many people, one charge may not even get them to and from work. Second, many of these batteries need eight or more hours to be recharged.

Some progress has been made. In 1992, the Advanced Battery Consortium, formed the year before by Ford, General Motors, and Chrysler; the Electric Power Research Institute; and the U.S. Department of Energy, announced the first contract to develop an advanced battery expected to propel an electric car farther and faster than today's lead acid storage battery.

There are currently two batteries being considered: Ford Motor Company has developed a sodium–sulfur battery, and Energy Conversion Devices is contending with a nickel–metal hydrid battery. These two batteries will allow the electric car to travel 120 to 150 miles on a single battery charge, more than twice the range of the conventional lead oxide battery.

The nickel–metal hydrid battery is considered a surpising entry. Developed by Energy Conversion Devices, Inc., in Troy, Michigan, until 1991 it was overlooked by the Advanced Battery Consortium. It promises 120 to 170 miles between charges (a little less than the miles old gas guzzlers could put on before refills). Some say this battery can be recharged in one hour or less.

If battery technology does not improve much beyond these projections, we may have to consider more creative methods to make electric cars a viable form of travel. For instance, we could develop a national system whereby drivers could swap batteries at a service station with about the same fanfare involved in filling a gas tank. Drivers would not necessarily own the battery but license the right to own a battery. The used batteries would be recharged at the station and later put in other drivers' cars. Another way to enhance the viability of electric cars would be to incorporate them into the "smart roads" system. Here, drivers would not be using the battery during the time their car sits on the smart road's conveyer belt.

Efforts are being made to solve the recharging problem. Companies such as General Motors, EHV Corporation of Manhattan, Kansas, and Norvick Technologies of Mississauga, Ontario, are in the hunt for development of a quick and efficient car recharging system. In mid-1993 the Boston Edison Company agreed to market electric vehicle chargers made by the GM-Hughes Electronic unit of General Motors. In this system the rechargers are plugged into a slot on the side of the vehicle and pass current into the car's battery. Hughes claims that its system can recharge a small electric car within fifteen minutes, and predicts that future systems will be even more efficient. Boston Edison plans to install the rechargers first at malls and corporate parking lots and later near restaurants, theaters, and other public places.

In spite of improvements in recharging time, the electric car still possesses many disadvantages. The electric car has a limited range, is relatively slow, and its price is about three times that of a comparable car powered by a conventional internal combustion engine. Although electric cars seem to be a possible short-term alternative to fossil-fuel-based automotive technology, they fall outside the definition of hyperprogress. The goals in developing any new technology must be consistent with the Imperative of Growth. The technology must enable us to accomplish more, to safely travel farther and quicker, with less drain on our time and energy. It is questionable whether a society whose transportation system largely depends on electric battery cars and trucks for the movement of people and goods will experience real economic growth. At present, electric car technology as currently conceived would decelerate societal progress.

Macromanufacturing

Hyperprogress will occur only if the species transforms current methods of producing goods, machines, parts, and materials. The emerging Era's productive capacity will very much depend on the development of *macromanufacturing*, the large-scale production of individualized and customized goods. This large-scale manufacturing will be made possible as the species applies computers and robotics to the production process. In addition, we will change the inherent nature of machinery by incorporating magnetism into its construction.

However, as we shall see, the success of macromanufacturing will depend on an educated work force and an ample energy supply to power its machinery.

The Cybernetic Factory

Computer-integrated manufacturing (CIM) not only allows entire industrial plants to automate production, but facilitates rapid transformation of the entire production line so that quite different and highly customized products can be manufactured in the same factory. This breakthrough in and of itself promises megagrowth in the production of goods.

The alliance of the computer with the manufacturing process takes many forms, so much so that even business leaders are sometimes confused by the seeming endless variety of technologies that are labeled computer-integrated manufacturing.

One example of CIM is computer-aided design (CAD). In the CAD process, an engineer or technician utilizes the computer to design a product to specifications established at the plant or possibly even by the customer. With the enhanced imaging abilities of today's computer at his or her disposal, the engineer can view a prototype of a design model before the model ever exists, often in three dimensions. With CAD, the design process has become so facile that the customer using computer imaging might literally sit at a home computer and inform the engineer what he or she specifically wants the product to look like.

Even relatively unsophisticated customers can utilize CAD technology when making a purchase. Homebuilders are using CAD systems to allow their customers to see model homes on computers and redesign the models on-screen before a brick is laid or a beam placed in position.

Computer-aided manufacturing represents another form of CIM. Here a computer monitors and controls the workings of an array of robots, who then actually do the manufacturing. Many who witness firsthand such operations are in an instant mentally jolted right into the Macroindustrial Era. They observe the manufacture of radios, televisions, or cars. Where, they ask, are the workers? The only human they see participating in this process might be one engineer/technician sitting at a computer screen, making some minor adjustments in the process, troubleshooting when needed.

Many systems now fully integrate both techniques. These CAD/CAM operations entail full computer participation in the entire design and manufacturing process. At Motorola's Paging Products Division plant in Boynton Beach, Florida, the world-class CIM facility allows Motorola to achieve high quality and quick response to customers. A rush order from a customer is relayed from an IBM mainframe in Schaumburg, Illinois, to the Stratus and Hewlett-Packard computers in the Florida plant. These computers instruct the "work force" of twenty-seven Seiko robots to begin constructing pagers. Within two hours of order entry, Motorola's BRAVO radio pagers, customized to mechanical and radio-frequency specifications, can be completed.

One of the most inclusive and sophisticated CIM systems is located at Texas Instrument's (TI's) Lewisville plant, which builds the guidance and control sections for the U.S. Navy/Air Force HARM (high-speed antiradiation missile) program. These missiles are capable of homing in on and destroying enemy radar systems. Since 1985, when the HARM system was first established, the CIM system has helped the TI plant boost production tenfold, while employment has risen only threefold. The cost of each missile produced has dropped by 58 percent. TI is especially proud of the fact that it has experienced seven straight years of on-time delivery.

TI's Lewisville plant illustrates how sophisticated CIM systems will play a critical role in the emerging Macroindustrial Era. Here TI employs a total of 250 personal and minicomputers, to control an assortment of plant systems.

For example, the plant has an automated material handling network. All aspects of the work, the inventory, and the material used are tracked by computer. Using bar codes similar to those found on items in supermarkets and retail stores, the computer can route various parts of the missile assembly units to different work areas. Six minicomputers run a network of testing stations that put completed missile parts through a series of vibration, frequency, and temperature tests. Four laser-inspection units check the 2000 solder joints on each printed wire board.

Humans do have a role in the missile assembly process, but even that role is guided by computer intelligence and judgment. Workers place and solder components on microwave circuit boards following text and graphics assembly instructions downloaded from a computer that contains TI's engineering database. They receive their instructions on terminals at their workstations.

This whole process uses vision-aided robots extensively for inspection and assembly tasks. These robots, part of a new generation that can see and hear, perform in two minutes some assembly jobs that used to take humans four hours by hand.

The Lewisville team has developed fourteen unique computer systems, but many of them are still essentially "islands of automation." The plan is to create linkages between those islands progressively through a total networking system. In this way, each subassembly unit would be connected with the whole.

Ironically, in spite of these technological breakthroughs and productivity gains, many observers cringe at the type of plant evolving at Lewisville. They feel that the new macromanufacturing seems to eliminate human input or at least relegates the worker to an unskilled, ancillary role.

Closer examination of the emerging relationship between human and manufacturing should allay such apprehensions. For one thing, the new role of the human is that of a sophisticated, scientifically oriented engineer, designer, or systems analyst. Initially, the entire process had to be created and planned. Obviously, humans, albeit highly educated ones, performed this task. For all the hoopla over artificial intelligence, no computer can plan, project, and create to the extent required for these macrosystems. Humans must breathe life into these machines in order to actualize what the human mind imagines: People, not robots, wrote the 750,000 lines of computer code that operate Lewisville's fourteen computer systems.

Second, although it is claimed that these robots are displacing workers on the assembly floor, in reality, they are relieving humans of the grunt work that dulls the mind and induces worker tedium. In Lewisville and around the globe, the computer allows us to pursue more sophisticated levels of production and creation.

This becomes more obvious when we see robots doing what humans hated to do. Dr. Rodney Brooks of MIT and his team at the Artificial Intelligence Laboratory have created a series of small robots that perform any number of tedious tasks, such as collecting empty drinks in the office, sweeping a room, or moving large objects. On the horizon are small insect-sized robots that can be let loose on a rug or under furniture to collect dust and grime, return to base, and deposit their booty in a waste bin.

Some critics claim that workers resent being replaced by dumb machines. The more germane question is why we have been satisfied for so long performing jobs that these brainless machines can master so effortlessly. In the future, more people will be involved in designing and improving machines that perform routine tasks than doing such tasks themselves.

Magnetic Machines

The greater productivity promised by macromanufacturing will be generated not only by the marriage of computers and machinery. The machines themselves will also undergo a fundamental change that will make them more durable and more efficient. To effect such a transformation, macromanufacturing will engage the services of magnetism and its special powers. As in the case of the maglev train system, the species will literally defy the laws of gravity to hasten the transition to the next Macroindustrial Era.

Aura Systems, in El Segundo, California, produces devices that, according to its president Harry Kurtzman, could one day replace ball bearings and actuators in just about every machine. Conventional bearings and actuators generate heat, need constant lubrication, are often noisy, and eventually wear out. According to Kurtzman, Aura System's machine parts possess none of these problems. They use magnetic bearings and actuators that actually float frictionless in an electromagnetic field. This lack of friction allows them to operate at superhigh speeds. Equally important, this lack of wear and tear allows them to last for an inordinate amount of time.

The key to making magnetics technology applicable to the operation of machinery is advances in microchip electronics. With such advances, magnetic forces can be controlled with precision and used to levitate parts in machines.

The technology has already spread to several industries. One company, Avcon Advanced Controls Technology, Inc., is developing lightweight magnetic levitation bearings for use in petrochemical and aerospace equipment. Varian Associates, of Palo Alto, is using Aura's technology to develop magnetic levitation turbo pumps used in semiconductor production.

Exxon plans to use Aura's computer-operated and monitored pumps at a Baton Rouge, Louisiana, pump in late 1993. General Motors and Toyota have contracted with Aura to have the company develop and manufacture suspension systems, fuel injectors, and other products using electromagnetic actuators. All of these systems will be composed of parts that do not touch other objects because of their suspension in electromagnetic space.

Like many companies in this field, Aura suspects that there is no limit to the applications of magnetism to the industrial process. Aura's most radical plans involve a magnetically controlled cutting device for cataract surgery that it is developing in a joint venture with Nestle S.A.

Many analysts agree that magnetism will play a major role in future industrial development. Some on Wall Street project that Aura, which claimed a mere $14 million in revenue in 1991, may increase its revenue to a half billion dollars within three years. The size of its work force may grow from its current 160 employees to 1000 in that time.

Of all the basic forces of the universe, gravity exerts the most control over our world. On the positive side, gravity keeps us reliably glued to the Earth and prevents the planet from hurtling out of the Solar System. However, it also restricts our movement and over time even causes our skin to sag. Some feel that gaining control over gravity, even in a limited sense, will be a necessary step for humanity in its quest to gain ultimate control of itself and its destiny. As a slogan on the office wall of Aura, president Harry Kurtzman proclaims, "The nation that controls magnetism will control the universe." If that is our goal, we can start by controlling the effect of gravity on our machines.

Spurred by CIM and zero-gravity technology, macromanufacturing will become the mechanism by which goods and parts are produced in the Macroindustrial Era. The final products will be superior in quality and highly customized, produced by incredibly efficient machines that require minimal human intervention. However, their conceptualization, design, and continual improvement will depend on humans who must be more educated and skilled than any previous generation. As we shall see, macromanufacturing, indeed the whole Macroindustrial Era, will necessitate a significant expansion of the energy and power base.

The Energy Explosion

Hyperprogress will bring us supertrains, macroengineering, macromanufacturing, lake-size waterways, and the construction and maintenance of artificial islands and underground cities housing thousands, perhaps millions, of people. Clearly, however, these developments, which will make possible an enhanced quality of life for the human species, will certainly require a more sophisticated energy production system than currently exists.

The Energy Needs of the Macroindustrial Era

Most of the advances discussed in this chapter and throughout the book are dependent on a cheap, abundant, and accessible energy supply. The megagrowth implied by the Macroindustrial Era will require an ever-increasing energy base.

Before 1973, most Westerners gave little thought to energy. Issues such as the overall availability of energy and the form that energy would take were considered the domain of policy makers and technocrats, but a series of wars and political upheavals in the Mideast and various actions by the OPEC cartel, including oil embargoes, and price increases changed all that. Confronted by long lines at the gas pumps and rising prices, consumers no longer considered themselves immune from the geopolitics of world energy production.

Most Westerners instinctively suspect that over the next two decades nations will be required to make fundamental decisions about how much energy we will need and how we will produce or acquire this energy. As we shall see, European and Asian countries have already registered an increased awareness of the swift changes in the supply of and demand for energy, and recently the U.S. policymaking establishment has also undergone a consciousness-raising over the need for changes in energy policy.

This sea change in our perspective on energy will be dictated by some unpleasant realities regarding the supply of traditional fuel sources. We know that we cannot rely on the world's oil supply to fuel our Macroindustrial machine. The Earth at most holds an estimated 1744 trillion barrels of oil, which would fill Lake Erie one and a half times. Based on current usage rates, we will run out of this resource in seventy-five years. In short, most of the children born in 1992 will live to see the oil supply diminish and then entirely dry up and will spend the latter parts of their lives dealing with this crisis. Conservation may extend this resource somewhat, but over the long run, oil will not be fueling our economy.

Natural gas has similar upper limits. According to Princeton energy analyst Robert Williams, the planet has perhaps a fifty- to one hundred-year supply of natural gas. And while many have portrayed coal as the ultimate energy panacea, if all the available coal was applied to the economic system, its supply would last at most for 200 years.

On a global and national level, companies, industries, and governments are beginning to realize that these fuels must be replaced if the world is to have any hope of achieving long-term economic growth. Indicative of this adjustment is the growing trend toward electrification of the industrial and public power grid. Electrification is specifically defined as the trend toward the use of electricity, regardless of its source, and away from the direct burning of fossil fuels like oil, natural gas, and coal.

Electricity increasingly plays a major role in the energy grid. Since 1973, the percentage of all U.S. energy consumption represented by electricity use has grown dramatically. All indications are that it will continue to grow over the next two decades. In 1960, 19 percent of all energy was produced from electricity; in 1970, 24 percent; in 1990, 36 percent; and by the year 2010, according to the Energy Information Administration, electricity will account for 40 percent of total energy consumption.

As an example of the megagrowth of electrical production over the last three decades, consider that the global output for all fuel sources in 1958 did not equal the electricity generated in 1991 just by nuclear power plants. Nuclear only represents about one-fifth of all electricity production.

In absolute terms, electricity demand in the United States is up 58 percent since 1973, with all three sectors of the economy—residential, commercial, and industrial—weighing in as major electricity consumers. American industry especially has demonstrated that it needs to replace fossil-fueled production processes with electrical power. In the late 1980s, as the world and U.S. economy rebounded from the recessionary 1970s, industries such as steel, aluminum, and chemicals, all electricity-intensive industries, underwent a dramatic resurgence. As they expanded, they sharply boosted their demand for electricity.

What the public has not been told is that continued economic growth, even at the current tame 2 to 3 percent gross national product (GNP) growth rates, will require much more electric generating capacity than the United States or the world can presently provide. The president's National Energy Strategy projects that even if society endeavors to conserve fuel and restrict demand, it will still require 190,000 to 275,000 megawatts of additional generating capacity to fuel economic growth.

Within the context of the evolving Macroindustrial Era, even these estimates are conservative. Such hyperprogress programs as supertrains and smart roads demand an ever-greater supply of power. Significantly greater amounts of electricity will be required to sustain economic growth. According to the Department of Energy, the country will have to increase its generating capacity by almost 40 percent by the year 2010, an amount of energy equivalent to the output of 250 large coal or nuclear power plants. If old plants are dismantled as scheduled by 2030, the need for new plants will most definitely skyrocket.

Conservation will not solve society's energy needs. These projections on global energy needs prove that no matter how well we insulate our houses or how carefully we recycle spent energy and waste, we will not escape the responsibility of constructing a reliable and productive energy grid. We cannot enjoy economic growth and raise our standard of living without dedicating ourselves to building a new generation of power plants. According to the U.S. Council for Energy Awareness, "Simply stated, if this [economic] trend continues, the U.S. would need more new electric generating capacity than is now recognized."

In spite of the monumental effort that will be required to meet such demand, there is one bright spot. The overall trend in the price of electricity production is downward. In fact, since 1984, real prices of electricity have fallen 24 percent, a downward trend experts believe will continue.

Nuclear Power: The Pendulum Swings Back

Policymakers agree that the coming era's energy source must be readily available, easy to produce, relatively cheap, and, to the extent possible, immune to international political and military developments. It is one of the great ironies of technological history that in this debate the pendulum of scientific opinion is swinging back in the direction of nuclear power.

Perhaps no energy source has been more the focus of controversy than nuclear power. Once heralded as the savior of humanity and the pathway to cheap energy, since the 1979 near disaster at the Three Mile Island plant, this energy source has been the object of media derision and public apprehension. Ironically, in spite of such controversies, the percentage of electrical energy supplied by nuclear plants, in the United States and throughout the globe, has risen dramatically during this period.

The Macroindustrial Era requires a fuel source that delivers the massive and abundant energy supply that nuclear power can provide. In March 1991, several governments, including Britain, France, Germany, and Belgium, reaffirmed their belief that nuclear power, if developed in conditions of "optimum safety, ensuring the best possible protection both for populations and for the environment," was the energy of choice. They agreed to participate jointly in the development of new, safer reactors.

Other countries, sensing the transition into a new era of supergrowth and hyperprogress, do not hesitate to use nuclear power to drive their electrical apparatus. For instance, France derives 75 percent of its electricity from nuclear sources; Belgium, 61 percent; Sweden, 45 percent; West Germany, 40 percent; and Japan, 27 percent. In fact, France has become a net exporter of energy. Germany, a major purchaser of France's energy, now desires to revive its own nuclear program.

Taiwan, Korea, and Japan are building their economic futures on a sound nuclear base. Japan, which as recently as 1990 enjoyed a 5.6 percent rise in GNP, seems to be in the vanguard of implementation of nuclear power, planning to construct a total of forty new plants over the next few decades. Using American technology, Japan is building the world's first next-generation nuclear plants. The two units, which will be built in less than half the time the most recent U.S. plants required, are expected to be operating by 1997. South Korea has also begun construction on two nuclear units based on a state-of-the-art U.S. design.

Ex-President Bush's energy policy unveiled in June 1991 explicitly made nuclear power a major focus of the United States' growth-oriented energy program. A combination of next-generation reactors and a new dedication to industry standardization will help the United States develop a robust nuclear industry that will underwrite its transition into the Macroindustrial Era.

The United States currently seems to favor the advanced light water reactor (ALWR) in its various permutations as the next generation of nuclear plant. The United States already utilizes light water reactors, such as the one located at Indian Point, New York. In all such plants, regular water serves as a coolant for the reactor shell.

ALWRs are evolutionary: They incorporate into their design several decades worth of accumulated knowledge about nuclear power. These new plants will employ technological improvements like instrumentation and control systems that use state-of-the-art multiplexed/fiber optics, superior fuel and reactor core designs, dramatically improved safety systems, and a host of design and structural changes that enhance maintenance and operation of these advanced reactors.

The smaller-sized ALWRs will be relatively simple to construct, maintain, and operate. They also rely on so-called passive safety features, such as cooling water, which depends on gravity instead of pumps for its delivery to the reactor shell. Such features require a decreased amount of pipe, control cable, valves, and pumps. The fewer the parts, it is believed, the less chance of mishap.

These plants will be standardized. According to the Nuclear Power Oversight Committee, for nuclear power to succeed and remain safe there must be a "comprehensive commitment to standardization." They insist that the United States should follow the French example and build nuclear power plants to standard designs. Because engineers and technicians would be familiarized with one basic design technology, they would find such standardized plants simpler to operate. Inspectors, having full knowledge of these plants, would be better able to evaluate whether a given plant is operating safely.

The European Community will not be left behind in the nuclear power research and development race. It has marshaled its collective research and economic forces to develop the conceptual design for the European Fast Reactor (EFR), a technology that will extract sixty times more energy from a given amount of uranium than other types of reactors. Plus, they use the more abundant plutonium as fuel. In addition, the reactors breed even more plutonium by converting the uranium that is left after the fuel has been converted.

Japan is also building a fast-breeder reactor. In 1992, France sent Japan the first of thirty shipments of plutonium by sea to help fuel Japan's first breeder reactor. Ironically, the United States abandoned this high-potential power source in the 1970s in an effort to prevent the proliferation of bomb-grade material. Japanese officials say that the United States will eventually regret not taking a longer-range vision regarding the breeder reactor. Japan seems unfazed that countries such as Great Britain are bowing to political pressures to eliminate their breeder reactor programs. According to the Japanese foreign ministry, "Were Japan to be the only nation working in this area, [it] would view its responsibility as even greater and redouble its efforts to contribute to the international community through technological development."

The evidence is clear. Many countries, such as France and Japan, are pinning their hopes for economic growth on nuclear power as a reliable energy source. However, countries are favoring nuclear power not only because it is efficient, but because it is a nonpolluting, environmentally clean alternative to coal and petroleum. Ironically, the

United States, having restrained nuclear power development at the behest of the environmentalists and the public they have so thoroughly unnerved, may become the world's number one polluter by increasing its dependency on coal and oil.

Recognizing that nuclear power has had some positive impact on the environment, some environmentalists, long the arch-opponents of nuclear power, have recently altered their position. For instance, since the first oil embargo of 1973, by turning to nuclear power the world has significantly reduced total global emission levels of carbon dioxide, sulfur dioxide (thought to cause acid rain), and nitrogen oxides, which contribute to urban smog and acid rain. Ample evidence exists that countries that depend on nuclear energy, like Spain, France, and South Korea, are among the lowest producers per capita of carbon dioxide.

In an astounding about-face, the Club of Rome stated in 1990 that coal and oil are "probably more dangerous to society, because of the carbon dioxide they produce. . . . There are, therefore, strong arguments for keeping the nuclear option open."

Some fears about disposing of nuclear waste should be allayed by advances in biotechnology. Scientists at the U.S. Geological Survey have identified several strains of bacteria that may help clean up radioactive uranium. These microbes reduce uranium to a precipitate, a concentrated form that can easily be disposed of or recycled.

In the Macroindustrial Era, national strength will largely be a function of a country's economic growth patterns, which in turn will be determined by a society's access to a cheap and abundant energy supply. Unless it embarks immediately on an aggressive program of new plant construction, the United States will not be able to support more than a minimal growth pattern, in the range of an annual 2 to 3 percent GNP increase. Even these increases will only be possible because many nuclear and other power plants contracted for before 1979 came on line in the 1980s. These plants allow the United States to maintain a fairly robust baseload energy system, the main power plants that run twenty-four hours a day and provide the major share of energy to industry and cities.

At the end of the century, however, the United States will find itself facing energy shortages, unable to embark upon and support the macroengineering feats, such as supertrain technology, that require large outlays of energy. President Bush's 1991 energy plan reflected such concerns and called for development of nuclear power and offshore drilling. However, well-organized opposition made some of the proposed program politically risky. During the 1992 election, all major candidates maintained an eerie silence regarding the disturbing possibilities of impending energy shortfalls in the coming years, nor would any politician publicly discuss the need for hundreds of new power plants.

Nonetheless, there are signs that the political sectors in the United States will respond to the nation's energy needs. In 1992, the energy bills fashioned by the House and Senate were overwhelmingly pronuclear, sharply reducing the waiting period for approval and construction of plants. According to Marvin Fertel of the U.S. Council for Energy Awareness, "This was actually a referendum on 'are you going to foreclose the option, or are you going to allow the option to continue.' The support was just overwhelming. Politically its looking better than it has in a decade." The legislation recognized that the next generations of reactors will be of standardized design and operation.

I interviewed Congressman Dick Zimmer in early 1993 on a number of technology issues, including the prospects for nuclear power in the United States. Zimmer, who sits on the key Science, Space, and Technology Committee, a conduit for information on energy issues, feels that although energy prices are still cheap, "I think we should look at all sources, including nuclear . . . it should compete with all other forms of energy on an equal footing."

Barring resistance from the Clinton Administration, nuclear power plant construction may enjoy a revival. According to Zimmer, "We somewhat streamlined the licensing requirements so there won't be a separate license required to begin operation if the design is the same as originally proposed and approved . . . I voted for that streamlining because there are plenty of safeguards." He suggests that with the new energy bill "it may be that there will be a revival of nuclear power."

Over the next five or ten years, only about five or six nuclear plants are scheduled to be built. If the United States wants to grow economically, it must quickly embark on plant construction, especially because it takes about ten years between the initial planning of a plant and its ultimate operation.

Industries of all types already sense the imminent shortfall in the ability of the utilities to deliver energy. To compensate for this deficiency, big companies are building their own power plants. According to Fertel, "We're seeing a change from where almost every kilowatthour you had in this country came from an electric utility. While at least for the next decade the great preponderance of electricity will come from utilities, a significant portion of new electricity will come from non-utilities."

Of course, DuPont and other mammoth industrial companies do not have the know-how to bring on-line a nuclear reactor. Hence, the power plants they privately build are generally powered by gas. Ironically, since these plants are private, the companies are exempt from the public service hearing process. Needing only to secure such documents as environmental permits, they can go on-line quicker.

The United States realizes that implementing a nuclear power program is contingent on its acceptance by the American public, which will be forthcoming only when Americans are convinced that nuclear fission is safe energy.

According to recent polls by the United States Council of Energy Awareness, American attitudes toward nuclear power are laden with contradictions. When asked which source of energy the United States should rely on most over the next ten years, fully 40 percent of the respondents claimed that we should go nuclear. (Oil was a weak runner up with 25 percent; coal, 22 percent.) When asked if we should build more nuclear power plants to generate this electricity, 52 percent said no; 40 percent, yes. Such polls indicate a conflicting attitude toward technology. People desire the benefits of growth, but fear the risks involved in acquiring such benefits.

The Macroindustrial Era is arriving, and a society without a firm energy base will rapidly devalue into a second- or third-class nation. The lurking danger for the United States and other nations if they forestall the development of a viable energy grid is that they will wait too long to begin construction of twenty-first-century power plants. Then, confronted with demand they cannot meet, they may turn to familiar technologies that can be quickly implemented. Many of these, however, such as coal and gas plants, increase our dependency on polluting and often inaccessible first resources.

Fusion Power: Fueling the Macroindustrial Era

In spite of its benefits, many see nuclear fission as a transitional energy source. By the middle of the next century, we should have at our disposal a form of energy that will dwarf the capabilities of even fast-breeder nuclear power plants.

When science finally cracks the knowledge and technological barriers that so far have prevented fusion power from becoming the energy source of choice, the Macroindustrial Era will finally have the power necessary to fuel its factories fully, its spaceships, and ultimately the entire society itself.

In principle, fusion power is the opposite of fission. Fission is based on the splitting of the nuclei of heavy atoms, like uranium, in two. In fusion, the nuclei of very light atoms, like hydrogen, are forced together to make a single atom. The sun is a primary example of fusion power generation. Here the gravitational strength of the sun forces heavy hydrogen (deuterium) atoms to fuse to make helium. This reaction releases heat, light, and neutrons.

At the JET (Joint European Torus) fusion lab in Culham, England, the first successful breakthroughs occurred at the end of 1991. The JET fusion experiment combined two forms of hydrogen, deuterium and tritium, which when fused form one helium nucleus. In this process, an extra neutron, a subatomic particle, is hurtled away, carrying energy with it.

In theory, the mass of extra neutrons released by fusion would heat a surrounding "blanket" and boil water, which would in turn power a generator. Instead of employing wood, coal, or petroleum to run power generators, we would theoretically use as our basic fuel anything that contained a basic element like hydrogen; for instance, water.

What keeps scientists chasing down this nuclear Holy Grail is the sheer energy potential of fusion reactions. The energy produced from fusion would be more than 10 million times more efficient than that generated by coal and 600 times more efficient than present nuclear power stations, without the pollution of fossil fuels.

The reactor, also, would be inherently safe. Any operating problem would result in an almost immediate halt to the reaction, since the quantity of fuel within the reactor can only operate for a few tenths of a second. In other words, any problem would be related only to the minute amount of fuel in the reactor at a given time. Also, fusion creates no radioactive by-products.

The current stumbling block is the difficulty in effecting reactor conditions that enable more useful energy to be created than that which is put in. To get these atoms to fuse, incredibly hot temperatures of 200 million degrees centigrade must be achieved. Throughout the late seventies and eighties, many reactors were getting close to the *break-even point*, the point at which they could generate some energy from the fusion.

However, in November 1991, at the JET Lab, director Paul-Henri

Rebut said that they achieved fusion for two seconds and produced about 1.7 megawatts of power for nearly a second. According to Rebut, "This is the first time that a significant amount of power has been obtained from controlled nuclear fusion reactions." He claimed that it was "clearly a major step forward in the development of fusion as a new source of energy." This breakthrough currently propels JET and therefore Europe way ahead of the American Tokamak Fusion Test Reactor in Princeton, New Jersey, and the Japanese JT60 reactor. The leaders at JET envision building an experimental station that will produce 1000 megawatts of power.

However, many believe that Princeton's Tokamak will be the site of the real breakthrough. It is here that physicists will fire up an experimental fusion reaction that could produce more energy output than input for significantly longer periods of time. By 1994, the Princeton Tokamak was expected to produce about 5 million watts of fusion power in experiments using tritium and deuterium, the very mixture that will be used in a fusion reactor. This power level will be triple the power produced at the JET lab. According to Dr. Ronald C. Davidson, director of the Princeton laboratory, achieving such a goal will be "quite a milestone in fusion energy."

Of course, the race for achievement of fusion power will be greatly affected by government funding. Billions have already been spent on fusion, but ominous cuts in the United States seem to suggest that America may fall behind in the race. In 1991 Stephen O. Dean, president of Fusion Power Associates in Maryland, claimed that U.S. government funding of fusion peaked early in the 1980s, and had only grown modestly in the last few years. Instead of being fifteen to twenty years away, a fusion-based U.S. economy now seemed thirty to forty years away.

In an effort to keep the United States competitive in this international effort, in May of 1993 the Clinton Administration gave its backing for design work and a second major experimental nuclear fusion project. Department of Energy official N. Anne Davis told the United States House that the Tokamak Physics Experiment would be located at the Princeton Plasma Physics Laboratory in Plainsboro, New Jersey. If all goes as planned, construction could begin in fiscal 1995 and be operational around 2000.

Davis said that the Fusion project could help maintain the "vitality of the United States fusion research program" because it would lead to a "cheaper, more compact, simpler fusion power reactor." The Clinton Administration requested an initial $13 million for starting up the To-kamak Physics Experiment. Davidson said the total project construction cost is estimated to be about $600 million. With added funding this new experimental project could hasten the development of a commercial reactor in the United States by the year 2025.

On the international level, fusion experimentation is progressing at lightning speed. And the fusion breakthrough, when it occurs, could potentially liberate economies by lifting from them the burden of fossil fuel dependency.

Cold Fusion: The Message in the Bottle

Of course, you can never predict when and where actual breakthroughs in the energy area will emerge. In March 1989, two chemists at the University of Utah, Stanley Pons, an American, and Martin Fleischmann, a British national, rocked the world when they reported that they had performed an experiment in which they achieved *cold fusion* of hydrogen atoms in a jar on a kitchen table! When they announced that they had actually produced energy and heat with such simple equipment, the scientific world was aghast.

They supposedly achieved fusion with tabletop apparatus that included battery-powered electrochemical cells with palladium and platinum electrodes submerged in heavy water mixed with salts and other chemicals. The "cell" was nothing more than a steel test tube, a Teflon-coated flask, about 8 centimeters in diameter and 20 centimeters tall, large enough to hold a quart of liquid. The flask was filled with half a quart of heavy water, at which point the platinum and palladium rods were lowered into the vessel.

Their experiments flew in the face of contemporary scientific wisdom, which claims that to achieve fusion we must reach temperatures up to about 200 million degrees centigrade. Now two scientists were claiming that they fused atoms at room temperature.

They were attacked that year by the scientific establishment, especially since they would not replicate their experiments in public. Others, however, have corroborated their results. A team at SRI International in Menlo Park, California, has claimed that it was able to switch power production on and off in three types of fusion jars by monitoring and controlling the electrochemical reactions inside.

In fact, although the findings of Pons and company have been regularly disputed, replications of their experiments periodically reappear around the globe. U.S. Navy researchers in March 1991 reported matching the production of nuclear products in cold fusion experiments similar to those of Utah scientists. Their experiments, involving heavy water and electrochemical cells similar to those of the Utah researchers, apparently produced more than half a watt of electricity.

The navy chemists, Melvin H. Miles and Benjamin F. Bush, claimed that the "excess heat" and helium observed in the experiment is caused by a fusion experiment. They said that the production of helium-4 in the experiment proved that the cell put out more energy than it took in.

Fritz Will, the director of the Cold Fusion Institute, labeled the navy results "a stunning finding." However, skeptics within the scientific community greeted the navy chemists' findings with the same derision and incredulity they previously aimed at Pons and Fleischmann.

In spite of such skepticism, research in cold fusion has suddenly erupted all over the world. Scientists in Russia and China claimed that they also observed the production of helium in their experiments. Japan boasts twenty-five government institutes furiously attempting breakthroughs in this field. The Italian and Indian governments are establishing cold fusion experiments, and many other governments are encouraging the entrepreneurial small scientist to forge ahead in his or her cold fusion research. It is rumored that a young Italian physicist received a quarter-million-dollar grant from his government for a cold fusion experiment.

The controversy over this technology has grown with every passing year. MIT now seems to have become the bastion of cold fusion skepticism. Scientist after scientist brings his or her data to a scientific meeting at MIT, only to discover that those present refuse to accept the validity of the findings. Scientists now openly clash in the press, one side claiming successful cold fusion experiments, the other side claiming that such experiments cannot and have not been replicated by other scientists.

In 1991, Eugene Mallove, former chief science writer in the MIT news office, filed an official complaint of scientific misconduct against the university's Plasma Fusion Center. He claimed that the center's director, cold fusion critic Robert Parker, along with his researchers intentionally distorted a data curve in one of their experiments to camouflage the fact that the experiment was confirming, not invalidating, the Pons–Fleischmann 1989 experimental findings regarding cold fusion. Mallove resigned his news office position at MIT to protest the "unfortunate way the [cold fusion controversy] has been dealt by MIT." (He still holds a teaching position at the university.)

The skeptics openly describe cold fusion researchers as suffering from delusions, and one writer included cold fusion research on his list of such delusions in an article labeled "Case Studies in Pathological Science."

This has become one of the most bitter scientific controversies in decades. After reporting their findings in 1989, Pons and Fleischmann went underground, continuing their experiments in Europe and Japan. Skeptics immediately suggested that the two disappeared due to embarrassment over their "discredited" research, but recent developments suggest that they are privately perfecting their cold fusion methods in preparation for applying for a patent for the process. A successful method for fusing atoms would be worth billions.

In the summer of 1992, Pons and Fleischmann gathered several Japanese companies together in closed-door meetings to discuss what the Japanese Ministry of International Trade and Industry labeled "new hydrogen energy." A Japanese scientist present at the meeting said that the two scientists presented "some interesting data, convincing us to accept that cold fusion is taking place." This came on the heels of the first successful replication of a Japanese cold fusion experiment that produced 70 percent more energy than was being put in. The replication was performed by materials scientist Edmund Storms at the Los Alamos National Laboratory in New Mexico. The Japanese experiment, performed by a Dr. Takahashi, is also being replicated in Japan and Italy.

Ironically, cold fusion may succeed using a completely different technology than the simple tabletop apparatus currently employed. Japan's Institute of Physical and Chemical Research, with a $12 million government grant, is collaborating with Britain's Rutherford Appleton Laboratory in an effort to use powerful atom-smashing-type equipment instead of electrolytic cells to coax deuterium atoms into fusing. The ingenious experiment involves changing the atom's structure so that they will be so attracted to each other that they will achieve fusion. Some are predicting that soon the Rutherford lab, working jointly with Japan, will develop a reliable cold fusion technology for commercial application.

Although the quest for cold fusion has become an international adventure, in the United States the only remaining source of funding for cold fusion research is the utility-supported Electric Power Research Institute. The institute has already spent about $14 million on these projects, whereas the U.S. Department of Energy dropped all such support in late 1989. The state of Utah, which had spent $5 million to support the Pons–Fleischmann experiments, terminated such funding in 1991.

By 1993, more and more companies and individuals were reporting successful cold fusion experiments. The Japanese in particular were pioneering a variety of cold fusion techniques. Researchers at Nippon Telephone and Telegraph Corporation and the Catalysis Research Center at Hokkaido University claimed that their fusion experiments were generating much more heat and energy than they were consuming. An American company, Thermacore Inc., in Lancaster, Pennsylvania, is already planning to capitalize on these experimental breakthroughs. Since 1992, it has been operating an electrolytic cell that produces sixty-eight watts of power for every eighteen it consumes.

By 1993, the spate of new research on cold fusion had led such magazines as *Popular Science* to at least consider cold fusion a viable source of energy. The magazine's July 1993 cover story on the controversy, entitled "Cold Fusion: Fact or Fantasy," demonstrated that many segments of the international scientific community had shed their skepticism and were maintaining an open mind regarding the cold fusion issue.

Regardless of the technology employed, if cold fusion accomplishes its goal of producing excess energy, the age of abundant and cheap energy may arrive more quickly than predicted. However, harnessing this energy for maximum economic benefit would require a country to retool its entire energy grid.

Any country that hopes to compete in the emerging macroindustrial arena must have an energy source that is reliable, safe, and powerful and can increase the nation's productivity and enhance its citizens' standard of living. All things considered, the balance will shift first to nuclear fission and then fusion. In the coming era, the litmus test for any energy form to be universally adopted will be whether it can fuel the macroengineering and macromanufacturing projects necessary for human growth and economic progress.

The World of the Tiny: Nanotechnology and Microtechnology

In the Macroindustrial Era the species will make incursions into as yet uninhabited space. But what space? Certainly outer space—the stars, the planets, and the galaxies. As we have observed, the species is redefining the very concept of living space by tunneling underneath the Earth and building artificial islands at sea.

However, the emerging era will witness the species entering and manipulating another level of space—the ultratiny, the molecular, the infinitesimal.

While the Macroindustrial Era by definition represents megagrowth and expansion, an interesting paradox presents itself. In order to achieve such growth, the species must learn to manipulate matter at almost inconceivably minute levels of existence. We must master the micro in order to dominate the macro.

Mastery of the world of the ultratiny will enable the species to make gains in a variety of fields including medicine, biology, advanced materials, general manufacturing, and computer technology.

The sciences and technologies related to the ultratiny are divided into two subareas. One is microtechnology, the miniaturization of objects with which we are familiar. Here science endeavors to create smaller transistors, motors, gearshifts, and computer chips. The other field is nanotechnology, or molecular technology, in which atoms are isolated and positioned in order to construct a particular molecule. Microtechnology's objective is to shrink objects, nanotechnology endeavors to fabricate objects one atom at a time.

Microtechnology: Our Journey to Lilliput

At places like AT&T Bell Labs, the University of California at Berkeley, and other laboratories in the United States, researchers are developing tiny gears and minuscule electric motors. Micromachining is also being successfully pursued by the Japanese and the Germans.

According to George Hazelrigg of the National Science Foundation, within thirty years "this technology is going to be everywhere." The first micromotor was produced at Berkeley in 1988 and spanned 0.001 of an inch across. That is large by comparison to the silicon motor developed by Mehran Mehregany of Case Western Reserve University. He thinks that within three to five years a commercial application may be on the way, perhaps to power little mechanisms that will chop up plaque on artery walls.

Many envision these micromachines motoring gnat-size robots that take toxic chemical from backyard wells or operating micropumps that float through the bloodstream straining out human immunodeficiency virus (HIV)-infected cells. Some think we will construct microlevel computers that can serve industry.

The international competition to build smaller and better micromachinery has intensified. In 1991, the Japanese Ministry of International Trade and Industry chose micromachines to be its next major national industrial effort and began to pour the first of a reported $200 million into a ten-year drive to research and develop both industrial and medical microrobots. By comparison, the U.S. government will spend $2.5 million in one year on micromachines, with private R&D adding another $2.5 million per year.

Electroneering

When the species fully develops the science of molecular technology, or nanotechnology as it is called, it will control matter in ways that we never thought possible. As we will see later on, with this new science we have the potential to build materials of unbelievable strength and durability, control the aging process, and restructure matter in any shape or form we desire. We will do this by developing methods to control the atomic structure of matter and by employing machines and computers that operate at the level of the infinitesimal.

When conceiving proportions, people have a more difficult time envisioning the incredibly small than the extraordinarily large. We experience the large everyday—buildings, the sun, the universe (or what we can see of it). When we imagine the small, however, our sense of perspective becomes distorted.

How small is an atom? We can start with the common mosquito. A bacteria, with which we are familiar, is 1/10,000th the size of a common mosquito. An atom is again 1/10,000th the size of bacteria. Matter is composed of trillions of atoms stuck together in a particular shape.

Nanotechnology hopes to manipulate matter at the level of the atom. Proponents of this new science believe that we will build nanomachines that will serve as devices for assembling molecular structures. These nanomachines—"assemblers"—will be able to bond atoms together in virtually any stable pattern, working from a small workpiece until a complex structure is complete.

One of the physical obstacles confronting this field is the tendency of atoms to career wildly at supersonic speeds, making them a challenge to manipulate. AT&T has developed a method in which beams of laser light can slow down these atoms so that they can be studied and possibly individually moved. Laser light has also been used as so-called optical tweezers to hold tiny molecules in place for further study and manipulation.

IBM's Research Division has developed a scheme for manipulating individual atoms of silicon to remove silicon atoms individually and in clusters from a surface and to deposit them someplace else. IBM sees this technology as opening the door for construction of electronic circuits out of individual components the width of one atom or molecule. In 1990, scientists at IBM's Almaden Research Center at San Jose, California, used a similar technology, the scanning-tunneling microscope, to pry atoms from the strong chemical bonds that tie them to move atoms of xenon gas. In this startling operation, the scientists rearranged these atoms to spell out the company logo.

The scanning-tunneling microscope has other uses, the most important of which is its capacity to provide incredibly accurate information about the atomic stucture of materials.

Prognosticators now believe that these ultratiny machines, including scanners and computers the size of molecules and atoms, will provide an array of amazing benefits. This technology could also be used to clean up the Earth's atmosphere by helping create specifically modified or enhanced organisms that could target and destroy pollutants that industrial plants have released into the air. As we shall see in Chapter 4, this technology has the potential for almost miraculous medical applications.

The implications of these technologies are overwhelming. The microgears being developed by Henry Guckel of the University of Wisconsin, all of which can fit on the head of a pin, may someday be standard parts of tiny rockets traveling to distant worlds or minirobots searching the innards of nuclear power plants for cracks. In the future, nanotechnology may allow us to assemble our own T-bone steaks, amino acid by amino acid.

Eric Drexler, nanotechnology guru and visiting lecturer at Stanford University, claimed at a scientific conference that "Nanotechnology promises a replacement for industry as we know it; a sustainable basis for global wealth; and an opportunity to roll back environmental crises." He told the audience of more than 200 scientists, engineers, and entrepreneurs that this new science will allow the species to make almost everything "cheaper, stronger, lighter, more efficient, more reliable, and more available."

This message has not been lost on Japan. That country's Ministry of International Trade and Industry (MITI) late in 1992 unveiled plans to invest $200 million in research in nanotechnology. Labeled the Atom Technology Project, this program's primary goal is the development of ultratiny semiconductor devices that would be built atom by atom. Lured by MITI's proposed goal of building a memory chip with 1,000 times the capacity of the latest 16-megabit chips, several high-tech firms are signing on to the project. Japanese companies such as Fujitsu, Hitachi, NEC, and Toshiba are being joined by Texas Instruments, Motorola, IBM, and other United States and European firms in a coalition with MITI to advance research in nanotechnology and its applications.

Micromachines and nanocomputers will allow us to work faster and, on a grander scale, manufacture more and to begin to green other planets as a prelude to colonizing them. To that extent, nanotechnology will be part of an overall technological thrust that will make us masters of the universe.

The issue is no longer how we will develop such technologies, but when. The curve on which nanotechnological development sits is an accelerating one. Many different technologies may emerge simultaneously to forge a unitary major breakthrough. Some claim a thirty-year curve, others predict the advent of nanotechnology within a decade. John Walker, founder of Autodesk, a leader in the molecular technology industry, claimed in 1991 that "current progress suggests the revolution may start within the next decade, perhaps starting within five years." If such a timeline is probable, we ought to be preparing for a traumatic cultural adjustment to a world that we, not nature, control.

Hyperprogress will be a landmark characteristic of the Macroindustrial Era. There can be little doubt that supertrains, smart roads, macromanufacturing, nanotechnology, and various projects that will reshape the Earth will enhance our quality of life. However, major societal adjustments will be required to achieve this higher standard of living. First of all, we will be required to produce greater amounts of energy to power these new projects and technologies. The maglev, although it will move material and people at incredible speeds, requires large energy-consuming generators. Smart roads will require similar large, efficient energy sources.

Second, the net contribution made by each member of society will have to improve. For these goals to be met, we will all have to become more educated, more diligent, and, most importantly, more dedicated to the principle of growth.

That will be the trade-off in the Macroindustrial Era—a higher quality of life in return for greater human effort. However, the rewards of hyperprogress are such that once the population comprehends the immeasurable benefits from such improvements, they will certainly accept the individual and societal effort necessary to achieve these marvels.

3: A Space of Our Own

In the Macroindustrial Era, the species will obliterate the restraints on human growth and expand human capabilities to a degree never before achieved. Nothing better personifies this process than humanity's exploration and eventual mastery of outer space.

On the day that we, humanity, lifted off the ground in a machine of our own design and manufacture, we changed our relationship to the planet and the universe forever. In demonstrating that gravity would no longer restrict our freedom of movement, we declared this basic law of nature null and void. We also proclaimed that from that day forward, the planets and the stars would now permanently be included in our travel plans.

Spacebase Earth

The Earth is humanity's birthplace. Yet regardless of any affection felt for the planet, throughout its history the species has restlessly searched for the means to free itself from the planet's iron grip. The mere fact that humanity immediately embraced aeronautical technology once it became available demonstrates that the species never totally accepted Earth as its sole domain.

As soon as humanity began to engage in space travel and exploration, it transformed its home into Spacebase Earth, a launching pad for the extension of the species into other worlds. To many observers, the possibility of space travel and space colonization still seems more science fiction than science fact. Considering the fact that the United

States and other countries have been involved with space activities for several decades, this incredulity regarding man's advance into space is surprising.

The history of humanity's efforts to explore space is a fairly recent one. From man's early primitive flights to the experimentation of German scientists with V-2 rockets during World War II to the space race between the post-Cold War superpowers, the United States and the former USSR, a certain linearity manifests itself. Progress was real and measurable. The space objectives remained the same: to launch a satellite into orbit, launch a person into orbit, and finally, to reach the Moon or other celestial body.

Only one country, the United States, has actually landed a human on another sphere, a feat it accomplished several times. Russia, which seemed so close to developing a crewed lunar program, instead retreated into a combination of long-range probes and Earth-orbit space station projects, such as their highly successful *Mir* enterprise.

Humanity will move to an entirely new plateau in the development of space exploration in the Macroindustrial Era. The fact that we have embarked upon a new stage of space discovery was first articulated in then-President George Bush's speech delivered July 20, 1989, in which he put the United States squarely on the side of not only space exploration but space colonization.

His speech that day, delivered at the Air and Space Museum, Washington, D.C., reflects the general consensus emerging within the scientific culture regarding the future direction of the space program. Bush forthrightly proclaimed that by 2010, the species, at least the American variety, will return to the Moon. However, as Bush claimed, this time we will be "back to stay." The next target, Bush stated, is Mars, both as an object of exploration and colonization. He couched this mission in terms of both humanity's and America's ultimate purpose, quoting William Jennings Bryan's remark, "Destiny is not a matter of chance. It is a matter of choice."

At that time, Bush named his vice president, Dan Quayle, the leader of the National Space Council, whose mission is to determine the requirements for the next round of space exploration, including money, work force and material. Bush asked that the National Space Council develop what he termed "realistic timetables" for reaching these milestones. Bush's mandate was unmistakable: He wanted the council to develop concrete recommendations to "chart a new and continuing course to the Moon and Mars and beyond."

NASA had already been studying five different scenarios for inter-planetary travel:

1. Establish a manned lunar base without later moving onto Mars.
2. Launch an Apollo-style one-time-only crewed expedition directly to Mars.
3. Establish a manned outpost on Mars directly, without using the Moon as a stepping-stone.
4. Build a manned lunar outpost that would evolve over time into a large base. Such a base would provide us with experience and scientific knowledge that would prove useful in a later Mars expedition.
5. Develop a lunar base primarily to serve as a launching pad to Mars exploration and colonization.

Scientists in NASA and elsewhere maintain the greatest enthusiasm for the last scenario and are affording this the most attention.

Politicians and NASA officials view such an endeavor as one that requires international cooperation. NASA officials are establishing connections with the European Space Technology Center in the Netherlands in order to determine whether the European Space Agency will cooperate with the United States on a human space flight mission to Mars and/or the Moon, and Japan may become a possible partner of the United States in the Martian adventure. Also, the U.S. government already has plans for several space projects performed in coordination with the Commonwealth of Independent States, including docking an American space shuttle onto the Russian *Mir* space station.

Why Space?

Modern civilization has exhibited an ambiguous attitude toward space exploration. In one sense, the desire to learn about other worlds and to expand our base of knowledge about the exotic and unknown is an inherent part of the species' psychological architecture. To be curious is to be human. On the other hand, the thirty-plus years of the various national space programs, although quite successful, are remembered by some for their failures as well as their achievements. After all, human nature does possess a more apprehensive side that fears change, abhors risk, and avoids the dangerous.

As the Macroindustrial Era unfolds, it will become evident that nations, corporations, and individuals are shedding this self-doubt and increasingly directing their energy to a myriad of activities whose ultimate purpose is the translocation of man and machine to distant spheres and unknown galaxies. What compels the human species to risk life and limb, time and money, to leave this planet and explore mysterious worlds?

Here are just a few of the benefits that will accrue to the species as it accelerates the international space effort.

Space Activity Will Foster Innovation

Various products for consumer and industrial application are spun off from the research and development activities of the space program. For instance, the new superlightweight materials now used in wheelchair construction are a derivative of NASA's advanced material research. The communications industry as we know it could not exist without the species' achievements in space satellite technology. Every space shuttle adds to pharmaceutical and materials research: Its zero-gravity environment makes possible the growing of crystals that may help in the fight against aquired immunodeficiency syndrome (AIDS) and other deadly diseases.

More importantly, there is every reason to believe that the Moon and probably Mars will themselves become sources of energy and material that will serve humanity on Earth.

Space Exploration Will Advance International Cooperation

As we will see, the exigencies of space exploration will compel nations to achieve a high level of cooperation. Because space projects need talent, resources, and knowledge from a variety of cultures, the entire space enterprise seems to be the one area of human endeavor that genuinely requires continual international coordination. The technological advances necessary for space exploration and colonization are just too daunting for any single nation to undertake alone, and Russia, the United States, and Europe have already admitted as much. It is curious just how cordial and accommodating presidents, prime ministers, and premiers can be when they conference over space matters. Those in power, examining closely the need for space exploration, realize they must suppress inclinations to subvert or antagonize the other participating parties to ensure the success of space projects. We rarely see these leaders and ambassadors exhibit such generosity of spirit when they discuss trade relations or fishing rights.

Such relationships, although oftentimes resembling "arranged marriages" more than true love, may even help to heal the centuries-old wounds inflicted on the planet by "natural" nationalistic ethnic enmities. When citizens from different nations are forced to pull together as one to navigate a spacecraft or survive on the planet Mars, they all begin to recognize their commonalities as well as their differences.

Space and Population Expansion

Zero population growth proponents consistently fret that a rampant population increase will eventually lead to global overcrowding. Although this does not appear to be an immediate danger, they contend, eventually the species will have to confront the possibility that we will simply run out of room for comfortable habitation.

The exploration and colonization of other spheres potentially offers limitless possibilities for the numerical growth of the human species. Ironically, as the species begins to migrate and establish settlements, the complaint may arise that we simply have too few people to populate these new worlds and staff the jobs in interstellar cities.

The Space Mission Will Link the Species over Time

Recent studies of the Pyramids and the Sphinx, architectural marvels of Egypt's Fourth Dynasty (about 3000 to 2000 B.C.), have uncovered some unexpected findings. Originally, historians assumed that these wonders were built primarily by thousands of slaves working under barbaric forced-labor conditions. However, Egypt possessed few slaves except for the occasional prisoner of war. As we examine the Pyramids more closely, we find inscriptions such as "Vigorous Gang" and "Enduring Gang" on the casing stone, declarations of workers' pride in their contribution to the monument's construction.

Such evidence suggests that these monuments were constructed over several generations by the Egyptians themselves, many of whom were farmers voluntarily lending their labor at various times of the year. In other words, the Pyramids and other stone monuments were first and formost long-term community projects.

When the members of a nation or community labor together over time on one project or set of projects, a fascinating social dynamic begins to evolve. For one, social integration increases: We are all in this together, and we are all contributing our brains and skills to the completion of this project. However, a more powerful force is unleashed: solidarity over time. Not only does one generation work together on the project; each succeeding generation inherits the project from the preceding one. A centuries-long project connects people through the ages: They all feel a responsibility to former generations to continue the good work and to succeeding generations to pass on to them the project in the best shape possible.

In the Macroindustrial Era, the space program, especially the Mars project, will play a role similar to that of the Pyramids. As we shall see later, colonizing Mars will be a complex process requiring at least two centuries of uninterrupted effort transcending the whims of administrations and the vagaries of history. Ironically, although the very essence of novelty and the apotheosis of change, endeavors such as the colonization of Mars will provide the species with generational solidarity and temporal continuity totally lacking in the modern age.

Further the Species' Growth

By extending our reach and loosening our ties to the home planet that nurtured us, we may launch the species into a new stage of development. Migration has always fostered growth, within the economic, social, or cultural spheres. Many cosmologists view space travel and colonization as an important developmental leap and refer to it almost with the same level of reverence reserved for the movement of organic life from sea to land.

No one can predict what types of evolutionary transformations may occur as the species begins to seriously migrate throughout the universe on a large scale. However, the species seems to sense that movement, travel, and exploration will on balance bear more positive than negative returns for the effort expended to succeed in this venture.

Still in its adolescence, humankind must begin to expand beyond the planet in order to mature as a species. Judging by past exploration experience, space travel will allow the species to experience the novel, to dismiss worn-out ideology, and to entertain new ways of thinking and acting.

The Immediate Benefits of Earth Orbit

The space program is an endeavor that reflects the combination of starry-eyed idealism and clearheaded pragmatism that so characterizes the culture of the Macroindustrial Era. We desire transcendence and similarly insist on a fair return on the dollar.

Although many view the species' extension into space as basically an exercise in adventure and exploration, there will always be a hard-nosed commercial aspect to this effort. The space programs of various countries have become incorporated into those nations' manufacturing and commercial needs to such an extent that progress and growth are increasingly dependent on space activities. The space programs have become inextricably linked with advancement in communications, military, and manufacturing technology.

Much of the commercial activity in space, which has become increasingly international in scope, occurs in orbit around the Earth. The first commercial application of an Earth-orbiting satellite emerged in the area of communications. Until 1960, it was literally impossible to broadcast a program to a worldwide audience. Because television broadcast signals travel in straight lines and tend to disappear into the atmosphere, even national broadcasts were carried by overland cable. However, satellites, which allow the broadcaster to bounce the signal off a *transponder* located on a satellite down to a different geographic location on the Earth, irrevocably changed the entire communications industry.

The success of such satellites as the United States' Telstar paved the way for a veritable revolution in international private and public communications. By enhancing the species' ability to experience events simultaneously, communications satellites made feasible the emergence of a global community that could begin to develop a common culture. They also expanded the ability of people to communicate privately on an international basis to the point where American soldiers stationed in Iraq during the 1991 conflict there could utilize videophones to establish visual links with family and friends on the other side of the globe.

Early successes have spawned a diverse industrial network servicing and supporting the commercial applications of space. This network includes such companies as Martin Marietta Corp.; Hughes Aircraft Company; Matra Aerospace of Paris, France; and Deutsche Aerospace. Some companies build the launching services, such as Space Services of Houston, Texas, which produces the famed small boosters *Conestoga* and *Starfire*. Other companies, like Scott Science and Technology of California, actually package an array of launch services for satellite owners.

The commercial space endeavor is now a thriving, vibrant international enterprise. The American shuttle program, featuring such colorfully named craft as *Endeavor*, *Discovery*, and *Columbia*, which garnered the lions' share of press and public attention in the 1980s, in part serves these commercial needs. Many other countries also are launching such shuttles. In April 1990, China launched its *Long March 3* rocket and put an American-made communications satellite into orbit. This satellite now broadcasts television programs and carries phone conversations across East Asia. Europe's Ariane series has taken a leading position in the commercialization of Earth-orbit space.

The Japanese are becoming more involved in Earth-orbit space science. Their H-2 rocket, which will be tested in 1993, will be able to put a two-ton spacecraft into a high Earth orbit, securing for that country a competitive position with the U.S. Titan rocket, Europe's *Ariane 4*, and Russia's Proton booster.

Nineteen ninety-three will see the launching of the first satellite to combine the communications capability of satellites with those of fiber optics. NASA will propel from the space shuttle *Discovery* its Advanced Communications Technology Satellite (ACTS) into geostationary orbit. This satellite will enhance the ability of land-based fiber-optic cables to route and reroute data to different users in rapid succession. The telecommunications switching system will therefore exist in the satellite itself. Although NASA plans to maintain this mission in an experimental mode for at least two years, it will eventually turn over ACTS to private industry.

The Microgravity Bonanza

If anything, the potential for the commercial rewards of space-based science is expanding. One of the key uses of low Earth-orbit satellites is projected to be in the area of microgravity manufacturing and experimentation. Because certain materials and products can be produced only in low gravity, shuttles serve as prime sites for manufacturing products that cannot be made on Earth.

One of the most successful applications of zero-gravity experimentation involves the growing of protein crystals for the development of powerful new drugs. Drug companies manufacture new drugs by first determining the molecular structure of different protein crystals. However, they require that these protein crystals be sufficiently large to reveal their molecular structure. Unfortunately, because of Earth's intense gravity, these molecules are difficult to grow. But zero gravity allows a perfectly formed crystal to be grown whose internal structures can be studied and then replicated.

It can take twenty to thirty years to determine and study the atomic structure of such crystals. However, access to a zero-gravity environment allows researchers to reduce to two years this process of cultivating crystals, mainly because these crystals are larger and more detailed.

Pharmaceutical companies such as Merck and Schering-Plough have utilized the Russians' *Mir* space station and the U.S. orbiter *Discovery* to conduct experiments applicable to drug research on immune system problems, high blood pressure, emphysema, cancer, and AIDS. Burroughs Wellcome Company and Wellcome Research Laboratories are growing crystals that could help to duplicate the AIDS virus in microgravity environments, a process that would obviously advance AIDS research. Biocryst, Ltd., a new company, launched proteins useful to cancer treatment research. A researcher at the University of California at Riverside experimented on certain crystals that may help grow nutritious foods.

Certainly, the orbital missions have shown that at least in the areas of pharmaceutical research and drug development, access to microgravity is critical. Possibly the next stage will involve not only the study of atomic and crystal structure, but the actual alteration of such structures to create the bases for the required drugs.

Under NASA's auspices, research is being performed that will allow the astronauts both to see the crystal formation and to modify it. On the June 1992 thirteen-day mission of the space shuttle *Columbia*, the astronauts performed a variety of experiments to develop pharmaceutically oriented crystals and advanced materials molecules.

Experimentation continues. In 1993, the space shuttle *Endeavor* flew a suite of experiments designed by private industry. For the first time the space program carried these experiments in a cylindrical module known as Spacehab, designed by the Italian engineering company Alenia Spazio. This pressurized module comes replete with racks for storing experiments and provides easy access to human manipulation and monitoring. The Spacehab will expand both the scientific and commercial advantages of the space program.

Freedom at Last

One of the crucial areas of development in the Earth-orbit area is space station *Freedom*, a joint venture cosponsored by the United States, Europe, and Japan. Then-President Reagan's original 1984 proposal envisioned this station as a multipurpose platform that would serve as a space observatory, a manufacturing facility, and a staging area for deep-space missions.

Over the years, the scope of this mission has been modified. The scaled-down version will study life sciences and conduct materials research. The first piece of station hardware will be sent into orbit in November 1995. By December 1996, astronauts will be able to board the station for a series of thirteen-day visits. Permanent boarding of this half-million-pound station will occur in September 1999. The station will then be in permanent orbit over 250 miles above Earth, its energy supplied by 64,000 solar cells.

Still, *Freedom* represents one of the most ambitious space projects to date. In preparation, many activities of future shuttle flights will be directed toward acquiring the knowledge necessary to complete this mission. The shuttle *Endeavor* in 1992 embarked on a pioneering rendezvous/extravehicular mission. After *Endeavor* linked up with an Intelsat satellite, three members of the *Endeavor* crew climbed out of the shuttle and after several unsuccessful attempts grabbed onto the Intelsat. They were eventually able to place a new motor on Intelsat and set it on a new supersynchronous transfer orbit.

Other shuttle missions will engage in similar learning experiences to facilitate construction of the space station. For example, at the end of 1993, a shuttle crew will attempt to repair the $2 billion Hubble space telescope, one of the most complex of such missions in space history. It will involve the largest number of space walks ever attempted in one mission, all to replace Hubble's flawed primary mirror with a set of corrective "eyeglasses" to be placed between the troublesome mirror and three of the telescope's instruments. Although currently operational, the telescope has been hampered in its mission to send clear images of the cosmos by faulty optics.

Like many other low and high orbital missions, the space station *Freedom* has been subject to a barrage of criticism, both on the issue of usefulness and the matter of cost. House member Richard Zimmer, a member of the Subcommittee on Space and Technology, fears that *Freedom* may siphon off funds from more worthy projects in NASA's mission statement. There are few life science experiments, Zimmer claims, that could not just as easily be conducted on Earth. Others like Gregg Easterbrook of the *New Republic* point out that this station will be dependent on the space shuttle for constant repair. Any downtime, such as the hiatus after the *Challenger* accident, might endanger the safety of the project.

Worse, many critics fear that concentrating so much energy on an orbital mission may be seen by many, including the schoolchildren that

Congress hopes to inspire, as a regression from the progress we have made exploring the cosmos. After all, the species had traveled as far as the Moon by 1969. They ask why we should then spend an exorbitant amount of man-hours servicing an Earth-orbit space station.

These comments do contain a large grain of truth, for it is becoming increasingly evident that although the commercial applications and rewards will be sufficient reason to embark on projects such as space station *Freedom*, their spin-offs and research breakthroughs are only a small part of the species' motivation to voyage into the heavens.

The species has a yearning not just to circle the Earth and manufacture in space—it wants to explore and expand. The space programs represent the actualization of some of the more basic desires embedded in the human psyche. We want to extend ourselves, make our presence felt in the cosmos, rendezvous not just with satellites, but with our destinies.

Still, space stations such as *Freedom* and the Russian *Mir* serve useful purposes as sites for experimentation and aeronautical experience.

Controlling Earth-Conditions from Space

Future proposals for projects in Earth-orbit are far more grandiose and ambitious than the *Freedom* and *Mir* space stations. In the early 1990s NASA began seriously to consider projects that embody the very spirit of the emerging Macroindustrial Era. The agency is developing plans to utilize Earth-orbiting space objects to control climate and energy production on the planet's surface.

Imagine 40,000 objects known as "solar sails" positioned above the Earth. Together these solar sails will block enough solar radiation headed toward the Earth that we will have the ability to regulate the temperature on our planet. In the near future the species may also deploy space mirrors and satellites that direct energy to low pressure areas that could ultimately develop into hurricanes. This energy will dissipate the incipient core of a hurricane, preventing the devastation of future Andrews and Hugos. NASA scientists also speculate that it is possible for a few thousand Earth-orbiting panels, each about 20 x 20 miles, to collect solar power and beam it down to the planet's surface to meet the species' energy needs.

The knowledge gained from these space projects will serve us well in our more ambitious forays into the solar system and beyond. After all, once we learn how to regulate our own climate, we should have little trouble manipulating the physical environments of Mars and Venus.

Unmanned Probes

Regardless of what other space activities humanity engages in, it will always attempt to extend its ears, eyes, and arms into the nether reaches of the Solar System, the galaxies, and the universe. Humanity's will compels it to stretch its capabilities to their limits in order to satisfy its inherent curiosity about the cosmos and its role and purpose within the continuum of matter. What drives this relentless curiosity? Is it a search for God? For humanity's origins? Or does our species unconsciously suspect that what it really will discover among the stars is its future?

Until 1957, all that homosapiens could do to satisfy its curiosity about the stars was to gaze upon them from the Earth. That year, however, the USSR launched the first Earth satellite, *Sputnik*, and began the age of space exploration. Within two years the USSR was probing the Moon. The 1960s witnessed the United States and the USSR competing to see who could probe the cosmos with greatest speed: The *Mariner 2* was sent to Venus, the U.S. *Ranger 7* captured the first close-range pictures of the Moon, and *Mariner 4* examined Mars.

By 1971 the United States had finally orbited Mars with *Mariner 9* and landed an unmanned spacecraft on that planet in 1976. Since the beginning of the 1970s, the species has encountered the planet Jupiter and explored its moons and sent *Pioneer 11* to Saturn, resulting in the discovery that the rings of Saturn are actually ice-covered rocks.

Now the probing of the cosmos is accelerating. The United States, for one, has an ambitious plan for space exploration: largely unmanned flights that will be launched from either Earth or a variety of artificial surfaces.

The spacecraft *Magellan* was launched from space shuttle *Atlantis* in May 1989. Its mission was to map the surface of Venus by radar in an effort to ascertain why the planet has evolved into a turbulent-type sphere marked by intense volcanic activity. In its highly successful Venera missions, Russia has landed on Venus's 817-degrees-Fahrenheit surface seven times since the 1972 landing on Venus to transmit photos and data back to Earth and scoop up samples of surface material for analysis back home.

By January 1992, *Magellan* was transmitting radar pictures of cloud-enshrouded Venus. It was able to map almost 97 percent of the planet's surface before its primary transmitter failed. Scientists then successfully switched on the probe's backup equipment. However, in an action reflective of today's current volatile mix of politics and science, Congress insisted that NASA cut the project from its 1993 budget.

Progress continues unabated, however. The *Ulysses* probe was launched from the space shuttle *Discovery* in 1990, using a West German-built spacecraft. Truly an international effort, the probe featured instruments contributed by France, Italy, West Germany, and Great Britain. In 1992, *Ulysses* made its closest approach to Jupiter, traveling 235 miles above the planet at a speed of over 61,000 miles per hour. Incredibly, it then used the gravity of Jupiter as a slingshot to position itself for a study of the Sun's poles in 1994 and 1995.

One of the most ambitious robotic spacecraft probes is the planned joint mission of the European Space Agency and NASA. The project has been labeled the *Cassini* mission, after the French-Italian astronomer who discovered several of Saturn's moons in the seventeenth century. It is scheduled to leave Earth in October 1997, fly by Jupiter in 1999, and arrive in an orbit of the planet Saturn in 2002. What makes this probe probably the most challenging of the unmanned space missions is that when the orbiting *Cassini* passes near Saturn's moon Titan, Huygens, an entry probe that it is carrying, will detach itself and plummet into Titan's atmosphere. Its descent will be moderated by a large parachute. After it lands, Huygens will conduct a chemical analysis of the surface and send the information back to Earth.

Many scientists theorize that the organic-rich nitrogen atmosphere may nurture chemical processes similar to those that were present on Earth long before life began. Many commentators speculated that the *Cassini* mission may finally unlock mysteries surrounding the origin of life, and especially human life, on Earth itself.

In NASA's plans is a craft called *Wind* that will orbit the Sun and measure solar wind at its source. The satellite will act as an early warning system predicting atmospheric disturbances on Earth caused by such solar patterns, including geometric storms and auroras. After its launching, the satellite will first swing by the Moon to receive an extra gravitational "kick" that will catapult the vehicle to the Sun. Earthbound personnel will continually assist the satellite to maintain a permanent orbital position between the Sun and the Earth.

These probes and missions are critical to an understanding of many questions related to physics, biology, geology, and a plethora of other sciences. However, the ultimate goal of space programs, even of the unmanned probes themselves, is to smooth the path for humanity's entry into the cosmos. The more we know about surface conditions of these planets, asteroids, and other orbs, the better suited we will be to land members of the species on these spheres for purposes of further exploration and eventual colonization.

The Lunar Base

The Moon is a prize coveted by the most knowledgeable scientists and policymakers and was mentioned as a prime astronautical objective by the Bush administration. This sentiment was reiterated by Thomas P. Stafford, chairman of the Synthesis Group, a study group formed by NASA to synthesize proposals from around the nation and infuse the agency's space exploration program with fresh ideas.

The Moon's unique strategic importance stems from several different factors. For one, most space experts assume that it will serve as a base of operations for other explorations, especially the Mars expedition. It is also a relatively convenient testing ground for space colonization and space habitats: Humanity can learn to "do it right" on the Moon before moving on to more distant spheres. Because of its low gravitational pull, it is a natural launching site for Earth-orbiting vehicles.

Moreover, humanity perceives the Moon as a possible energy source for a fusion-based economy. Although the Earth could barely produce more than a few kilograms of helium-3, the proposed basic power source for fusion power, the Moon has plenty of it in the soil. For eons its crust has been absorbing helium that has been cast off from the Sun. And helium-3 could be sent back to Earth at a reasonable price, analysts say. Once fusion reactors are in operation, our ability to garner helium-3 from the Moon's soil would hasten the onset of the Macroindustrial Era.

Congressman Dick Zimmer, a member of the Space subcommittee, mentioned to me that "there are those who say we can meet all our energy needs by mining the surface of the moon for an isotopic version of helium-3, a very efficient form of fusion." Some university professors have testified before his subcommittee that mining the helium-3 and then shipping it back would be economically feasible considering the remarkable cost efficiency of fusion power.

A permanent lunar mission requires thorough planning, and NASA and its contractors have started to examine a new class of heavy-lift boosters that could place about 300,000 pounds of material in orbit to support manned mission operations on the Moon. NASA's plan is to assemble a lunar outpost by first sending an unmanned cargo vehicle that would transport a small habitation module and supplies to the surface.

According to this scenario, four astronauts would land near the cargo vehicle several weeks later, deploy the habitation module, and spend a month on the surface. These crews would be followed by another small crew, which would spend about six months in the module. At this point we would be well on our way to the establishment of a permanent settlement. After five to six years in this mode, NASA foresees the program making the transition to a "utilization" phase, in which lunar resources could be processed to produce liquid oxygen for life support or perhaps even as a rocket propellant.

With all of the inherent benefits of establishing a permanent Moon base, it is hardly surprising that other countries have their eyes on the Moon. Russia has launched an unmanned probe to the Moon, their first lunar mission since their *Luna 24* in 1976. Equally notable is Japan's thirst for lunar exploration, as demonstrated by the launching of their *Muses-A* probe in 1990.

The mission was fraught with symbolism; after all, Japan is the first country outside of the now-ancient Soviet–American rivalry to launch a Moon-orbiting rocket. One of the curiosities of the Japanese venture lies in the fact that they have rewritten the rules of protocol of astronautical development. Whereas most nations' space programs evolve from military technology and research, Japan's scientists had to develop their space apparatus literally from the ground up. Because of constitutional curbs on military activity, that country has no substantive military aeronautics program from which to draw upon.

From a purely technical perspective, Japan's program could be described as primitive, borrowing heavily from other countries' technologies. The main launcher, the H-1, is modeled after a relic of the U.S. space program, the Delta rocket.

In other areas, however, Japan's program excels. Its independent companies like Shimizu, the construction firm involved in the construction of subterranean cities, have started to develop plans for a Moon base. Shimizu has assigned twenty-five of its engineers to begin conceptualizing a method for making concrete from lunar soil to form large structures on the sphere. Ohbayashi, a Japanese construction company, will enter into a joint venture with American companies to build a research facility in the United States to further lunar colonization.

Thus, most countries acknowledge that the Moon is valuable as an area to manufacture in low gravity, as a source of energy and minerals, and, most important, as a launching pad for missions to Mars and beyond. It is becoming increasingly evident that any country or group of countries that has the resources and knowledge to explore and colonize the Moon will pursue this goal ambitiously.

Mars: The Next Step Beckons

The overriding mission, not just of the United States but of the global society itself, is the exploration and eventual colonization of the planet Mars. This feat may be one of the crowning achievements of the Macroindustrial Era.

How important is Mars? Many nations now have Mars on their agendas for exploration and/or colonization. After all, Mars is believed to be laden with minerals, ore, and a variety of other valuable commodities. If Mars was as close to Earth as the Moon is, more than one politician has noted, nations would already be staking territorial claims and battling among each other for land on this incredible planet!

Mars and the Earth share so many qualities that many scientists refer to Mars as "Earth's double." They suspect that Earth and Mars were formed about the same time and began on the same biological journey about 4 billion years ago. About 3.8 billion years ago life first appeared on Earth in the form of microorganisms. Although on Mars, similar microbes may have simultaneously developed, for some unknown reason Mars never developed the rich variety of life forms that we enjoy. Some scientists theorize that because Mars is only half the size of Earth, it did not possess sufficient gravity to hold onto its own atmosphere. When Mars lost its gaseous covering, the planet's ability to retain the Sun's heat diminished. Instead of retaining its wet warm climate, Mars developed into a freezing desert, minimizing its potential to serve as an incubator of life forms, human or otherwise.

The fact that Mars is so similar to Earth suggests to many scientists and space enthusiasts the possibility that Mars can serve as a permanent or temporary home for the human species. By transforming Mars into another Earth, we can provide the species with an additional place to live. At the very least, many feel that a Mars project will spark a revolution in science and technology even more dramatic than did such missions as the Apollo project and the Manhattan project. The Mars project may generate technological spin-offs that we can only dream of.

Moreover, biologists, anthropologists, and a variety of social scientists are intrigued by the possibility of humanity once again embarking on a new venture that will require renewed experimentation in human cooperative living and social interaction. We can only speculate as to what the human species will learn about itself through such an experience.

Timetable for the Trip

This project is moving at a faster pace than the general public imagines. If the European Space Agency, the United States, Japan, and Russia have their way, exploration and eventual colonization of Mars will begin in only a decade.

In 1992, the United States lofted the *Mars Observer*, a 5600-pound satellite that will settle in an orbit around Mars. The sophisticated measurements and images of that planet that will be returned to the Earth will provide the basis for further Mars exploration. In 1994, the *Mars Observer* will link up with a balloon probe of French, American, and Russian origin that will be carried aboard a Russian rocket. Barring an economic cataclysm, the Russians will launch rockets to Mars in 1994, 1996, 1998, and 2001 that will carry orbiters, weather stations, soil samplers, and land rovers and return them to Earth.

According to Michael Griffin, former NASA associate administrator for exploration and now NASA Chief Engineer, in 1996–97, the United States will launch a series of automated landers that will touch down on the Moon. The land sensors would package a number of useful scientific instruments and astronomical sensors. He thinks that these instruments can be used to churn out fuel and oxygen from lunar soil and rock and perhaps perform other tests to clear the way for human beings living on the Moon.

From Griffin's perspective, the United States and its partners can have people on the Moon by the turn of the century. They would remain on the Moon for forty-five days, during which time they would groom an ideal site for a follow-up group of lunar colonizers. In effect this would mark the inception of the permanent presence of humanity on the Moon.

The last half of the 1990s would also feature increased robotic exploration of Mars, followed up by a human visitation and colonization in the early twenty-first century. In his historic 1989 speech, President Bush expressed the wish that there should be a Mars human landing no later than July 20, 2019, five decades to the day after the *Eagle* landed on the Moon.

Terraformation: The Greening of Mars

To most observers, Mars appears intimidating, a planet whose climate and topography are overwhelmingly uninviting to human habitation. The usual vision of humanity's sojourn on the planet involves either living in the actual landing craft or in modules similar to those that will house our astronauts on the Moon. It is assumed that colonization will entail establishing structures such as bubblelike biospheres to ensure human existence on these planets. In fact, there is an experiment in biosphere living taking place on Earth at this time to determine whether humans could survive in enclosed space for a one- to two-year period.

In all probability the early stages of the Martian experience will require living in such accommodations. However, the miracle that humanity will perform on that planet may change not only Mars, but the very image that the species possesses of itself and its capabilities.

Establishing a permanent base on Mars will be perhaps the greatest feat of the coming Macroindustrial Era. Key to this incredible accomplishment is a bioengineering process gathering support within scientific and political circles in the advanced industrial societies: terraformation. A radically different approach on both the technological and conceptual levels, *terraformation* involves transforming the climate and ecology of a sphere or other location so that its environment resembles that of planet Earth.

The timetable for this major Macroindustrial project is ambitious. According to leading space scientists, the first step in Mars colonization should occur early next century, possibly around 2015 to 2030. In this phase, the first earthlings, most likely members of a multinational force, will arrive on Mars in nuclear-powered spacecraft. They will grow experimental crops, analyze the atmosphere, drill geological cores, explore the surface of Mars within a radius of 500 miles of the landing site, and monitor their own physiology. They will live in biospheres and venture outside only when wearing pressurized suits.

In the second stage, covering the period 2030 to 2080, we will initiate the terraformation process. One or more methods will be used to warm the planet from its current −76 degrees Fahrenheit to −40. One way to accomplish this gargantuan task is to build orbiting solar reflectors, Mylar mirrors, that will melt the ice caps by reflecting sunlight on them.

Another entails building nuclear-powered chemical factories that will pump out greenhouse gases such as carbon tetrafluoride or sulfur hexathoride on Mars itself. As the atmosphere thickens, the hope is that the temperature will rise, and if all goes well, an ozone layer will form that will filter out the deadly ultraviolet rays. If an ozone layer fails to materialize, the alternative plan would be to pump into the Martian atmosphere an ozone substitute.

In this second stage, Mars would be inhabited by perhaps 10,000 individuals, mostly scientists, engineers, physicians, and mechanics, living in biospheres and occasionally venturing out for a walk in pressurized space suits.

The third stage of this scenario involves a continued warming of the planet through a basic alteration in the atmosphere. The temperature may reach as high as 5 degrees Fahrenheit, quite livable from the point of view of human survival. Carbon dioxide, nitrogen, and water will emerge from the planet's crust, and as the atmosphere thickens, the settlers, now about 50,000 in number, will witness white clouds forming in a sky undergoing a transmutation from its original pink to royal blue. Water will cascade into the deep canyons that dot the red planet and vegetation will be able to survive.

Major questions revolve around the timing of the creation of a truly breathable atmosphere. Some scientists theorize that we might be able to derive an oxygen-based atmosphere from the carbon dioxide that now exists on Mars at this stage. They also speculate that if the carbonate rocks and deposits of iron oxide are heated, they may generate millions of tons of oxygen into the Martian atmosphere.

In the fourth stage, not expected to occur until 2115, the temperature of Mars will rise from 5 degrees to 32 degrees Fahrenheit. The oxygen level will approximate that of Earth, vegetation will increase, and small oceans will be in their infant stage. Immigration will increase—people attracted by the predictable temptations of freedom, a better life, even wealth. New industries and service businesses will multiply on the planet.

During the fifth stage, around the middle of the twenty-second century, the mean temperature will reach 32 to 40 degrees Fahrenheit. In the sixth stage, colonists will be able to walk around the planet without "rebreathers" or other mechanical apparatus. Mars will be suitable both as a vacation spot and a colony. Because of the plenitude of raw materials and cheap labor, Mars will become a target for investment from countries, institutions, and venture capitalists. High-tech products such as computer chips will be manufactured there. And importantly, Mars, with a weaker gravitational field than Earth's, will become the launching pad for other space projects.

Although some of the aspects of the terraformation process seem daunting (as is the case with many Macroindustrial feats), it will be feasible to complete the project in two to three centuries. As Dr. Mel Averner, manager of biospheric research at NASA headquarters in Washington has said, "There are many, many barriers, but none of these are insuperable in the sense that you have to breach a law of nature . . . you don't have to reverse gravity." Although terraformation is not possible everywhere in the universe, certainly a kindred planet such as Mars presents intriguing possibilities.

Terraformation will represent not only the accomplishment of a critical macroengineering feat, but a major watershed event in human history. True, the species has migrated throughout its history, but this will be the first time that humanity will extend nature itself onto spheres and into sections of the universe that it could never have reached on its own.

The greening of Mars, the extension of Earth-bound nature, will demonstrate that the species, through the application of its own technology, can create organic life in corners of the universe where none existed before. Flora and fauna would have been trapped on Earth if not for the wise intervention of human purposive action.

Space Colonization: Prospects and Possibilities

To explore and colonize Mars or any other space destination physically, several technological advances must be made.

For one, we must somehow solve the problem of the effects of prolonged weightlessness on the health and well-being of astronauts. To reduce the effect of weightlessness on, among other things, blood flow and breathing, physicians and trainers have suggested medicines, exercise, and special garments that can keep crewmembers healthy for a year in space. A different solution would be to rotate the entire space vehicle in order to create artificial gravity. In 1993, a joint U.S.–German Spacelab mission will further study this problem: Crewmembers will participate in studies of the heart, blood pressure, and blood flow. Lung functioning will also be extensively analyzed.

A second critical scientific advancement must be the development of a spaceship that can provide massive shielding to insulate the inhabitants from cosmic rays. A trip from Earth to Mars and back would require a ship with ten times the submerged endurance of a nuclear submarine.

The most important advance of all may be the development of a giant rocket with tremendous propulsion power to get the astronauts to Mars. One idea now currently in favor is to build such a rocket in low Earth orbit, piece by piece, and jettison the vehicle from outside the Earth's gravitational pull. However, the United States would still need to develop a rocket to deliver the material to this orbital construction site.

Some feel that the Russians already have a heavy-lift vehicle that may facilitate a Mars project. The United States decommissioned its one heavy-lift vehicle, the Saturn 5, and dismantled its support facilities after the last Apollo astronauts returned from the Moon. However, the Russians have tested a Saturn 5-class rocket, the *Energia*, which flies automatically into space and is not reused. Ironically, although the Russians have no human space exploration experience outside of the low Earth orbit, in some respects they are more advanced than the United States. To no one's surprise, Mars exploration and eventual landing is one of the top priorities of the Russian space program.

Many scientists strongly support utilizing nuclear-powered spaceships to get to Mars, a proposal that had garnered much political support during the Bush administration. A study produced for the White House by the National Space Council shares the feeling that nuclear-powered ships would reduce the round-trip travel time to about 320 days from 400. The rocket would boost from Earth using conventional fuel, but another stage would be propelled to Mars by a second nuclear blast. This nuclear stage would be jettisoned into solar orbit on the return trip to Earth.

In the future, the very concept of propulsion may undergo a radical transformation. An exotic technology may emerge from the Strategic Defense Initiative program. According to Jordin Kare, a program manager at the Lawrence Livermore Laboratory, lasers may someday propel rockets into outer space. In this scenario, laser beams will be directed from Earth at small projectiles to vaporize the fuel and blast it into orbit, thereby eliminating the need for rockets to carry oxidizers. The rockets will thus be much lighter than those presently used. Kare hopes to boost a small payload into a suborbital trajectory within the next three years using an already existing laser called MIRACL.

Mars exploration and colonization are attainable goals, but it is evident that a whole range of technological problems will have to be overcome. International cooperation and information sharing would hasten the resolution of such problems.

We Can Reach the Stars

Although concepts such as Mars colonization and lunar bases are novel and somewhat unsettling, there are cadres of space proponents in the social and natural sciences as well as in the policy sectors who strongly feel that such goals do not go far enough. They say that humanity should set its sights on reaching the stars.

Traveling to the stars introduces a range of technological and resource problems not encountered on trips to nearby spheres. For instance, the round-trip to Mars in a nuclear-powered rocket is forecast to take as little as 320 days, less than an Earth year. Relatively speaking, Mars is our next-door neighbor. A trip to the stars would take eons, well beyond the lifespan of the spaceship's crew.

Many feel that this problem could be solved if we could develop a vehicle that could travel at or near the speed of light. Vehicles at such speeds could reach some nearby stars in a few years. The question, of course, is whether we can build spacecraft capable of reaching near light speed. Although physicists regularly propel subatomic particles at or near the speed of light, 186,000 miles per second, the fastest rocket today moves at a velocity of 2.7 miles per second. Obviously, we would have to develop machines operating along principles of physics that we have not even begun to conceive of, let alone mastered.

Because the carrying vehicle's mass will increase almost without limit as its speed approaches that of light, more and more energy will be required to push this increasingly larger and more massive vehicle to the limit of the light barrier. Therefore, many physicists claim that we will have to devise more exotic methods for our assault on time and space. If such technological limits can be breached, however, star travel is a distinct possibility.

Some would argue that there is a greater limit on star travel, the limited lifespan of the human space travelers. They concede that a crew could reach some stars in their lifetimes. Within the confines of classical physics, a perfectly efficient rocket traveling at the speed of light would require only 4.3 years to reach the nearest star to our Sun, Proxima Centauri. However, it would take even this light-speed vehicle a full 30,000 Earth years to reach the center of the Milky Way. Do not such daunting distances and travel times preclude the possibility that the species can ever explore the entire universe?

Many have countered that the classic laws of physics may not actually apply to spaceships traveling near the speed of light. According to many scientists, the time dilation effects of relativity would change the way that the crew on the interstellar voyage experiences the unfolding of time. They cite Einstein's special theory of relativity, in which the experience of space and time is dependent on the observer's relative motion.

Physicist Eugene Saenger calculated that because of the way that speed decelerates the passage of time, a trip of 2 million light years, the distance to the Andromeda galaxy, would require no more than twenty-five years for a crew traveling near the speed of light. Incredibly, this time dilation would allow a human to reach the edges of the known universe within forty Earth years.

While many scientists admit Saenger's math is theoretically solid, they concur with physicist Max Born who called Saenger's calculations "a victory of intellect over reason." On the other hand, Werner von Braun in 1965 claimed that Saenger's concept of the relationship of space flight and the passage of time is an incredibly important theoretic and scientific advance. He called the series of papers establishing this theory one of Saenger's most important works. In fact, von Braun claimed that Saenger demonstrated "the infinite possibilities of space flight and the vast technological and scientific challenge for Man of the cosmic age."

Although the theory that motion can slow down time seems counter-intuitive, it should be indicated that we already have empirical evidence that time dilations do occur in ultrahigh-speed conditions. Sensitive atomic clocks aboard aircraft and spacecraft have exhibited minute time dilations even though their carrying vehicles travel nowhere near the speed of light. Time dilation effects have also been demonstrated in high-energy physics experiments.

As Paul Davies and others have indicated, the social problems of traveling to stars at the speed of light must be considered. The astronaut who experiences these time dilation phenomena may find herself in the awkward position of returning to Earth thousands or even millions of Earth years after she has departed, although she may have aged only two or three years. What would she find? How much of the world she knew would still exist?

Even if current technology will not allow us to reach certain spheres within one lifetime, the species can still gradually migrate throughout the universe, planet by planet, over a period of centuries. This scenario differs from those that portray the space venture as an Earth-centered process in which space voyagers eventually either return to Earth or become permanent colonists in continual communication with and indefinitely dependent on the social and political structure at home.

Earlier global migration patterns bear out this scenario. For example, although many American citizens regularly communicate with former relatives in their countries of origin, in reality most Americans have switched allegiances, frames of references, and, importantly, cultural identity. Their very concept of home has been translocated from Europe, South America, and Asia to America. Likewise, the experience of space exploration, colonization, and eventual migration and settlement will eventually transform the identities of the migrants. If a Mars civilization develops its own unique culture, frame of reference, goals, and identities, we must expect that its relationship to Earth will change.

On the other hand, communications technology has improved to the point that the divisions and alienations that characterized earlier Earth-bound colonizations will not occur. After all, it takes only one second for a message from Earth to reach the Moon.

Regardless of the political and social implications of migration, this movement to the Moon, the planets, the stars represents a transcendent process in which the species fulfills its destiny. Extending ourselves through space and time, we bestow life on the universe, not only through terraformation, but eventually *hominization*, the exportation of human consciousness and culture.

The Time Is Now!

The creation of a space of our own is a paramount goal of the Macroindustrial Era. We now possess much of the technological proficiency necessary to explore the cosmos and establish at least biospheric settlements on Mars and the Moon.

Countries are quickly realizing that the time for talk on establishing a space program has long past. Nation after nation is taking actions and adopting strategies to ensure their participation in the Macroindustrial Era's voyage into the cosmos. Moreover, meaningful planning and action must be taken on the political, economic, and sociological level to accelerate the accomplishment of our space objectives.

The Benefits Must Be Explained to the Public

Throughout this chapter, we have explored the benefits of the species meeting its destiny in space. The government and the scientific establishment should promote space exploration on the basis of such benefits. Government and science will win the support of the general population for these space megaprojects when the citizenry believes these programs to be technologically and economically viable.

Public support wanes when citizens suspect that the government perceives the space mission as simply another program competing for resources with the military and educational and social welfare agencies. Unfortunately, too often that is the image communicated to the public. The general population will begin to take space exploration and travel much more seriously when its leaders do.

Congressman Zimmer mentioned that in spite of Congress's recent reluctance to fund some major space project, "I and others would love to go explore deep space." Understandably they want these projects to have real economic payoffs. Zimmer claims that the Space Studies Council has suggested that "we should use as our motivation the same things that motivated the discoverers of the New World who were looking for gold and spices, which means sources of energy, or other resources that you can use to live in the deep space environment or which you can in certain cases bring back to Mother Earth for uses here."

Ultimately, the ability of humanity not only to reach Mars and the stars, but even to conceive of the process itself, requires not only an enhancement of the general skill level but a veritable transformation in the way people think about humanity and its relation to the cosmos. We have to be open and accessible to new ideas and have to be willing to surrender the comfort of the ideas that surround us. Only strong visionary leadership can serve as a catalyst in this process.

As I will make clear in later chapters, though, visionary leadership need not be of exclusively governmental origin. Privately owned and run theme parks such as Disney World serve as stunning advertisements for space travel. Japan's Hyperion Project is a proposal to build a theme park in Takasaki, Japan, based on the concept of a Martian city of the future. Visitors to such a park will experience the architects' conceptualization of life in a future self-contained biosphere colony on Mars. It is conceivable that those visiting such parks will come away from these experiences believing not only in the possibility of human colonization of distant planets, but also in the need for this interplanetary migration.

Space Must Become the Large-Scale Employer of Choice

In 1991 Congress and then-President George Bush agreed to a massive highway bill that promised not only to improve the transportation infrastructure, but also to provide thousands of jobs, including both professional/skilled and construction-type semiskilled/unskilled positions. President Clinton similarly offers billions for mundane road construction jobs.

The potential for space as a large-scale employer must be promoted. In other words, government and industry, if committed to a Moon/Mars project, could employ thousands of people in the design, construction, and development of rockets, colonies, buildings, and so on.

Importantly, space provides a payoff for all of the resources poured into training and development. We have seen how space provides jobs, energy, and manufacturing/industrial benefits. At the very least, we will be creating jobs with no greater tax on our GNP.

Coordinate Space Objectives and the Educational System

These projects will need to employ highly educated individuals. Unfortunately, currently we are confronted by a shortage of those skilled professionals we need most, including engineers, architects, physicists, and software specialists.

The space projects will require that a sizable minority of people be knowledgeable in the natural sciences. As will be discussed in Chapter 7, the educational system is not producing the number of people needed to fill such positions. If truly committed to a permanent future in space, government and industry will see to it that the best and the brightest are prepared for careers relevant to such goals.

There is no reason why the government cannot offer to retrain large numbers of people for the skills needed for aeronautics as well as other Macroindustrial projects and fields. In fact, the time may be ripe for planning to transform those people in sales, marketing, and middle management who lose their jobs in subsequent recessions into engineers, planners, architects, technicians, and so on. After World War II, the GI Bill prepared an entire generation for the professional and managerial jobs emerging in the postwar period. A similar program can help the population develop skills for the Macroindustrial Era.

The current lull in hostilities between the superpowers and former superpowers could provide an historic opportunity for the space mission. What if much of the work force, development, technology, and funding that was devoted to training personnel for defensive and offensive concerns could be rechanneled into space efforts? There is no time better than the present to discover the answer.

Internationalize the Effort

As we have seen, space has generated an unprecedented amount of joint international cooperative efforts. The formation of the European Space Agency is one such indication of this new era of cooperation as is Japan's willingness to become a technological partner in various space ventures.

The United States and the Commonwealth of Independent States both realize that they will not be able to reach Mars or involve themselves in any ambitious space project without closer cooperation. Because of such complementary needs, they have agreed to a series of joint missions in several different space-faring areas.

The first indications of serious bilateral cooperation on space matters between the United States and Russia occurred in early 1992. Yuri Semenov, general director and chief designer of Russia's scientific and industrial complex, suggested to the U.S. Senate that Russia and the United States initiate bilateral efforts in space efforts. He proposed several projects, including joint satellite efforts to monitor the weapons and missile technologies of each country and the use of the Russian RD-170 rocket engines to launch a joint space platform. (As mentioned earlier, the Russian engines far exceed the carrying capacity of current American rockets.) That space platform would have several goals. It would be equipped with mirrors to divert radiation from the Earth and reflect more sunlight to the Earth for solar energy. It could also be used to clean up space debris.

Semenov told the Senate Appropriations Subcommittee that oversees NASA that he envisioned a two-country venture to explore Mars, with the Moon serving as a takeoff point. He proclaimed that "our two countries will be the first to jointly step on Mars." There were even suggestions that the United States buy the *Mir* space station as an alternative to continuing work on the $30 billion *Freedom* station. NASA believes, however, that the proposed downsized *Freedom* station is more capable than *Mir* of accommodating research projects in life science, microgravity, and medicine.

In June 1992, Presidents Bush and Boris N. Yeltsin agreed to more cooperative efforts, including arrangements for American and Russian astronauts to fly aboard the other nation's spacecrafts. Both countries will also study how Russian technology can be incorporated into other projects, especially the proposed international space station. NASA will sign a contract with a Russian space firm to study ways to adapt Russian technology for American projects. The U.S. agency will also examine the feasibility of adapting a Russian docking system for American spacecraft such as the shuttle and using an advanced version of the Soyuz spacecraft as interim emergency rescue vehicles on the space station. One of the more exciting short-term projects centers around a planned U.S. space shuttle meeting and docking with the Russian space station *Mir*. *Mir*, of course, has been up and running for several years.

Mars is a critical focus of the agreement. It opens the way for the United States to supply experiments on a Russian unmanned mission to Mars in 1994 and increases the likelihood of a joint U.S.–Russian interplanetary travel.

Although nothing like a global space program exists, international cooperation abounds. The European Space Agency is increasingly looking to the American shuttle program for technological assistance. They also launched in 1992 a three-year $127 million study to develop mechanisms for working with the Russians on development of a shuttle to serve European space stations. In October of that year, Russian scientists and business people formed an association called Motoraviafond to develop rocket engines for *foreign* orders. A Russian program for the exploration of Mars will depend on extensive scientific interface with both German and U.S. agencies.

From a purely technological point of view, it is no longer feasible for one nation to possess all the resources, knowledge, talent, and experience necessary for a major space initiative. Necessity, not sentiment, will internationalize the species' foray into outer space.

Organize!

In spite of their accomplishment, space projects of all nations demonstrate an overwhelming tendency toward duplication of effort, research, and knowledge. These programs ought to look to the business world for a model of how to produce a successful product or project. They must set specific goals, decide how the goals will be accomplished, assign responsibility for fulfillment of each role and function, set timetables for the goals, and establish which resources will pay for the projects.

Most importantly, the guiding concept for all space projects must be continuity. Once a project is established, for example, by Congress and the president, succeeding administrations and subcommittees must honor the commitment to these projects. Such commitment must be written into law so that the space endeavor has the same status as Social Security and other untouchable programs.

The agencies and individuals involved must determine early on just how much they can handle from the perspective of personnel and budget. Concern has already been voiced that NASA may not have the resources to construct space station *Freedom* and pursue the Moon/Mars projects simultaneously. International cooperation must be solicited whenever several large projects are commissioned.

Encourage Privatization

Because of the technological and financial demands inherent in all undertakings in space, outside input must be encouraged. Fortunately, ideas, talent, and money for space exploration abound in the free market. There is a growing space business, a market currently expanding into areas that were once considered the exclusive domain of government and the military.

One unexpected area of entrepreneurial activity is the development and design of powerful rocket launchers. Some entrepreneurs claim to have developed cheaper and more efficient methods of delivering payload into the stratosphere. They are assisted in their pursuits by the 1984 Commercial Space Launch Act, which called for the elimination of some of the red tape surrounding private sector space development.

Bruce Roth, president of the Arizona-based commercial space company Orbital Transport Services, wants to actualize a number of ingenious ideas. He and others are targeting the Pacific Rim and other equatorial sites as points of departure for space flight. At the equator, space vehicles can take advantage of the Earth's high-speed rotation of more than 1000 miles per hour to catapult into orbit, saving fuel and increasing the chance of mission success. Also, many of the Pacific islands, like Christmas Island, have mountains suitable for launching whose higher elevation allows the spacecraft to avoid the thick lower atmosphere. These islands are also remote, lessening the chance that a malfunctioning rocket will wreak havoc on populations and property.

The Arthur D. Little firm did a study of the Pacific Rim that indicated that two points on Hawaii, Palima and Kahilipali, are feasible launching sites. Cape York, Australia, is also considered an advantageous Pacific Rim spaceport. These entrepreneurs are coming up with novel rockets that drastically reduce the price of building and using such craft. One innovation is the space gun, a cannon that shoots payloads of supplies and machinery to distant spheres. Some of the pioneering work for this ballistics approach was done by Gerald Bull, who later gained notoriety as the man constructing the "supercannon" for Saddam Hussein. Bull, in coordination with the U.S.–Canadian effort known as HARP (High-Altitude Research Project), actually built an enormous space gun prototype in Barbados. However, he encountered pressure from rocket makers, who saw this novel technology as a threat to their own businesses.

The key is that the new generation of launchers is reusable. Four aerospace companies, General Dynamics, McDonnell Douglas, Rockwell, and Boeing, have designed prototypes of reusable rockets. Some take off and land horizontally like airplanes, others like the space shuttle lift off vertically but land horizontally. These designs call for a fully loaded rocket to weigh about 1 million pounds and lift a 10,000-pound payload to orbit.

Another potential launch breakthrough is the EML, the electromagnetic launcher. It uses the technology of the magnetic levitation trains now under development in Europe and Japan that we encountered in the last chapter. The EML would use a long tube with magnets, just as the trains do, but instead of propelling trains, it would propel a projectile at more than 25,000 miles per hour, the velocity needed to escape Earth's gravitational pull. The proposed launching site is Hawaii's Mauna Kea volcano.

The most important issue for development of space and the high frontier is whether to keep this the exclusive domain of government and the military or to allow private industry to invade this territory. Many feel that without entrepreneurial input the space program will never reach its potential.

Unless the space establishment radically changes, this nascent industry will experience difficulty overcoming the combination of government red tape and the attitude that official channels are adequate to handle space traffic and aeronautic projects in the future. Critics are quick to indicate that under current leadership there has been a paucity of lunar orbiters, the *Mars Observer* has been postponed five times, and the Hubble space telescope has been plagued by problems. Congressman Zimmer mentioned that in contradistinction to how the space enterprise operated in the 1960s, when the United States was trying to get to the Moon, the governmental space program today has "just completely bogged down and ossified." There is a growing feeling in policy circles, Zimmer says, that the cure for this overbureaucratization is the privatization of many space projects. As with all Macroindustrial projects, entrepreneurial input will be critical to success.

In the final analysis, the species will permanently reach out into space when the population understands the need to do so and accepts responsibility for the overall initiative's success. Nineteen ninety-two was deemed the International Space Year, intended as a worldwide celebration of humanity's future in the space age. Hundreds of space science projects and public events were held with the support of the U.N. and individual nations. In retrospect the Space Year may be heralded as the beginning of an organized grassroots movement to propel the species to the next stage.

The international space movement, composed of a loose web of space support organizations, numbers around 500,000 individuals worldwide. Although representing a small proportion of the population, these people, if formally organized worldwide, could serve as proselytizers to the rest of humanity. The media can also help. Positive coverage of space flights, endorsements of the space mission by key political/celebrity role models, even science fiction, will foment the cultural changes necessary for global support for the species' extension into the cosmos.

As John Logsdon, the director of the Washington-based Space Policy Institute, has claimed, "It's going to take a collective decision by society expressed through government that [space exploration] is our people's or the planet's future."

Space and the Destiny of Humanity

It has been postulated that the movement of humanity into space has initiated a new era that will help us transcend our ties to the home planet. According to physicist George Seielstad, the movement of the species into space is comparable to the movement of life out of the sea: We are beginning a transition into an entirely new sphere of existence. As was true during that process, this next migration will change both the new lands we inhabit and the species itself.

The literal extension of the human species into outer space will change the spheres that we colonize. The process of terraformation will occur in tandem with what Teilhard de Chardin called hominization. At one level we will export Earth's atmosphere and geophysics to locations like Mars, but by our presence, we will extend ourselves and our capabilities to these planets. As far as we know, we are the only intelligent life form in the universe, and by its very nature, the extension of that intelligence elevates the quality of the spheres and orbs that humanity inhabits.

In the process of interstellar expansion, we as a species will change. Every challenge becomes a learning experience, a chance for growth, making us smarter, more able to cope, more adaptable.

In a challenging and original book on the fifteenth- and sixteenth-century exploration of the New World, German Arciniegas makes a startling and original claim. He states that the act of traveling to the New World, exploring and experiencing the novel, led to a host of social innovations, including the Renaissance itself, back in Europe. He demonstrates that exploration and colonization served as catalysts to a host of new cultural forces including democracy, faith in progress, and individual freedom. He thus speaks of exploration itself as an inherently liberating experience for the human psyche, permanently changing it for the better.

Will exploration of Mars, followed by immigration, transform humanity in subtle ways that we cannot even comprehend? We know that astronauts who engage in short orbital flights return with a variety of new impressions of humanity, the Earth, and their relationship to the cosmos. I strongly believe that this experience of regularly, and permanently, extending ourselves beyond our current sphere will strike fundamental changes in humanity's perception of itself and the universe it inhabits.

At the fourth Case for Mars Conference held in Boulder, Colorado, in 1990, a scientist from a large Japanese corporation, Joi Ishikawa, articulated his rationale for Mars exploration. "Going to a new place, making a new home, this is what is exciting about going to Mars." It is the extension of the human species that seems to many in Japan as the ultimate goal of space exploration and Moon/Mars colonization.

Hopefully, the thirst for adventure and the yearning for human progress and growth will become the prevailing ethos of the Macroindustrial Era.

4: Breaking the
Biological Constraints

Health and Longevity in the Macroindustrial Era

Until this century we envisioned time as an absolute, a fixed period or set of periods within which the species lived out its history. Time provided the stage upon which the human drama unfolded. Throughout the twentieth century, however, our concept of time has changed. Theoretic and experimental work in physics has led to such notions as parallel universes, relativity, and the emergent idea that time and space are perhaps equivalent aspects of existence. These new ideas forced the species to reconsider the nature of time as not so much a fixed quantity, but a variable one.

Although physics changed our concept of time, it did not provide us with the mechanism to control it. Time continued to exercise its iron will over the species. We lived our lives within the confines of days, months, and years, with no hope of changing this immutable force.

In the emerging Macroindustrial Era, the fabric of time will be torn asunder as the combination of scientific expertise and individual human activity will obliterate known limits on the quantity and quality of the years nature bestows on humanity. In fact, the species will usurp control over the temporal order.

Reinventing the Life Span

Within less than a century, most industrialized and developing countries have experienced sharp increases in the average life span. In the United States alone, the average life expectancy at birth has increased from forty-seven years in 1900 to almost eighty years in 1993. Since the midnineteenth century, the average life expectancy at birth has nearly doubled. It is not uncommon for people to live past 100, with some of our oldest now living to 115 or 120. Japan, which supposedly is working itself to death to maintain its high level of productivity, features the longest life expectancy in the world at seventy-eight. This miracle of longer life has extended to countries that only a century ago had extremely high death rates, like Kenya and Nigeria.

In the United States, it is now predicted that one-third of today's baby boomers (those born between 1946 and 1964) will live to age ninety. Already the United States has 1 million nonagenarians, 50 percent more than just ten years ago. Only one-third of them are in nursing homes. Stories in the popular press abound about nonagenarians who go kayaking, work twelve-hour days in family businesses, compete in marathons, and pursue professional dancing.

Worldwide increases in life span have been generated by improvements in medicine and public health. These advances first appeared in the West and are now part of the global health matrix.

In the nineteenth century, science, along with other interested parties such as insurance companies, deduced that germs and disease could be spread through sources like sewage, water, and personal contact. Eventually, public health law changed to reflect this heightened awareness of how disease spreads from person to person, location to location. The nineteenth and the twentieth centuries also saw vast reductions in infant mortality rates. The reasons for this drastic reduction are usually linked to the advent of more hygienic hospitals, greater medical knowledge of the birthing process, and better prenatal care to ensure the health of the baby at birth.

Antibiotics also have contributed to an increase in the human life span. The elimination of many diseases such as small pox, measles, and a plethora of other life-threatening ailments is a major accomplishment of the twentieth century. Hundreds of thousands of people who in earlier times would have been killed by such dread diseases survive childhood and adolescence unscathed. The fact that large numbers of people escape early illness and death helps skew statistics on life span upward.

As extraordinary as these gains have been, they pale by comparison to the increase in life span that will occur during the Macroindustrial Era. As this chapter will demonstrate, the anticipated explosion in medical discoveries is so extraordinary that we can envision a future not too far off in which the human species extends its life span by years if not by decades and beyond.

This process will involve more than making old people live longer. No, on the horizon is a far more exciting and intriguing possibility: life expansion. The breakthroughs that we will discuss deal not only in making sick people well, which extends the life span, but in improving the very fabric of the human body, making it less susceptible to disease in general and thereby extending youth. Quite simply, as the Macroindustrial Era evolves, we will each experience a longer period of high-quality, healthful living.

There are compelling reasons for society to strive to loosen the biological constraints on the human life span. Most people want to live as long as possible and generally include longevity in their definition of personal happiness. (One recent survey found that over half the respondents wanted to live past 200.) Who would not seize the chance of living a life free of pain and disease?

In this chapter we will encounter medical and technological break-throughs—genetic therapy, superdrugs, fetal surgery, and cell and molecular repair—that are helping society extend the life span and improve the quality of our physical existence. The advances are as striking as any of the Macroindustrial Era, and their implications are revolutionary.

Genetics and the Assault on Disease

Increasingly, we are discovering that our medical fate lies in our genes. Once we achieve the ability to diagnose medical problems at the genetic level and replace faulty genes with healthy ones, we will eradicate a great number of diseases before they ever start. The onset of what has been labeled the "genetic age" of medical research will revolutionize medicine and help us increase life expectancy and minimize human suffering.

At the center of this new age of biological manipulation is the gene, found in every cell of the body. The cell, of course, is a basic unit of life. Each human cell possesses twenty-three pairs of chromosomes, each pair consisting of a chromosome from the father and another from the mother. These threadlike chromosomes house the deoxyribonucleic acid (DNA), the blueprint for producing the host of proteins and chemicals that carry out life functions. A gene is simply a stretch of

DNA that contains the actual instructions for making proteins or a particular trait. If the gene is damaged or sends the wrong signals, the body simply will not function correctly. This bodily dysfunction is what we know as disease.

Genetic Mapping

The excitement generated by recent research emanates from the fact that we are beginning to identify each gene and which function in the body it specifically controls. So far we have identified only a handful of genes, perhaps 3000 of the 100,000 or so genes in the body. The United States and other countries will be able to expand that knowledge quickly through research endeavors such as the Human Genome Project, which will cost billions but eventually will lead to an understanding of the genetic roots of health and disease. Through the use of computer progams such as Cal Tech's genetic sequencer, we will eventually catalog the 100,000 or so genes that direct the making of proteins in the body.

French geneticist Daniel Cohen and his colleagues at the Center for the Study of Human Polymorphism in Paris claim that through a series of brilliant shortcuts they will complete a map of the genetic system in late 1993. In the true scientific spirit, Cohen and company will donate their genetic map to the U.N. for study by other biologists. The only drawback of the maps currently under construction is their lack of precise detail. The French version, for example, is a broad cartography that describes fragments of DNA aranged in the proper order as they would appear on the chromosomes. Within ten years, we will have at our disposal the ultimate genetic recipe book, which accurately locates all 100,000 genes and correctly identifies their functions.

This expansion of our knowledge of the genetic composition of the human body will enable us to predict an individual's proclivity for disease, even at the fetal stage. We may then be able to treat disease before it occurs. Hopefully, we will be able to inject into a patient the correct version of any of his or her genes that happen to be flawed. The injected gene then will find diseased cells, insert itself into them, and make the cell operate correctly, curing the disease.

The possibilities are mind-boggling. According to geneticist Michael Hayden of the University of British Columbia, "We're looking at a totally new form of medicine, preventive medicine." According to Hayden, the hope is that we can employ genes first to predict the risk of a disease and then to modify the genetic makeup to prevent the disorder.

This process is illustrated by our recent experience combating heart disease and emphysema through genetics. In 1987, scientists at the J. David Gladstone Foundation of the University of California discovered that one of heart disease's causes can be traced to the absence of a protein that cleans cholesterol from the blood. In 1 in 500 people, a genetic mutation creates a defective protein that disrupts the process in which bad cholesterol is brought to the liver and broken down. According to Gladstone director Robert W. Mahley, we can test people for the flaw and inform those people afflicted with the mutation that they ought to begin dieting and exercising to save their lives.

For years we have blamed a patient's emphysema exclusively on the fact that the person smoked. Now we have found that a genetic defect plays a decisive role in the onset of emphysema, especially when the disease strikes early in life. In 95 percent of the cases studied, one mutated gene has been found to be the culprit. This gene prevents the development of a key protein in these patients' blood, leaving the lung's sensitive lining vulnerable to a destructive enzyme made by white blood cells. Researchers are now cloning the gene that has the ability to make this crucial missing protein. At a clinical trial at the National Institutes of Health (NIH), 1000 people are being treated with the manufactured protein that helps prevent lung damage.

Because genetic testing indentifies people with this genetic defect, and thus a vulnerability to develop emphysema, it provides clinicians with a powerful preventative weapon. Doctors can warn those with the defective gene to avoid activities such as smoking, which will surely trigger the disease in their case.

Although gene mapping is in its infancy, the number of disease-related genes we have already identified is impressive.

• *Fragile-X mental retardation.* Scientists are diagnosing the defective X chromosome and may soon find the gene that causes this hereditary disorder.
• *Muscular dystrophy.* The flawed gene that causes this disease, which kills by gradually wasting away the muscular system, has been recently identified.
• *Hemophilia.* In this disease the patient's blood refuses to clot properly and therefore leads to profuse bleeding. The gene was cloned in 1984.
• *Cystic fibrosis.* The faulty gene for this disease, in which mucus

accumulates in the patient's lungs causing eventual suffocation, was discovered in 1989.

• *Sickle-cell Anemia.* A genetic mutation was identified in the mid-1980s for this disease, which leads to severe anemia.

Other diseases for which specific defective genes have been identified are eye cancer, colon cancer, and coronary atherosclerosis.

To the nonscientist, it may seem curious that disease is more than something you just "catch," that it is in reality a tendency to which you are born. This genetic concept helps explain why certain diseases cluster in families, nationalities, and nations. For instance, we now realize that in many cases the reason that mental retardation often occurs in several children from the same family is a shared inherited genetic flaw.

Ironically, our enhanced knowledge of the genetic map has also helped scientists determine the absence of inherited flaws where we thought we should find them. Because the females in her family demonstrated a tendency to develop early-onset breast cancer, a thirty-two-year-old Michigan woman assumed that she would inevitably become a victim of this particularly pernicious form of breast cancer. Although neither diagnosed with cancer nor plagued by any of the disease's symptoms, she decided to have her breasts removed as a preventive measure.

A recently developed test for the defective gene saved this woman from making a tragic mistake. Just days before she was to undergo a prophylactic mastectomy, results from genetic testing revealed that somehow this woman had missed inheriting the elusive gene that causes this type of breast cancer. Later, all the females in her family underwent genetic testing, many breathing a sigh of relief upon learning that they had escaped what they had come to consider an inevitable family curse.

Coming Soon: Gene Therapy

The species wants to transcend mere genetic mapping and diagnostics. We want to treat faulty genetics by replacing bad genes with copies of normal ones. Why not cure muscular dystrophy or heart disease by simply injecting properly functioning genes into the diseased cells?

Gene therapy, as the process has been labeled, is an idea whose time has finally arrived. One of the first targets for gene therapy may be cancer. In 1989, three researchers, W. French Anderson, Steven Rosenberg, and Michael Blaese, began to track the progress of cells in terminally ill cancer patients. The information they gathered about the functioning of tumors will serve as a launching pad for an ambitious plan to add a gene for a cancer-fighting substance to the tumor-killing cells that already exist in the human body. They hope that the gene will induce growth of the cancer-fighting substances and begin to erode the tumors.

These researchers also wanted to treat the so-called bubble-boy disease, the genetic condition in which children lack a functioning immune system and must live in antiseptic plastic bubbles or risk dying of a number of diseases. They felt that the disease, which afflicts these children because they lack a specific enzyme (ADA), could be cured if the right gene for the enzyme was added to their blood cells. They theorized that as the gene flowed through the body, the cells would make the correct enzyme, and the disease would be cured.

In 1990 an NIH team led by Blaese performed the first successful genetic treatment of this disease on two young girls. The team was able to extract the girls' immune system T-cells, insert normal ADA genes into the cells, and reinject them. As Blaese and company had hoped, the reinjected T-cells began churning out natural ADA, helping the children's immune systems to function effectively.

Unfortunately, this treatment was not a cure. Because the new T-cells die out after several months, the children had to return to NIH periodically to repeat the treatment.

But in a two week period in May 1993, three youngsters afflicted with this disease (also known as Severe Combined Immunodeficiency, or SCID) underwent treatments that are considered tantamount to a cure for this ailment. Different teams of scientists, including one led by the pioneer Michael Blaese, were able to insert the missing enzyme, ADA, into "stem-cells" which were painstakingly extracted from the patients' bloodstream. Researchers then reinjected the genetically engineered stem-cells, which have the unique ability to continually give rise to new blood cells, back into the patients' bodies.

It is believed that these powerful stem-cells will now pass the ADA gene to all newly formed immune cells. Miraculously, these patients, who previously would have had to return to the hospital weekly or monthly for a new supply of ADA, may now be assured that their own bodies will produce a permanent supply of the enzyme. Because their bodies can fight disease and overcome infection, these patients will not be forced to live their lives in the reclusion of a plastic bubble.

We may see such a breakthrough in the battle with AIDS. What makes AIDS so difficult to treat is the tendency of these viruses not only to insinuate themselves into cells, but also to splice their own genes into the genetic code of the host cells. The cells then become tiny factories for the production of more viruses. Beginning in 1992, Anderson and others worked to develop strategies to introduce a number of genetic mutations into the virus that may fool the AIDS virus into not reproducing itself inside the cell.

This is only the beginning. Biologists now confidently envision "reengineering the embryo." Genetic engineering has reached the point where changing the genetic makeup of human embryos is possible. Germ-line therapy enables geneticists to intervene directly in the development of fetuses, making genetic changes at the preembryonic stage that will affect future generations.

We will probably get to the point where we will modify the genetic composition of an infant so that as a parent he or she will pass on such changes to future generations. That means permanently altering the genetic blueprint inside the human embryo so that it no longer passes on defects to future generations.

According to Charles Scriver, a professor of human genetics and biology at Montreal's McGill University, to effect any of this, "the genes will have to be put in at the right time. This may mean putting the gene inside the fetus, inside the mother, during an early point in fetal development."

As with most of the medical breakthroughs discussed in this chapter, genetic engineering in humans and human embryos brings the species closer to total control not only over its health, but over its very evolution. We are conditioned to think of genetic and hereditary tendencies as fixed and immutable and to realize suddenly that through such novel technologies as germ-line genetic therapy we are the controllers of our own biological destiny is at one time thrilling and daunting. After all, we will not stop at merely producing a more efficient, disease-resistant body. We will probably attempt to customize our own children, determining the future child's height, sex, weight, and eye and hair color before birth. Many are disturbed by this possibility.

Joan Rothschild of the University of Lowell asked in a paper, "As genetic science and reproductive technology create a new health hierarchy of birth, we need to ask if the perfect child will ever be female —or black." Although such fears have a basis in truth, the benefits of genetic engineering will overwhelm them. Ask the parents of a child with cystic fibrosis (CF) or muscular dystrophy whether they would have exercised the option of correcting their child's genetic makeup to spare their child this misfortune! Ask families that are plagued with a tendency toward cancer and other diseases whether they will thwart science's brave forays into the netherworld of genetic engineering to squash their family's scourge forever!

For all the Sturm und Drang surrounding the onset of this and other technologies, the argument may be moot. The species has always chosen longer life and better health, and when the medical breakthroughs that facilitate the abolition of disease and suffering become available, most will grasp the opportunity to live a longer, better life.

The Diagnostic Revolution

To be sure, in the best of all possible worlds, an easy method of extending the life of an individual is through early detection of disease or, as we have just seen, identification of particular genetic vulnerabilities that a person may have. Early detection leads to successful early treatment.

One method transforming the way doctors detect dozens of ailments is called *gene amplification*. Cetus Corporation, one of the pioneers in this field, has developed a sleuthing technology known as PCR, short for polymerase chain reaction. With this technology, technicians can locate and identify specific genes much more quickly and precisely than using other methods and hence identify the bacteria, viruses, and mutant genes that cause disease.

The PCR method itself is ingenious. It plucks a gene from a sample of blood or tissue through the use of DNA probes and brackets the target much like a bookend. It then replicates it a trillion times in a PCR machine. Through gene amplification—replicating the DNA segment millions of times over—the machine can help doctors detect the possibility of relapses after treament and also serve as an early warning system for new viral infections.

According to Jack Crawford of the Centers for Disease Control in Atlanta, "Rapid detection using PCR offers the possibility of early intervention." In a variety of medical centers and research programs, PCR has been used to detect the genes responsible for diseases such as sickle-cell anemia, CF, fragile-X syndrome (a type of retardation), and cancer. It is particularly useful in diagnosing AIDS and can detect HIV in a newly infected adult before the virus makes antibodies. Importantly, because of its ability to amplify genes, PCR is seen as a tool for efficiently screening donated blood for HIV. The American Red Cross claims that the ability of PCR to screen blood donors quickly will add thousands of individuals to their list of potential blood donors.

The list of PCR-diagnosed diseases goes on—herpes, the Epstein–Barr virus linked to mononucleosis and lymphoma, and the papiloma viruses linked to genital warts and tumors. Importantly, PCR can also detect cases of virus-borne diarrhea before antibodies are produced, making it potentially easier to prevent outbreaks in hospitals and day-care centers by locating infected individuals earlier.

The diagnostic revolution is further augmented by breakthroughs in fiber optics. These new technologies will allow us to view internal anatomy plainly, analyze blood reliably using sensors, and perform surgery inside the body safely with laser systems.

Most of us have heard of optical fibers. They are superthin fibers used to transmit data, voice, and video images from phone to phone, computer to computer. Medicine now uses them for diagnosis. Physicians insert optical fibers into the body and then thread them along any of numerous body pathways. They can then peer into any number of body areas, including the lungs, the folds of the intestines, and others that have been heretofore inaccessible to science's diagnostic probe.

The first fiberscope was invented at the University of Michigan School of Medicine in 1957. Since then, the devices have been refined to the point where they can be used to inspect virtually every organ system of the body. The modern fiberscope is uniquely adapted to its mission. It consists of two bundles of optical fibers: One, the *illuminating bundle*, carries light to the tissues and the other, called the *imaging bundle*, transmits the image to the observer.

This new technique makes available to physicians a level of measurement precision previously unknown. New sensors have been developed that can analyze blood chemistry by measuring the hue and florescence of various biomolecules, making it possible, for instance, to determine the blood's oxygen content directly. By studying the colors reflected inside various organs, we can detect whether a patient's blood has the capacity to supply sufficient oxygen to his or her heart and lungs for these organs to function. Physicians and technicians thus perform instant blood tests without taking blood samples from patients.

This tool represents medical progress at two different levels. First, it clearly enhances the ability of physicians and technicians to peer into the innermost parts of the human body. Also, because fiberscopes represent a noninvasive technique for exploring the body, the patient is spared the medical risks involved in old-style incisions and cutting. Diagnosis can be done without performing surgery.

Finally, technology will help pathologists perform long-distance diagnosis of various diseases. Clinicians will have at their disposal a "telepathology" system that combines a robotically controlled microscope, high-definition television cameras and monitors, and customized computer software.

A pathologist simply puts a slide on the microscope located somewhere in the United States. Broadband microwave satellites transmit the image automatically to a recipient in some other locale. Using a key pad to control the focus and illumination of the enlarged image on a high-resolution screen, the receiving pathologist can manipulate this image as easily as if he or she were directly hunched over the transmitting microscope in the lab.

The net effect of gene amplification, fiber optics, and long-distance diagnosis will be profound. We no longer need experts in a particular pathology, say, blood diseases, clustered in one geographic area. Doctors in remote regions can perform fiber-optic explorations and even show an expert in a major medical facility the results via satellite. Video conferencing is not an unlikely derivative of this technology—several key experts from different regions simultaneously commenting on, perhaps even controlling through joysticks, the fiberscope's journey through a patient's intestines.

The application of distance diagnosis to space travel and colonization may further extend the benefits of this breakthrough. Earth-bound specialists will be enabled to diagnose Moon-walking astronauts' blood and skin samples to determine their overall health.

Pharmacology as a Panacea

Regardless of the incessant shibboleths warning of the dangers of drug usage and dependence, we are moving into a world in which drugs will increasingly be enlisted in the assault on both physical diseases and diverse psychological maladies, such as depression, anxiety, memory loss, addiction, and schizophrenia.

A whole new approach to drugs and drug making may finally help the species overcome problems related to health and longevity. One company, Vertex Pharmaceuticals, Inc., has embarked on a new wave of R&D to assist in what has been labeled rational drug design. This union of biotechnology and chemistry may streamline and enhance drug development and reshape the biotech and pharmaceutical industries.

These new superdrugs are synthetics and relatively inexpensive to manufacture. The new drug designers use biotechnology to help them work backward from what biologists know about a disease and how the body fights it. Utilizing this production strategy, Genentech, Inc., has now developed a drug that patients may take orally so that they can prevent heart attacks.

Other superdrug designers are investing millions of dollars to fight a myriad of diseases. Arris Pharmaceuticals is targeting atherosclerosis and heart and pulmonary disease. Agouron Corporation has sunk $43 million into finding a synthetic to overcome cancer, AIDS, and psoriasis. Biocryst of Birmingham, Alabama, is looking to overcome diabetes, and British Biotechnology has spent over $70 million to fight AIDS, arthritis, and heart disease. This company also wants to discover a drug to induce wounds to heal more quickly than they would under natural conditions.

All this research and monetary investment in superdrugs is beginning to pay off. In early 1993, a U.S. Food and Drug Administration panel approved for sale in the United States Imigran, an antimigraine drug produced by British company Glaxo Holdings PLC. What makes the appearance of Imigran a watershed event in pharmaceutical development is the fact that the drug introduces a radically new way of treating a variety of brain-related disorders.

The underlying principle behind Imigran involves serotonin, a neurotransmitter substance in the body that flips nerve cells on and off by slipping into receptors that reside on the nerve cells' surfaces all over the body. Importantly, these receptors affect mood, appetite, sexual arousal, and a number of other human activities. Each receptor responds to the substance serotonin.

Scientists have discovered drugs that mimic the effects of serotonin on specific nerve receptors and can thus affect functions such as mood and appetite. Imigran acts on one type of serotonin receptor involved in these headaches. The real breakthrough, however, is that Imigran does not affect the myriad of other receptors and therefore has no side effects on memory, alertness, and so on. The drug effectively thwarted migraine attacks in 75 percent of the people tested but, because of the nature of migraine headaches, must be taken within an hour of the onset of a migraine attack.

The development of Imigran presages a whole range of new wave drugs that can improve bodily functioning by manipulating receptors. One of their drugs, Zofran, shuts down receptors that cause muscles in the gut to go into spasm. This drug, when taken by cancer patients, permits them to receive high doses of radiation during chemotherapy without experiencing the severe vomiting usually associated with these procedures.

At the University of Bradford, experiments are demonstrating the ability of drugs to modify serotonin's effects in a number of areas, including memory. Glaxo is utilizing some of these research findings in the development of some of their newer drugs such as Ondansetron, a superdrug that promises to increase people's memory and eradicate memory loss. Imagine the rush for serotonin drugs when word emerges that these drugs can make an individual smarter!

The ability to manipulate serotonin may also help in the cure of schizophrenia. This dread disease, which usually begins to appear between the ages of fifteen and twenty-five, is a frightening experience in which the sufferer withdraws from friends, hears voices, and becomes paralyzed by irrational fears. For years, we believed this to be a strictly mental disorder caused by a combination of life experiences and mysterious personal demons residing in the psyche. Increasingly, evidence suggests that body chemistry is the culprit.

The original breakthrough occurred with the development of thorazine, which helps hundreds of thousands of schizophrenics by minimizing the chance that they will suffer the more outrageous symptoms, such as hallucinations. Unfortunately, thorazine, which operates by blocking the neurotransmitter dopamine, contravened the proper functioning of some other neurotransmitters, leaving the patient listless and passive.

A new drug, clozapine, was developed by the Swiss drug giant Sandoz to overcome thorazine's worst side effects while helping "cure" schizophrenia. Clozapine, which affects serotonin and dopamine, allows the patient to function normally. Patients still need "talk therapy" especially if they have suffered from the affliction for several years. However, clozapine's success at least demonstrates that even so-called mental illness can be partially ameliorated by pharmacology. Many of its users have been awakened from their hellish years as schizophrenics to live productive lives.

Biogenetic Drugs to the Rescue

Reported breakthroughs in genetics will lead to the development of drugs that will transform the species' ability to overcome disease. Recently, a story ran about Nadine Jenkins, who suffered from a chronic kidney malfunction. For over twenty years, she was being kept alive by a dialysis machine that cleansed her blood of the toxins that kidneys normally process. However, dialysis, though a lifesaving device, is ultimately only a salve. Its ultimate shortcoming is that it cannot replicate the kidneys' ability to secrete a key hormone that produces red blood cells.

Because of this blood deficiency, Jenkins endured constant fatigue. She required blood transfusions just to survive. However, in 1991, Jenkins's luck changed. She began injecting herself with a prescription dose of a genetically engineered form of a hormone that raised her blood cell count to near normal levels. Although still on dialysis, the injection of this blood hormone has eliminated the debilitating effects of chronic fatigue.

She is the beneficiary of a process that has taken science by storm over the last fifteen years—the splicing and cloning of genes in order to create copies of the proteins in the human body that control human bodily functions. There are now about a dozen of these new genetically engineered substances on the market, a trickle that many observers feel could turn into a flood. One of these new genetically derived drugs, developed by Genentec, mimics human insulin and another is a clone of the human protein that regulates physical growth. Under development is a new set of genetically derived substances that may cure AIDS, several types of cancer, and Alzheimer's disease.

These so-called designer genes are primarily genetic weapons to fight disease. According to Philip Leder, chairman of the genetics department at Harvard Medical School, "We are suddenly presented with a whole new set of tools for curing disease."

One of these drugs uses genetically engineeered human growth hormones to treat pituitary dwarfism. Dr. Robert Collu, a pediatric endocrinologist at Montreal's St. Justine's Hospital, uses this genetically produced hormone to spur young victims of dwarfism to reach normal or near normal heights. Until the appearance of this drug, these young children would have been relegated to lives of coping with extreme shortness.

The list of companies involved in research into the applications of genetics to drug development is proliferating. Vancouver-based Pacific Pharmaceuticals, Ltd., is currently testing the protein interferon as a cancer treatment, and Bio-ega of Quebec is investigating ways of treating heart and nervous system disorders. Genentech has developed Activase, a substance used to dissolve blood clots.

Pharmacology and the Attack on Aging

The human species desires not just long life; it wants a life whose quality as closely as possible resembles that of youth in appearance, functioning, and mobility. In fact, the Macroindustrial Era requires a population that functions at peak performance levels physically and mentally.

Pharmacology is bursting the bounds of the aging process, according the species more control over its own growth process than it was ever thought possible. Genetics again emerges as a key player.

The assault on aging takes many forms. For instance, scientists are beginning to inject elderly individuals with a synthetic growth hormone. Originally an approved treatment for dwarfism, this drug is now being used as a treatment for the elderly and infirm. This new application of the growth hormone started in 1990 when Dr. Daniel Rudman of the Medical College of Wisconsin published an article in *The New England Journal of Medicine* that maintained that this growth hormone, when administered to the elderly, turned their flab into youthful muscle. The men injected with human growth hormone registered enormous gains in this six-month experiment: They regained 10 percent of their muscle mass, 14 percent of the body fat, and 9 percent of their skin thickness. Rudman claimed that the treatment reversed changes in body composition that would occur in ten or twenty years of aging.

Not unexpectedly, people flooded health clinics all over the world with requests for the treatment. Just as predictably, the media are increasing their scrutiny of these startling results. Even though the positive results were found in many to be temporary, researchers are pressing on.

Some growth hormones are scoring large victories in the fight against emphysema. In its later stages, this dread disease wracks the patient's body to the point that it languishes in a muscle-wasting state. Growth hormone treatment was found to induce weight gains and strengthen chest muscles. Because of that enhancement of chest strength, more than merely cosmetic changes take place; there is a measurable increase in breathing power. According to researcher David Clemons of the

University of North Carolina, such results indicate that the increase in muscle mass leads to significant improvement in patient functioning.

According to Carl Coleman of the University of California at Irvine, human growth hormone study is merely the beginning of a trend in the development of technologies to improve the functioning of the elderly. Daniel Perry of the Alliance for Aging Research claims that "we're learning to divine the chemistry of human aging, and we'll learn in the next five years how to [replace] parts of human chemistry to restore function and maintain tissues . . . that otherwise would be lost to aging." Genentech and Eli Lilly, two U.S. pharmaceutical giants, are already testing a variety of growth hormone drugs to combat aging.

Among the new technologies in the offing are a host of synthetic versions of other natural human proteins called *neurotrophic* (or nerve growth) *factors*, which may be able to restore brain and nerve cells to youthful states. Each separate neurotrophic factor has a different target cell in the body, and each possesses a possible role in protecting the body's nerve cells against damage from a number of diseases.

These synthetic drugs, when infused into the brain, actually increase the size of shrunken neurons, physically changing the way the nerves work. These nerve growth hormones are now on the drawing board in a number of labs.

• Syntex Corporation, Synergen, Inc., and Genentech are slating clinical tests of a nerve growth factor that may combat the more debilitating effects of Alzheimer's disease.

• Johnson & Johnson, among others, is investigating the development of basic fibroblast growth factors involved in Parkinson's disease and stroke.

• Cephalon, Inc., is developing a compound that stimulates the gene that triggers production of the nerve growth factor. This would actually use the body itself to produce the factor that can prevent or reverse Alzheimer's disease.

• A host of other companies are searching for ways to attack Parkinson's disease and the fatally degenerative ALS, better known as Lou Gehrig's disease.

By eliminating diseases, we extend life.

Pharming

Several companies believe that a better method for developing human hormones or proteins exists than the use of bacterial cultures. Companies are utilizing what is known as "pharming" to alter relatives of common breeds of cattle, sheep, and goats genetically in order to endow such livestock with human genes. These genes enable *transgenic* animals, as they are called, to produce human hormones or proteins in large quantities. The process has led some scientists to label such animals *bioreactors.*

The transgenically produced hormones closest to being sold commercially are α-1-antirypsin, a hormone that helps to fight emphysema; hemoglobin; and lactoferrin, a substance in the milk of nursing mothers that helps babies fight infections.

The first step in pharming is to isolate the human gene for a desired protein. (The Human Genome Project is making identification of such genes possible.) Then a string of genetic materials must be engineered that tells the host (perchance a goat) when and where to make the protein. Then we must selectively breed these transgenic males and females that produce the desired protein.

The difficult stage in the process is the development of methods to separate the protein from the blood or milk extracted from this transgenic goat or cow. If this is accomplished and the safety and effectiveness of the transgenically produced protein is assured, companies can then begin to breed whole herds of animals to produce a single gene.

Companies in this field go by such exotic names as Genpharm International, Inc., and Genzyme Corporation. Genpharm expects its thirteen-month-old Friesian bull (who currently lives at the Dutch Ministry of Agriculture) to produce female offspring who will inherit the gene he bears governing the production of lactoferrin in the mammary gland. The female offspring who do inherit this gene are expected to produce large amounts of this hormone in their milk as early as 1994. If Genpharm can then develop a large herd of transgenic cattle rapidly, sufficient amounts of lactoferrin may be available for use as a nutritional supplement for baby formula and as an antibiotic agent for hospital patients. There are encouraging indications that this milk may serve as a therapeutic agent for those with weakened immune systems, like AIDS victims and chemotherapy patients.

Another company, Pharmaceutical Proteins, is developing a flock of transgenic lambs carrying the genes to fight emphysema and hopes to mass produce the genes by 1994. A company called DNX of Princeton, New Jersey, has reported that it has genetically altered pigs to produce human hemoglobin. The possibilities of increasing the world's blood supply by using transgenically produced material warrants optimism at DNX's laboratories.

Zoopharmacology: Animals as Druggists

It seems that the animal kingdom has yet another role to play in the development of human pharmacology. Although not anticipated to be a major aspect of drug development, the behavior of some lower primates such as chimpanzees may help us discover some medical practices to help us in our search for better drugs.

For instance, chimpanzees in Tanzania's Gombe Stream National Park were recently observed eating leaves off a fruit tree known as aspilia, removing only the small young leaves. They would fold the leaves and swallow them whole, grimacing while they ate the bitter substance. Based on these chimps' negative response to the taste, researchers quickly surmised that the goal of ingesting this substance was not so much nutritional as medical.

As it turns out, the plant contains thiarubrine-A, a potent compound that may help chimps rid themselves of internal parasites. When sick, the chimpanzees eat the aspilia plant but only at dawn, when the active compound is most concentrated in the leaves. This behavior was also observed in nearby Mahale Mountains Wildlife Research Center. There, primatologists found that a lethargic chimp sampled another apparently medicinal plant and within twenty-four hours was well again.

Observing the medical habits of members of the animal kingdom has led to a new field of study, zoopharmacology. Harvard researchers discovered bears rubbing medicinal oils on their fur; and pregnant female elephants about to give birth will often go looking for a plant that induces labor.

Such findings may help humans extend lives and overcome disease. For instance, it is suggested that thiarubrine-A could be mixed into the feed of livestock in developing countries, making these animals less vulnerable to parasites and safer for human consumption. It may even protect crops.

How useful will a field such as zoopharmacology be in helping humanity break the biological restraints? Chances are synthetic drugs and genetically designed drugs will probably represent the major contributions to medical breakthroughs, but this new field indicates that we should consider all possibilities for research and knowledge.

The Perfection of Surgery

Regardless of the genetic and pharmaceutical advances that will lengthen the species' life span, we are still plagued by accidents and dysfunctional organs. Breakthroughs in surgery that allow physicians to achieve surgical perfection undreamed of only a decade ago will help us continue our assault on disease and mortality even in this area of medicine.

Every day new advances make dissection and repair more precise and hence more safe. Surgery, whether to remove a diseased organ; correct a fairly healthy though dysfunctioning one, as in the case of a heart bypass; or insert a valve or other bionic device such as an implant, has ordinarily involved cutting through a mass of tissue, muscle, and organs in order to reach the surgery's target. Now, because of the use of palm-sized videocameras, miniaturized scissors and staplers, and minute incisions, the ancillary damage and pain that usually occurs during surgery can be avoided. Urological surgeon Dr. William Schwessler claims that these new approaches, which displace the dreaded knife and scalpel, represent the greatest surgical revolution in the past fifty years.

Enhancing surgery are the instruments, some of which we have already encountered, that help surgeons peer inside the body before surgery even takes place. Long fiber-optic tubes can be inserted deep inside the body through the smallest of incisions. In addition, the surgeons use tiny telescopic lenses, a miniature light source, and a videocamera in the tube that projects onto a screen images of the patient's internal organs. The surgery team also sees the various tiny instruments they must manipulate in order to perform the miniature-level operation with pinpoint accuracy.

The mere names of these instruments convey the manner in which they are employed: The laparoscope is used in abdominal surgery, the arthroscope is applied to the joints, the thoracoscope is used in the chest, and the angioscope, for blood vessel walls.

Fiber optics, when blended with laser technology, brings surgery ever closer to perfection. Optical fibers, composed of exotic materials such as quartz, have been developed to transmit the variously colored laser lights. Lasers generated through optical fibers can cause many different types of reactions in the body: Lasers can make blood coagulate and cause proteins to congeal. In 1973, the first medical device incorporating lasers and optical fibers was designed to control bleeding from peptic ulcers. Now lasers are available to remove arterial obstructions that lead to strokes, heart attacks, and gangrene.

The combination of lasers and optical fibers not only increases the precision with which lasers can be applied to a local area. The lasers will also bypass any tissues not set at their frequencies. (A laser set at the correct frequency can harmlessly pass through a human hand while incinerating a piece of paper directly behind the hand.) Hence, they can penetrate noninvolved tissue to reach the target organ or tissue.

Further challenges will involve the problem of manipulating the laser beams inside the artery and distinguishing between normal and diseased segments of an artery before using the laser to vaporize tissue. The visual improvements, however, should make this more achievable.

This type of instrument can dramatically reduce surgical trauma. In 1990, Dr. Ralph Clayman of Washington University devised a technique for using a laparoscope to remove dysfunctional kidneys. Clayman wanted to reduce the size of the incision needed to remove a kidney, which is the size of a fist, to no larger than 2½ centimeters. He utilized an ingenious procedure: Clayman went in with a small incision, cut the kidney free, sealed it off from the main artery, moved it into an impermeable sack that he had placed inside the patient's body, and chopped it up with a minuscule rotating blade. The sack, now containing the pulverized remains of the kidney, was removed from the patient through the tiny incision.

Amazingly, this entire procedure took place inside the patient. This technology is diffusing rapidly. In the past four years, over 28,000 U.S. surgeons have learned how to remove gallbladders utilizing the laparoscopic technique, and nearly three-quarters of the 600,000 gallbladders removed are done so laparoscopically. Soon, every procedure from hysterectomies to hernia operations will be performed utilizing video-surgical techniques.

The lasers are also being utilized in ear, nose, and throat surgery for treating blocked tear ducts and chronic sinusitis, removing tattoos, breaking up kidney stones, and removing genital warts. The technology is also being used in prostate surgery, face-lifts, and the treatment of herniated lumbar discs.

Robots in the Operating Room

The introduction of technology into surgery transcends the use of lasers. Soon robotics will be aiding physicians in the performance of their medical duties in the operating room. In 1992, a machine called Robo-doc, a collaborative effort of International Business Machines and Integrated Surgical Systems, debuted as a doctor's assistant in a hip replacement experiment. This marked the first time a robot helped perform invasive surgery in the United States.

The aim of Robodoc is essentially to augment the skills of the surgeon, not replace them. Even so, the robot exhibits an impressive range of skills. In the hip replacement procedure, the machine uses imaging data to portray a patient's bones, enabling the surgeon to map out a strategy for creating a cavity. Once surgery has begun, the doctor first cuts through the soft tissue, and then under the surgeon's watchful gaze, the robot mills the bone.

Imagine the surgeon as only one player in the operating room. In addition, a robotic arm may be hunched over the patient, and the surgeon will have visual access to computer printouts and video apparatus. During surgery, computers will analyze, diagnose, and plan treatment and provide the physician medical images and patient data as well as lab data and real-time monitoring of the operations. In the future, robots may also serve as operating room minimanufacturing plants, making customized hip joints and other body parts during the operating procedure. Soon we expect that most of this apparatus will be activated by the surgeon through voice commands.

European medicine may be ahead of the United States in the application of robotics to surgery. In England, the University of Bristol developed a robot for operations on the deaf. The robot can neatly drill a tiny hole just 0.2 to 2.5 millimeters deep into the interfering bone, opening a passage from a tiny device that helps restore hearing. Surgeons at Grenoble, France, now perform computer-assisted brain operations and plan on using robotics in spinal surgery. James M. Drake, a Toronto neurosurgeon, relies on customized industrial robots to remove brain tumors in gravely ill children.

Surgery Before Birth

In 1990, doctors endeavored to perform surgery to correct a lethal birth defect, a diaphragmatic hernia, which afflicts about 1 in every 2000 babies. The defect involves a hole in the fetus's diaphragm that fails to grow shut, causing the stomach, intestines, and other organs to squeeze into the chest cavity. The otherwise healthy baby is born unable to breathe, and three-quarters of such babies die.

What differentiated this particular form of surgery from other procedures was the fact that it was performed on the baby before the baby was born. In this highly controversial procedure, the doctors partially removed the fetus, rearranged its internal organs, and returned it to the womb to develop into a normal, healthy baby.

The first six times Dr. Michael R. Harrison, who developed the technique, performed the surgery, the fetuses he attempted to save died. However, he experienced success with this technology in the next two operations. The doctor cut into the mother's uterus and then pulled the fetus's arm out through the hole, immediately attaching wires to the fetus to monitor its heart and oxygen levels. He made an incision in the now partially exposed fetus; put the misplaced organs, including the stomach and intestines, back where they belonged; and then sealed the hole in the diaphragm with a Gore-Tex patch. In the original successful case, the mother carried the 24½-week fetus for seven more weeks and then gave birth to a premature baby boy.

Ethical considerations abound. First, the operation is performed on a fetus that does not have a completely developed immune system to fight possible infections caused by such surgery. Second, because one-quarter of the afflicted babies live anyway, the doctors must know which of the babies will be doomed without such surgical intervention. Since the operation itself can be dangerous, doctors must weigh the fact that they may be exposing to unnecessary medical dangers a baby who might have overcome diaphragmatic hernia without such surgery.

Interestingly, one serendipitous result of this surgery demonstrates the second corollary of the Imperative of Growth. This corollary states that when a system pursues growth, in this case the elimination of a birth defect through innovative procedures, not only will it progress along the lines it intended, but it will expand, perhaps even redefine, its very concept of progress and growth. We are not aiming for a pre-defined state of perfection, but a new level of achievement that becomes a launching pad for further progress.

This point is illustrated dramatically by fetal surgery. Harrison's group was stunned to discover that the fetus, after being subjected to this ground-breaking surgery, heals perfectly, "seamlessly," literally without a scar! In humans, seamless healing is supposedly an impossibility: accidents, cuts, and surgery leave adults with ugly scars, strictures, and abdominal adhesions.

Harrison and others observe that the fetus seems to deposit collagen in a unique way. This chemical process, which helps the seamless healing, may be lost after birth. According to Harrison, "The fetus is going to teach us how to heal wounds without a scar." Now that we have enlisted fetal surgery to attempt to save the child's life, we can apply it to more expansive needs. Perhaps we can utilize fetal cosmetic surgery to tackle serious deformities like cleft palate or craniofacial abnormalities before birth.

At the frontiers of this surgery are techniques to transplant healthy cells from one fetus to another. One promising area involves the possibility of transplanting the bone marrow of a healthy unborn into fetuses doomed by blood disorders to an early death. The healthy stem cells from one fetus, injected into another, will migrate untouched to the bone marrow of the recipient before the recipient's immune system has matured enough to reject them. (Rejection remains a problem in such transplants from adult to adult.) Importantly, these donor cells may produce a lifelong supply of healthy blood cells for the recipient.

A critical point here is that since fetal surgery is a direct assault on infant mortality, it will directly lead to an increase in the human life span.

Taking Health into Our Own Hands

In the Macroindustrial Era, improvements in health and life span will not be generated by medical and biotechnological breakthroughs alone. The public will demand and assume a more proactive role in its own health care. This is truly a cooperative venture between the public and science. By changing their life-styles—eating better, exercising, reducing stress—individuals are doing their part to help science improve their chances of living longer to an optimum.

A powerful example of this trend lies in the attempts to eliminate heart disease. Coronary heart disease (CHD) still remains America's number one killer, but the battle against this disease is being won in part by people changing their high-risk behavior.

Causes of CHD vary, but we know that fatty diet, cigarette smoking, and sedentary living are primary suspects. Changes in life-style and personal habits forced CHD rates down by 46 percent from 1968 to 1988. Although much of this decrease is due to drugs that prevent or even reverse atherosclerosis (the buildup of fatty deposits in the arteries that leads to heart attacks), we know that the reduction in cholesterol intake has had some effect.

Because of this increase in exercise and lowering of cholesterol, life expectancy has risen by five years, to seventy-five, since the 1960s. It is estimated that 420,000 Americans alive today would have died in 1989 alone if the CHD death rate had remained what it was in 1963. In general, these benefits affect races and classes differently.

Besides changing their life-style and food intake, individuals can take health into their own hands by becoming better medical consumers. For instance, consumers now have technology available to them that will predict CHD risk earlier and more accurately. Tests can demonstrate the potential for future heart problems in seemingly healthy senior citizens, and computer programs can develop profiles for CHD risk based on a variety of medical and demographic factors. People can then modify their behavior accordingly.

Genetic tests will soon demonstrate which genes predispose certain people to heart disease. Thus, even before we can correct such genes through gene therapy, we will be able to indicate to such people that dietary and life-style changes are certainly in order.

The Vitamin—Health Connection

People in the West have taken synthetic and natural vitamins in moderate amounts for years. "One-a-day" vitamin dosages have been a staple of the Western diet for decades. An evolving trend today is the self-administration of megadoses of key vitamins both to alleviate and to prevent a range of medical complaints.

Research has uncovered a plethora of substantial relationships between specific vitamins and medical benefits. Vitamin A prevents night blindness and may reduce the risk of breast, lung, and other cancers. Vitamin B_{12} prevents pernicious anemia, vitamin C prevents scurvy and loose teeth, and vitamin E inhibits anemia.

What has scientists excited currently is a group of vitamins that include C, E, and β-carotene, the chemical parent of A. These vitamins are antioxidants, able to defuse the volatile toxic molecules, oxygen-free radicals, that are a by-product of normal metabolism in cells. These toxins are also created in the body by tobacco smoke, car exhaust, and sunlight. These free radicals can wreak havoc by damaging DNA, altering biochemical compounds, and even killing cells outright.

Some biochemists now feel that people should have themselves screened for the existence of free radicals in their bloodstream as they do for cholesterol. If the person discovers that he or she has too high a rate of free radicals, antioxidant therapy composed of the above vitamins should be considered. There have been suggestions that healthy seniors boost their immune system by ingesting megadoses of vitamin E. In this way, they can reduce their chance of acquiring life-threatening infections.

In 1993, two separate studies seemed to confirm the special benefits of vitamin E. The studies reported that people who ingested large doses of vitamin E in pill form, about ten times the average person's intake, had a 40 percent lower risk of heart disease than those who consumed more modest doses. Together the two studies followed more than 120,000 people for a period of four to eight years, and controlled for such variables as lifestyle and heredity.

The likelihood is that Westerners will adopt vitamin self-therapy to the same extent that they began to perform aerobic exercise and reduced their cigarette smoking and fatty red meat consumption. As Westerners become more convinced that health is partially dependent on taking health into their own hands, they will gradually adopt a vitamin-oriented diet.

Thinking Good Thoughts

People are showing an extensive interest in incorporating meditation and various mind-alteration or mind-control techniques into their health regimen. While we will deal with this at greater length in Chapter 8, medical benefits of such practices deserve mention here.

According to a study performed by Dr. Jay Glaser, older people who practice transcendental meditation for at least one hour have higher levels of the hormone DHEAS (Dehydrogpiandrosterone) in their blood. The absence of this hormone in the body has been linked to heart disease, osteoporosis, and other maladies of age. Secreted by the adrenal glands, high levels of the hormone serve as a good index of general health and well-being.

Although the link between meditation and increased life expectancy is not understood, the effects of altered states of consciousness on bodily functioning may form new ground for medical research. We know from one study, for instance, that long-term meditators score better than nonmeditators on the Morgan Scale, which gauges blood pressure, vision, and auditory threshold. On average, long-term meditators' scores indicate that they possess the blood pressure, sight, and hearing of a person twelve years younger.

Does meditation slow down the aging process? Objective testing seems to indicate this distinctive possibility!

Bringing Doctors Up to Speed

In the Macroindustrial Era, people will realize that they must get the most from the medical system: they will adopt more proactive behavior regarding doctors, the medical establishment, and their right to information.

Self-education has become an integral part of the species' assault on mortality. Knowledge and skill are unequally distributed throughout the physician population; patients often perceive acquiring a knowledgeable physician as a matter of luck. One physician knows how to cure a disease, whereas another does not even read medical journals or popular periodicals and newspapers to keep abreast of medical news.

The public is gradually realizing that an immense chasm exists between medical breakthroughs and practicing doctors' knowledge of these breakthroughs and/or their willingness to employ them. According to Dr. Thomas Chalmers, a researcher at the Harvard School of Public Health, clinical experts are often behind the times in treating heart attacks. In his study, he found that patients were often not informed by their doctors of new lifesaving therapies and given outdated medical advice that had been shown to do more harm than good.

In another study, it was found that many physicians persist in offering only mastectomies for breast cancer even though radiation and a lumpectomy could be equally useful. Men with localized prostate cancer could get relief from radiation therapy but were usually referred automatically to surgery.

According to Dr. Jeffrey Isner, cardiologist at Tufts University School of Medicine, doctors generally are reactionary when confronted with new ideas. Although studies have consistently revealed that ulcers can be cured with antibiotic therapy, rarely will doctors take this route when dealing with ulcer patients. Instead, they inform patients that medication that suppresses stomach acid is the best method. Dr. Cornelius Doley, a Sante Fe gastroenterologist, claims that doctors just find it "very hard to accept that some kind of bacteria could fit into this whole thing."

According to Dr. Charles Hennekens of the Harvard University School of Medicine, drug companies and their advertising and promotion campaigns undermine adoption of research results. For instance, such pharmaceutical company advertising has led doctors to use calcium channel blockers as a way to prevent heart attacks even though data do not support such use. On the other hand, because drug companies have not trumpeted the relationship between heart attack reduction and aspirin use, only a minority of heart attack victims receive such therapy.

An underlying cause of this reluctance to adopt new therapies is the fact that many doctors do not take the time to read or understand journal articles. Insurance money also influences the eventual decision to choose one therapy over another. Isner suggests that doctors will not embrace a superior treatment that takes twice as much time to perform but is reimbursed at the rate of the old treatment.

In the Macroindustrial Era, the mystery that has enshrouded medicine and science in general will dissipate, empowering members of the public and divesting the medical establishment of much of its control over health. The aura of the medical establishment as a modern version of a priesthood will be shattered, liberating the population from its role as passive beneficiary to active participant in the curative process.

Once a person contracts a dread disease, he or she acts with amazing rapidity to accumulate a massive amount of highly technical information and data on the etiology of the disease. Ordinarily, the patient would have considered such technical information beyond his or her grasp, but necessity acts as a powerful catalyst on our ability to learn and understand previously incomprehensible material.

In the Macroindustrial Era, this level of patient involvement in his and her health will be the norm. Computer data bases make the information much more available. Software is making information on diseases, symptoms, and doctors themselves much more commonplace. Importantly, support groups and networks spring up almost immediately when new diseases occur and serve as excellent conduits of information.

The AIDS experience may be instructive. As the disease spread throughout the 1980s, patients and supporters refused to accept the medical and pharmaceutical establishment's dicta on the disease's etiology, therapy, and cure. Many of these groups even influenced the speed at which the United States and other governments approved drugs such as AZT. Such new patient behavior was celebrated in the 1993 movie *Lorenzo's Oil*. The movie dealt with the painstaking labors of parents of a child stricken with a dread disease to find a cure for the disease themselves. Refusing to accept the medical establishment's death sentence for their child, they rallied themselves and patients plagued by the disease to engage in a variety of actions to discover the etiology of the disease and possibly its cure. They established worldwide personal and electronic networks and superseded the efforts of the medical establishment itself to fight this disease.

The last obstacle to medical self-help may end up being the tenuous relationship among doctors, pharmaceutical companies, and the medical consumer. At this point, the medical establishment serves as a gatekeeper to drug distribution among the population. Most drugs can only be acquired by the patient if his or her physician writes a prescription. Early signs have developed that suggest that this relationship has begun to weaken. Dr. Thomas Szasz, a well-known medical writer, in his most recent book, *Our Right to Drugs: The Case for a Free Market*, attacks the monopoly that the medical establishment has on drug therapy in the hospital and outside. He presents cogent reasons for loosening such a stranglehold, the greatest being that this monopoly prevents people who need certain drugs for valid medical reasons from ever acquiring them.

In the coming Era, people will commandeer the resources, medical and other, that they need to progress. Events today presage a coming consciousness of the fact that people will live longer when they demand to live longer.

Nanotechnology and the Promise of Continual Regeneration

For eternity, humanity has wrestled with the ultimate question of life and death. We know that the technologies and biological methods explored up to this point will extend life and make it inherently healthier.

But *nanotechnology*, the science of the molecular and ultratiny, brings to the table a unique solution to life and death. In medicine, it will represent an industrial engineering solution to the problem of mortality—the use of tiny machines to repair, renew, and regenerate damaged or "aging" cells. This inventive science, which we encountered earlier, literally defines the term *hyperprogress*.

Again, nano- and microtechnologies operate at the most minuscule levels of matter—the molecular, the atomic, and the subatomic. According to micromatter researcher John Roland, molecular machines could be used to rebuild damaged organs, make cosmetic alterations, or provide people with wholly new body parts capable of dramatically enhanced powers. According to Roland, missing limbs could be regenerated, and defective eyes and ears could be restored to their previous state or could perhaps even be improved.

In fact, medical researchers envision these molecular-size nanodevices augmenting the immune system by finding and disabling unwanted bacteria and viruses. They dream of pumps no bigger than a printed period that would stream through the human bloodstream straining out HIV-infected cells.

Expert K. Eric Drexler waxes eloquent about these new devices to rearrange atoms and set them right. Nanotechnology will mean that physicians will be able to use molecular machines directed by nanocomputers to examine and probably repair small components of human cells, such as the molecule.

In a sense, we already have in our possession a method of molecular repair, namely, drug therapy. As we have observed, these pharmaceutical breakthroughs will certainly make their mark. However, it is important to note that drugs and surgery at most encourage tissues to repair themselves. The molecular machines guided by nanotechnology will enable physicans and technicians to repair the cells directly.

The technology at this level is intriguing. The cell repair machines will be comparable in size to bacteria and viruses. They can travel through tissue much like white blood cells, enter cells (just as viruses do), and take whatever action they are programmed to perform. They will be guided by nanocomputers no larger than $\frac{1}{100}$th the volume of a typical cell. In such a repair system, these nanocomputers will direct simpler computers, which in turn will direct machines to first examine molecular structures, take them apart, and repair any damage.

The implications are stupendous. Floating through the body and powered by the body's cells themselves, these tiny machines will have the capacity to repair whole cells, tissues, and organs, eventually bringing a patient back to total health. Even though the machine is working cell by cell, tissues or whole organs can be repaired within days or weeks.

Applications

Where will this nanomedicine ultimately lead? Most observers agree that nanotechnology's benefits will change the way we think about medical care and will force the species to confront the concept of eminently extended life span and possible immortality.

Although essentially a building technology, one of the more extraordinary benefits of nanotechnology may derive from its ability to achieve "selective destruction" within the body. Because the human body is prone to cancers and infectious diseases, it requires a mechanism that can destroy dangerous replicators such as bacteria, cancer cells, viruses, or worms. Some think that these molecular-size repair devices can cure such diseases. For instance, the herpes virus splices its genes into the DNA of the host cell. The nanotechnological repair device, replete with computer and minuscule robotic arms, will read the cells' DNA and remove the additional gene that spells *herpes* without affecting the host cell's inherent integrity.

Nanotechnology will also play a major role in postoperative healing. Quite simply, repair machines will help the heart grow fresh muscle by resetting cellular control mechanisms. Stroke victims will be helped to regenerate fresh brain tissue even where there has been significant damage.

The ultimate goal here is not merely to cure diseases, but rather to establish lifetime health, perhaps even immortality. This will transpire when we have achieved a complete understanding of the molecular structure of healthy tissue. Then we will have the knowledge to diagram, as it were, the structure of a healthy heart cell or a healthy liver and transfer to the tiny machines the accurate information about that organ's molecules, cells, and tissues.

Suppose we want an ultratiny machine to repair a defective liver. The researcher only has to describe to the machine the specific molecular and atomic structure of a healthy liver. Armed with this information, the repair machine explores the liver for differences between the picture we provide it and the cells and tissue that it encounters in the defective organ. The machine begins to make the liver right again by changing its molecular and atomic structure to correspond to the diagram it possesses of the "perfect" liver.

Of course, this technology currently lies beyond our ability and scientific expertise. The programs in these ultratiny machines must contain detailed information on hundreds of types of cells and perhaps hundreds of thousands of molecular structures. They must also be able to restructure these damaged cells to correct them.

The End of Aging

The medical establishment increasingly considers aging another disease that must be overcome. We have made remarkable progress in increasing the life span, mainly through better drugs and diet and more sanitary living conditions.

In lab experiments, combinations of drugs and special diets have extended the life span of mice by 25 to 45 percent. Many companies are joining the fray in the battle against aging. In the 1980s Eastman Kodak and ICN Pharmaceuticals joined in a project costing over $45 million to produce drugs such as Isorinosine to extend the life span.

Now, nanotechnology will launch a whole new era in the quest for longevity. To many observers, cell repair machines will be able to improve cell function for as long as the distinctive structures of the cells remain intact. They cannot create new cells, but they certainly can regenerate existing ones.

Once we realize that the effects of aging, including brittle bones, wrinkled skin, slow wound healing, poor memory, and other "signs of aging," are just so many misarranged cells and molecules, we can instantly recognize how a machine with the right program could potentially rearrange those structures so that we can maintain and restore youthful health.

It is not coincidental that a cornerstone of the Macroindustrial Era, an increased life span, will result from a gradual translocation of the medical process from the world of the physician to that of the engineer, albeit the computer engineer. These nanocomputers and ultratiny cell repair devices know no distinction between organic and inorganic. They will rearrange atoms and molecules in coordination with sets of commands originating with a preset program, or vision, of the correct arrangement of such structures.

The reconstitution of livers, hearts, and damaged organs will in essence become an industrial, no, a Macroindustrial process, overseen by technicians and medical engineers.

The question of when such technology will arrive on the scene is a hotly debated one. When dealing with computer-based technology, the machines themselves become part of the design and creation process. Artificial intelligence systems, which mimic human thinking, can very well help us make several of the creative leaps necessary for us to perfect this technology.

We do know that whenever this breakthrough occurs, our basic concepts of health, healing, and life itself will undergo a dramatic transformation.

The Full-Pronged Attack

The most encouraging aspect of the Macroindustrial Era's campaign against disease is the fact that it does not involve just one technology or therapy. This is a full-pronged assault on aging and disease: relentless, thorough, and determined.

The battle against cystic fibrosis most typifies the way that disease in general will be challenged and overcome during the Macroindustrial Era. Cystic fibrosis afflicts 25,000 Americans, killing at least 500 mostly young people per year. Most chilling is the way this disease kills. Its victims experience a gradual accumulation of a thick bluish mucus in their airways, including the lungs. Over a period of years, the victim's air passage system increasingly clogs. This mucus buildup in the lungs, pancreas, and liver serves as a fertile ground for potentially damaging infections and also blocks the flow of vital digestive enzymes to the intestines. Even sperm stops up in the testes. By the teen years, or sometimes in the early to late twenties, the victim dies.

The usual treatment for cystic fibrosis, while moderately effective, is surprisingly primitive: clapping young patients on the back and chest several times a day to clear the lungs, administering nutrient-rich diets, and other palliatives. These therapies have extended the average life span of victims from just five years in the 1950s to as much as twenty-eight years.

As we approach the next era, however, pharmacological discoveries may provide better solutions to cystic fibrosis. One such drug may prevent the protein elastas, which CF patients produce, from attacking the lung tissue. Another drug, DNase, dissolves leftover DNA from dead immune cells, allowing the body to use its own self-cleansing mechanisms to clear away thinner residual fluids.

Researchers feel that they can even more effectively overwhelm this dread disease by stopping the production of this thick mucus at its source. We have discovered that cystic fibrosis is caused by cellular malfunctions that induce cells to produce an excess of salt that "leads" water out of the mucus. The remaining mucus is the excessively thick fluid that eventually kills the patient. Now two drugs have been discovered that repair this cellular malfunction: The repaired cells no longer produce salt, and the thick mucus no longer forms in the patient's body.

However, the most promising technique of all will not be pharmacological, but genetic. Two researchers, Francis Collins and Lap-Chee Tsui, discovered the CF gene on chromosome 7 in the summer of 1989. The challenge now is to transport correct versions of the DNA into the lungs of the victims of cystic fibrosis. Several methods have been suggested. Some scientists have devised methods to utilize ordinary cold viruses as vehicles for transporting the corrected version of DNA. Another method utilizes an aerosol spray containing the corrected DNA that patients would use every two or three months. Discussion already has developed about using goats as a virtual embryo for mass production of the corrected DNA.

In late 1992, the NIH's Recombinant DNA Advisory Committee voted to allow three medical teams to squirt solution of the cold viruses containing the CF gene into the nasal passages and lungs of patients. Each team will test the gene therapy in roughly ten patients over the age of twenty-one with mild to moderate cystic fibrosis symptoms. Says Robert K. Dresing, president of the Cystic Fibrosis Foundation, "We're very excited about the prospects of these experiments. [CF patients] should be extremely encouraged by the speed with which things are going . . . this could have a real effect on their lives."

The total cure may include a combination of drugs, genetic engineering, and nutrition, reinforced by life-style changes. That the medical profession seems willing to take risks and consider new and unorthodox therapies in the fight against cystic fibrosis presages a fundamental change in their attitude toward acceptance of innovative solutions to medical problems.

This full-pronged approach is also proving effective in medical and scientific research, as demonstrated by the divergent methods now being developed to create a bona-fide "blood substitute." To be useful, artificial blood must be able to carry oxygen to the body's tissues as efficiently as human blood does. And these substitutes must be able to perform other blood functions, such as clotting.

As we have already seen, DNX Corporation through gene pharming has created lines of pigs that carry the genetic code for human hemoglobin. Somatogen, Inc., fashions its approach after methods currently used to produce megadoses of human insulin. Its vats of genetically engineered bacteria produce large quantities of a mutant form of human hemoglobin. Following a totally different research approach, Biopure Corporation extracts hemoglobin from cow blood and chemically treats the molecule so that it safely carries oxygen in humans.

Some companies believe that the real goal should not be to reproduce hemoglobin but to develop substances that function like hemoglobin. Hence, Alliance Pharmaceutical Corporation in San Diego specializes in producing in quantity perfluorocarbons (PFCs), molecules unrelated to hemoglobin but which once injected into the bloodstream have the ability to pick up oxygen in the lungs and let it off in the tissues of the body.

At present, blood substitutes have not achieved the lifetime of normal blood. Once infused, real blood lasts for three weeks in the body, but artificial blood, lacking red cells' protective membrane, must be replaced within twenty-four hours. The company that can provide a substitute as hardy as human hemoglobin will succeed in what Somatogen vice-president Gary Stetler describes as the "Mars landing of biotech."

The healthy competition among diverse approaches to this problem will only hasten the development of an abundant blood substitute. In 1993, DNX chairman Paul Schmitt predicted that within ten years "tanker cars of product" could be delivering blood substitutes all over the world.

The Will to Live

As we approach the Macroindustrial Era, we are developing technologies and pharmacological wonders that will upend our concept of the species' natural life span. Humanity will suddenly confront a myriad of medical advances—the advent of superdrugs, the minimization of disease, the elimination of genetic fragility, advances in surgery, and the possibility of regeneration through nanotechnology. It would be naive to assume that these advances will not reconstitute social institutions, personal expectations, perhaps even the meaning of life itself.

The Immortal Society

As we have observed throughout this chapter, medical breakthroughs are not only adding years to life, they are adding life to those years. If the breakthroughs in nanotechnology perform as expected, people will not experience their two century-plus life spans as old people getting older but as young people at their physical peak.

What will be the effects of significantly longer life spans? We can only speculate, but longer life will bring with it momentous benefits to the human species. As people live longer, their individual wealth of knowledge and their ability to use this knowledge and experience makes them more valuable to their organizations, communities, and families. The individual's life extends through a greater proportion of a society's existence. For instance, imagine how longevity, say, a life span of 200 years, would affect the average American.

If these medical breakthroughs had occurred in 1776, many Americans living today would be as old as the country. What an overview of America's history, its values, its accomplishments, and its mistakes! A society would have as members individuals with memories sweeping its entire development. Because these people would still be physically and mentally sound, they could continue to play a critical role in the country's development but with an historically unprecedented sense of perspective.

The longer people live, the more they become significant stakeholders in society. Because they will probably be alive to see the results of their actions, they perceive their behavior as having greater personal consequences. A person at age seventy or a hundred will understand that, barring accident or homicide, he or she will probably enjoy many more years on the planet. We will not see people "bailing out" of the activities that constitute a society—work, family, culture, and politics. They will be required to remain personally involved, because people will not retire from their jobs and mainstream cultural activities.

Society benefits when its members believe that they will be significantly affected by events unfolding in their midst. They are less likely to feel apathetic and have a greater tendency to take actions that will positively change society. We can speculate with a degree of surety that Americans today who knew for sure they would be living and working in the year 2092 would make more concerted efforts to reduce the national budget deficit. Currently they fret about shouldering their grandchildren with debt. In the Macroindustrial Era, they will worry about personally paying off the national debt of a century distant.

We can only speculate about how people will confront not the prospect of getting old, but a personal future in which they will either resist age or remain young for a significantly longer time. The 200-year-old in the new society, although by current standards chronologically old, will not be "aged." Regeneration of organs, cells, and tissue will create a society of "young" people, at least as gauged by physical condition.

Individual perceptions of themselves and their place in the world will undergo a radical transformation. For one thing, they will suddenly be presented with a much longer time frame in which to accomplish certain goals. On the other hand, since they will be living with the results of their personal decisions for a greater period of time, they must be more diligent in their quest to achieve financial and personal success.

Sources of Resistance

In spite of the fact that the species may be at a critical juncture in its battle with mortality, there remains an underlying uneasiness in our society about any substantial increase in the life span. Certainly, change of any sort will encounter a measure of resistance. Considering the fact that death has been humanity's most dreaded companion since time immemorial, it is surprising that people are apprehensive about its demise, however.

The sources of resistance vary.

Do We Want to Live an Extremely Long Life?

The first negative reaction to life expansion is a strictly personal one: People are not sure whether they would want their own lives as they are now experiencing them to extend indefinitely. Although over half the people surveyed recently claim that they would welcome living for 200 years, others see such an eventuality in a far different light. Most of these negative reactions to longevity originate in a belief that a 200-year life would entail living the second century of existence in a physically impaired state. Most people assume that they would spend their latter years in the body of a 1994-style ninety-five-year-old individual.

In truth, integral to the achievement of longevity would be the plethora of breakthrough techniques discussed earlier, including cell regeneration, tissue repair, limb replacement, and the eradication of most degenerative diseases. In a world where these feats are commonplace, the ninety-five-year-old person will not look like anything that we have currently encountered—he or she will be young! So extending this person's life for another century implies the continuation of youth and health.

People resistant to the idea of extreme longevity are reacting within a perspective shaped by the species' current experiences with aging and disease. They will change their opinion when they come to realize that in the new Era a long life is a healthy life.

Another personal source of resistance to protracted longevity is people's tendency to project their personal current life experiences into the future. People who have had a difficult time of it so far cringe at the thought of more of the same for another century.

Certainly, this reaction warrants understanding and sympathy. In the Macroindustrial Era, the period in which radical life expansion will first appear, change, both social and personal, will become an integral part of the social fabric though. For the individual, this means that each decade presents to him the opportunity to train for new skills, live on another planet, and make novel contributions. Because the life span itself will be expanded, the period of adulthood, even young adulthood, will include many more years in which he can redeem himself, change and improve his fortunes, and perhaps find a spouse.

In contradistinction to the fear that longevity will only extend our troubles, a longer life will ultimately prove to be each person's greatest source of hope.

Longevity Is Impossible

It may seem ironic that although medical breakthroughs explode in our midst, many members of the scientific establishment maintain that the species has reached the upper limits on its life span. Some seem almost comfortable envisioning human existence bounded by an upper temporal limit.

In 1990, demographer S. Jay Olshansky, gerontologist Christine Casels, and biostatistician Bruce Carnes of the Argonne National Laboratory utilized a number of measures to try to prove that the era of rapid increases in human longevity had come to an end in the developed countries. Using simple mathematic formulas, they concluded that even if we eliminate heart disease, cancer, and other maladies, we would only minimally affect the death rate. By their calculations, the upper limit on the average human life span is eighty-five.

Other scientists vehemently disagree, postulating that tomorrow's children could reach 130, 150, and even 170. They conclude, however, that we would have to discover the secret of aging by overcoming the limitations exhibited by the human cell itself. In controlled laboratory experiments, human cells divide only about fifty times before they disassemble like worn-out machines.

Although the cells left to their own devices are limited in the number of times they can replicate, in the true spirit of the Macroindustrial Era, humanity is only too willing to help the body transcend the limitations of its own cell repair strategy and mechanisms.

How will we help nature achieve its personal best? Some have suggested that eventually we will use nanocomputers to inform the cell simply to stop replicating, thereby eliminating the main cause of cellular deterioration. Another innovative plan would be to repair the cell before it had a chance to disassemble. As indicated, cell repair machines may resuscitate brittle bones, wrinkled skin, low enzyme activities, slow wound healing, and poor memories. As we have seen from experiments in nanotechnology, these cells can be reconstructed through microindustrial engineering.

It is predicted that those whose cellular structures survive intact until such time as we have at our disposal cell repair machines will have restored their youthful health with a youthful physical structure.

As we have seen, the major degenerative diseases of old age, including Alzheimer's disease and osteoporosis, may be subject to genetic engineering at birth or at some point in the life span. Some even feel that such research endeavors as the Human Genome Project may eventually uncover an aging gene, which could be reprogrammed to reverse the aging process.

Researchers at the University of Texas Southwestern Medical Center at Dallas have discovered two separate genetic programs, Mortality 1 and Mortality 2, that seem to cause human cells to become senescent. Both these programs cause the cell to decay and eventually die. In special experiments performed on human cells, the team discovered that when they inactivated one of these programs, Mortality 1, cells in culture lived 40 to 100 percent longer. To their astonishment, when they inactivated Mortality 2, the cells became immortal and continued to replicate indefinitely. A California research company called Geron has identified a group of genes that promote aging in brain cells, skin cells, and blood vessel cells and is developing a number of compounds called *senstatins* that reverse the aging process in such cells. They believe that such senstatins will form the basis of a treatment for halting or reversing the aging process, restoring aging skin to its youthful texture.

The Natural Order of Things

We discussed the possibility that people would resist life expansion because of deep reservations about the effects of such changes on their own lives, but resistance to hyperextended life exists at a much deeper cultural and philosophical level. There seems to be a shared assumption that all things have a natural, predetermined span of existence that humanity will only violate by tampering with rudimentary processes such as cellular and atomic behavior.

The belief that there exists a natural order that humanity ought not change or attempt to control exists throughout the culture, in science, religion, and environmentalism. Such a belief often obstructs the progress of the species.

Consider the reaction of one scientist to the use of drug hormones to extend the life span. According to Stanford's Dr. Robert Marcus, "The whole concept of life extension is patent nonsense . . . to help people age gracefully and with less disability is the only goal worth pursuing."

We can only wonder how the good doctor would respond to the radical effects of nano- and microtechnologies on life expectancy!

Let us suppose that scientific and technological breakthroughs advance to the point where superlongevity or even near immortality are on the horizon. Would the powers that be merely say enough and with the cooperation of antigrowth forces such as Jeremy Rifkin and colleagues pull the plug, so to speak, on the entire longevity enterprise? Will the cultural bias toward noninterference with the natural order of things ultimately sabotage technology whenever it approaches a godlike mastery of nature?

The distaste for humanity's transformation of nature manifests itself in surprising ways. Consider the reaction of some to modern humanity's success in reducing the incidence of heart disease. They focus on one of the paradoxes of this success: By reducing heart disease in people in their forties and fifties, we increase the chances that they will develop arteriosclerosis when they reach their eighties and beyond. Some have employed this fact to denigrate our success in eradicating the early onset of heart disease. In discussions of medical progress, this same argument reappears continually: If we extend life, are we not increasing the possibility that humans will develop other problems such as arthritis or Alzheimer's in later years?

This convoluted logic will never triumph, but it becomes another legal and philosophical argument that Rifkinites and others can use to slow the rate of progress in the medical field. It means little to these critics that each time we improve health at any point in the life cycle we enhance the species' long-term prospects for survival. The eradication of early heart disease proves as much. According to Kenneth Manton, a Duke University demographer, over time "reducing the number of early [nonfatal] heart attacks may mean less degenerative heart disease later" in people with weakened hearts. So, to that extent, treating heart problems early may lead to better health later on.

If the culture truly adheres to the concept of the natural order, though, such scientific findings will be considered irrelevant. Ultimately, culture is as important a factor in determining continued societal progress as is the technology we discover. Technology residing in an inventor's mind and a breakthrough sitting on a scientist's table will be actualized only if the culture accepts the technology's legitimacy and desires to apply it.

The cultural sanctions against violating the natural order may also have a religious foundation. Here, the negative feedback regarding the achievement of longevity is rooted in the fear that we are truly playing God. Once humanity gains control over life and death, has it not usurped the Creator's role?

In reality, the attainment of life everlasting has been a goal specifically articulated by numerous religions. Some would argue that such theological statements actually refer to attaining eternal spiritual, not physical, life. This point has been routinely debated in intellectual circles. Regardless of the outcome of such philosophical arguments, the species long ago crossed the Rubicon regarding restructuring pieces of the universe, including the human body. The natural order has receded into mythology.

Fear of the Ultimate Generation Gap

One of the unconscious fears regarding the achievement of longevity involves that uncomfortable transitional period in which the key discoveries of cellular repair and rejuvenation will have been made, but for a number of medical reasons will not be able to be applied to everyone.

This conundrum will certainly confront the species for a number of years and further complicate the longevity issue. Suppose there emerge cellular regeneration technologies that can save intact cells, ensuring long life to the beneficiaries of such techniques. Doubtlessly certain people will be too far gone to be helped. We see this in the case of cystic fibrosis, wherein many adolescent sufferers possess lungs already too damaged to benefit from the pharmaceutical breakthroughs and genetic strategies.

In the early stages of the introduction of these medical miracles, we will have a portion of the population that will have been born too late to enjoy the medical salvation that others in their midst will.

For a brief period in our history, we will witness the ultimate generation gap between those who might live forever and those who will surely die. Will the nonelect, invidiously comparing their own mortality to the anointed's gift of life everlasting, attempt to slow down science's progress in the life expansion field? Probably not consciously; overtly destroying others' ability to live forever would be perceived as the ultimate manifestation of selfishness. However, they may enlist the other aforementioned arguments, such as the natural order, to decelerate progress in this area. In any event, some hostility or jealousy will emerge during this transitional period.

·   ·   ·

Technology holds the long-term promise of extending life and, more immediately, providing us with a better standard of health. However, the biological future will not be determined so much by our ability, but our desire. We express a certain trepidation at exploring the nether world of near immortality. Death, although a source of fear and horror, also provides each of us with a sense of comfort, a well-defined boundary around our lives that gives us a feeling of closure and completeness.

Ironically, we may finally have the dream that we claim to have wanted for the last 30,000 years and probably since time immemorial —immortality. Once we gain immortality, the eternal youth promised by breakthroughs in cellular regeneration, will we want it? Or will humanity begin to conjure up centuries-old edicts about the appropriate upper limits on the the species' life span? Will we finally reach this critical juncture and surprise ourselves by thundering in unison a resounding no?

Certainly, as we approach development of the means to reprogram our cells and our genes fundamentally, we must achieve a consensus on the methods and strategies for introducing such technologies. Society's leaders would have to begin to alert the citizenry to such possibilities and initiate a much-needed national dialogue on the immortality issue.

The danger inherent in such a dialogue is that those opposing progress in this area would use this debate as a platform to subvert the entire project. It would probably provide them a soapbox from which to condemn biotechnology, nanotechnology, pharmacology, and longevity in general.

Regardless of the decibel level at which these arguments will be waged, the human species will ultimately take advantage of the opportunity to live a longer, healthier life. By acquiring true longevity and ultimately defeating death, we are finally taking our destiny into our own hands. We will surely seize the future when we can extend ourselves into infinity.

5: Fields of Plenty

The Coming Era of Material Abundance

Throughout its existence, the human species has been plagued by shortages of food, material, and natural resources. Now, as we move into the Macroindustrial Era, we are about to experience a transformation in the production of goods and food that will liberate the species from the threat of scarcity and expand the very concept of abundance.

Advances in technology are enhancing our capacity to create the resources we need to survive and thrive. We will look at the processes by which we will produce and design a whole new world of materials for homes and industry, and we will examine the breakthroughs in agricultural science that will feed the world. In contradistinction to the Malthusian predictions that humanity will outstrip the available food supply, we are actually on the verge of increasing the species' net nutritional and caloric intake and improving the overall quality of foods available to the human species.

Such exponential increases in food and goods can form the material base for an even larger population than exists at present. As we shall see, a case exists for the actual continued expansion of the world population base.

The Food Supply Revolution

As the Macroindustrial Era unfolds, innovations in vegetable and animal production are enhancing the ability of the species to feed itself at a level previously considered impossible. Contrary to the barrage of misinformation in the popular media, world food production has increased considerably faster than has the population in recent decades. According to such sources as the U.N. and the U.S. Department of Agriculture, between 1950 and 1977, per capita food output increased by somewhere between 28 percent and 37 percent. Recent data bring more good news: The world food output has continued to match or outstrip population growth since 1977.

In 1991, the world output of rice, wheat, corn, and other grains swelled to 1.7 billion metric tons, about 260 million tons more than in 1981. Such a quantum leap in agricultural productivity amounts to the creation of another Midwest farm belt in just a ten-year period. Over the last four decades, some of the more encouraging increases have occurred in the less developed countries that have quickly applied many of the recent advances in agricultural and food-related technology.

Five major factors motored the so-called green revolution: the hybridization of corn; the ninefold increase in fertilizer use between 1950 and 1984; the near tripling of irrigated areas in that same period; the spread of new high-yield wheat and rice seeds in the Third World countries; and the use of chemical insecticides, herbicides, rodenticides, and fungicides. The last category alone, the protection of crops through chemistry and nitrogen fertilizer, has been of particular value to world agricultural production. Is it any wonder that during the green revolution world grain output multiplied 2.6 times?

India's recent experiences in agriculture concretely illustrate the impact of the green revolution. In India's notorious famine of 1943, 1.5 million citizens of that country starved to death. By 1977, however, India not only fed its own population, but became a grain exporter, even as it doubled its population. Rice and wheat production in India in the 1980s was almost three and a half times as bountiful as in 1950, outstripping India's population increase by over 1900 percent. So dramatic was India's reversal of fortune that by the 1970s other developing regions actually coveted Indian farm products; farmers planting improved wheat laden with seed had to protect their riches lying in the fields from international poachers!

By 1993, the continuing increase in world grain production was so pronounced that it began to change the relationship between producer and consumer. The United States possesses the largest area on the globe featuring the valuable combination of rich soil, good climate, and good river transport. Historically, the United States has been a net exporter of food to a hungry planet, accounting for four-fifths of the world soybean trade and half of the wheat business as late as the 1970s. By the 1990s, however, improvements in food production techniques have helped many former importers become agriculturally self-sufficient. Even the European Community has utilized agricultural breakthroughs to revive its moribund farm industries and now challenges the United States in many world food markets.

The green revolution itself demonstrates the extent to which the human species has expanded its control over nature and its products. Miraculously, these great increases in the world food supply in recent decades have brought humanity to the point where only 2 percent of the world's population suffers from hunger. According to the U.N., the number of malnourished people in poor countries has dropped by 150 million over two decades, and much of the remaining hunger and malnutrition results more from wars and capricious governmental policies than agricultural shortfalls.

As the Macroindustrial Era evolves, the species will completely eliminate the scarcity of food. Farmers have barely scratched the surface of the available food-raising resources: Some experts claim that scientists are using less than half of the Earth's arable land and only a minute part of the water supply to irrigate dryer land. That dry crop land, about one-fourth of the globe's total acreage, ultimately will be made arable by macroengineering irrigation projects.

How Large a Population Can the Earth Support?

The population of the world is currently around 5 billion, and it is expected to grow to 8.5 to 11 billion sometime in the next century. Colin Clark, former director of the Agricultural Economic Institute at Oxford University, classified world land types by their food-raising capabilities and claimed that if all farmers were to use the best food-growing methods, enough food could be raised to provide an American-type diet for 35.1 billion people, about seven times the present population. The American diet is a very rich one, featuring high-cholesterol foods, meat, and other delicacies. If the goal is to provide the world's members with a more modest Japanese diet, we could possibly feed three times again as many, or twenty-two times the current world population.

Roger Revelle, former director for the Harvard Center for Population Studies, has determined that world agricultural resources as they now stand can provide an adequate diet (around 2500 calories per day) for

40 billion people. Surprisingly, according to Revelle, we can feed these people with an average world yield per acre *one-half* that presently produced in the American Midwest.

Revelle has estimated that the less developed continents are capable of feeding 18 billion people, or six times their present population. Africa alone, according to Revelle, has the capacity to feed 10 billion people, twice the number of the present world population and more than twenty times Africa's 1980 population. Revelle also believes that agricultural yields in Asia could be greatly increased and reflects some sentiment that India alone could feed the entire population of the world.

The Expanding Land Base for Farming

A key factor in the food supply revolution is our ever-growing agricultural land base. Examples abound of how human imagination is effecting an exponential increase in the world's farm acreage.

For instance, humanity is literally "greening the desert." The canal currently labeled the Indira Gandhi Canal was launched in 1958 to bring life-sustaining water to the northwestern India state of Rajasthan, and it now helps to irrigate more than 1.5 million acres of once-arid land. The main canal, running parallel to the Pakistani border, was completed in 1987, but this fine example of macroengineering is far from finished. A network of tributary canals, more than 5000 total miles in length, is slowly spreading across the desert at the main canal's southern extremity. This work, which costs $41.4 million annually, will take another fifteen years to complete.

The price is well worth it. These areas have been barren for centuries and are now becoming arable once again. Supplementing this process is a state-sponsored land distribution program providing newly cultivated land to the landless. In 1989, 370,000 tons of crops, including cotton, sugar cane, and food grain, were produced on land irrigated by the canal.

The species is developing a plethora of hardy plants that thrive on salt, called *halophytes*, which the National Research Council claims could "improve food or fuel supplies, help stem desertification, and contribute to soil reclamation." A four-year study by the council identified hundreds of plants that can survive in the brackish waters and arid lands of the world.

Experts believe that halophytes could be a valuable commodity in developing countries where millions of hectares of land are damaged from high salt content and in areas like the western United States, where periodic droughts threaten irrigation supplies for conventional crops and where some irrigated lands have become loaded with salt.

Saline agriculture is creating a quiet revolution around the globe. Israeli farmers irrigate specially bred tomatoes and cotton with saline water; Pakistanis grow kalar grass in water-logged, high-saline soils as food stuff for livestock; and Mexican farmers harvest salicornia, a succulent plant that thrives in seawater and produces a safflower-type oil.

According to a Food and Agriculture Organization study, we have not even begun to utilize available land. The organization estimates that there are in the world nearly 8 billion acres of arable land lying idle —four times that now being cultivated, just waiting for humanity's ingenuity and imagination to transform them into farms and gardens. Tropical lands, for instance, allow multiple cropping. If that fact is taken into account, then the fourfold potential increase balloons to tenfold.

Occasionally we hear arguments that a variety of factors will actually reduce the land area available for farming, thus reducing the species' ability to grow food. The main culprits in this argument are the growth of cities, increased populations, and desertification, the gradual expansion of deserts into previously arable land.

Facts show that the fear of urbanization/population sprawl is overstated. The total land area on the globe used for urban purposes is minuscule—less than 3 percent in the U.S. (and that is counting a large number of homesites that literally sprawl on for several acres).

The biologist Francis P. Felice claims that the sum total of the world's population could be placed in Texas, forming one giant city with a population density less than that of many existing cities and leaving the rest of the world empty. Incredibly, even if one-third of the space of this city were devoted to parks and another one-third to industry, each family could still occupy a single story dwelling of average American size. In other words, this city would house the entire planet's population and still be a pretty nice place to live, more spacious than cities like London, that are famous for their open park areas.

Even though these changes are dramatic, the future will bring even greater increases in food supply and quality, an exponential supply-side explosion that provides proof positive that we are quickly approaching the historical juncture where we can produce enough food to feed not only the current population, but a much larger one as well.

The Biotechnological Breakthrough

Breakthroughs in the science of biotechnology will deliver an array of powerful new agricultural techniques that will vastly enrich the global food basket. In fact, advances in biotechnology will literally reconfigure the very method of growing things.

Biotechnology is simply the use of living systems—plants, animals, microbes, or any part of these organisms—for the production of useful products. We have been using this method for some time. For instance, the nectarine, which most people would consider a natural-growing fruit, is a combination of the tangerine and the peach; the tangelo combines the tangerine and an orange; and modern strains of corn and wheat reflect more simple biotechnological alterations. In their simplest forms, cheese and bread could be classified as biotechnology products, because they are fermentations that rely on living organisms—bacteria and yeast—for commercial production. Domesticated animals have also been genetically altered using classical breeding and selection techniques. For instance, the mule is a hybrid animal.

The Impact of Genetics

Significant breakthroughs in the Macroindustrial Era will emanate from genetic engineering, a form of biotechnology that provides the most exciting possibilities for commercial applications.

As we have seen, in humans, genes determine an individual's eye color, hair color, and other traits. They also determine what diseases a person may develop or what viruses he or she may be susceptible to. Genetic engineering is the use of precise biological techniques to rearrange these genes, removing them, adding them, or transferring them from one organism to another. This technique involves the transfer of DNA (the universal code of life) between living organisms, crossing natural species barriers. For instance, DNA inserted into bacteria can produce human insulin, interferon, and other lifesaving medications. Bacterial genes can also be inserted into plants to make them insect resistant!

The first successful example of genetic engineering occurred only twenty years ago, when Herbert Boyer of the University of California teamed with Stanley Cohen of Stanford to splice genes from a South African toad into a species of bacteria. Now it has become quite commonplace for scientists to snip a gene from one organism into another with the hope that the recipient organism will carry out the instructions of the new gene.

Genetic engineering holds the promise of not only creating wholly new foods and drugs, but of facilitating the mass manufacture of substances and products. Key to this food production revolution is the ingenious incorporation of bacteria into the manufacturing process.

Consider how insulin is manufactured genetically. Scientists locate the gene in the human chromosome responsible for the manufacture of insulin. That gene segment is removed and implanted into a bacterium, a single-celled organism that has the convenient tendency to reproduce at a dramatically high rate. The bacterium then not only reproduces the insulin (following the instructions of the gene), but passes the manufacturing instructions on to other bacteria it spawns. In this way, insulin is manufactured for human ingestion.

Gene implantation occurs through a number of techniques. One utilizes a biolistic apparatus, which literally fires DNA into a colony of cells at tremendous velocity so that the particle enters the cell wall. Once inside, the DNA can start reshaping the organism. In a more subtle approach, a electrostatic repulse device sends particles into cells.

Redefining Cornucopia

The impact of biotechnology on agriculture can and will be dramatic: It will obliterate hunger and even force the human species to reconceptualize issues like scarcity and abundance. Crops will be grown that will be resistant to disease and drought, tolerant of herbicides and salt, and immune to attack by insects. Humanity will transform agriculture and liberate it from the ills that have plagued it from time immemorial.

There is a new technology on the horizon, antisense RNA and DNA, which allows products to retain their vine-ripened flavor and enjoy a longer shelf life. Importantly, it may also provide a means to lower the level of natural toxicants in foods and increase the nutritional value of crops that serve as staples in our diet.

The impact of biotechnology on the food industry is dazzling:

• Genetic engineering may improve bacteria and yeast for the production of fermented dairy, meat, vegetable, and cereal products.

• Microorganisms can provide a variety of components to be used as ingredients in processed foods—vitamins, amino acids, sweeteners, and flavor enhancers.

• Protein engineering will improve enzymes used by the food industry as processing aids.

• Raw material conversion will convert more of the raw material into finished products, leaving less bones, blood, and collagen to be discarded into the environment.

• Biotechnology will also help in the area of food safety.

The potential for agricultural biotechnology is impressive. Already on line is a highly productive corn that grows without fertilizer. Reports have also become public of a marsh grass that cheaply desalinates seawater, changing it to drinking water needed by a growing population. More than a dozen U.S. companies have developed at least seventy new crops by utilizing innovations in genetic engineering:

• A wide variety of cantaloupes, potatoes, tomatoes, peppers, and cucumbers that contain new proteins, enzymes, and other substances that make them superior in several diferent ways.

• Grains that resist the effects of drought. Such crops may have further uses in space colonies or in other areas that have little or no access to water.

• Cotton and other products that are immune to infestation by insects.

• More plentiful milk and lower calorie meat. The milk production has been accelerated by the utilization of bovine somatotropin (BST), an additive that increases cows' milk production by up to 10 percent. Monsanto, a producer of BST, has donated large quantities of BST to Russia, to offset that country's chronic food shortfalls.

For many companies, the 1990s are the biotech decade. Among those planning to introduce genetically improved tomatoes with extended shelf life are Calgene and Monsanto. The latter company, along with Frito-Lay, is also involved with developing a modified-starch potato that resists starch. Many companies, including Monsanto, Upjohn, American Cyanamid, and Eli Lilly, are developing a cow growth hormone that boosts milk production.

According to Winston Brill, vice president of research and development at Agracetus, in Middleton, Wisconsin, a pioneer in the genetic engineering of plants, we will be mixing and matching genes from different kinds of organisms. Brill claims that by the century's end, the bacterial genes that serve as natural pesticides and have been already added to many plants, may soon be added to corn. According to the U.S. Office of Technology Assessment, U.S. corn production may thus rise from its current level of 8 billion bushels to over 10 billion by the year 2000, a short time to increase production by 20 to 25 percent.

According to Brill, by the year 2001 we may see corn with built-in insect resistance, soybeans with greater protein content, and higher yields for both crops. And why not? One variety of modified bacteria has already proven successful at preventing frost from forming on leaves. Another could turn out to produce natural weed-controlling chemicals, thus replacing some of today's toxic herbicides. Another may improve a plant's ability to absorb fertilizer and further reduce chemical use.

As is the case in so many areas of development in the Macroindustrial Era, the key to forwarding human progress is not so much technological as political and cultural. In this regard a critical obstacle was cleared in May 1992 when the Bush Administration adopted a regulatory policy that would allow bioengineering forces to jump a number of bureaucratic hurdles to reach the market. The deregulation evolved under the watchful eye of the President's Council on Competitiveness, then headed by Dan Quayle working in coordination with the U.S. Food and Drug Administration. The council tries to ensure that the U.S. industrial and Macroindustrial bases can compete globally.

This change was expected to spur investment in agricultural biotech stocks and help this industry reach its full maturation. The United States would be assured of possessing one of the cornerstones of the Macroindustrial Era, a large and multiproduct food supply. According to Richard Godwin, president of the Industrial Biotechnology Association, "It's a long-awaited road map which will tell us what we need to do to commercialize our products."

The crux of this new policy is a set of procedures that will spare agricultural biotechnology companies from having to obtain FDA approval for every new or modified food product they develop from genetically engineered varieties of plants. The important component here is the safety issue. The FDA intends to invoke its power to regulate food additives only if a totally new substance has been added to a food or if the composition of the food has been altered sufficiently for the agency or other interested parties to be concerned about the safety issue.

Such deregulation, with a careful eye on safety, will lead to a veritable explosion in newer, more healthful foods—sweeter tomatoes, longer-lasting peppers, leaner pork, healthier cooking oils, and the aforementioned drought-resistant grains.

Immediately, industry responded positively to this ruling. Within two weeks of the ruling, companies began publicizing their patents for genetically engineered plants. One such company was the New Jersey-based DNA Plant Technology Corporation. According to John Bedbrook, the company's vice president and director of science, they had just received a patent for antifreeze protein, similar in structure to naturally occurring proteins that protect certain organisms from freezing. The antifreeze proteins they developed attach themselves to "seed" ice crystals and prevent the crystals from undergoing the explosive growth that occurs during repeated freeze–thaw cycles.

This will have the effect of reducing what has become known as freezer burn, the tendency of products such as frozen desserts, ice cream, and ice milk to have an undesirable grainy texture. In other words, the company has found a way to stunt the growth of ice crystals that affect texture and flavor. It will also inhibit the tendency of freezing to reduce the quality of doughs by destroying the dough structure and reducing the viability of yeast. According to Bedbrook, "We have engineered yeast to better survive through freezing and thawing." The company has a patent pending for a transformed yeast that produces antifreeze proteins.

Interestingly, the FDA policy already spells out which characteristics in a new or altered substance would trigger premarket regulation. Before they can launch a new product, the companies will have to address a series of questions about the level of natural toxicants in the food, the tendency of the food to cause an allergic reaction, and changes in key nutrients.

If this policy holds, the United States will move to the forefront—or perhaps hold an insuperable leadership position—in this field for years to come. More importantly, it will be able to contribute to two critical dimensions of the Macroindustrial society, quantity and quality, in this case of agricultural products.

Deregulation clears the way for such unique genetically engineered products as natural pesticides, which will help crops increase dramatically. These new products, although still in their infancy, are expected to reach market by the second half of the 1990s. Driven by safety concerns about traditional pesticides, biotechnology is prepared to attack problems that are currently controlled by chemical pesticides. They will also be in position to replace many of the conventional pesticides to which insects have become resistant.

The market for pesticides is expected to grow to an astonishing $10 billion by the year 2000, with biopesticides claiming an ever-greater share. Companies like Sandoz Corporation and Monsanto Chemical expect to have genetically protected products on the market by 1995.

Coming Soon: Cell and Food Factories

At Washington State University a team of research chemical engineers has set up clusters of plants and animal cells which are suspended and agitated within *bioreactors*, tank-like fermenters in a liquid solution of carbohydrates and salts.

These clusters are the newest biotechnological innovation: cell factories. Once these cell factories' biological products are separated from their fueling solutions, many different types of agricultural and medically useful products will be generated. In order to meet commercial demands, engineers plan to perform this genetic manipulation of cells on an industrial scale by enlarging the bioreactors and separators.

Disney World's Epcot Center houses the Plant Biotechnology Laboratory, one of the United States' major public showcases of plant biotechnology. At present, they have made significant advances in plant tissue culture technology to the extent that whole plants are being regenerated from cells or sections of leaf tissue from a mother plant. The lab has an ever-increasing storehouse of perhaps a half-million cells or tissue cultures growing under sterile conditions in cylinders, tubes, and flasks containing media formulated to meet the nutrient needs of the plant species.

Some of the tissue cultures will be used to nurture plants that have been slow and expensive to grow and may carry diseases from generation to generation. This tissue culture technology has been successfully applied to strawberry plants, pineapple trees, carrots, potatoes, and peanuts.

One of the more amazing aspects of Epcot is the exhibit displaying *hydroponics*, plants that grow in waterless soil. The agricultural implications of hydroponics are overwhelming. For instance, think of the ability of populations living in desertlike conditions to grow food and develop an agricultural base. Also, the space colonization endeavor suddenly will no longer be plagued by one of the major obstacles to the establishment of permanent space bases, the food production issue. If dependence on water is lessened, the probability of a successful mission should be enhanced.

Breakthroughs in tissue culture technology may lead to a revolution in agriculture destined to become a landmark of the Macroindustrial Era—food factories. The underlying principle of such factories has already been successfully demonstrated in the lab. At this time, laboratory scientists can take a slice from a tree's leaf and place it in a medium of hormones and nutrients that cause it to grow into a mound of undifferentiated cells called a *callus* (which looks by some to be a helping of green mashed potatoes). Every single cell in that callus has the genetic information to become a whole plant. It is felt that in the proper medium, the callus can produce a hundred or a million copies of a single tree.

Scientist Brent Tisserat demonstrated that you could create food in vitro. In one experiment, he placed half a lemon in a lab container, fed it the proper nutrients, and found that the lemon began to sprout juice vesicles, the fluid-filled pouches we find in most citrus fruits. He then discovered that he could grow juice sacs from other vesicles.

In short, scientists are learning to grow fruits or at least their products without using the fruit itself. The implications for food production are enormous.

Two U.S. Department of Agriculture scientists are actively involved in promoting what would seem to be a logical extension of this phenomenon, a revolutionary food production system. These two researchers, Martin Rogoff, a microbiologist, and Steven Rawlins, a soil scientist, ask disturbing questions, like what would happen if erosion caused by desertification wiped out America's breadbasket region? How, they ask, would the nation substitute for its lost food?

The answer is food factories that operate on entirely different principles than the farm system of today. A visitor to a food factory that produced orange juice would be surprised to find no farms, no oranges, no orange trees. All she would see are rows of juice sacs grown in culture. Another factory would fabricate flour, real flour, without using wheat, corn, or any grain. Another factory would make tomato sauce or fruit juice. No tomatoes or fruits are employed in this process, only enzymes to regulate the growth of the plant tissues and a basic nutrient feedstock from which the plant tissues produce food for people.

Rogoff and Rawlins envision this factory system as able to produce a wide array of foods—everything from a fruit or a nut to a vegetable.

The one stumbling block in establishing such factories immediately is the availability of cheap and abundant "feedstock," the nutrition that will help grain and fruit grow. In these factories, juice-making sacs must be fed a constant supply of sugar, the ingredient from which all parts of plants and animals are made. As it happens, biotechnologists are currently working on turning wood and straw, which are composed mainly of chains of glucose molecules, into simple sugar syrups. Once this process is perfected, the food factories will have available the feedstock necessary for full scaleup.

Because of these breakthroughs, the Macroindustrial Era will feature an agricultural system unlike any we have known before. The system will have several components. Instead of farms as we know them, with annual crops, the species will develop plantations of trees and brush (and environmentally sound perennials at that) that would be periodically harvested, broken down into sugar syrup, and transported to food factories, thereby supplying the missing link in the production of juice and grain.

We have any number of sources of wood for this system. At present, the planet is awash in trees, with forests covering almost a third of the Earth's land surface, as in 1950. However, our need for trees and brush can also be met by genetically engineered forests. Recently, David D. Ellis, a University of Wisconsin horticulturalist, successfully inserted foreign genes into embryos of the white spruce. Many of the genetically altered embryos have now sprouted into seedlings that have quickly grown to three or four inches.

It would appear that we are on the verge of genetically altering trees and brush in order to speed up their growth. Researchers are already beginning to accelerate the growth of conifers and pine trees. Once such procedures are perfected, our food factories should have an endless supply of feedstock for the food factory process.

Improving the Animal Kingdom

In the Macroindustrial Era, the ability of humanity to improve the quantity and quality of living things will extend to the animal kingdom. Already, genetic engineering has been successfully applied to a variety of animal species.

Because of the advances made in embryo transfer technology, which involves the splitting of embryos at very early stages, we can now produce genetically superior animals. In a sense, this process is considered an extension of classical breeding techniques such as selection and artificial insemination. Genetic engineering has been used to clone the aforementioned BST gene from cows, which, when injected into other cows, increases milk production and feed efficiency. There is a pig gene, PST, which when injected into the pig produces offspring with more muscle than fat. This results in a leaner meat with less marbling and less carcass fat. Certainly, this will be welcomed in a country like the United States so concerned with the amount of fat and cholesterol in the diet.

The potential of this exciting new technology to feed the billions and improve life on Earth is encouraging, especially considering the power of genetic reprogramming to increase animal size. In experimental situations, for instance, mice have been given rat genes to make them grow larger. The technology has also been successfully applied to fish. Scientists effected a miracle when they introduced a gene that controls growth in rainbow trout into a common carp, thereby creating a new, larger fish that grows as much as 20 percent faster than normal carp. The researchers had isolated a single gene from the rainbow trout's pituitary gland that produces a growth hormone protein that regulates how quickly the fish grow. They then duplicated the gene and injected the clones into carp eggs. Although carp have their own growth hormone, the trout gene added to the carp accelerates the growth process.

This technology is about to explode. Imagine the common catfish, a delicacy in some regions, able to be raised to maturity in twelve months instead of the eighteen months it now takes. Quality is not sacrificed; witnesses attest to the fact that the reengineered fish tastes as good as the former version.

An even more daring biotechnological technique is the process of cloning large numbers of identical animals from a single embryo. The goal is lofty: to realize the same quality in farm animals that we have achieved in manufactured goods. Beautiful in its simplicity, cloning has been achieved as a result of the combination of several technical breakthroughs and an increase in our knowledge of the fundamental workings of genetics.

Scientists are already applying this technology to cattle. In this case, a prize bull produces semen, which in turn is used to inseminate a prize cow. This artificial mating yields ten embryos each composed of 323 cells that each contain the entire package of genetic instructions necessary to compose a complete calf. Next, recently developed delicate microsurgical techniques are used to remove the nuclei from the embryonic cells, which are then transferred into the cavities of unfertilized eggs taken from ordinary cows. The new embryo is then transplanted into surrogate mothers, who give birth to genetically identical calves, the product of prize bulls and cows.

The beef and dairy industries are now enthusiastically anticipating a vast number of superior animals that can be produced in a given year. The pork industry has already produced larger, leaner pigs.

Biotechnology in the Third World

In contradistinction to the incessant complaining heard throughout the developed countries about inevitable food shortages, it is encouraging to see that the Third World has completely ignored such doomsaying and is taking a headlong plunge into the incorporation of biotechnology into its agricultural growth program.

Recombinant DNA techniques are expected to accelerate traditional plant breeding methods and help farmers reduce their dependence on pesticides and herbicides. In the highlands of Vietnam, for instance, thirty families have been reaping profits from crops of potato plants they have grown with the assistance of some biotechnological tools. With an average investment of as little as $250, these farmers, many without formal education, have set up makeshift laboratories in their backyards and bedrooms, where they use tissue culture techniques to propagate potato plants. This earns the families $100 to $120 a month, which in rural Vietnam is certainly enough to make one prosperous. Some of the farmers are using the same techniques to grow other vegetables in vitro.

The impediments to full-scale introduction of this technology in developing nations are not so much scientific as cultural and economic. These constraints include suspicious farmers who worry that the developed nations will use such technology to genetically replicate Third World exports such as sugar and cocoa butter. The farmers perceive that such an eventuality would sabotage local African and Asian economies. Another problem is that biotech companies have little financial incentive to transfer such technologies to the Third World, mainly because the legal structures there do little to protect the large companies' patents from being stolen and "readopted" by third parties.

In a move that presages the new economics of the nascent Macro-industrial Era, Third World leaders have already taken the initiative in nurturing a homegrown biotechnology industry, one that will be established according to their rules and conforming to their unique agenda.

They want to invest in their own technologies and products, using scientists more sensitive to the needs of the country and the needs of native farmers. They will not rely on the developed countries unilaterally deciding for them what genetically engineered crops to develop. More startling to First World agricultural companies is the fact that these Third World upstarts may be stretching regulations. Whereas U.S. scientists spend an average of a decade to engineer plants genetically and test them in federally regulated field trials, developing nations may already be harvesting the fruits—or vegetables and meats, for that matter—of the major biotech companies' labors.

Third World countries have made strides in original research and experimentation in the biotechnology field. Several countries, including Nepal and Bhutan, have established biotechnology laboratories to support original research and spawn new farm products. The World Bank has been quite generous in its support for the establishment of such scientific centers. Is it any wonder that China has suddenly emerged as the world's second largest corn exporter or that Brazil, growing seeds that flourish in acidic soil, now has become a global soybean power?

In reality, genetic engineering has evolved into a worldwide enterprise that is creating a phalanx of newer, better breeds of crops, animals, and life forms of all types.

In light of the fact that biotechnology and genetic engineering have enhanced our capacity to produce food, it is surprising that people still go hungry. However, the hunger and malnutrition seen today have little to do with the state of agricultural technology and much to do with cultural, political, and economic factors.

An illustration of this paradox occurred in the 1980s. U.S. farmers offered an African country a year's crop of surplus raisins free of charge, asking only that the country pay the shipping costs. However, because this African country was so impoverished, even paying freight charges seemed formidable. Sadly, the raisins went to waste.

In truth, some Third World countries' foreign debt impedes their entrance into the Macroindustrial world structure. Such countries use their entire output not to feed their people, buy essentials, or develop their economic infrastructure, but to service the debt owed to developed countries and major international banks. For these countries, merely paying the interest on these loans, let alone repaying the loan itself, is equivalent to an individual attempting to raise himself from a prone position with a two-ton weight resting on his chest.

Nevertheless, these less developed countries can overcome their current economic and political quandary. Once these countries master advanced food-growing techniques such as biotechnology and mega-irrigation, they will not only achieve agricultural self-sufficiency. They will harvest food surpluses that they can sell and trade and will begin generating real national wealth. China, Brazil, and Mexico are testaments to the power of food to reestablish economic health.

Living in an Abundantly Material World

Nothing will more characterize the activities of the human species in the Macroindustrial Era than its conquest of scarcity. In addition to dramatic increases in the production of food, we will witness a veritable revolution in the creation of materials. Advances in ceramics, new metal-based materials, and synthetics are providing the framework for progress in the areas of energy, health, dentistry, space exploration, and a host of other fields.

Humanity has traditionally depended on better materials—bronze, iron, and stone, to name a few—to improve the human condition. Today, we are transcending our dependence on the adaptation of naturally occurring materials and minerals for our purposes. We now have the ability to design and produce from scratch the materials that we require.

This advanced material revolution will also make us less dependent on the current necessity of mining material and then transporting it halfway across the world. The advanced material of the Macroindustrial Era begins its life not in the ground but in the mind of the laboratory scientist. According to Rustum Roy of the Materials Research Laboratory of Pennsylvania State University, "We can make materials to predesigned specifications. We can configure molecules to do the jobs we want."

Most of us already have firsthand experience with such artificial materials as ceramics, but the new ceramic products, made out of alumina, titania, and sand, are harder, stronger, lighter, and more durable than many metals. We already see these advanced materials showing up in ceramic scissors, knives, fishhooks, batteries, and artificial limbs. Engines made of ceramics, such as those conceived by the Isuzu and Toyota car manufacturers, will be able to withstand temperatures of up to 1500 degrees Fahrenheit without coolant or lubrication, thereby reducing the West's dependence on oil and boosting fuel efficiency by 30 percent.

Plastics will also reduce our need for so-called natural resources. By

1979, plastics had already overtaken steel as the number one material used in production. Now, new manufacturing processes make possible high-performance plastics and advanced composites. We can literally design new materials on the computer and then produce them. These resulting composites are produced from the bottom up, as it were, molecule by molecule, and can be designed to literally disappear after sixty days in sunlight (the ultimate in biodegradation) or be washed away with water if we choose.

Encouraged by the fact that these new composites will be lighter and more durable than older materials, General Motors says that 20 percent of its cars and 50 percent of its vans will have all-plastic bodies by the mid-1990s.

New materials such as gallium and arsenica are creating a new generation of computer superchips, faster and more powerful than today's variety. This new material has helped spawn the field of photonics in which light pulses are generated by lasers and transmitted by fiber-optic cables.

The field that may receive the greatest immediate benefit from the growth of manufactured materials is medicine. Polyurethanes, silicones, rubbers, and carbons are being incorporated in the composition of artificial arteries, synthetic blood, and entire artificial ears. Of course, bone implants, tooth implants, and hip replacements, all unknown a few decades ago, have become rudimentary procedures thanks to new materials. In addition, repairing the muscular system is easier because of the availability of tendons and ligaments made of polymers and carbon fibers. And artificially produced lens implantation is saving the sight of millions of elderly cataract victims.

Breakthroughs in the development of new metals are part of the revolution in advanced materials. Atomic engineering holds the promise of designer materials whose properties are achieved by blending elements that could not be combined utilizing traditional methods. Scientists claim that these new materials represent a wholly new state of matter. By combining such metals as copper and zirconium, researchers have produced materials that are as thin as a sheet of paper but more resilient, retaining their shape after excessive bending. They also may be more resistant to corrosion.

The miracle products are endless—diamond films for unscratchable glass and zero-expansion ceramics for power telescopes—all dream materials that pioneer designers have been turning into reality.

Of course, such breakthroughs are facilitated by new tools for analyzing the inner structure of materials. If we want to design plastics, ceramics, and new metals atom by atom, we must understand the spatial relationship of atoms in basic materials. The scanning-tunneling microscope, which we encountered in Chapter 2, can uncover incredibly accurate information about the positions of individual atoms on surfaces. According to Frank Fradin, associate director of physical sciences at Argonne National Laboratory, by combining the scanning-tunneling microscope with advances in computer modeling "we can model how molecules place themselves on a substrate without doing exhaustive hunt-and-peck experiments." The marriage of the computer and the scanning-tunneling microscope will provide the necessary information to fashion many of the new materials of the Macroindustrial Era.

These new material sciences incorporate recycling into their building process. One example is the innovative use of fly ash, a residue of the burning of coal, in the development of new forms of concrete. According to Ronald Levy, a vice president at Arthur D. Little, the consulting company, "using fly ash from coal-fired power generating plants as an additive to concrete has been discussed for twenty years and nothing has happened. But environmental concerns about urban sprawl and a growing shortage of building lumber may finally bring about fly ash's use in concrete to build high-rise buildings for efficient housing."

Fly ash concrete is finally on the horizon, made possible by better design principles, polymer additives, and process improvements. Levy thinks that fly ash concrete is so strong that it should open the way for the construction of 200-story skyscrapers and other structures only recently considered impossible to build.

Biomemetics: The Imitation of Life

Many of these breakthroughs have as their inspiration nature and life itself. To help develop more durable materials, Ilhan A. Askay, a professor of materials science and engineering at the University of Washington, used as his model the abalone. Askay wondered why the shell of this mollusk is so hard to break. Viewing the shell under an electron microscope, he was intrigued to discover that the atomic composition of the shell was a near perfect imitation of a ceramic composition. Askay used the abalone shell as a model for arranging the molecules of a new material, which is now being tested for use as an impact-resistant tank armor twice as durable as artificial ceramics currently employed.

Askay and others find themselves laboring in a brand-new field of materials development labeled *biomemetics,* in which science imitates the structures found in nature. The proposed national aerospace plane mentioned in Chapter 2, which would enter low orbit during its two-hour trip from New York to Tokyo, will benefit from biomemetics. Such a plane will carry a greater weight load than the shuttle but must itself weigh less than the shuttle in order to quickly reach the speed necessary for its unique flying mission. Researchers are studying the strong, yet lightweight exoskeleton of the horned beetle, hoping to replicate the material in the beetle's shell for use in the construction of the aerospace plane.

Why this beetle? According to air force researcher Fred L. Hedberg, "When nature builds a protective coating for an insect, it also permits the animal to breathe through it, insulates it, and provides all kinds of sensing devices." Researchers are also intrigued by the beetle's resilience and its entire damage control system. They suspect that the beetle's exoskeleton, composed of fibers that themselves are often composites, may be far more complex than the materials we have developed so far.

Nature will continue to provide an enormous amount of information about the structure and uses of advanced materials.

The Advent of Smart Materials

Some engineers want to impart to materials a crude sort of intelligence, replete with artificial nerves and muscles. At Michigan State University, two researchers are developing an adaptive helicopter rotor that can not only sense turbulence, but can swiftly stiffen in response to these atmospheric changes. A professor of solid-state science at Pennsylvania State University is developing a "stealthy" material for submarine hulls that can flex to change shape, thereby reducing underwater turbulence. Such an improvement would make submarines undetectable by underwater listening systems.

The key here to making a material smart is to embed in it other nonmechanical materials that have the capacity to change their physical shape or state without using moving parts. The helicopter rotor blade operates on this principle. The researchers utilize what are called electrorheological fluids that can change from a liquid to a solid within milliseconds of receiving a small electric current. By scattering such fluids throughout a ceramic, the scientists can build a rotor blade that can immediately stiffen when informed of damage or turbulence by sensors.

Scientists and engineers are already embedding sensors and actuators in the materials used to build cars and bridges. Researchers have also developed what are labeled smart suspension systems in cars that dampen vibration. Smart bridges, laden with sensors, will be intelligent enough to alert engineers if a girder is about to fail.

Growing Materials: Nanotechnology Again

One of the keys to this material revolution will be the emerging miracle nanotechnology. We observed how this new technology would expand the species' control over the very basic building blocks of matter and examined its application to such fields as medicine. As we shall see, nanotechnology will not just help to rebuild skin and internal organs in the human body; it will redefine our very concept of material scarcity and abundance.

Again, we are speaking of tiny machines able to grasp and reposition individual atoms. A machine that can do that, with its molecular size arms and atomic size computer, will be able to build almost anything by bonding the right atoms together in the correct patterns (a process we otherwise label as growth).

Expert K. Eric Drexler imagines this approach being used to "grow" a large rocket engine inside a vat in an industrial plant. The vat, made of shiny steel, stands taller than a person, because it must accommodate the completed engine. The chamber is then flooded with a thick, milky fluid that submerges the plate. The assemblers, replicators, and nanocomputers would go to work "growing" material. The result would be an engine but not a massive piece of welded and bolted metal, rather a seamless thing, gemlike.

This manufacturing process has the potential to become cheap, fast, clean, and efficient. It involves precise machines that will handle matter in molecular pieces that make it easy for nanotechnology to operate. Molecular manufacturing equipment can be used to make all the parts that are needed to build more molecular manufacturing equipment and can even build the machines needed to put the parts together.

Other machines in this nanotechnology universe include assemblers of various flavors, nanocomputers, disassemblers (to analyze a material's inner structure in order to then replicate it), replicators, and others. Nanotechnology's ability to engineer products from the atomic level on up may lead to a manufacturing cornucopia. Some of the applications are truly astounding.

• *New products.* Because we can build products atom by atom, nano-technology will bring thorough control of the structure of matter. We will literally just have to imagine a product shape, size, and resiliency; design it in a three-dimensional framework on a mainframe computer; and issue instructions to assemblers and nanocomputers.

• *Reliable products.* Imagine creating products ten times stronger than steel and more resilient! Because molecular manufacturing allows the species to arrange atoms to acquire these properties, we can now conceive of airplanes that are spared the sometimes disastrous results of current manufacturing practices, such as wings being ripped off airplanes.

• *Intelligent products.* Nanotechnology promises materials and ob-jects that contain trillions of microscopic motors and computers, form-ing parts that work together to perform a useful function. For instance, we already have predictions of tents that can be made of parts that slide and lock and walls and furniture that can be made to repair themselves instead of deteriorating. At present, these capabilities are simply beyond our imagination, but once these become part of our physical landscape, we will wonder how we could have survived without them.

• *Clean, inexpensive production.* Industry's chief enviromental con-cerns are the actual by-products of manufacturing—pollution, toxic waste, and so on. The nanotechnological vision is one in which even sophisticated parts of the manufacturing process, including the nano-computers and assemblers, are biodegradable.

The country that moves to the forefront of these abundance-creating technologies will have gone a long way toward achieving global leader-ship in the Macroindustrial Era. Japan's Science and Technology Agency surveyed some 2000 Japanese scientists for their predictions on just what kind of major materials advances we may expect in the near future. The commercialization of ceramic superconductors and the widespread use of micromaterials figure prominently in their list of predictions.

Whereas Japan has increased funding for such technologies as nano-technology, U.S. support for nondefense funding for materials research in general has waned. During the 1990s, the U.S. government and American industries must increase R&D in this critical area if the coun-try is to maintain economic viability in the Macroindustrial Era.

Plants into Energy

The increase in material abundance will not just occur through nano-technology and material recombination. Biotechnology will play as mighty and powerful a role in material growth as it already has in increasing food production. A new biotechnology breakthrough could mean an almost unlimited supply of clean-burning fuel for automobiles. Furthermore, this fuel will be cheap.

According to Lonnie Ingram, a professor of microbiology and cell science in the University of Florida's Institute of Food and Agricultural Science, "for the first time bacteria have been genetically engineered so that they are now able to convert sugar in plant materials to ethanol." Technicians have been able to modify organisms that produce organic acids as fermentation products and simply divert their metabolism to ethanol production.

We are at long last looking at a way to produce a substitute for petroleum to fuel our automobiles on a large scale. Currently, ethanol production depends on corn starch or cane sugar as a biomass source. Now, by cloning the genes of a bacterium and inserting them into another bacterium, we are in a position to convert inedible vegetable waste, stalks, stems, leaves, and woody materials into ethanol.

Ethanol fortuitously is a clean-burning fuel that can be used to reduce air pollution and the need for foreign oil. In 1990, producing ethanol cost $1.20 per gallon, while gasoline cost about one-third as much. By producing ethanol utilizing biotechnological methods, however, the price of this clean-burning fuel will be cut in half. This non-polluting substance, already used in premium-grade gasoline instead of lead additives, may eventually eliminate the need for gasoline altogether.

This is another example of the multipronged attack on scarcity and the creation of abundance. The fact that biotechnology, oft criticized by self-styled environmentalists, will actually contribute to the purification of the atmosphere demonstrates again the third corollary of the Imperative of Growth: We improve the environment by adopting more sophisticated technologies, not by reducing our technological skills and techniques.

Progress the Old-Fashioned Way

Although we have concentrated on the more exotic materials-related breakthroughs, the fact is that in the Macroindustrial revolution we will still continue to utilize the classic mineral and metal sources with which we have built civilization—copper, iron, ore, zinc, platinum, silver, even gold. While we continue to develop more sophisticated technologies and materials, the good news that confronts us at the beginning of the twenty-first century is that in spite of recurrent predictions that all basic metals will be exhausted, data simply do not support such pessimism.

In the 1980s, a group of distinguished resource experts reported that the cost trends of nonfuel minerals during the period 1950 to 1980 quite plainly do not support the hypothesis that we are approaching a scarcity of basic mineral resources. In fact, the price of raw materials has decreased when compared to what we pay for consumer goods as measured by the consumer price index.

Although the asthenic argument that minerals will soon become exhausted is being sorely tested daily, many zero-growth advocates cling to the belief that materials of all types are on the verge of disappearing. In 1980, there was a famous wager between Paul Ehrlich, the famous prognosticator of doom, and demographer Julian Simon over the future price trends of raw materials. Simon challenged Ehrlich to a $100 bet that materials would be cheaper in 1990 than they were in 1980 relative to the price index. Simon won the bet hands down.

In 1980, Julian Simon was confident that these key metals would become cheaper because he understood that over time our use of these materials would become more efficient and technology would improve. Considering the breakthroughs in advanced materials and nanotechnology and the possibility that asteroids and the rest of the universe might possess minerals such as helium-3 and titanium, Simon would doubtlessly increase the size of his wager today. Assuming, of course, he could find any takers.

The Case for a Larger Population in the Macroindustrial Era

The Imperative of Growth states unequivocally that in order to ensure its continuation, systems must grow. This tenet holds true whether applied to material, aesthetic, social, or economic growth. This principle certainly applies to population growth as well.

This chapter has shown that the material and agricultural infrastructure, combined with the ingenuity of the human species to create higher forms of energy and greater amounts of food, can and will support a population several times that of the current human family. Although this chapter has demonstrated that a larger population can be supported, many still question whether we should encourage demographic growth. Do we not, many ask, have a sufficient amount of people, if not an overabundance of them?

The answer is an unqualified no. Population expansion, long the pariah of ecologists and zero-growth advocates, actually benefits societies. In the nineteenth century, population growth went hand in hand with the rapid expansion of the economy. The case can be made that we need more, not fewer people, to continue this qualitative enhancement of our living standards and quantitative expansion of the goods and services available.

In contradistinction to the current zero-growth orthodoxy, a strong case exists for encouraging population growth.

Population Growth Stimulates the Economy

The first reason for encouraging population growth stems from the positive relationship between population increase and economic prosperity. Although the barrage of media sentiment is biased in favor of the view that zero population growth is a rudiment of sound economic policy, empirical studies have failed to demonstrate such a relationship. Observe such densely settled countries as West Germany, the Netherlands, and Japan: They have both very high levels of per capita income and productivity. Also, Singapore, Hong Kong, and Taiwan boast the highest outputs per capita in the world. Countries with lower population densities, such as India and China (yes, they actually have lower population densities) have much lower levels of per capita economic output.

This relationship is due to the fact that the more densely settled populations make better use of their transportation and communication systems as well as other parts of their economic infrastructure. More importantly, members of such groups have enormous opportunities for the face-to-face contacts that encourage innovation and productivity. It hardly qualifies as an accident that the Renaissance of sixteenth-century Europe was preceded by late medieval town fairs and the growth of urban areas. Human interfaces and communication that took place in the towns (and the trade fairs that they spawned) facilitated the intellectual explosion that we label the European Renaissance.

Julian Simon's research reaches two unconditional conclusions regarding population growth. Although admitting that research has not detected an "ideal" demographic growth rate, in economic terms, a declining population always does badly in the long run, and second, all birth rates above the replacement level raise future income. These have been proven in a variety of empirical studies. A faster-growing population produces a larger labor supply, which implies output. In addition, capital, machines, and other commodities increase in proportion with the labor force.

As early as 1967, Simon Kuznets had shown that rapid population growth was no impediment to rapid economic development, citing as examples Thailand, Mexico, Panama, Ecuador, and Jordan.

Larger Populations Attract Investment

A second reason for encouraging population growth is that growing populations attract outside investment and simultaneously pour more of their own money into building the economy. For example, Malaysia, with a population growing at a very high clip of 2 to 3 percent per year (and regularly scolded for such audacious breeding), achieved investment in 1985 amounting to 28 percent of its gross domestic product, compared with 19 percent for the low-growth United States.

People invest when they expect profit from their investment. Profit is a function of the efficiency of resource development and education rate, not the birth rate. No matter how densely populated, a country blessed with a growing highly educated population will attract investment.

Population Growth Increases the Human Genetic Pool

A third reason, and considered by some the most important, relates to the human talent pool. Larger numbers increase the chances that the next Einstein, Freud, or Beethoven will be born. As we have seen, the Imperative of Growth implies an exponential increase in the net total of benefits that an individual can bestow on a society. One Einstein does not benefit only one other individual—his knowledge extends to all society.

The common rejoinder to this argument revolves around the fact that small populations like Switzerland and Germany and nongrowing populations such as the United States are dominant in the world of science, business, and education. The response is simple: Yes, observe how these societies are enlarging their talent base by tapping into the genetic pool being developed in India and Taiwan. They increasingly supplement their dwindling talent base with the best and the brightest from developing countries.

Large Populations Are More Efficient

Research offers incontrovertible evidence that the larger the population, and the more densely settled that population is, the more likely the members of the group will practice good land management: They will take care of the land, attempt to ensure more hygienic practices, and provide for land stewardship practices such as sewage. These findings directly contradict the common assumption that larger populations somehow overburden land, materials, air, space, and other natural resources.

Other factors make population growth an attractive path to follow. Studies have shown that large populations make more efficient use of the infrastructure, in everything from modern transportation and communications systems to education, electricity, irrigation, and waste disposal systems. More importantly, such growth presents business with a sizable market, encouraging corporations to specialize and enlist cost-saving methods of large-scale production.

The validity of the above argument is admitted, often unconsciously, by most observers, even those who under ordinary circumstances may support zero population growth. In fact, the internal contradiction in the zero population growth argument can be detected in current discussions over the decline of population in the West and its concomitant effects on the labor supply.

After rising throughout the 1950s and 1960s, the size of the labor force in the West is beginning to stagnate. The United States from 1985 to 2000 will undergo some growth in the labor force, but in most other Western countries, such numbers will stabilize or begin to decrease. In short, the West confronts a stagnant labor force that is rapidly aging.

Reacting to such figures, a *Harvard Business Review* report on Global Work Force 2000 asked an intriguing question: "Can the developed countries sustain economic growth as their work forces stop growing?" What makes this such an amazing statement is the fact that only twenty years ago the Club of Rome reported that population growth would undermine global stability and economic health. As the barren zero population growth policy begins to demonstrate its more pernicious effects, policymakers are forced to wonder: Where will we get our engineers, software designers, and business and scientific leaders?

The case can even be made that larger populations actually increase the aesthetic quality of the human condition. Some of the world's most beautiful cities—San Francisco, Paris, New York, Boston—are the most densely settled. High density spawns unique architecture and ingenious design.

In fact, perhaps the time has arrived for the species to reconsider the very concept of density altogether. The Macroindustrial society's stupendous ability to construct artificial islands, underground cities and city-buildings, obliterates timeworn and obsolete notions of "population" density in much the same way that skyscrapers rewrote earlier concepts of overcrowding. In fact, when people want more land, it is within their ability to go out and create it. Israelis are reclaiming the Negev Desert through the use of hydroponics, the agricultural technique that recycles all water and nutrients, is nonpolluting, and needs little land and no soil at all. Holland has been reclaiming land from the sea for centuries.

Between 1951 and 1971, India's total cultivated land acreage increased by 20 percent. In fact, it would surprise most Westerners bombarded with dire media predictions about that country's fate to discover that India is not now densely populated. Measured by the number of persons per acre of arable land, Japan and Taiwan, neither of which can be considered suffering from malnourishment, are about five times as densely populated as India.

So it would seem that the argument that a growing population will outdistance the supply of food, materials, and energy cannot withstand empirical scrutiny. Nonetheless advocates of zero growth periodically revive such alarmist arguments, exploiting fears harbored deep inside the human psyche since the dawn of the human species: mass starvation, drought, and ecological Armageddon.

The arguments can be safely ignored. The world population, which at present stands at about 5 billion persons, will peak over the next century and a half at around twice that. What conditions must prevail for a population to add another 5 billion individuals to its ranks? For one, its members must be sufficiently healthy to reach puberty, must be physically resilient enough to bear healthy children, and must remain in good health to care for the children and to produce goods and services to support this next generation.

In a sense, the zero-growth advocates have turned the argument on its head to produce a concept that is ultimately illogical. How could a starving, unhealthy, disease-ridden society, which we supposedly will become if we keep increasing our population, even sustain itself to double in size? Such societal breakdowns—famine, drought, and plague—are the very factors that prevented humanity from reaching any sizable population level until A.D. 1800, after 30,000-plus years of attempted expansion.

In other words, our expansion from 5 billion to 11 billion, instead of being a harbinger of shortages and deterioration, will be proof positive that the Macroindustrial revolution has delivered what it promised—a healthy, well-fed, technologically advanced global society that supports 5 billion more people than lived on the planet at the era's inception!

In truth, the decision to consider the newborn child as a mouth to feed instead of a being whose brain will contribute to the world's knowledge and whose hands will help build the universe more reflects the observer's own prejudices and pessimism than any reality we know.

From the above, it is obvious that the technological breakthroughs and material improvements of the Macroindustrial Era will sustain a much larger population. At the same time, that growing population will contribute the labor and creativity necessary to support the continued progress of the species.

Implications for the Human Species

As we have seen, these advances in the agricultural, energy, and materials fields demonstrate the species' ability to overcome the restrictions of nature and to recast the concept of limits and boundlessness. The implications of these advances are many.

We can finally see the light at the end of the tunnel in terms of eliminating hunger and malnutrition from the face of the planet. As agricultural and medical breakthroughs continue to serve humanity, we can predict that the species' members will live longer, healthier lives. As more members of the species lift from their shoulders the twin burdens of malnutrition and poor health, they can begin to become net contributors to the next scientific and technological breakthroughs that will improve the human condition.

Of course, cornucopia will not be achieved without the species encountering a plethora of economic and sociological changes, some of which will be cataclysmic. For one thing, most technological advancement, no matter how beneficial to the species in general, displaces some members. A hundred years ago a man invented a synthetic blue dye that replaced one of the world's leading cash crops, indigo. Today, high-fructose corn syrup, manufactured by a biotechnologically assisted process, has negatively impacted such sugar-producing countries as the Philippines.

So, too, will the advances in agriculture have economic and social impact. It has been predicted that in 2001 there may be as few as 1.25 million farmers in the United States, 900,000 fewer than there are now. Although it will be thriving at the turn of the century, agriculture will be more an engineering project than a family-run rural business. Increasingly, the growing of food will be turned over to biologists and technical specialists.

However, the goal justifies such transformations. The agricultural and materials revolution may spell the beginning of the end of poverty. If poverty originates in scarcity, then both biotech and nanotechnology should play an active role in relegating scarcity of resources and food to the realm of mythology and ancient history.

Only the Beginning

The battle to achieve these goals is only beginning. The world must maintain its diligence not only in the production of food and materials technology, but also in encouraging a world economic system that ensures that the species as a whole participates in the benefits.

Most importantly, the culture must support the continued expansion of the knowledge, resource, and talent base. Critics in politics, academia, and the media maintain a consistent barrage of negative campaigning against advances in biotechnology and genetic engineering. In spite of our enhanced ability to increase the food and materials base, the media, including Cable News Network (CNN) and *Time* magazine, continue unabated their dire predictions regarding drought and shortages. The alarmist harangues about the "dangers" of population growth go unchallenged to the point that the public accepts even the most inaccurate statements.

Orville Freeman, former governor of Minnesota and U.S. secretary of agriculture under both Presidents Kennedy and Johnson, made some prescient statements about the issues of food, population, and the developing countries. Viewing the alarmist tendencies of environmentalists and others, he claims that we face bigger risks if we do not proceed with agricultural growth and experimentation.

Freeman states that "the United States must keep its productivity high in order to provide food assistance to starving people and also to stimulate emerging agriculture in the developing world." In other words, the United States must serve as both a source of food, and more important a source of knowledge about how to grow food.

According to Freeman, "any effective blueprint for increasing agricultural production worldwide must incorpoate development and application of crop and food related technology." In short, to adopt so-called ecological outlooks and ban biotechnology will be equivalent to condemning millions of Third Worlders to subsistent living standards or worse. If anything will lead to starvation, it is the adoption of an anti-technological viewpoint!

Needed: Another Green Revolution

Many developing countries are now only striving for subsistence and beyond, whereas in the United States agricultural production is currently *40 percent over domestic needs*. This surplus has been achieved even while we allow millions of arable acreage to sit idle and encourage farmers not to develop their land. Obviously, some countries have mastered the techniques that lead to agricultural and material abundance, whereas others have not.

Obviously, the Third World as a whole needs another green revolution. In the Macroindustrial Era, however, such a revolution will involve application of technology and skills to Third World problems. In certain countries when food supply cannot support its population adequately, it is not because of drought or natural causes, but because of the lack of technology. Much of the progress that has occurred over the last two centuries in the Third World was due to the importation of skills developed in the more technologically advanced countries. This trend must continue if the Third World as a whole is to come up to speed in terms of skills and technological achievement.

Although many have suggested wholesale exportation of food to developing countries, others have cautioned that such aid be considered at most temporary relief of emergency situations. This view emerges not from a reluctance to help others, but from a belief that such so-called charity has begun to undermine the development of the recipient countries' home-based agriculture. In many cases after a continued influx of food, arable land in the recipient country goes begging for development. The cheap charity food has been found to underprice native farmers, inadvertently driving them out of business and out of the environment in which they could develop and apply innovative agricultural techniques. Over the last few years, such foreign aid has serendipitously sabotaged Third World development.

The good news, however, is that the global society, at the dawn of the Macroindustrial Era, has the technology and resources to help the world feed itself and meet the needs of a growing population.

Although we most definitely have the physical capability to meet these needs, there is still the question of whether we have the will to succeed in this venture. The promise of the Macroindustrial Era is that it will be an age in which people will live 200 years, live better and healthier than we ever imagined, and begin to populate the cosmos. To achieve this state, both society and individuals in general must undergo a series of transformations. Among these changes are the acceptance of risk as a part of growth and an enhanced image of the human species and its possibilities.

We have already begun to clear many of these cultural and psychological hurdles. For example, genetic engineering and nanotechnology represent a key turning point in humanity's cultural development— they typify the key Macroindustrial Era notion that the species can and will exert control and direction and help develop areas that have been unreachable on a physical level and unfathomable on a cognitive level.

People find these new sciences unsettling, mainly because they perceive that when we probe and manipulate at the genetic and subatomic levels we are operating in some sense out of our rightful domain. (The issue of whose domain those areas really are varies by individual persuasion and ideology. People choose God, nature, or animus of their choice.)

I have repeated throughout that the movement into this next era will not be restrained by technology. The only possible substantial obstacles to the ultimate achievement of human progress and growth lie in the culture and the individuals who inhabit it.

In the next chapters we will explore the cultural and social foundations of our species' continued progress and conclude our exploration in Chapter 10 with a look at the practical method for achieving this growth.

Part Two

The Pathway to the Macroindustrial Society

As the previous chapters demonstrate, the species possesses the technology, science, and resources to achieve momentous breakthroughs in the fields of space exploration, medicine, agriculture, macromanufacturing, and energy. To be prepared to take its place in the next era, however, a society must possess not only the resources and technology, but also social, political, and cultural institutions that will facilitate its transition into the next era.

Part II will explore these issues. Chapter 6 will deal with the family unit necessary to create the creative, intelligent risk taker so important in the Macroindustrial Era. Chapter 7 will propose a model for the educational system required to prepare individuals to contribute to the fundamental activities of the Macroindustrial Era. In Chapter 8, I will describe steps the individual may take to engage in constructive self-development to prepare him- or herself for the challenges on the historical horizon.

Chapter 9 describes the basic components of what I have labeled the Expansionary Culture, a set of social and cultural forces required by a society to advance into the new world of the Macroindustrial Era. The Expansionary Culture will provide society's members specific values and behavioral cues, such as a valuation of risk taking, necessary for our emergence into the Macroindustrial Era. The final chapter presents the specific stepping-stones to be taken at the governmental and individual level to propel our society into the next era.

6: The Family as a Catalyst for Growth

Creating the Macroindustrial Generation

The progressive advances envisioned in the earlier chapters—traveling to Mars, exponentially increasing the food supply, and breaking our biological and medical restraints—require the effort of humans with superior knowledge, intelligence, confidence, and motivation, not to mention the courage, to take the necessary calculated risks to move a society forward. The society also needs people who are simultaneously cooperative and individualistic.

Society depends on a number of institutions and structures to develop its members. Some of these agents of influence, the media, for instance, the culture, even religion, shape the human personality indirectly. However, one institution profoundly and directly molds and develops the individual's character, values, and attitudes. We are speaking of course of the family unit. The members of this unit—parents, siblings, and relatives—provide the child his or her earliest memories and most meaningful developmental experiences.

To support our early physical development, nature has ensured that each of us enjoys nine months in a relatively protected state, unfettered by the challenges of the world. In our mother's womb, we evolve from a unicellular organism to a being that at birth can function at minimal life support levels—we can breathe, eat, digest, eliminate, and develop some level of mobility.

However, after birth, the real challenge begins. The suckling infant must be transformed into a creative, productive, autonomous, feeling individual with a unique identity and set of abilities. Therefore, the human species early in its history developed and perfected a structure for this purpose, the family, which provides a protective environment, a veritable second womb for the evolution of the organism into a person.

The family exerts a profound effect on its individual members and, hence, on society. In the best of situations, the family unit provides the nation's children with both a skill base and an emotionally supportive environment that will help them develop to their fullest potential.

The family teaches the individual how to speak, think, and interact with others. It also instills in the individual a set of values and expectations that hopefully will match those of the society's educational and occupational systems. The family possesses mechanisms that teach the child that he is special, accords him the necessary rewards for good behavior and punishment for bad, and provides him the strokes necessary to inspire him to higher performance levels. To provide the necessary experiences for the child to grow to the fullest potential, the family may arrange access to a network of contacts and support outside of the immediate family, including friends, relatives, schools, and churches.

In general, the higher the quality of family life, the more likely this environment will produce a coherent, self-respecting, and capable member of society. Judging by the rate of progress in Western society and the spread of the benefits of progress to the non-Western world, we may deduce that the family system, at least until recently, has fulfilled its role as generator of productive and creative individual contributors.

Nonetheless, in order to compete in the Macroindustrial Era, society must develop an ever more efficient and stable family unit, one that can nurture, motivate, and deliver a generation more intelligent, innovative, and adventurous than any preceding cohort. In this chapter, we will examine the extent to which the current family is meeting the mandate to provide society with the person endowed with those qualities needed in the emerging Macroindustrial Era.

Why a Strong Family Must Power the Macroindustrial Era

The Macroindustrial Era requires individuals who are productive, creative, adjusted, and self-confident. Research seems to suggest that the intact, stable family structure provides the optimum environment for the cognitive and emotional development of children. We also find that children in this environment have fewer problems with the law, have better school attendance records, and are more productive throughout the life cycle.

As we enter the new Era, the public as well as professionals in policy and academic circles seem to be increasingly aware of the importance of these facts. As we shall see, the data overwhelmingly support these conclusions.

Cognitive Development

Societies must develop individuals who can creatively contribute to societal growth in the coming Macroindustrial Era. Quite simply, in the next era, individuals will be required to be smarter than they were fifty or a hundred years ago. As we will learn, the family is a critical link in the developmental chain.

In a study of several early-development programs, Miles D. Storfer, president of the Foundation for Brain Research, determined that the quality of the intellectual environment in the first two years of life can make "a dramatic and lasting difference in [children's] measured intelligence".

Storfer's theory rests on the fact that the biochemical activity of neurons in the brain centers, keys to the development of higher intelligence, is activated soon after birth. Hence, intelligence can be enhanced by exposing the baby to certain critical stimuli early in its development. During this period, parents can involve the child in activities that may make it easier for the child to learn things quickly and easily throughout his or her lifetime. In other words, during this period, we are not just trying to teach the baby specific facts, identities, names, speech, and so on. We are attempting to *sensitize* the child to stimuli in order to accelerate its cognitive development.

Storfer's specific techniques for improving the baby's chances of becoming a lifetime quick learner can best be employed in a stable, caring environment. He suggests that the parent engage in nurturing behaviors such as rocking and soothing. Eye contact is important, especially when enhanced by vivid facial expressions such as widely opened eyes and a broad smile. The caregiver should engage in dialogue with the baby, imitating its vocalizations, behaviors, even its facial expressions. Importantly, Storfer suggests that the parent encourage the baby with praise when she in turn mimics the parent's expressions and sounds. The baby, feeling that it has the power to affect its own surroundings, will begin to develop a sense of self-esteem. This is reinforced by the fact that this constant attention by the parents informs the child that the parents and hence the world highly values her.

The key to this set of behaviors is that it occurs in one-to-one relationships and situations. The baby is being trained within the context of caring, nurturing relationships with people who can react to the person as an individual, not a member of the group. We can only intuit that the fewer the opportunities for one-to-one behavior, whether due to divorce, single parenthood, or two-incomehood, the less time there will be for the baby to receive this type of attention. Data support this contention.

In a 1991 survey of 27,000 elementary and middle school principals in the United States, the educators supported the contention that positive family experiences develop good students. The principals said families build their children's self-esteem by paying consistent attention to children's questions and feelings, listening when they talk, and making it a point to praise a job well done. According to Samuel G. Sava, executive director of the school principals national association, "even the best school can't help a child who's not getting the right family support."

The principals complain that today's family seems to be abdicating its role in the education of its offspring. The responding principals claimed that fewer than half of the students nationwide are receiving adequate preparation for school within their home environment.

One study carried out by the Baldwin Wallace College faculty in Ohio concluded that by comparison to children from divorced or single-parent homes, preschool children from intact families have a lesser chance of ever developing problems producing speech or grasping comments from others. According to the study, although the overall number of children having such speech or thinking skills problems has skyrocketed from the 3 to 5 percent range a few decades ago to a current level of 35 percent, the majority of children with such deficiencies come from nontraditional households. The study traced speech and comprehension problems to the fact that the child in some of these nontraditional home settings, such as the single-parent household, is left to "learn" almost exclusively from TV or video games.

A recent national study of 47,000 households by the National Center for Health Statistics presented some interesting insights into how different types of living arrangements affect children's cognitive and emotional development. Deborah Dawson, a demographer for the National

Center for Health Statistics, examined four types of family arrangements: both biological parents present; mother and stepfather present; formerly married mother, no father present; and never-married mother, no father present.

Her finding was striking: children living in a household with both biological parents had a dramatically lower chance of ever repeating a grade or getting expelled or suspended from school than children from other family situations. This study, which examined children ages five to seventeen, found that only 12 percent of those in intact original families ever repeated a grade. Those with never-married mothers showed a 30 percent chance of repeating one or more grades. Only 4 percent of those living with both natural parents had ever been suspended as compared to 11 percent of divorced children and 15 percent of children living with never-married mothers.

Studies consistently demonstrate the positive effects of an intact environment on learning ability. For instance, in a recent study in Britain, researchers found a significant difference in the reading and spelling ability of 500 thirteen-year-old children based on family background. The researchers found that the children of divorced and separated parents lagged behind children from intact families in such skills as reading comprehension and spelling.

Another study dealing with so-called learning disabilities demonstrates that intelligence is determined far more by home environment than innate predisposition. The data revealed that learning disabilities, though present in all types of families, were less prevalent in children in intact families. Only 5 percent of children in intact families were reported to have learning disabilities, 7.5 percent in mother-only families, and 9.1 percent in mother–stepfather families. Such studies seem to suggest that such disabilities are less biological than environmental.

We have found that the educational effects of family living arrangements can be long-term. A recent Canadian study that analyzed the life course of 45,000 Canadians between the ages of eighteen and thirty-four demonstrated that the intact family has a more positive effect on long-term educational attainment than have mother-only or father-only households. This may also have economic implication. After reviewing the data on educational advancement, the main researcher, Marianne D. Parson, concluded that "children raised in lone-parent families in Canada are socioeconomically disadvantaged in adulthood . . . all indicators point to a worsening situation for the children raised in this family structure."

What properties of the intact family help produce higher grades, lower dropout rates, and greater learning proficiencies? A University of Chicago study examined fairly intensively the processes inside family life that lead to such positive results. It found that students whose parents talked with them about schoolwork usually achieved noticeably higher grades. These conversations achieve two goals. For one, the parent explains the homework to the child, making possible higher comprehension rates of the material and thus higher grades. Also, the child realizes that an adult, whose approval he desires, is noticing his academic performance, if only on homework. In order to maintain that adult's approval, the child must continue to do well in exams, quizzes, projects, and, ultimately, his grades.

The study also discovered that TV restrictions at home lead to higher grades. As we shall see in the next chapter, the more TV ingested by students, the lower their grades. According to the study, such restriction can only be placed on the child by a guiding parent; in the intact family, there is a greater chance that at least one parent will be on hand to regulate the child's TV viewing.

Creating the Emotionally Stable Individual

In the Macroindustrial Era, to fulfill his or her role in societal growth, the individual will have to be more than intelligent and creative. Emotional stability will be necessary. The stable individual has a greater tendency to perform well at school and work, refrains from wasteful and destructive criminal behavior, and contributes meaningfully to society and family. He or she will also possess the self-confidence to take risks and explore new intellectual avenues.

Studies show that a definitive relationship exists between early childhood family experiences and overall emotional and physical health. In an Australian study of 2100 adolescents, it was found that those in intact families were reported to be healthier, less neurotic, and more extroverted and had better perceptions of their bodies than adolescents from nontraditional homes. They were less recklessly impulsive and had a more positive view of their school performance. In addition, they were less likely to report alcohol-related and psychological problems in their families and used health professionals such as psychologists and social workers less.

In a recent study of over 20,000 individuals under the age of eighteen, men and women raised in intact families were doing better than those reared by divorced mothers on a number of measures: satisfaction with life, happiness, sense of personal control, trust, and friendship. Some of these differences were a direct result of the economics of divorce, which tends to depress the income of the child and mother; but even after taking into account differential household income, the university researchers discovered that adult children of divorced parents were worse off emotionally than peers from intact families.

The emotional effects of destabilized family structures on young children are devastating. Deborah Dawson at the National Center for Health Statistics discovered a correlation between family instability and the need for psychological treatment. Only 2 percent of children three to seventeen years of age are likely to have needed treatment for emotional or behavioral problems in the preceding twelve months. Children living with formerly married mothers were more than three times as likely as those living with both biological parents to have received such treatment. Almost 5 percent of those living with a never-married mother sought such help.

The Impact of Divorce on the Next Generation

Any society wishing to foster a generation that will successfully compete in the Macroindustrialization must take into consideration emerging data on the deleterious effects of divorce on children's cognitive and emotional development. Divorce has effects on children's emotional and cognitive development that adults often overlook when contemplating leaving their spouse. These effects very often only manifest themselves in therapy sessions or large-scale research projects.

The effect of divorce on academic performance is pertinent here. Society will increasingly require an influx of intelligent high achievers in the next era. According to a recent study with a relatively affluent population sample, one-third of the children experiencing parental separation demonstrated a significant decline in academic performance. Most troubling is the fact that these problems persisted for at least three years after the divorce for both boys and girls and in all grade levels.

This and other studies reveal that children living through parental separation have a higher probability of being distracted, upset, perhaps even traumatized. Such children are hardly the people required in the next era who can concentrate on their studies and who have a fixed stable base on which to mature intellectually and emotionally.

As we will see in Chapter 9, the emerging era also requires people equipped with an optimistic worldview and a positive national outlook. Research illustrates the critical role that a stable family unit plays in developing optimistic, forward-looking individuals. Unfortunately, studies show that young people who experience divorce exhibit lower positive views of themselves and the world than their intact-family counterparts.

Recently an Eisenhower Army Medical Center investigation of 134 psychologically disturbed children revealed that most of the subjects had parents with a history of separation and divorce. After investigating 400 white fifteen-year-olds, researchers at the Simmons College School of Social Work in Boston concluded that those in divorced housholds were much more likely than those in intact households to become delinquents, report depressed behavior, and use drugs to excess.

The behavioral patterns of divorced fathers may in some way explain the adverse effects of divorce on the young. A recent University of Pennsylvania study of children from a variety of family backgrounds shows that over time contact between divorced fathers and children declines sharply. By studying one group of children in 1976, 1981, and 1987, they were able to measure the amount of regular contact that these children had with their fathers after the actual divorce. Early on, the amount of regular contact between father and child decreased sharply. Only 10 percent of the children originally surveyed in 1976 had weekly or monthly contact with their fathers between 1976 and 1981. Only one in five had any contact at all during that period.

A high-quality relationship between father and child helps the child form a stable personality, but this study shows how divorce undermines the ties between father and child. By 1981, only 38 percent of the 1976 divorced group described their relationship with their fathers as "very close" compared to 79 percent of the children from intact families. By 1987, a full eleven years after the divorce, intact-family children were three times more likely to have a strong high-quality relationship with their fathers than were the children of divorced parents.

At the time of the breakup, most fathers insist that they are divorcing the mother, not the children, and fully intend to maintain a close relationship with their child after the divorce. What then leads to the gradual alienation of father from child? According to the researchers, when the father leaves the wife, he effectively abandons the children. "They find it difficult to maintain bonds with their children at the same time they relinquish ties to their former spouse."

Such data suggests that we are deluding ourselves when we assume that after a divorce a father either feels like returning to the nest for quality time with the young ones or that he perceives that he is welcome to do so. Most disturbingly, the data reveal that the younger the child at the time of divorce, the less chance the father will retain any relationship with his children.

Family Stability and Economic Health

Part of the reason that intact families provide such a nurturing environment for the development of the young is purely and simply economic. A stable family unit for the most part is more economically viable than an unstable one. To the extent that money can buy him or her if not happiness, access to better schools, a predictable life, and a feeling of well-being, the child in a prosperous home has a better chance of doing well intellectually and emotionally than a child in a poor one.

The relationship between family stability and economic prosperity, though a strong one, is hardly understood by the public. For instance, intriguing statistics have emerged concerning the economic differences between intact two-parent families and the single-parent family. In 1982, for instance, the poverty rate for a married couple family was only 7.6 percent, but for female-headed families, the figure stood at an astounding 36.3 percent. This reflects a persistent economic pattern—by 1991, although only 8 percent of married couples lived below the poverty line, 47 percent of female-headed households were officially poor.

Marriage, especially when it mirrors the nuclear family model, stands as a powerful defense against poverty. According to U.S. Census data, a married couple, both able-bodied adults, regardless of their race or educational background rarely stays below the poverty line for a period longer than one or two years. Compare this to the long-term poverty demonstrated by the household of the single parent (read single mother), which usually stays below poverty and on the national dole for a period of eight years or more.

In addition, the intact family enjoys higher per capita incomes, is buffeted less by the vagaries of inflation, and withstands the winds of recession more easily than nontraditional family units.

What do these statistics indicate? They suggest that children in non-nuclear families, besides being deprived of the emotional and cognitive benefits of the intact family, must also do without its economic benefits. Money certainly helps open the door to educational opportunities, including private tutors, computers, and tuition at a good college. It can also buy the child peace of mind: She does not have to worry about the family's economic situation, nor does she have to listen to her parents argue about it. Her world is at peace, and she can get on with her life.

Is Institutional Day Care Meeting the Next Era's Needs?

If we are in fact concerned about the productivity of the next labor force, we must ensure that children develop intellectually and cognitively. They must possess several character traits in order to contribute to society in the coming Macroindustrial Era, including creativity, intelligence, and emotional stability.

We depend on social units such as the family and school to imbue our children with these qualities. Due to changes in family structure and new demands on its members, however, parents are increasingly sharing the nurturance and development of their children with other adults. Children today are more than likely to live with parents who work full-time or with a working mother who is either divorced or has never married. In the United States, where over half the mothers are employed, a large majority of the children must spend part or all of their day in some form of nonparental day care. By 1990, it was estimated that 20 percent spend their days in some form of neighborhood day-care facility, 28 percent stayed with the mother's parent, another 19 percent were watched by another relative, and 28 percent of the children spent time in commercial day care.

The nonhome day-care facility format warrants special interest here because it is quickly becoming the preferred child-care alternative for parents who choose to pursue their careers instead of rearing their children full-time. Corporations are besieged by employees to establish a plethora of institutional child-care programs, such as on-site day care or financial assistance to pay for outside day care that will make it easier for parents to work full-time.

If institutional day care is to become a substitute for family socialization, we ought to ask some hard questions about the efficacy of these new arrangements. We know that day care is convenient for the parents. However, is it beneficial for the children? Although people in the United States and in most of the West generally believe that institutional day care has fulfilled the goal of providing child care equivalent in quality to that of full-time parents, the evidence indicates that their judgment in this matter is decidedly premature.

One study demonstrated that kindergartners who have spent a substantial amount of time in the care of people other than their parents exhibit a myriad of negative characteristics. They display a low interest in and respect for other children and teachers, show symptoms of stress, and have elevated tendencies toward aggressiveness and a low tolerance of frustration.

In a study of eight-year-olds in Texas, for instance, those with extensive institutional child-care histories exhibit a number of negative tendencies as early as age one. According to the study, those children who had been in nonmaternal care since their first year of life were worse off on a number of measures, including school achievement, social behavior, and self-esteem than peers who had received maternal care.

Wherever one looks, the judgment on day care is less than positive. One assessment of all day-care children studies up to 1990 revealed a chilling analysis of where we are headed as a society if we continue to pursue the nonparental developmental model. It found that children in day care are less cooperative with adults, more physically and verbally aggressive with peers and adults, and are less able to manage their frustrations.

Researchers have also studied the impact of day care by age cohort. By eighteen months, 50 to 70 percent of infants in day care demonstrated weak attachments to their mothers. By two years of age, the children in day care since infancy were less enthusiastic and persistent in fulfilling tasks than those in full-time parental care. Some long-term studies have found that teenage boys originally reared in day care display a more aggressive nonconformity to parental requirements than those reared by parents. The day-care experience also has been increasingly linked to problematic behavior later on, including drug and alcohol use, delinquent behavior, adoption of morally permissive attitudes, and early withdrawal from school.

Social scientists and concerned policymakers ponder the dynamic underlying the negative consequences of nonparental childrearing. Some feel that the effect of interrupting attachment bonds between parent and child during the first two years of life prevents the child from developing a basic trust in constant human relationships and an impaired ability to form committed relationships with other people.

Researchers such as Professor Jay Belsky of the University of Pennsylvania claim that the child placed in day care may experience a daily sense of abandonment at being turned over to the care of strangers. In his research with such children, Belsky detected a definitive loss of both trust and what he labels a "sense of order in the world" among day-care graduates. Ought we to be surprised? Research has shown that in the day-care setting, with its group-care orientation, the child receives a low level of stimulation, less attention, and less response and affection from adults.

Most worrisome is the fact that infants spending more than twenty hours per week in day care develop a tendency to avoid contact with their real mothers. Boys have particular problems attaching to either parent. We can hypothesize that while the child initially experiences a sense of loss of parent during the bonding stage, he or she eventually simply learns to live without parents on a full-time basis.

According to primary research performed for this book by one of my researchers, children from such backgrounds lack direction and what her respondents label a "moral center." Viewing the behavior patterns of such students, these respondents, directors of a grade school with 250 children, labeled many of them "kids without conscience." These children, who had spent the first two years of their lives in nonparental settings, present a real challenge not only to the teachers, but to the other students.

According to one director, literally anything such children want to do seems all right to them; they are aggressive, self-centered, and easily angered. He claims that each year his classes are filled with more and more children like these—unattached to another person and bereft of any genuine sense of self-worth but with a tenacious sense of self-survival.

We can easily see how such people might become noncontributors to the societal Macroindustrial effort. As mentioned earlier, in this new era, the requisite culture will be based on optimism, a positive outlook toward the future, a mature attitude toward risk, and a sense of dedication and long-term purpose. We cannot construct such a culture upon individuals who are mistrustful, uncooperative, intolerant of frustration, and unable to defer gratification.

It is also doubtful whether the day-care experience is preparing the next generation for the intellectual challenges of the emerging era either. Every year politicians and educators are confronted with declining scores on such standardized tests as the SATs and national math and reading exams. They make public promises to improve the educational system, usually with a fresh infusion of money. Yet rarely do they publicly acknowledge the influence that childrearing arrangements have on the test taker's cognitive development and hence his or her test score.

A University of London study found that children reared at home by parents learn to use words in combinations more quickly than those reared in day-care centers. According to the study, which compared the language usage of eighteen-month-old children reared at home by parents with that of children of the same age reared in day care or "nursery," the home-care child was linguistically superior. Children in group care were "less likely to have language records indicative of advanced language development" and used a lower number of word combinations and exhibited inferior vocabulary. Surprisingly, the lower-performing day-care children came from a relatively advantaged position in terms of parental income, occupational status, and education. According to the researchers, more advantaged groups would be expected to show better language development than less advantaged groups. The day-care experience eliminated such an advantage.

Other studies support this contention. In one study that looked at children in a variety of care settings, it was found that third graders who spent their preschool years in day care have lower academic grades and demonstrate poorer study skills.

In spite of this evidence, the media continue to heap praise upon the "new dawn of day care" as though all of this evidence simply does not exist. For most commentators, the "more perfect" day-care system is always just around the corner.

A recent newspaper article on the subject addressed such issues as the extent to which government and business will support day care, the cost of top-drawer child care, the quality and salaries of the aides, certification of practitioners, and center accreditation. At the purely descriptive level, the article, like most mass-media discussions of day care, is remarkably thorough (it even listed recommended centers, with names and addresses). However, evaluation of the societal and individual effects of day care are absent. Because the need for and advantages of day care are already accepted, parental responsibility then easily becomes redefined in terms of choosing the best day-care center. This particular article mentioned only one case in which day care was criticized—an ABC special on *Prime Time* that painted negative pictures of day care—and then quickly dispensed with this presentation by describing the whole effort as an exercise in "back-stabbing" by program host Diane Sawyer.

In truth, the majority of media discussions over day care subtly establish an agenda. Questions regarding the efficacy of this child-care modality or research supporting such suspicions are rarely addressed; instead the issue becomes one of availability and affordability of this type of care.

Supporting the Family

In the last few years, sociologists, interest groups, activists, and politicians have realized and acknowledged both the important role that the family plays in a country's economic growth and, conversely, the pernicious effect that family breakdown and instability have on society and the individual. By the time the 1992 U.S. presidential campaign arrived, most politicians had undergone a near religious conversion to the belief in the sanctity of the home. The family had suddenly become a national resource, "family values" a national crusade.

No country can take a leading position in the Macroindustrial Era without a stable family unit to provide the occupational and educational system with the next generation of world-class scientists, engineers, managers, and leaders. Hence, it is little wonder that politicians and policy planners are growing increasingly uneasy about the overall condition of the family unit, not just in the United States, but in the West in general.

The American family has undergone a traumatic transformation over the last several decades, a change reflective of patterns in major Western countries. For example, of all children in the United States who were born in 1980, 70 percent can expect to spend part of their lives in single-parent homes. The most significant reason for this increase is the fact that approximately 22 percent of all children born in the United States are born to unmarried mothers; among American blacks, that number has skyrocketed to 62 percent.

Another contributing factor is the high divorce rate. This rate, calculated per 1000 married females, fluctuated throughout this century. In 1920, the divorce rate was 6.6 per 1000 married females, increasing to 17.9 in 1940 and declining in 1957 to 8.9. It is in the recent past, the period between 1960 and 1990, that divorce has become pervasive. The divorce rate went from 9.2 per 1000 females in 1960 to 22.6 in 1980 and has stayed high during the 1990s. Since 1970, over 1 million children per year have seen their parents divorce. Between 1963 and 1988, the rate of children experiencing the disruptions of divorce doubled.

Sad to say, children living in single-parent households will not find themselves back in a two-parent household marital situation any time soon. According to investigators Larry L. Bumpass and James Sweet, "For most children, living in a single-parent family is not a brief, transitory situation on the way to a reconstituted family. . . . For the majority of children—white and black—who live in single-parent families, this situation is likely to persist for the remainder of childhood."

Only 36 percent of children whose parents separate or divorce or who are born out of wedlock will become part of a two-parent family within five years. According to calculations of Bumpass and Sweet, 35 percent of children born to unmarried women and 50 percent of children from divorced families will never live as part of a two-parent household before the age of sixteen. Under current conditions, hundreds of thousands of young children will have little or no idea of what it means to live in a typical nuclear family arrangement.

But change is on the horizon. The fact that the public and institutional leaders have noticed the decline in the intact family and its concomitant traumatic effects on individuals and society is a necessary preface to fundamental change. We know we have to revive the intact family. The question is how. We will examine a variety of insights into how society, polity, and culture can nurture back to health the family structure needed in the Macroindustrial Era.

Structural Solutions

When politicians and policymakers speak of curing the ills of the family and reinstating familial stability, they usually are referring to programmatic solutions which entail government and corporations taking some type of formal action to stimulate the family unit. We will first examine and evaluate the best of these structural solutions. However, the answers are not all programmatic. The weakening of the family unit has its roots in the culture and the individual also, and we will consider solutions from those perspectives.

Economic solutions to the family instability problem usually involve a variety of government and corporate programs that look both to present incentives to people to remain in marriage and to provide disincentives to leave children, remain single, or remain childless.

Critics and policy analysts are divided on correct solutions to these ills. However, many are coming around to the thinking articulated by social critic and writer David Blankenhorn. In his *Rebuilding the Nest: A New Commitment to the American Family*, a multiauthored tome on action plans to help the family, Blankenhorn echoes an emerging theme regarding government family policy. He proclaims that when government takes any action on any program that involves family and family life or any question that affects children, there should be one and only one issue: Does the program strengthen the parent–child bond, or does it contribute to family fragmentation? Many experts are beginning to realize that the groundswell of data and opinion has brought back to prominence the reality of what and who help children develop into mature, stable, creative individuals.

Many of the following proposals are aimed at different sources of family instability and are based on specific philosophical interpretations of why the family unit has deteriorated.

Provide Tax Credits for Families

The solution most often proffered to save the family unit involves reworking the tax structure in such a way that tax benefits accrue to those who are married with children.

Proponents justify such proposals on the premise that married parents are making sacrifices to provide society with the next generation of workers, taxpayers, and parents. They also help to pay for the current generation's old age through Social Security contributions. Some have even labeled parenting a form of personal sacrifice for the national good. As Harvard sociologist Mary Ann Glendon says, "It's legitimate for the law to accord special preference to child-rearing households, for all of us have a stake in the socialization of each new generation."

The United States lags behind countries like France, which aid the parenting process by providing couples with maternity benefits, tax breaks, maternity and paternity leave, even cash bonuses for having children. In the United States, suggestions abound regarding the utilization of progressive taxation, deductions, and other mechanisms to encourage both marriage and fertility. In the United States, many experts support a high out-and-out tax exemption, say $6000 per child, as a way to strengthen the family.

All indications are that political pressures will eventually force government to change the tax structure somehow in favor of married couples with children.

Change Divorce Laws

Legislators are beginning to include in their thinking about marital law the proposition that being "married with children" brings unique responsibilities. Legislators now seem to comprehend the effects divorce has on the children, and sentiment is beginning to rise for the toughening of divorce laws for parents.

Many critics complain that the so-called no fault divorce laws, in which both members can sue for divorce without bringing formal complaints against the partner such as mental cruelty or adultery, are causing family disruption. They reason that the easier it is to obtain a divorce, the more prone people are to ignore alternatives, such as counseling. History does bear out such a contention.

It is not unreasonable to predict that over the next five to ten years legislation will be introduced and most likely passed that will place some restrictions on divorce between parents with younger children.

Enforce Child Support

Five years after their divorce, not only do the majority of fathers no longer see their children, they also discontinue their court-mandated child-care payments and alimony.

Most family activists focus on the enforcement of child support payments as a primary mechanism for either reducing the incidence of divorce or minimizing its damages. Democratic presidential candidate and now-President Bill Clinton, no flaming conservative, has emerged as a proponent of inducing divorced fathers to live up to court-mandated alimony and child support payments. Proposals usually include beefing up the courts, increasing penalties for nonpayment of child support or alimony, and utilizing computer technology to track down child support "deadbeats."

There are several assumptions underlying these proposals. Many believe that there now exist few economic sanctions against leaving the marriage. In fact, fathers may know that they will not be penalized by eventually withdrawing monetary support; the legal system is overworked and cannot pursue all negligent fathers. Hence, the way the system is currently constructed, fathers can opt out of supporting their children by divorcing the mother. By enforcing child-care payments, the legal system can make divorce a less attractive alternative to fathers. The hope is that potential divorcers, recognizing that divorce will cause them economic pain, will think twice about pursing this option.

Proponents of such legislative changes argue that even if the new laws do not eliminate all divorce, they will minimize the damage divorce visits upon the children. Because the children of divorce will actually receive monetary support from the absent parent, the chances that they will live their formative years in poverty are greatly reduced.

Restructure Social Welfare Systems

In his 1984 book, *Losing Ground*, Charles Murray claimed that changes in federal social policies and court decisions that were made between 1965 and 1975 made single parenting and other nontraditional parenting behaviors profitable. Some even claim that the child benefits paid by welfare agencies to a parent exceeded the costs to that parent of raising the child, sometimes by as much as $3000 per year per child. The implication is that a mother could actually turn a profit by having children, that profit increasing incrementally for each child she bore.

A study by Robert Plotnick of the University of Washington demonstrated that government welfare programs do provide economic incentives to mothers to have a child out of wedlock. According to Plotnick, the only cost to the mother would be the social stigma surrounding illegitimacy, but "the broad social controls that inhibited out-of-wedlock childbearing had declined relative to their strength in prior times."

A 1991 PBS special, "Childhood in America," highlighted the debate over the relationship of the welfare system to destabilized families. Madeline Cartwright, principal of Blaine Elementary School in North Philadelphia, claimed on the program that she knew of many girls who have additional babies for the express purpose of increasing their welfare supplements. Others on the program denied ever witnessing or even hearing of such a situation; but Allan Carlson, president of the Rockford Institute, a social policy think tank, argued that the welfare system was indeed economically rewarding poor women for having more children.

Although originally considered a "conservative" point of view, this perspective has increasingly been incorporated into the programs and platforms of the reborn "centrist" Democratic party. All now look for solutions to ameliorate this situation.

The draconian alternative, complete elimination of welfare, would spell disaster for millions of parents and children. The reasonable solution involves retaining the social safety net for worthy recipients while eliminating some of its more deleterious elements. The system must encourage the recipients to form stable households, regardless of the number of children they have. Some have suggested rewarding stability by increasing the welfare payment to the parents if they are married and living together. Currently, payment schedules seem to reward people for staying unmarried. The system could also allow tax credits to those on the program who are married.

A simpler proposal would be to return the system to its original Depression-era focus: a safety net for children who have lost their fathers through death. Such a system would reinstate the original philosophy that the social welfare net exists for the benefit of children, not parents.

Encourage Child Care by Relatives

In a recent RAND Corporation study comparing the effectiveness of regulated day-care facilities and private arrangements, such as child care by relatives, several unexpected findings emerged. According to the RAND study, child care by relatives may potentially provide the small group sizes (about five children to one adult), loving environment, and transmission of family cultural and religious values that most closely correspond to mother care.

In other words, if both parents have to work, they can most closely replicate home care for the child by enlisting as caregivers relatives, such as the child's grandparents or aunts or uncles. One suggestion is to provide parents with child-care vouchers that they can apply to any number of child-care alternatives. Many insist that one of those alternatives should be child care by relatives.

Change Corporate Policy

One of the targets for structural change in family policy is the parents' employer, namely, the modern corporation. Controversy surrounds this issue. Some argue that the corporation has no business developing practices and policies that affect its employees' family behavior one way or another. Others emphasize that corporations have a stake in the development of the next generation of workers and hence must help their employees nurture their children.

The litany of corporate programs that have been suggested to help employees lead a stable family existence is endless. Some suggest that companies provide on-site day care so that mothers can be with their children while they work. Others counsel corporations to offer employees who become parents at least a temporary home-based job assignment that they can perform through home–office computer interfaces.

Solutions such as flextime, job sharing, compressed work weeks, and long-term paternity and maternity leave all require cooperation by the employer and also the parent's co-workers.

In truth, corporations will help employees maintain stable family relationships for either of two reasons. The first reason would be their recognition that it is in their economic self-interest to do so. Because corporations benefit by retaining key employees, companies act in their own best economic interests by accommodating the maternal decisions of talented women in key positions. The second reason would be government mandates that the corporation must provide flextime, maternity leave, work-at-home opportunities, and other such benefits to those wanting to start a family.

Corporations, acting in their own best interest, perhaps with government encouragement, will incorporate some profamily policies into their overall human resources framework. The 1993 Family Leave Bill addresses some employment issues. For instance, companies of fifty employees or more must permit their employees to take unpaid leave of up to twelve weeks per year to tend to family emergencies, including childbirth and family illness. Ironically, many large companies had policies even more liberal than those stipulated by the bill. About half of U.S. workers would be affected by this bill.

Cultural Change

The greatest trap that all modern analysts fall into when analyzing any human behavior, from purchase decisions to family decisions, is to overemphasize the role played by governmental and business policy. It gives us the false hope that all solutions lie in a more improved legal structure or a revised employee handbook.

I have emphasized throughout this book the powerful role culture plays in all areas of human behavior, and its influence certainly extends into the family arena. Although we may attempt to encourage family stability through tax credits, tougher divorce laws, and enlightened corporate policy, the cues that the culture sends to the individual about appropriate behavior will exert an equal if not greater influence on him or her as structural change.

A strong case can be made that the culture, at least as it now exists in the West, and more specifically in the United States, mitigates against any lasting commitment to either marriage or children.

Change the Message

According to social historian and clinical psychologist Edward Hoffman, the social values that circulated and stabilized in the late 1960s and early 1970s transformed society's perspective on marital institutions. A combination of Hollywood movies, network television, popular music, mass market advertising, and pop psychology/self-help books conspired to undermine the Westerner's preference for marriage and traditional parenting and childrearing practices.

These media routinely extolled as preferable life-style choices singlehood, open marriage, creative divorce, and, in general, the childless state. Movies were quick to emphasize the joys of the single life, and books such as Ellen Peck's *The Baby Trap* comtemptuously depicted what she labeled "baby raising" as an almost prisonlike condition. Peck proclaimed voluntary childlessness as the ultimate state of freedom and self-fulfillment.

The O'Neills' *Open Marriage,* a best seller in 1972, recommended that husbands and wives live together in a sexually liberated manner (so that both could live the best of both worlds). According to the O'Neills, couples ought to be more concerned with "commitment to personal growth" than monogamy or loyalty to spouse. Influenced by such arguments, many counselors and psychotherapists actually began recommending to their married and engaged clients that they explore open relationships as a means for achieving a fulfilling life.

In 1973 and 1974 books with titles like *Divorce: The New Freedom, The Courage to Divorce,* and *Creative Divorce* gained a mass following. In *The Courage to Divorce,* the authors described divorce as a "wholly liberating and positive experience."

Many would agree that the attitudes and values evolving during these years have held sway in Western society even to the present. Although such critiques smack of conservative rhetoric, the Right certainly has no monopoly on the emerging critique of "liberation culture." Barbara Ehrenreich, a liberal to left-of-center social thinker, in her book *The Hearts of Men* acerbically describes how cultural forces, especially media-generated pop cultural forces, gradually weakened Western males' adherence to the stricter norms of marriage and fatherhood. Her list of culprits includes *Playboy* magazine, the "do your own thing" message of the sixties, and the decades-long emphasis on sexual freedom.

Influenced by a culture that has sold them on the "virtues" of the single life, men, not women, have been continually seeking liberation from the bonds of matrimony. The proof, Ehrenreich claims, is the ever-decreasing marriage rates and increased divorce rates. It seems that American men have heeded the call of the single life: As of 1993, an astounding 18 percent of men in early middle age, between the ages of thirty-five and thirty-nine, had never married, up from 7.8 percent in only eleven years.

These figures for the never married among the older age groups are particularly important, because a large portion of this group has now made its permanent life choices. In contrast to the "never-married" twenty-five-year-old, the thirty-eight-year-old bachelor will most likely never get married in the future. Singlehood then has become a legitimate permanent life-style choice for a sizable group of people. In 1991, the proportion of Americans getting married hit the lowest point since 1965. In 1991, one in four Americans age eighteen and older, about 41 million people, had never married. In 1970, that figure stood at one in six adults.

Furthermore, the men who do marry and become fathers are surrounded by a constant media-oriented reminder of the better life outside of marriage and the family. This other life promises much more than sex; it offers freedom itself.

It is under the weight of this cultural baggage that today's men and women endeavor to achieve the familial stability and continuity critical to their society's success in the Macroindustrial Era. They must bear and nurture the creative scientific workers, thinkers, and inventors of the next era in a culture that provides scant ideological and moral, not to mention financial, support for their efforts.

Certainly, the culture must change, but such a transformation requires that culture bearers transmit a new set of messages and signals to members of the society. The media will play a part in this solution. Perhaps the media ought to begin to highlight parenting as a job, a career in which young adults can accomplish something really worthwhile. Sitcoms and movies must begin to reshape the image of parents as individuals who can be teachers and caregivers in ways that others quite simply cannot be.

To a great extent, the overwhelming evidence in favor of the intact nuclear family as a source of societal growth is already generating books and articles that are promotherhood and profamily. Sylvia Hewlett in her best-selling *When the Bough Breaks* wrote against the supermom syndrome, which leads to parental neglect of children, and psychologist

Brenda Hunter wrote of the emotional trauma that children suffer when they are neglected by working parents.

The publicizing of such research through the media becomes part of a campaign that can change, or reclaim, the intact family. However, many researchers and writers who take such positions too often discover that the culture itself becomes an obstacle to the acceptance and transmission of their ideas. Hunter and Hewlett have been attacked by a variety of feminists, politicos, and others who claim that they are attempting to dictate to women how they ought to live their lives.

Scholars who publicize research findings construed to be supportive of a profamily position undergo similar treatment. Savage reactions greeted Professor Jay Belsky's work on the deleterious effects of day care on child development. After his troubling studies of post-day-care graduates surfaced, the academic wagons circled almost immediately. Fortunately, Belsky was already tenured at his university and had to fend only against the judgments of colleagues, not threats to relieve him of his teaching post.

The movie *Parenthood*, which highlighted the joys of being a parent in an intact family and celebrated multigenerational cohesion, was not so much attacked as ignored by the cultural establishment. In spite of the movie's overwhelming success, it was relegated to cultural Siberia by those who considered its profamily message out of step with prevailing Hollywood standards.

In fact, it is sometimes difficult for well-meaning people either to support the nuclear family or to point out the weaknesses of its alternatives without being sharply attacked by the media. On popular talk shows, the position is trumpeted daily, through anecdote and personal testimony, that the words *dysfunctional* and *family* are truly synonymous.

Certainly, the mass media ought to begin a reexamination of itself, pondering whether its primary role is to expose the family's weaknesses or work toward strengthening that institution. Popular culture could help the individual to make better decisions regarding family and child-care issues. Disseminating information about the negative consequences of familial destabilization might encourage parents to stay married and choose home care over institutional day care for their children.

The Divorce Industry Must Change

Other cultural institutions have a major impact on the family. Clinical psychologist Diane Medved partially blames the high divorce rate on the growth of what she labels "the divorce industry," a coterie of lawyers, counselors, psychologists, and other professionals who are making a profit on divorce and hence encourage it.

In Medved's eyes, lawyers and psychologists are the worst offenders. She feels that divorce lawyers often exacerbate an already bad relationship between husband and wife by becoming involved in the marital version of "ambulance chasing." By pursuing their legal quarry so voraciously, egging on their client to go for the jugular, they actually reduce the likelihood of reconciliation between the partners. Of course, lawyers rejoinder that if the partners were not so intent to exact their pound of flesh, lawyers could not enjoy such a profitable practice.

Medved particularly blames the counseling segment of this industry for high divorce rates. She feels that many of these counselors and psychologists do very little to help their clients consider any alternative to divorce. In fact, it has already become part of the folk culture that the marriage counselor is more concerned with helping the couple adjust to the fact that they will separate than preventing the disengagement. According to Medved, "A troublesome number of my colleagues tend to avoid 'value judgments' at the expense of marriages and the long-term needs of the individuals involved."

Both the psychologists and the lawyers take their moral cues from the culture: Since the culture proclaims that individual satisfaction and self-expression warrant maximum consideration, priority should be first given to the personal wishes of the bickering members of the couple. The culture has already proclaimed the sanctity of divorce, so the professionals in the legal and therapeutic communities act in ways essentially reflecting the moral ambiguity emerging from the media.

Perhaps every psychologist and counselor working with an individual or couple pondering divorce should provide them with information on the traumatic effects divorce can have on their children and their own lives. Certainly many couples would at least attempt reconciliation.

Individual Change

The legal system, media messages, and tax and penal codes all can play a role in inducing family stability. Ultimately the decisions to get married, stay married, have children, and provide those offspring with a nurturing environment are made by individuals. Nothing can force people to do what they are unwilling to do.

A Massachusetts Mutual American Values study found that 81 percent of Americans claimed that family was a primary source of pleasure in life. Yet a survey conducted by General Mills found that although some people espoused a belief in a traditional family model, 43 percent of those polled represented what the researchers labeled a "new breed" of parent.

This emerging breed of parents displayed a new set of beliefs about the obligation one generation owed to another. For one thing, this new breed did not believe in sacrificing career or economic goals for their children. Nor did they believe that unhappy parents should remain together for the sake of their children. Consistent with these beliefs, this new breed does not expect their children to assume any future obligation to them.

In a 1989 study, Americans were asked to imagine that they were thirty-eight years old and were offered a new job requiring more work hours and less time with their families. This new job would provide higher rewards such as greater prestige and more pay. Two-thirds of the respondents said that they would be "very likely" or "somewhat likely" to take such a job. Out of the 1200 respondents, not one person said that he or she would be "very unlikely" to take the job. Although Americans claim to support family values, obviously spending time with children does not rate very highly when compared to career priorities.

It is this attitude of nonattachment and indifference that must change. Merely providing an intact family structure may not be sufficient to produce the brave innovators required by the Macroindustrial Era. Parents must become committed to participating fully in the development and education of their children. In the coming era, a laissez-faire attitude toward our children's welfare will just not do. We cannot expect government and outside agencies to provide the love and caring necessary for their nurturance.

One of the reasons that the Japanese will take a leading position in the new Era is that Japanese parents recognize the role that they play in child development. The Japanese mother drills her children in their studies; helps them understand their homework; and provides the necessary encouragement, emotional support, and confidence building that produce the quality individual.

Americans are surprised when first-generation children of Vietnamese and Cambodian refugees, many of whom entered the country with nothing but a willingness to work, walk off with the lion's share of the prestigious Westinghouse awards for original scientific projects by high schoolers. However, an examination of the family dynamic in which they are raised reveals just why the Asian youngsters perform so well.

The parents assume a proactive role in the education of the children. In fact, recent studies have revealed that many Asian-American parents in the United States purchase two sets of textbooks each year—one for their child and one for themselves, for the express purpose of learning and mastering the subject along with the child. They can then supplement their children's learning experience by coaching and teaching them.

According to a recent Department of Education landmark survey of 25,000 eighth graders and their parents, in spite of claims to the contrary, American parents are not providing their children with this type of educational assistance. Although four out of five of the parents surveyed boasted that they "regularly discussed schoolwork with their children," two-thirds of the children surveyed claimed that their parents rarely or never talked to them about homework, school programs, or their classes.

This laissez-faire attitude manifests itself in other areas related to child supervision. Most of the parents portrayed themselves as strict enforcers of limits on television viewing, but the large majority of the students claimed that they were placed under no such restrictions. This probably explains why eighth graders spend four times as many hours (twenty-one) per week watching televison as they do on homework.

The media, the schools, and perhaps interested corporations and foundations can provide parents with some of the necessary knowledge and tools to be better "education" mothers and fathers. However, ultimately the decision to establish and maintain stable and productive home units will be made by individuals.

The Family and the Global Macroindustrial Race

Ironically, society seems to be denying that practices and policies we consider necessary to run our organizations and businesses smoothly ought to be applied to our families. The management literature of the last three decades is permeated with admonitions to managers to treat workers warmly and make each one feel special. This human relations approach claims that managers who want to increase their workers' productivity would be well advised to pay close attention to each worker's needs.

How strange that we have literally taken the reverse approach in the raising of our children. Suddenly the depersonalization of childrearing has become acceptable; we entrust our children's development to nannies, day-care workers, their peer group, even television.

Of one fact we can be certain: The country that assumes a leadership position in the Macroindustrial society will rest on the solid bedrock of a stable family structure. To succeed in this era, a society must be capable of meeting extreme challenges and mastering complex knowledge. A society whose families neglect the growth of their offspring will produce offspring too emotionally unstable and intellectually deficient to meet the skills levels required in this awesome era. Such a society will be relegated to a secondary role, either as a blue-collar services second-tier nation or as a nation providing the rest of the world support services such as entertainment.

The impact of family on economic competitiveness in the Macroindustrial Era has already been noted. Researchers at Stanford and Harvard have linked what they label the "Japanese advantage" to "correlations between the mother–child relationship and school achievement." George Gilder, in an interview on the Family Channel in January 1992, claimed that the United States certainly could not compete with a well-disciplined society such as Japan, which maintains a family life characterized by stability and integrity.

The U.S. Department of Education in a 1987 study noted that the stability of the Japanese family and "the strong parental commitment of and sustained support for the education of the child" acted as a catalyst for Japan's economic growth. Many analysts have even linked the trade deficit between the United States and Japan to the ability of the Japanese family to produce better workers and innovators who can outdistance their counterparts in the United States.

Demographics illustrate the relative stability of the Japanese family. In 1985, the crude divorce rate in the United States was over three and a half times as high as Japan's. In 1984, 21 percent of all American births were out of wedlock, but in Japan, only 1 percent was. Although America's population is only twice the size of Japan's, the United States has twenty-five times as many births to teenage mothers.

The United States' divorce rate does not strengthen its position in the international economic arena. As we have observed, divorce disassembles an economically efficient household, transforming the couple into two inefficient and warring parties. Some economists even feel that high divorce and illegitimacy rates contribute to one of America's greatest weaknesses, her inability to save. Such a causal relationship stems from the fact that the single-parent households resulting from divorce possess very little disposable income to save.

Family instability affects a nation's economic competitiveness in other more subtle ways. Although most studies focus on the effect of family life on the children, recent studies have revealed the pernicious effect that family disruption and dissolution have on the husband and wife. For instance, one study found that workers experiencing marital problems, including divorce, separation, arguments, and family dissension, became less productive. In fact, marital problems had a more deleterious effect on worker productivity than had drug or alcohol use.

So the stronger the family unit, the better off the society. Many countries, however, including the United States, are confronted with a paradox. To compete in the Macroindustrial Era, societies will have to utilize the talents of the best and the brightest in the work force. Yet they must simultaneously maintain an intact family nest to nurture the era's next generation of thinkers and creators.

Society must develop some strategy for allowing parents to pursue careers and still provide the children with the time and attention required for their positive intellectual and emotional development. Those who suggest that women withdraw from the work force en masse in order to raise children must think of the implications of such an action on the economy. Women's productivity is such that Western economies as currently constructed would be crippled if the women who are managing, inventing, and designing withdrew from the work force in any large numbers.

However, there do exist solutions to this conundrum. It may eventually be considered normal for women to marry and bear children early, spend time with the children during their formative years, and then pursue a career. They can rear the children while pursuing further education, a process made much easier by many of the advances in distant education discussed in the next chapter. The wife/mother continues her education while rearing the children and by her late twenties, when the children are entering grade school, enters the work force as a newly minted employee.

Although such a system sounds radical, it may make a lot more sense in the emerging Macroindustrial Era than the current sequence in which the woman goes to college, pursues a career, perhaps interrupts her career to bring up a child, and then struggles to reinitiate her career. Many women following such a scenario, in order not to interrupt careers, may opt for putting the children in day care. This new sequence seems like the perfect win–win scenario.

Although a country ought not to develop family systems solely to maintain international competitiveness, it is quite clear that the society that can develop the most stable family structures while tapping the fullest potential of its current work force will certainly be in position to lead in the next Era.

It must be emphasized, though, that all governmental attempts at resurrecting and strengthening the familiy will succeed only to the extent that the culture supports and encourages such efforts. A culture that rebels against family responsibility and that envisions family as an obstacle to liberation will ultimately frustrate any government attempt to revive the family.

Individual will is the ultimate determinant of the direction of society. The family will succeed when we decide to reject divorce and choose to spend more time with our children.

7: Revving Up the Knowledge Machine

In order to thrive in the Macroindustrial Era, a society must be blessed with a strong and flexible educational system that can produce the next generation of software engineers, genetic biologists, organizational specialists, computer developers, and academics and teachers, as well as a population able to read, write, reason, and analyze.

In this chapter we will explore unique methods countries are adopting to create these skills in all areas—engineering, science, even reading, writing, and simple computation. There is a veritable revolution occurring in the educational system, rooted in the ability of technology and technique to deliver a level of information and knowledge undreamed of only a decade ago. The educational system will not patiently wait for presidents, prime ministers, and national commissions to devise ways to make schools and universities more competitive. It is forging ahead with its own novel plans to prepare the population to succeed in the emerging Era.

New Skills for a New Era

The Macroindustrial Era will witness the virtual elimination of routine, dangerous work requiring brawn and physical effort and the addition of new jobs that require brains and ingenuity. Jobs that entail simple task performance and repetition will be replaced by those that require the worker regularly to perform diverse tasks with little supervisory direction.

Quite simply, the Macroindustrial Era will necessitate training generations of workers who can think, create, write, calculate, and master the rudiments of computer applications. As we transit into this next Era, each of us will be required to act and work smarter than in any prior historical epoch.

How will work change? The textile industry provides a good example. For generations, this industry relied on low-skilled, low-paid labor to manufacture and process fabrics. Now, mechanical looms have been replaced by microprocessing equipment. In order both to operate and repair the new equipment, workers must familiarize themselves with written material in complex manuals and then must employ abstract thinking to carry out these instructions. Sadly, many workers simply do not have an adequate education for this more complex work.

We see greater expectations and more complicated tasks challenging the work force in every sector. At one New Jersey surgical supplies company, assembly-line workers performed their tasks within the confines of an extremely circumscribed job description. Adding a part here, shaping a part there, each worker executed functions that could hardly be considered mentally demanding. However, as over time the company's major customers, physicians and surgeons, required more customized instruments, the company's assembly-line production system proved archaic.

The company met customer demand by introducing a CAD scheme: Each instrument could be customized right at the worksite to meet each physician's request. The nature of the job changed dramatically. Although workers still sit on a line, they are confronted not by a switch, pulley, or lever, but by a computer pad awaiting their intricate instructions for reshaping and redesigning the physicians' tools. The workers were transformed from assembly-line operators to innovators and designers, a change that demanded the development of skills for which their education had little prepared them.

The educational system must adjust itself to the fact that at all levels of the organization and in all sectors of the economy, the Macroindustrial Era will require a new type of worker that is more skilled and creative. We observe this transformation occurring in the clerical area, where computers are quickly replacing people in the processing of reams of paperwork. Jobs such as claims examiner have become wedded to the computer, and tellers, because of the introduction of automatic teller machines, are expected to transform themselves from money exchangers to marketing and sales representatives.

Even the area of management has been affected by the enhanced skill requirements. Managers now are expected to arrive at a company already equipped with a working knowledge of the computer as a tool for collecting and transmitting information, analyzing data, writing, calculating, and communicating. Because of this, many managers no longer merely manage; they process information and make decisions.

The following reveals how complex the requirements of the Macroindustrial Era will be.

Language

In the Macroindustrial Era, the greater a person's proficiency in reading, writing, and speaking, the more adaptive the person will be to the demands of these challenging times.

The U.S. Labor Department classifies language skills into six different levels of proficiency. At the lowest level, level 1, the person possesses the ability to recognize the meaning of 2500 two- to three-syllable words, can read at the rate of 95 to 120 words per minute, and write and speak simple sentences. As we move up each level, people have larger vocabularies, can read more complex sentences, and can write with more sophistication.

Various jobs, including travel agent, janitor, insurance sales agent, assembly-line worker, and toll collector, require their occupants to possess language proficiency at no higher than the first three Labor Department categories.

People classified at levels 5 and 6 can summarize reports and read literature, books, play reviews, scientific and technical journals, financial reports, and legal documents. Biochemists, social psychologists, lawyers, tax attorneys, mathematicians, corporate presidents, and other such people, in general, the science, business, and academic elite, must possess levels 5 and 6 language skills.

The Macroindustrial Era's requirements are quite clear. By the year 2000, 13 percent of all jobs will require that their occupants possess language proficiencies at the two highest levels, a doubling of such needs in six years. The expansion of the scientific and industrial sectors will require workers educated in the nuances of languages, able to read and digest enormous amounts of information that they then may have to interpret and transmit to others. In a world saturated with reports, memos, manuals, books, computer mail, proposals, and faxes, the ability to read and write will ultimately determine the success not only of the individuals involved, but of the system itself.

Math

The Macroindustrial Era must be populated by those who are comfortable with and understand mathematics. The Labor Department's categories of math skills demonstrate the eventual evolution of jobs into ones requiring ever more complex mathematical skills.

Workers in lower categories can add and subtract two-digit numbers and perform simple calculations with money and basic units of volume, length, and weight. Unfortunately, in the emerging Era, few jobs will be so simple that a worker with only such skills could efficiently perform them. According to the Labor Department, the jobs at this level are equivalent to that of a laundry worker.

It is at the higher levels that a society will succeed or fail in the coming Era. Not only must the person be able to perform basic mathematical operations like computation of ratios and rates; interpretation of a bar graph; and calculation of discount, interest, profit and loss, markup and commission; at the higher levels, the person must have a familiarity with statistics, calculus, econometrics, and possibly modern algebra. Again, here we find the scientific, academic, and business elite —corporate president, biochemist, social scientist, and computer-applications engineer.

In this changing environment, future individuals will have to master both the language/cognitive skills and develop their mathematical aptitude. There is no other choice for a society wishing to meet the challenges of the Macroindustrial Era.

The Worker as Problem Solver

The contributor to the Macroindustrial Era will be part worker, part creator, part designer. He or she will have to think at abstract levels, create new ideas, and bridge the gap between what is and what ought to be. The next chapter will describe at length methods of creativity enhancement, but suffice it to say that many management, scientific, and other jobs will require creative thinking, inventiveness, innovation, and the ability and courage to break with traditional patterns of thought.

As we will discover, companies and a wide spectrum of organizations stand at the forefront of nurturing worker creativity. They have already sensed that an era that entails breakthroughs on the level of quantity, quality, space, time, scope, and size requires individuals able to disengage themselves from routine thought patterns. Not unexpectedly, in the next Era, intuition will be as highly valued a skill as proficiency with charts and numbers.

The Ability to Learn

In the Macroindustrial Era, learning will become a lifetime activity. The time is quickly passing when an individual could undergo a predetermined amount of training for a set number of years, in only one particular field.

As people progress through their lives, they will be confronted with a changing economic landscape that will require them to periodically switch jobs and careers and acquire new skills. It will not be uncommon for an individual to finish college, become an engineer, decide after ten years in that profession that he or she desires to become a manager, and then return to school for a completely new career direction. More commonly, even to retain membership in their current field, people will have to acquire new skills and "relearn their trade."

Regardless of a person's chosen line of work, he or she will have to confront several incontrovertible truths about becoming a contributor to the Macroindustrial Era. First, to operate successfully, workers will constantly have to upgrade their skills, expand their occupational vistas, and keep pace with the veritable explosion of data and knowledge necessary to perform their jobs. Second, employees will have to possess or develop the ability to recognize learning opportunities when they present themselves. These opportunities may be courses, seminars, television programs, or articles that may help the person gain an edge in performing the job successfully.

Third, the person must become familiar with the tools of knowledge acquisition. People will excel if they know how to access pertinent information. They must be comfortable with using libraries, and they must become familiar with the world of computers, data bases and electronic information.

Because work in the coming Era will require continual training, schools may provide one of their most precious services to their students, the future workers, by endowing them with the ability to take responsibility for their own lifelong education. For instance, students must be taught how to use available tools to access information and how to enhance their knowledge and skill base constantly.

Early on students must be encouraged to continually upgrade their proficiency in mathematics, language, and science. The schools and the culture must instill in the individual the notion that formal education should be pursued. According to the U.S. Labor Department, the new jobs that will be created by the year 2000, both in the United States and across the globe, will require four years of college or more. The number of jobs requiring high school education or less will be diminishing.

The remainder of this chapter will reveal the remarkable advances that are at hand for educating individuals and cultivating those talents necessary to succeed in the Macroindustrial Era.

Digitized Schools

We have good reason to be optimistic that the learning goals of the next era will be met. One of the best reasons is the linkage of education to modern information and communications technologies. This revolution in education places knowledge and information literally at the teachers' fingertips for delivery and dissemination to students.

This new development includes a number of technological innovations. Computer-based training is increasingly used to raise the knowledge level of students, managers, and technicians, revolutionizing the way people learn both in and out of school. Students can sit in front of computers and learn math, guided by programmed learning techniques that allow them to learn at their own paces.

A plethora of new electronic technologies—computers, electronic data bases, simulations, on-line communication, video, satellites, and CD-ROM—are changing the way children learn. The results are sometimes dramatic. A coalition of Texas school districts called the Texas Learning Technology Group developed the 9th Grade Physical Science Project, which uses sophisticated interactive video technology to present about 60 percent of the material formerly presented by teachers. The technology, computers connected to videodisc players, has reduced the students' failure rate in science courses from 50 percent to 5 percent.

Computers are helpful in teaching students in areas that we might think to be totally unapproachable by the computer method. In Dayton Elementary School in South Brunswick, New Jersey, students are learning to compose music and perform musical pieces on Macintosh computers. The school initiated this project as part of its five-year program to immerse its students totally in computer technology. According to schools superintendent Dennis Daggett, "Computers are soon to be seen as the new pencil."

The computer's unique ability to extend the human capacity to create seems well suited to music performance. Through a program called Finale, kids can write music and view their finished compositions instantly on the screeen. This lightning-fast process eliminates the tedious handwritten composition techniques that often stymie the creative process, especially in enthusiastic but impatient youngsters.

This new type of technology will help overcome the passivity children often exhibit in the classroom setting. For one thing, when sitting at the machine, children are not competing with others for the teacher's attention. In addition, at the computer, the user has little fear of suffering the embarrassment of giving the wrong answer. After all, who would know? The student is more prone to learn by trial and error when the situation is devoid of the social stigma usually attached to being incorrect.

There are other benefits to linking electronics and education. Through satellite communication, videodiscs, and video tapes, truly gifted teachers can reach a larger number of students. It has been predicted that electronic communication may help alleviate the current teacher shortages in some school districts by allowing some lectures and instructional sessions to be handled over the television system, so that hundreds of students can benefit from a given teacher's knowledge.

The political sector is beginning to realize that the government must accelerate the rate at which schools adopt computers. One bill called the Excellence in Mathematics, Science, and Engineering Education Act would require the Smithsonian Institution in Washington, D.C., to serve as a catalyst in the adoption of advanced technologies by schools.

Another suggestion is for the establishment of a National Research and Education Network, a multigigabit fiber-optic computer network that would connect more than 1000 schools and research laboratories around the country, allowing students, researchers, and others to share and gain access to information. The National Research and Education Network could transmit billions of bits of data per second, which is the equivalent of sending the *Encyclopedia Britannica* over wire almost instantaneously. It would link more than a million students, teachers, librarians, and researchers in high schools, colleges, and universities.

Access could even be gained to the Library of Congress's millions of electronically stored books.

Of course, the digitizing of the classroom impacts the role of the teacher. In the Macroindustrial Era, teachers may become less presenters of information in the traditional sense and more managers of the learning environment. We can foresee a day when the teacher's main role will be that of coach, facilitator, and overseer of the information environment of electronic transmissions, computer-based training, and other self-teaching methods. Teachers, of course, will have to learn how to be better motivators, encouraging students to learn on their own and share information with fellow classmates.

Ironically, the private sector may very well upstage the government-based school system in the electronics area. In 1992, the Edison Project was founded by a group comprised of Whittle Communications, Time-Warner, Philips Electronics N.V., Associated Newspapers of Britain, and a small cadre of investors. The project involves opening 1000 schools on a for-profit basis, schools that will tap into an array of electronic and new age pedagogical techniques.

The Edison Project plans to pay teachers at a salary level considerably higher than the norm but does not intend to employ as many teachers. The reason is that the students will do much of their learning privately, using an interactive computer system in conjunction with help and advice from coaches, other students, and volunteers. As we will observe later, the combination of the electronic with the mentor/coaching paradigm may be the wave of the future.

Whittle's technological matrix may establish the next standard for quality education. Each student will be equipped with his or her own "learning partner" both at school and at home, which will consist of a monitor, a computer, a printer, a videocassette recorder, a fax machine, a paintboard, a stereo, and a telephone. Through modems and other gadgets, such as a centralized CD-ROM system, the student will have unlimited access to an electronic library of books, films, lectures, speeches, and a myriad of learning games.

The Edison Project plans a school year lasting eleven months, and early estimates suggest that such an electronically based school may cost the student about $5000 per year to attend.

A pertinent issue is the cost of digitizing the entire American school system. Jack Bowsher, an expert in training systems, estimates that in the United States the initial cost would be in the area of $250 billion over the next ten years. In the long run this expense would be offset by labor savings (e.g., digitization requires fewer live teachers) and the increased future productivity of the graduates of such an advanced educational system.

To survive and thrive in the Macroindustrial Era, a society must be willing to pay the costs necessary to upgrade its educational infrastructure, to take the necessary steps to cultivate a more skilled and creative population.

Building the Scientific Skill Base

In the Macroindustrial Era, nations will be competitive only if they can produce a scientific talent base, including not just people who will practice in various fields, but a population that understands the rudiments of both science and math. Increasingly, regardless of an individual's chosen career, proficiency in and knowledge of science and math will be required for acceptable performance.

The Younger, the Better

The earlier the individual is exposed to science, the greater the chance that the person will achieve a comfort level with math, biology, and physics. However, as educators have learned through the ages, children have a difficulty responding to science and science lessons as currently taught. How, then, do we begin to engage the hearts and the imaginations of our children?

First, education must get children to like science in general, whether or not they intend to pursue careers in scientific fields. In an *Omni* magazine article, Keith Ferrell writes that we ought to heed Jacques Barzun's statement that we should endeavor to make science entertaining to young people. We must begin to show students, and the population in general for that matter, that science is not just a series of facts that they must master to do well on the SATs, but a unique and valuable way of thinking about the universe. The object, then, is not merely to teach science, but more to spark in the student a curiosity about fundamental issues—the origins of the universe, the future of humanity, the environment, and space.

Education must make science relevant to the students' lives. We must show students that science is a "glorious entertainment," something that fascinates. Electronics reemerges as a powerful pedagogical tool. Television, especially, in tandem with video recordings, can be used to deliver to the students the images of science—space walks, nature, machinery, technology, as well as verbal descriptions of such subjects.

One teacher in Louisiana has discovered a very convenient linkage between the students' propensity to watch television and the teaching of science. She assigns her students a television program dealing with a scientific subject and requires them to write a detailed scientific report on the program.

The computer can be a boon to the teaching of science, too. One researcher has developed novel methods of combining play and computers to help children learn math and science. Several years ago, MIT physicist Seymour Papert developed Logo, a computer language for kids that helps them learn math by writing computer programs that produce geometric shapes and pictures. If the child wants to "draw" the picture on the computer screen, he must master the math necessary to write the program that will produce the picture.

The research on Logo stands as testament to the power it has to enhance children's knowledge of math and science. When the child engages the Logo program, he or she in effect is engineering his or her own learning. With minimal assistance from their teachers, young students discover mathematical concepts like the number of degrees in a circle.

Now Papert has created LEGO/Logo, a system that connects simple robots made of common LEGO plastic bricks and special light and touch sensors and motors to a computer equipped with Logo. The child must correctly program the computer to have the computer then direct and guide the robots to accomplish a simple task, such as reversing direction every time it bumps into a wall. Importantly, children using LEGO/Logo discover that true learning is not the "right or wrong" approach taught by the school system, but a series of trial and error procedures in which we debug our system until it functions properly. Because the rules are more fluid and the child is invited to use his or her imagination, the child experiences this process not so much as learning, but more as play.

The object of much of the educational process in the Macroindustrial Era will be not only to teach the population how to perform science, but how to think scientifically, that is, logically and coherently. To that extent, games and simulations like Papert's will play a major role in upgrading the population's knowledge and capacity to think in the Macroindustrial Era.

Perhaps one of the most challenging activities that the human mind can encounter is the game of chess. It involves a perfect admixture of logic, linear thinking, creativity, intuition, strategy, tactical maneuvering, and sheer courage. To many, the game so reflects the faculties of human mental capability that it has become the ultimate measure of the intelligence of the evolving generations of computers. The fact that computers now defeat human chess grandmasters becomes proof positive that the machines are approaching human intelligence.

Some feel that chess can help students develop several cognitive skills, including reasoning, concentration, and long-range thinking. To this end, in 1992, the state of New Jersey, with the encouragement of the New Jersey Chess Federation, passed a bill to allow New Jersey grade schools to offer chess instruction as part of the regular curriculum (not just as an extracurricular activity).

Games in general serve as cognitive trainers. For years, such companies as Avalon Hill in Baltimore, Maryland, have designed ever more complex war games that simulate every known battle and war in history, from the battles of Caesar to the war in Iraq, for precocious adolescents and preadolescents. A cursory review of the ponderous and intricate rules surrounding these games would be enough to regenerate faith in the young: Participants have to apply themselves rigorously to digest the thirty to fifty pages of often arcane rules needed to play some of these games.

These games simply make the player smarter. He or she learns the rules and then is forced to compete with others on a playing field where knowledge equals power. Players internalize a wealth of skills—a facility with spatial arrangements, mathematical proficiency, sheer memorization, and strategic thinking.

The transcendent issue is not whether the players eventually become physicists or mathematicians. Rather, these sophisticated games enhance the cognitive ability to think at a variety of levels, from the practical to the abstract. This is the type of mind that society will most need in the Macroindustrial Era.

Other approaches can be utilized to enhance learning. In both primary and secondary New Jersey high schools, interest in the study of Latin has suddenly come alive. This revival began when educators noticed that students who study Latin in grade school and high school score considerably higher on SAT exams. Latin increases students' vocabularies and reading skills as well as teaches them logical thinking. Colleges such as Rutgers and Montclair report an upswing in the number of students majoring in Latin, and many high schools have made Latin mandatory in some grades.

Colleges Must Produce More Scientists

Countries must improve scientific study at the university level and must also convince people to major in biology, physics, engineering, and chemistry.

In the United States, one society, the National Society of Professional Engineers, has been using various methods to increase the number of grade school and high school students who choose scientific majors in college and then pursue scientific careers. One favorite method involves representatives of the engineering profession visiting schools and spreading the message that scientific careers are interesting and rewarding.

The association is attempting to establish a link in young students' minds between scientific pursuits and tangible rewards. To that end the society runs Mathcounts, an annual competition in which seventh and eighth graders from across the United States, in teams and as individuals, attempt to win prizes such as personal computers and college scholarships.

Once people enroll in college to study science, they must be encouraged to stay. According to the National Science Foundation, some 42 percent of those who enter college professing an interest in science or engineering careers withdraw from the science track after their freshman year, and another 23 percent defect before graduation. Although this dropout problem is not new, it seems to be getting progressively worse.

We do know that the method of teaching college science must change if we are to eliminate what is developing into a chronic dropout problem in the sciences. Faculty members express frustration with students who exhibit short attention spans and a distaste for hard work. The students respond that college lectures are dry, packed with scores of incomprehensible formulas, and illustrated with confounding diagrams.

Many have offered suggestions to ameliorate this chronic lack of participation of American students in the scientific enterprise. One is to engage the students in the classroom actively, perhaps using real-life examples to illustrate some of the abstract principles that many initially find unfathomable. Another suggestion is to allow university students to learn through computer-based training in much the same way that grade school children are learning. There has been much praise for the efficacy of some computer packages to train students successfully in even the most arcane subjects, such as calculus. These packages are based on much experience with the way that people process information and learn. Unfortunately, although many professors know their subjects, teaching ability is not distributed uniformly throughout the professorial ranks.

Most importantly, colleges should reexamine their policies on retaining what they consider marginal science students. Too often colleges use a student's performance in one or two courses to remove that student from the major. A longer evaluation period should be considered. In the future, universities should focus on how to increase and sustain enrollment in the science and math majors, not reduce these numbers.

If we do not begin to make some of these changes at the grade school, high school, and college levels, the country will not produce the numbers of scientists and scientifically literate individuals needed in the Macroindustrial Era.

The University of the Future

The university recognizes that it must change drastically if it is to provide society graduates sufficiently educated to function in the Macroindustrial Era. In fact, the university of the future will undergo a transformation so profound as to make it probably unrecognizable by current standards.

For one, the curricula will be radically different. The subjects will be less theoretical and more practical, oriented toward preparing students for real careers. Even liberal arts majors will be required to demonstrate a robust scientific literacy. Also, there will be a greater emphasis on acquiring a facility with reading and speaking foreign languages. In the near future, students may be under pressure to become fluent in Russian, Japanese, and Spanish, as well as English.

It is becoming clear that in order to enhance the education of young people in the institutions of higher education, professors must be more prepared to fulfill their role of teacher. Over the last several decades, both U.S. and foreign universities have followed the lead of such major institutions as Harvard and the University of Michigan and fashioned themselves into primarily research organizations. Because of this institutional bias, professors in the colleges feel pressured to live up to this mandate and devote the major portion of their energies to research and publishing. The instruction and intellectual development of students is largely tended to by graduate assistants and part-time instructors. In such an atmosphere, teaching suffers.

However, the trend in many universities is beginning to change. Many of these research-oriented institutions are encouraging their full-time professors to spend more time with first- and second-year undergraduates. In this way, students will be exposed to the bright minds and original thinking of the more seasoned professors.

Universities are now catching up to industry in the application of electronics to the training and learning process. In one school, the University of California at Los Angeles, senior professor Maha Ashour-Abdalla is using computers to teach physics to 140 students. The computers simulate numerous experiments, from the measurement of sound waves in a pool of water to a three-dimensional multicolored representation of molecules colliding. The college sees this as a way to encourage students' interest in science.

At Ball State University in Muncie, Indiana, electronics are similarly utilized to imbue students with a thirst for knowledge and an enhanced ability to acquire such knowledge. Ball State has equipped some 200 classrooms and labs with a fiber-optic video information system, complete with color monitors. In this way, professors can, right in the middle of a lecture, push a button and access data, images, and sound to illustrate their concepts.

One of the more striking and radical changes in the university of the future will be the concept of distance learning. Students will not necessarily be required to spend most or any of their educational career in the classroom. Ball State, George Washington University, and others have already established a program in which students at a variety of locations receive instruction via fiber-optic transmissions. The students, both at the college and advanced high school level, can watch from distant locations a professor teach a course, replete with additional graphics that make chemistry and the other sciences more comprehensible.

One harbinger of the startling transformation of the university is the Englewood, Colorado-based Mind Extension University, created by cable entrepreneur Glenn Jones in 1987. With the guidance and approval of such institutions as the University of Minnesota, Penn State, and the University of Maryland, the Mind Extension University broadcasts college-credit courses to thousands of students throughout the United States.

Through Mind Extension University, or ME/U as it is known, students can take such courses as Oklahoma State University's American Poetry Post-1900, New Jersey Institute of Technology's Introduction to Computer Science, and Western Michigan University's Non-Western Societies in the Modern World, all for credit. You can even earn an M.B.A. from Colorado State University through this cable system. If students need to conference with the professors regarding grades or course material, they can reach them through an 800 number provided by the university.

Universities will increasingly become internationalized. American University in 1992 signed an agreement with Japan's Ritseumeikan University to offer a joint master's degree in international relations. To complete the degree students spend one year in Washington, D.C., and one year in Kyoto. It is predicted that more joint degrees with an international focus will be offered as we move into a more global society.

In the Macroindustrial Era, the university will have to "get with the program" or become obsolete as a learning institution. We do know that much learning will take place on the individual's own time, be taught by educational entrepreneurs, and involve several self-teaching mechanisms that the student will use outside of the classroom environment. The university must adapt to these changes or become a passive player in the emerging educational game.

The Corporation as Teacher

In the Macroindustrial Era, schools will no longer monopolize the area of training and education. Other institutions, such as the modern corporation, will participate in this process of development.

The corporation is assuming a major role alongside universities and public schools in the education not only of its own workers, but of the citizenry in general. As we shall see, corporations are fomenting a veritable revolution in educating the work force of the Macroindustrial Era, introducing a plethora of changes and innovations that will transform the educational landscape.

Making Workers Smarter

Companies are demonstrating a commitment to increasing the knowledge base of their workers. They realize that they require a highly educated work force, one that not only has mastered basic skills, but more sophisticated levels of knowledge and technique.

Getting Down to Basics

Firms first and foremost are concerned about enhancing the verbal and mathematical literacy of their employees. Companies are strongly responding to recent studies that predict a skill gap between the needs of the emerging era and the quality of the current work force.

According to recent surveys, an estimated 23 million Americans are functionally illiterate, plagued by deficient reading and computation skills. In the United States, the chasm between the skill requirements of the emerging era and the skills that the work force possesses is both wide and deep. Michael Higgins, president of Cox Educational Services, says that most workplace materials are written for those with a twelfth-grade literacy level, well beyond the typical worker's proficiency. Only 65 percent of the work force can be considered even "intermediately" literate, able to read at between fifth-grade and ninth-grade levels.

The effects of these deficiencies directly impact the work place. For instance, TI, a major computer electronics company, found that its high rate of product defects was caused by the fact that too many workers could not read well enough to interpret blueprints correctly.

Companies whose workers lack basic skills find themselves unable to upgrade their factories' operation, because this would involve installing advanced technology, including computers, robotics, and other forms of automation. A company whose workers cannot read manuals, blueprints, and other printed material; perform calculations; and handle a computer will find its path to high productivity and efficiency blocked. This problem is hitting many companies in the South—textile manufacturers, for example—particularly hard, according to a report by MDC, Inc., a North Carolina research firm. They claim that "a shortage of people who can read, write, compute, communicate and think critically has left the South in the jaws of a new economic trap."

Many of these companies find themselves in a paradoxical situation: They have customers, produce a useful product, and are well capitalized, yet must restrict production for lack of a labor force that can do the work. To remain competitive, many of these companies opt for using larger amounts of cost-effective cheap labor to get the product out the door. Unfortunately, most of that labor exists in Mexico, China, and other overseas countries.

However, a large number of American companies have decided to keep their production facilities in the United States. But these companies must upgrade their workers' skills.

At the Collins and Aikman carpet plant in Dalton, Georgia, the owners discovered that a third of the 560 factory workers were high school dropouts and many could not read or write. Collins and Aikman has spent an average of $1200 for each worker's often grueling training, which requires the employees to spend hours in the evening on homework after a full day on the job. They learn to read, calculate, and use the computer. The payoff has helped Collins and Aikman tremendously: The better-trained workers can now operate advanced equipment that is increasing productivity at the carpet giant.

Seventy percent of the Fortune 500 companies recently surveyed, among them Polaroid, Aetna Life and Casualty Company, and Ford Motor Company, plan to spend more on education and training in the literacy area. Simon & Schuster's new Workplace Resources Division is developing a program for the American Bankers Association that will train financial services employees in basic reading and math skills.

In order to teach employees 300 new skills, Peavey Electronics Corporation in Meridian, Mississippi, has adapted the U.S. Army's Job Skills Education Program to their corporate setting. Peavey claims that the forty hours of classroom instruction, which includes math, English, graph reading, and blueprint interpretation, is beginning to show the desired result of enhanced worker productivity.

Polaroid has always tried to improve the literacy level of its employees. Its Technology Readiness program enrolls 800 of its 8000 workers at any given time. After course completion, the employees are certified as being qualified to perform certain jobs that require a specified level of knowledge and skill. To accelerate learning, the company tailors instruction to the factory situation. For instance, the reading teacher uses flashcards with words that correspond to camera parts the students assemble on the job. The results are encouraging. Workers who previously could not learn to handle certain work-station operations because of their inability to read the operating instructions can now function in these independent work situations. Productivity at Polaroid has climbed, and the workers have become more versatile, able to transfer their skills and attention from one job and work station to another.

Training for the Future

Corporations understand that the Macroindustrial Era will require people trained in ever more complex skill areas, well beyond mere language and mathematical literacy. Workers must constantly upgrade their skills and augment the knowledge base in order to succeed in ever more sophisticated jobs.

At Nationwide Insurance Company's training center outside of Columbus, Ohio, new sales agents practice selling by means of a self-study system that combines a personal computer with a laser videodisc. The laserdisc interfaces with the computer, allowing the learner to progress through increasingly difficult sales situations. The computer actually teaches the user to make a sales call by allowing him or her to enter into a dialogue with the computer that plays the role of a prospective client. This dialogue is videotaped so that the prospective agent can examine his or her own performance. Whenever the user makes a mistake, the computer informs the learner and analyzes his or her error.

To increase its workers' knowledge base in the computer and high-tech areas and to increase employee productivity, International Business Machines Corporation (IBM) is currently training and retraining 22,000 of its employees using computer-based training. This training adds up to more than 7 million student-days per year at a total cost of $1.5 billion. In spite of the cost, IBM has been able to save between $200 and $300 million a year. The cost savings are generated first by avoiding the expense of live instructors and also by the fact that IBM students use self-study to master their lessons 25 percent faster while retaining more material. In other words, the trainees spend less time receiving instruction and more time on the job.

Chrysler is also bringing training to the factory. It is setting up video work stations in forty of its manufacturing plants to instruct 65,000 production workers. Chrysler feels that the video alternative will save the company an estimated $1.9 million over standard training procedures.

High tech has made its presence felt in other areas of corporate training. For instance, satellites have helped companies like GTE train large amounts of people simultaneously, as when the company recently assembled 800 salespeople at thirty sites for a six-hour satellite briefing on a new PBX product. This training is interactive: Students use microphones at their desks to question the instructor, and they punch keypads to respond to questions from the instructor. Students are quizzed every fifteen minutes, and their responses are collated instantly and displayed in a multicolor bar graph on-screen. Eventually, fiber-optic technology will enable voice, data, and image to be carried two ways simultaneously via cable.

Within a week of the satellite course, sales volume of the new product reached a level that normally would not have been approached for a month or two.

One company fully utilizing electronics and satellites is AMP, Inc., a Harrisburg, Pennsylvania-based Fortune 500 manufacturer of electrical and electronics connection devices. To reduce training costs, the company teamed up with the local Public Broadcasting Service (PBS) affiliate to deliver a high-tech interactive training course beamed to company engineers. The training programming would originate at headquarters and be broadcast to five AMP facilities in North America. AMP supplied the program content and training course participants, and PBS in Harrisburg supplied the necessary capital equipment and broadcasting expertise.

Companies like AMP are quickly discovering the subtle advantages of satellite training. Training courses can be delivered to small and remote operations, so trainers do not have to be sent there. Instruction is also more consistent. A company has only to train a few instructors in the substance and process involved, and it can uniformly deliver the same material to many participants at a high level of pedagogical proficiency. Companies like AMP can use the savings to employ full-time in-house experts instead of expensive external experts to develop and teach new courses.

Educating the Citizenry

Ordinarily, companies have invested their billions in the training and development of their own workers, but there seems to be a growing recognition on the part of corporations that present institutions such as the family and education are not delivering the creative and literate individuals needed for the coming Macroindustrial Era. Companies are realizing that if they want to select from a pool of well-educated, highly skilled workers, they will have to contribute to its creation.

Thus, corporations are expanding their role in the education of the citizens of their home country. For example, corporations are involved in designing new ways to teach children and run schools. In one such project, Time-Warner, the YMCA, the Smithsonian Institution, the

Weekly Reader Corporation, the College for Human Services, and the National Urban League have formed a network of educators, policymakers, and business and social services organizations that are hoping to improve the educational system.

Much of the impetus for this project was generated by President Bush's organization, the New American Schools Development Corporation. He established this (with the advice and consent of Wal-Mart's Sam Walton) as part of his mandate to be the "education president." Bush hoped to attract the sharpest minds and most capable thinkers in a project to rectify the educational dilemma. The corporation is an attempt to centralize what often becomes a piecemeal attempt by business to improve the educational system.

This New American Schools Development Corporation is using a system of competitive bidding to dole out money to about thirty design teams, all of which are expected to develop innovative programs to enhance education. The corporation itself is using a mixture of fund-raising techniques to raise the $200 million it needs to function and will additionally receive all the royalties from the 1992 biography of Sam Walton.

The response has been encouraging. Apple Computer has submitted an application to become partners with the National Center on Education and the Economy, Xerox, and a number of local school districts. The project will combine $8.6 million of funds donated by Apple, the Melville Corporation, the MacArthur Foundation, and others with $3 million from the New American Schools Development Corporation to devise a plan to overhaul classroom curricula, student assessment, and school management completely.

One of the private institutions drawn into this effort, the National Center on Education, claims that the effort ultimately will represent a total rebuilding of the whole educational system. According to Marc Tucker, the president of the center, rebuilding the educational system in the United States is akin to rebuilding an automobile corporation. "It would be absurd to expect that General Motors could build the most effective auto assembly plants in the world and not change the corporation around it."

Some of these companies want to apply their own successful management principles to the school system. For instance, Xerox plans to work with state and local school officials to teach school administrations their total quality leadership management strategy that saved the photocopier company from failure in the early 1980s.

Apple Computer will lend hardware and software plus personnel to assist schools across the country in establishing a telecommunications network. The National Center for Standards is offering to establish a new testing and assessment system for students that transcends the usual multiple-choice paradigm utilized by most schools. They will help schools develop indicators that more validly measure performance and intelligence.

Corporations are not awaiting government's approval to foster the enhanced quality of the emerging work force. New Jersey Bell, for instance, is also intensively involved in educating children. In coordination with the Protestant Community Center, Inc., New Jersey Bell has initiated a project in which it donates its facilities for employees who have volunteered to spend an hour every Tuesday tutoring Newark schoolchildren in grammar. This is a small but growing program of fifty students.

Over the years more than 200 employees have volunteered their time for the project, participants ranging from an assistant vice president and several company directors to clerical employees and servicepeople.

According to coordinator Julie Rogers-Martin, the program succeeds because the tutors encourage the children to turn every activity into a learning experience. The employees show the children how to read maps, improve their grammar, and add numbers. The employees are using their own creativity to devise new ways to teach the children, turning egg cartons into a math game and transforming a newspaper into an information-gathering scavenger hunt.

The results have been inspiring. Children starting the program with a D after three years in the program become B students.

The Power of Mentoring

The fact that the one-on-one paradigm can serve as a powerful force in the education of future workers has led a multitude of companies to utilize the mentor concept as a developmental tool. Hence, companies have developed mentor programs in many inner-city schools to provide personal and financial support for intelligent, ambitious students.

In 1988, Fannie Mae, the nation's largest home mortgage investor, introduced a mentor program at the H.D. Woodson High School in Washington, D.C. In the program, the most promising students are enrolled in Fannie Mae's Futures 500 Club, which provides them with a mentor, $500 a semester, and the possibility of getting one of twenty summer jobs that Fannie Mae offers. The mentor becomes involved with the protégé in a number of areas, including leisure activities, college applications, and general advice on how to succeed in life.

Businesses also look to mentor programs to develop the next generation of leaders from the current student crop. The University of Puget Sound matches its business students with corporate leaders from companies like Boeing, Weyerhauser, and Microsoft. Each fall thirty to thirty-five four-year college students are assigned a mentor, with whom they meet at least six times a year to discuss firsthand business problems, ethics, and other topics.

Mentoring's effectiveness as a development tool stems from a few different aspects of human behavior. First, it is important to note that the protégé in these programs perceives that someone—the mentor, the institution, society—cares. The role of caring in the development process often becomes lost in our obsession with high-tech solutions to learning. Although we have emphasized the necessity of the computer and fiber-optic technology, the human element in learning and personal development must be included for effective adaptation to the Macroindustrial Era.

Second, individualized teaching has always proven effective. The mentor can customize the entire learning experience to the personal needs of the protégé, from the choice of which information to disseminate to the actual style of teaching.

One program originating in the state of Washington combines all three proven educational techniques—business participation, electronics, and mentoring. The HOSTS program strives to increase the reading levels of barely literate students through computer-based training. The computer program is designed so that it can literally teach the child to read at his or her own speed.

However, the program developers realized that one reason people fail in their attempts to learn to read is not so much cognitive as emotional. The learners, especially young children, become discouraged, possibly because they have developed patterns of failure and dejection or simply because they do not believe that they can succeed. So HOSTS provides each student with a mentor, usually a businessperson from a large corporation or a small company, with whom the learner develops a personal relationship. The mentor sits at the computer with the child, not to tutor the student (the machine does that), but to provide encouragement, building the confidence of the student to the point that the child no longer fears failure.

The program's results are uniformly astounding. Previously "unteachable" students are reading books within several months. The critical determinant of success is quite obviously the one-on-one caring experience of the mentor relationship.

Business Goes to College

Business is also helping support and refine the university education system. For one, it provides colleges and universities with part-time and temporary teachers and professors in the sciences, engineering, mathematics, and computers. Corporations realize that they themselves may have helped contribute to the shortfall in college faculty by offering lucrative salaries to Ph.D.'s in these fields, and if they do not recycle some of that talent back into the universities, there may be no one left to teach the next generation of scientists.

Business also is using its facility with high technology to help universities. A large group of business ventures, including AT&T's Distance Learning Network and GTE's World Classroom, offer what many call state-of-the-art distance learning networks to schools. These large companies can offer students in these schools a variety of programming in many subjects to assist teachers in delivering the best education possible. CNN, the Cable News Network, is now working hand in hand with schools to provide closed-circuit on-the-air programming that can be broadcast into schools to enhance learning in such areas as politics and current events.

Most encouraging about corporate involvement in the education process, both inside the company and out, is that it helps education regain the holistic properties that it possessed until the last two centuries. Education was a part of the life process; individuals did not spend the initial stage of the life cycle in school and then the rest of life applying this knowledge. By fostering such processes as workplace training, the corporations are helping to establish a de facto continuum between personal development, formal education, and work.

To the extent that business is helping society reconfigure its perception of learning as a process that continues throughout the life cycle, it will contribute mightily to society's transition into the Macroindustrial Era.

The Role of Apprenticeship Programs

The Macroindustrial Era will primarily feature jobs that focus on the utilization of people's higher cognitive powers, their ability to manage, organize, create, and perform mathematical functions and scientific experimentation. However, in any era, no matter how advanced the general needs, we still need individuals who can fix appliances, service jet planes (and spaceships), and repair the machinery of the Macroindustrial society.

Even these so-called lower level jobs are requiring greater and greater proficiency. At the lower echelons of the job market, there will be fewer positions that require only simple skills. Unfortunately, just at the time when the high-tech world of work needs high school graduates with skills to perform such jobs, sadly many graduates are less prepared than previous generations for the world of work.

The groundwork is being laid in America to provide vocational training to those individuals without the interest in going to a four-year college. Business and the educational system agree that the approach that ought to be taken to ensure a smooth transition of this "forgotten half" into the world of productive labor is the apprenticeship program.

The growth of youth apprenticeship programs is remarkable. In Boston, eleventh graders are working in hospitals, receiving on-the-job training for positions such as surgical technician and medical secretary. In Oklahoma, a program exists that allows the students simultaneously to pursue their regular high school diplomas and also acquire a special certificate that will help them secure a job in the metalworking industry. California has established an academy to prepare students for jobs in fields ranging from accounting to printing.

Sears has spearheaded a program in which it hopes to link many of its 750 nationwide service centers with local high schools. High school students enroll in the program as apprentices and are coached by senior technicians in skills ranging from cosmetology to jet-engine maintenance to appliance repair. After training, many apprentices are offered jobs with Sears.

These programs have been supported by economists, community leaders, and politicians. The Clinton Administration has widely advertised its support for a variety of prototype apprenticeship programs.

Of course, while these programs are laudable, several caveats must be offered. First, of course, is the undeniable fact that many of these jobs, like air conditioner repairperson, may be transitional, both from the point of view of the worker's career and the evolving economy itself. Many service jobs can and will become automated. In addition, we cannot predict whether the appliances that these apprentices are learning to repair will even exist in their current form in the future.

The occupational trendline reveals itself quite clearly: We are moving into an era requiring millions of software engineers, biomedical engineers, managers, decision makers, and pure and simple creators. Therefore, the appropriate institutions should continue to make other career tracks and life possibilities known, and accessible, to the apprentice. Perhaps the organizations that eventually employ the new workers could link them periodically with a mentor from the professional and managerial groups so that they can get a closer look at how the other half lives, thinks, and performs. Exposure to this other perspective, this unknown world, can create novel vistas for someone who imagined that the only job he or she would ever hold would involve "fixing things."

Second, the Macroindustrial society cannot allow the development of a permanent underclass. These apprenticeship programs can appear extremely seductive to a young person overchallenged by the rigors of academic life, especially since a quick payoff lies just beyond the program. The apprenticeship model currently extant in Germany, often lauded in governmental and educational circles, has subtly helped solidify that country's class system so that youths in such programs can become permanently pegged as members of the worker caste. We need fluidity in the occupational structure so that the best and the brightest can move when needed and when ready into the higher work levels.

Third, and most important, we must realize that the current college completion rate is entirely unacceptable. The fact that 75 percent of the American work force enters the next era without a college education could prove to be an economic disaster. The rates are equally disgraceful in Great Britain and Europe in general. If these apprenticeship programs merely turn out to be methods of giving currently less ambitious people "something to do," the society may inadvertently be siphoning off talent that should be finding its way into more demanding positions and into higher education.

Importantly, completion of college allows the person entry into other educational areas, such as the pursuit of second master's and doctoral degrees, which make the person more flexible and able to respond to the changing demands of the Macroindustrial Era. Hence, our first emphasis must be on inducing the population to complete not only a college education, but a master's and/or doctoral degree. It is the only way to ensure that a growing economy possesses the necessary skills to continue to expand.

People Educating Themselves

In the Macroindustrial Era, education will evolve into a continuous process not limited to school or job situations. Individuals, having greater access to information that will be packaged in more creative ways, will be able to engage in continuous self-education throughout their lives.

The opportunities for people to access information are literally exploding. We have already encountered numerous examples of colleges utilizing satellite communication and public television conduits to deliver formal degree-bearing courses to remotely located students.

As mentioned, plans are afoot to build a fiber-optic network that will connect every home, office, and school in the United States to such facilities as the Library of Congress. However, many people are not waiting for fiber optics to deliver information to their homes. By adding CD-ROM players to their ordinary home computers, they are accessing a mind-boggling array of information, such as encyclopedias, dictionaries, and reference books, replete with cross-referencing capabilities. One baseball encyclopedia maker decided to incorporate the full potential of the CD-ROM technology to include film and voice in the learning experience. As the user sifts through the statistics, he or she can additionally access films of some classic plays. *Time*, when constructing its 1989–1991 almanac, used a similar concept to enhance its mainly text-based program: The reader could summon up films of the Iraq War as a backdrop to the textual experience of reading *Time* magazine on disc.

Many diverse formats of what has been labeled interactive media have appeared in the marketplace. Computer makers such as Leading Edge and NEC are already incorporating the CD-ROM drive into their personal computer line, thereby encouraging software designers to develop a plethora of intriguing CD packages. For instance, IBM designed a Columbus Project that enables the user to learn any and everything about the fifteenth-century explorer. The program allows the user to digitally navigate through an extensive collection of maps, documents, and narrated films stored on a videodisc. He or she merely moves a pointer to a picture of any topic, for instance, Columbus himself or one of the islands he explored, and the program will deliver on-screen an article on the subject along with films and narration relevant to the chosen topic.

One company, Seybold, publishes a quarterly CD-ROM publication that is actually an interactive seminar with experts in a given field. The user chooses a speaker and topic and can hear the expert present his information and point of view in his own words. The program even allows the user to type in specific questions that the on-screen expert then verbally answers.

Broadcast TV's role as an information medium is expanding. Although PBS held center stage in the educational realm for decades, we now see the introduction of veritable teaching networks such as the Discovery Channel, Lifetime, CNBC ("The Channel You Can Use"), the Learning Channel, and a host of programs that are finding an audience hungry to acquire the skills and information necessary to thrive in the new era.

A variety of new media are transforming the meaning of self-education. The skills that people can learn on their own, outside of the formal educational structures, are having profound effects on people's ability to meet the demands of the Macroindustrial Era.

Business Self-Taught

Business people and entrepreneurs are no longer waiting for business schools and corporations to deliver the information they require to succeed in the world of money, finance, and management. They are now devouring self-help computer software programs, sometimes called not-so-humorously MBA-ware, to help them expand their knowledge base. These programs, which cost anywhere from $100 to $500, are adding to knowledge available in self-help books and university courses. They go by such names as Business Insight and the Art of Negotiation and are considered by many to be an indispensable aid to improvement of business skills.

Entrepreneurs use a variety of software programs that support their efforts to develop models of cash flow, balance sheets, and income. Many users of MBA-ware are literally teaching themselves how not to go bankrupt. They believe that they are receiving the education they would in a course or an entire curriculum. To many, such software seems as good as an M.B.A.

The New World of Cassette Learning

Audiotapes have entered the self-education arena. Because such tapes are so accessible, individuals can use periods that were previously defined as leisure time—in the car or on the beach—to "read" books, magazines, and newsletters on audiocassette players.

Although this technology has been around for many years, new applications are drawing audiocassettes into the self-education field. One innovative program called the Teaching Company, created by entrepreneur Tom Rollins, captures the wisdom of the best minds in the country on video and audiocassette and makes these tapes available to the public. Now the public at large can hear lectures and talks by top professors from Harvard, Yale, and other top universities—Barnard College's Dennis Dalton on political theory from Plato to Gandhi, Brandeis's Allen Grossman on poetry, and others.

His "invisible university," available to anyone with a Walkman or VCR, has become quite popular. Rollins believes that adults over the age of thirty-five will make up the fastest-growing audience for the tapes. Interestingly, although Rollins predicted that lectures dealing with politics and current events would be among his best-sellers, he finds that the public has an incredible thirst for topics such as philosophy, religion, poetry, and literature. From the comments of his customers, Rollins has been forced to conclude that his customers want tapes that provide "rational insight into the meaning of life."

Rollins will next target the children of the people who are using these tapes for enrichment—high school students who are probably not receiving a quality education in the classroom.

The public response to the exploding market of self-education technologies serves as testament to people's innate hunger for knowledge. It also demonstrates that the population may be far ahead of the educational establishment regarding the coming need for continual enlargement of their personal knowledge base. Individuals innately sense that the coming era will place a premium on information, and they are taking personal responsibility to do whatever necessary to meet the demands of our evolving society.

Culture Is the Key

Ultimately, the underlying cultural climate will determine the success rate of these attempts at education. The culture can either support or sabotage institutional and entrepreneurial attempts at upgrading the societal knowledge base. Hence, cultural phenomena such as the family, the media, and inherent social values all exert enormous influences on the individuals' educational achievement.

An Eye on TV

Individuals are confronted by myriad cultural distractions that can inhibit their cognitive and intellectual development. Not unexpectedly, when searching for root causes of the decline in literacy and decreases in SAT scores, experts frequently focus on television.

As we have seen, television can serve as a medium for instruction, imparting information, classes, and data, and can even allow the user to interact with others. When experts speak of the pernicious effects of "television," however, they are referring to commercial television—the network and syndicated programming that maintains almost a hypnotic hold over both young and old.

For instance, some experts castigate network television for encouragement of short attention spans. According to Ernest L. Boyer, president of the Carnegie Foundation for the Advancement of Teaching, "We're raising kids to have two-minute minds."

In a national survey of 38,000 students, the Education Department found that one-quarter of the fourth graders surveyed watched more than six hours of commercial television a day, and nearly two-thirds of eighth graders claimed to absorb more than three hours of programming daily. The effects of TV watching were clear. Students watching the least amount of television a day (0 to 2 hours) had significantly higher reading scores than did students watching the most television. The studies indicate that television definitely distracts the child from pursuing reading and other endeavors.

The state of California has conducted a number of studies on the relationship between television viewing and reading skills. According to the superintendent of public instruction, "The more television you watch, the lower your reading skills." The results mirror other studies' findings: Literacy skills of those who watch two hours of television or less per day seem unaffected, but as the amount of TV time increases beyond the two-hour point, we notice a discernible decline in reading scores.

Some critics feel that the process of continual absorption of information and sense data, both visual and audial, without an invitation to respond or for dialogue, induces a passivity in the mind that leads to dullness. Some feel that the mind becomes lazy because it is not being actively engaged. Of course, networks defend their programming and its content, but it would seem that the sheer act of passive disengagement for hours on end on a daily basis seems to be positively correlated with low reading scores.

Bring the Family Back into Education

Although studies seem to indicate that students prefer spending time watching television to reading books, television is not entirely to blame for the students' lack of interest in reading. The family influences the child's literacy rate as much as the mass media does. Research indicates that children will acquire the literacy habit if their parents routinely read out loud to them as toddlers. The Education Department 1992 study on educational trends is adamant about the effects of family behavior on reading skills. The best student readers, according to the survey, are those who live in homes where books are accessible, the adults in the home read a lot, and these adults talk with each other and the child about what they have read.

In the current economic environment, parents are hard-pressed to find room in their schedules to devote the time and energy to regularly engage in this activity. Although this is a problem in the two-income family, the single mother is truly torn between supporting the child economically and devoting time to his or her development.

This lack of attention can be observed in other areas of parent–child relationships with equally deleterious effects on literacy and learning. As we have seen, the preschool period is a key developmental stage for the child. It is at this stage that children will hear, usually over dinner, words and conversations that they ordinarily would not be privy to in day care or with peers. Adult conversation and input are important. Countless studies confirm that day-care and single-parent children, exposed less to adult conversation, have more limited vocabularies than those in intact families.

Japan's experience illustrates how critical is the role that the family plays in the child's education. Japanese parents have high expectations of their children and ensure that the child has enough study space, books, time, and emotional support to meet these expectations. According to researchers, American parents are satisfied with lower grades for the children than are Asian parents. In Japan, the teachers encourage the parents to become an ally in helping the child reach his or her potential.

The parents, of course, are transmitting to the children values that they themselves have absorbed from the culture. The Japanese culture has for over 1000 years emphasized the core value of perfectionism, a trait reflected in all sectors of the society, from the zero-defects programs of its industry to the flawless architecture evident in the famous Japanese gardens. Achieving high grades and performing well in school are similarly reflections of this value.

School Versus Jobs

For many young adolescent students, family issues pale by comparison to the external influences that they encounter. Of course, school has traditionally competed with the world of leisure and entertainment for the attention of its students, but increasingly, high schools and colleges are encountering students whose intense involvement with their jobs interferes with their educational achievement. At present, an estimated 55 percent of all sixteen- to nineteen-year-olds are in the work force either full- or part-time, and many of them are full-time students.

Many educators complain that their working students are sleeping through class, not studying, and have discontinued outside reading. The jobs they hold—hamburger flipper, fast-food worker, checkout clerk (where the electronic scanners calculate change)—are essentially mind dulling. Worse, the jobs do not prepare the students for higher-level occupations or bestow upon them more sophisticated skills.

The effect of these jobs on both cognitive development and basic energy levels should be noted well by various pressure groups who would have us increase the amount of volunteer work that high schoolers perform. Many who would make such volunteer work a mandatory part of the high school curriculum imagine that we are improving students' character by forcing them to spend part of their school day visiting orphanages and senior citizen shelters or helping the homeless.

In the end, these programs will divert students' time and energy from their studies. The business of schools ought to be education, and the curriculum of the Macroindustrial Era ought to be emphasizing skills and activities that upgrade the conceptual, cognitive, and linguistic capacities of the emerging work force.

The culture itself, the society's value system, will determine the nation's academic performance. Individuals take their cue from a variety of sources in order to make their life choices and create their values. If students perceive that the culture values intellectual ability over sports prowess, brains over physical beauty, substance over charisma, and diligence over cleverness, students will respond to the culture's message and strive to succeed at school.

Because the culture can exert such a force on attitudes and behavior, cultural agents, including the family and the media, must endeavor to emit positive messages about the worth of attending school and pursuing lifelong education. This must be part of a conscious effort on the part of the cultural powers to encourage the population to pursue the excellence ethic.

Educating Ourselves for the Macroindustrial Era

The major mission of the educational system should be to prepare individuals for the complex scientific jobs and managerial and academic/teaching positions that will be required to help societies and nations adjust to the emerging sociological epoch. Only through a dedication to improving the mind of the individual will we be able to accelerate his or her learning capacity to the point where he or she will direct society's ultimate progress and survival.

We have to fundamentally redefine our concept of education. We must dispense with the idea that education is something that happens only in the classroom, at a certain stage of a person's life, but rather that it is a pervasive aspect of everyday existence.

The next steps are clear. Schools must emphasize math and science in the core curriculum so that all have an opportunity to experience these subjects. Creativity must be openly nurtured in the school environment, even as we teach the rudiments of science, math, and the culture itself. The electronic revolution must be permitted to contribute its power to increase the individual's ability and motivation to learn and experiment.

We must develop more sophisticated interpersonal methods to enhance the learning process. Certainly, the mentoring process must be applied to the educational environment, both within the school framework and outside it. The family must be brought back into the intellectual developmental process, even if the educational institutions must individually train the parents to be better teachers.

Regardless of the programs we initiate or the behavioral patterns we attempt to change, we must realize that the ultimate determinant of educational proficiency is the extent to which the culture values knowledge and glorifies and encourages the process of learning. If cultural forces conspire to encourage simplistic thinking and low literacy levels, any attempt to educate children and make them value education is like forcing them to swim without life jackets in a sea of mediocrity.

8: On the Frontiers of Human Potential

Purposive Self-Development in the Macroindustrial Era

Humanity's forward thrust into the Macroindustrial Era reflects the collective will of the species to progress, to forge ahead to a new stage in human development. We will succeed in this venture because we are determined to expend the massive amount of energy that this accomplishment mandates.

It should be obvious by now that this next Era will place greater requirements on us all in terms of our net contribution to the creation of the better world. The last chapter documented the changes that must be made in formal and informal educational structures in order to produce individuals able to contribute to societal growth in this new epoch. These sophisticated methods of transmitting knowledge and information to individuals are certainly impressive.

However, the species' success in the Macroindustrial Era will ultimately depend on the willingness and ability of all members of society to innovate, create, and contribute breakthroughs in space, medicine, and the social and physical sciences. Facilitating this process is the veritable explosion of techniques and technologies that are enabling the "average" person to tap into his or her own creativity and actualize his or her own ideas and inventions. Such technologies will ensure that we will expand the pool of individuals from which we will draw the ideas for the next maglev supertrain or breakthrough in biotechnology.

These technologies that stand on the furthermost frontiers of human potential will not only add to each individual's storehouse of information; they will enhance each person's ability to enrich and extend the pool of knowledge. The mass of people will be transformed from information consumers into *producers* of knowledge and wisdom.

We will now explore the newest developments on the very frontiers of the expansion of human potential, novel technologies that will enhance every person's ability to think, create, work, and innovate on these new levels. These techniques are being adopted by individuals, artists, corporations, schools, and universities.

Some of these techniques of human enhancement, like positive thinking, are familiar. Others, like virtual reality (VR) and biofeedback, are decidedly high tech and avant-garde. However, the totality of all these developments signals a quantum leap in the species' ability to achieve goals and exceed expectations.

Positive Thinking

Although some of these new techniques and technologies for expanding human potential border on the esoteric, one of these, positive thinking, is quite familiar. From books such as Norman Vincent Peale's *The Power of Positive Thinking* and, more important, Napoleon Hill's *Think and Grow Rich*, the conviction arose that an individual can induce positive occurrences in his or her own life and in others simply by believing in their possibility. This theory launched a worldwide revolution in the way people envisioned their capabilities and themselves.

Hill's book particularly impresses because it sparkles with data derived from rich biographical summaries and interviews with leading entrepreneurs. Yes, Edison did literally will himself into a state of believing that he possessed the ability to tap nature's secrets and utilized his infectious positivity as a catalyst for others' creative breakthroughs. Carnegie and other entrepreneurs were infused with a seemingly overabundant supply of positive affect.

Now, at the dawn of the Macroindustrial Era, we are discovering that scientific evidence abounds that a state of optimism and hopefulness actually leads to positive results. Psychologists are discovering that hope plays a potent role in helping people achieve academically, cope with tragic illness, accomplish difficult tasks, and tolerate and succeed at onorous jobs.

For instance, Dr. Charles R. Snyder, a psychologist at the University of Kansas, has found that freshmen's positive feelings about the future more accurately predicted their college grades than did their SAT scores or high school grade point averages. A study of nurses found that the more optimistic they were about the future, the less likely they were to quit their jobs or suffer burnout.

A study of people suffering from paralysis from spinal cord injury found that the more optimistic the person, the more physical mobility they were likely to experience regardless of the severity of their injury. This astounding relationship between optimism and recovery from spinal cord injury was dramatically illustrated by the case of New York Jets defensive lineman Dennis Byrd. In a December 1992 football game, Byrd sustained a vicious injury that left him almost totally paralyzed. The damage was so severe that several prominent neck and head specialists who examined Byrd unequivocally proclaimed his case hopeless: The prognoses ranged from permanent paralysis to at best eventual recovery of some feeling in his extremities.

Eleven weeks after his "devastating" injury, Byrd walked out of the hospital on crutches. Moreover, now his attending physician would not rule out even the possibility that Byrd would someday acquire the agility to play some noncontact sports such as tennis.

Most people who visited Byrd in the hours immediately following the accident were amazed to find the twenty-six-year-old brimming with optimism about his recovery. He simply refused to accept the prognosis that he would spend his life as a cripple and never lost his profound optimism in his eventual complete recovery. Did Byrd will himself into a healthy state? Doctors seem befuddled, but more than one has suggested that the power of positive thinking is the only remaining explanatory variable in Dennis Byrd's recovery.

In one recent study of factors contributing to some Americans' ability to live past one hundred years of age, researchers soon had to abandon physical explanations of long life, such as diet, exercise, and family history, and turn their investigation to psychological causes. They discovered that all centenarians shared a certain common mind-set: They all possessed a strong social support group, and most of them demonstrated *engagement*, a high state of involvement with both local and national events. However, more than anything, this group exhibited incredible optimism about themselves, their future, and the world in general. In interview after interview, they betrayed an unflappable sense that the world is a good place and will get better.

According to Snyder, such people induce positive thinking through a variety of methods. They turn to friends for advice on how to achieve their goals, they tell themselves they can succeed, they convince themselves that things will get better as time goes on, they focus on and stick to their goals, and they find substitute goals if they fail to accomplish their original objective. Importantly, they show an ability to break up tasks into specific, achievable chunks.

The relationship between positive thinking and health is well documented. In one experiment, British scientists injected volunteers with a virus purported to cause the common cold. Their discoveries told them more about mental causes of illness than about physical ones. Although all subjects were injected with the virus, individuals anxious about participating in the experiment tended to develop severe cold symptoms; those without such apprehensions remained cold-free. The researchers also discovered that volunteers who had recently suffered a stressful event in their lives—bereavement, divorce, even a traumatic house move—acquired worse colds than those who had not undergone such experiences.

Another group of British doctors reported a clear linkage between stress events and the recurrence of breast cancer. A study found that women who react to the diagnosis of breast cancer with a fighting spirit or even a blank denial of its existence are less likely to suffer a recurrence of the disease than those whose response is one of helplessness or hopelessness.

Positive thinking establishes the conditions for positive results. After reviewing much research on success and feelings of well-being, two sociologists concluded that people receive bona fide results in their projects by engaging in such illusions as overly positive self-evaluation, exaggerated perceptions of control or mastery, and unrealistic optimism. In other words, participating in a bit of self-delusion about one's skills and potential can actually lead to positive results.

These research results seem counterintuitive, but if we assume that the process of achievement involves some amount of self-delusion— about your own ability to achieve and the inherent difficulty of the task —research findings that tell us that people succeed by at least temporarily "throwing reality to the wind" make absolute sense. After all, limits to growth, both personal and societal, are largely illusory. So why not impose your own reality, the feeling that almost anything can be accomplished, onto a given situation?

With the onset of the Macroindustrial Era, the reason that positive thinking has been emphasized can be traced to the overwhelming responsibilities and requirements for succeeding in an increasingly complex work and educational environment. In a progress-oriented, activist society, expectations of individual performance, from age four or five until retirement, are enormous. The population senses that it must learn to develop habits that accentuate the positive in order to perform effectively in this demanding environment.

Reflecting such early demands, the educational system has absorbed positive thinking technology into its curriculum and philosophy. An organization known as the Power of Positive Students (POPS), funded by the Norman Vincent Peale Foundation, has established programs throughout the United States. A principal of a Catholic school in New Jersey related to me how the program effectively raises students' feelings of self-esteem and induces them to have hope in the future. Using a series of video- and audiotapes that emphasize problem solving and positive actions, the program encourages children to flaunt their positive features and eliminate negative thinking.

The sociological reasons for such organizations as POPS are numerous. The school has replaced the family somewhat as a socialization mechanism, especially in terms of personality development, confidence building, and ego enhancement. More importantly, the educational system seems to be sensing that a student's performance on school tests and statewide exams and overall absorption of knowledge, in general depends to a great extent on the student's sense of self-worth, optimism, and enhanced sense of potential.

An experimental program in New Zealand, Reading Recovery, utilizes positive thinking techniques to increase literacy in grade school youths. The teachers are specifically trained to work personally with the child and consistently demonstrate a positive attitude about the child's progress. Marie Clay, a New Zealand teacher-educator who developed Reading Recovery, claims that we must orient teachers away from concentrating on the failings of the child they are tutoring. Children notice teachers' heavy sighs and furrowed expressions and react poorly to tutors who invidiously compare them with others. All these actions signal to the child that he or she is not succeeding. In Reading Recovery, the tutors are advised to show confidence and express positive encouragement to help the child reach maximum performance.

One educator suggests that schools use health education courses as a locus for inducing positive thinking in students. Techniques should include thought stopping—each time a negative thought comes to mind, students immediately say to themselves "Stop." The idea is to interrupt the flow of self-defeating thinking, such as "I'm so stupid," and replace it with statements such as "I am smart" and "I can do it."

Children are encouraged to write down personal positive affirmations about themselves and carry index cards that remind them of their own positive self-feelings. By utilizing written and spoken methods of self-suggestion, the students can internalize these positive self-feelings.

A plethora of companies worldwide have subscribed to positive thinking as a method of increasing productivity. Charles Garfield in his book *Peak Performers* relates that companies no longer consider as downtime two-or three-day retreats in which employees are lectured by motivation experts, engage in outdoor survival exercises, and relearn can-do attitudes that they may have forgotten while performing day-to-day routine and unchallenging tasks.

Positive thinking has quietly established itself in the world of business as a useful tool. For instance, when engaged in performance appraisals, managers and supervisors are instructed to emphasize the employees' good behaviors instead of criticizing poor activity. It is felt that constant emphasis on the positive serves as a better motivator. In this environment, there are no problems, only challenges.

The Macroindustrial society will succeed to the extent that its members retain a positive outlook. They feel good about themselves and their prospects and demonstrate a decided willingness to take risks and challenge the unknown.

The bedrock of this national outlook is the society's members themselves—individuals imbued with hope, optimism, and self-confidence. The positive-thinking movement can only help in the creation of such individuals.

Creativity Can Be Taught

The Macroindustrial Era requires that individuals do more than believe that they can achieve the difficult. It also needs people who can think in innovative and novel ways, articulating problems and envisioning solutions outside of the normal realms of human consideration.

The elusive quality creativity is considered by both business and society as a magic elixir that generates prosperity and an overall enhanced quality of life, but few can actually define it. Some consider creativity to be a spark that allows an individual to develop a book, an opera, or an invention seemingly out of thin air. Others relate this concept to holistic thinking—the ability to ignore the pitfalls of fragmentary thinking and to envision processes in their entirety.

The enthusiasm with which business has embraced creativity training suggests that we are in the throes of a social trend. According to *Across the Board* magazine, a bible of corporate development, 32 percent of the large companies surveyed in 1991 offered some version of creativity training to their employees, up from 22 percent only two years earlier. Institutions such as the Center for Creative Leadership in Greensboro, North Carolina, have found themselves inundated with requests from corporations that wish their managers to think and act innovatively.

The underlying assumption is that the creative spark does not belong solely to "geniuses." Evidence supports such a contention. Frito-Lay claims that after it involved its 25,000-plus workers in creativity training they increased their ability to find different and better ways for the organization to function. According to James O'Neal, the director of the Frito-Lay Company, one employee even came up with 137 new ideas that were used to cut costs and improve quality, productivity, and safety. Corning Glass Works in Corning, New York, trained its 26,000-plus workers, spread over eleven countries and speaking six different languages, in the art of creative problem solving.

Making It Work

The methods featured in creativity training sessions may vary, but they are all established with the goal of helping participants perceive issues and processes differently than they normally would.

The Center for Creative Leadership employs brainstorming sessions to encourage participants to express any idea that comes to mind, regardless of how irrational or alien that idea may seem to its owner. In this environment, concepts that would be deemed too offbeat in the normal corporate framework are openly solicited. Unfortunately, in these sessions, it occasionally happens that the loudest individual dominates the session. So the center has developed a technique labeled *brain-writing*, which is merely brainstorming on paper. It allows the participants to formulate their thoughts uncensored by others' criticisms or counterpoints.

One of the center's most impressive techniques is what they label *guided fantasies*. The group leader guides the small group through a fantasy trip: for instance, a vacation on Mars. He asks the participants to envision what provisions he or she would need on the planet, what sights he or she would care to visit, the problems that might arise. The center feels that by sifting through ideas and images necessary to survive in this guided fantasy world, the group members may have their perspectives sufficiently unfrozen to take on a particularly daunting task, like introducing a new product or restructuring their organization.

One creativity consultant, Tony Buzan, has developed mind mapping, a graphic method for stimulating free thought. Managers and others are encouraged to draw on paper a diagram capturing the flow of thought: Start in the middle of the page with a circle or square and draw branches or spokes that radiate from the square or circle. The subject sees his ideas grow on paper from beginning to end. Managers at such companies as Boeing and Fidelity International find mind mapping a perfect way to help write speeches, plan meetings, and develop strategies.

Possibly one of the more intriguing methods of inducing creativity has been used by Ann McGee-Cooper, a Dallas-based creativity consultant. She uses ten-year-olds to help her teach her clients how to get past mental barriers to discover new possibilities. Her feeling is that children are more creative than adults and are tuned in to their inner creativity most of the time. As strange as it may seem, she literally has these little people sitting with corporate executives in brainstorming sessions, attacking real corporate problems. These children, recruited from the Dallas school system, have helped companies brainstorm solutions to problems such as how to improve meeting effectiveness. Under McGee-Cooper's direction, executives at such organizations as the Texas Utilities Company play with children in an effort to loosen up and become more inventive.

The use of children in such efforts is not as unusual as it may sound. In his exhaustive studies of creativity, Berkeley scientist Donald MacKinnon discovered that creative people have developed the facility for getting themselves prepared to operate creatively. He calls this facility "an ability to play" and describes the optimal mood for creativity as "childlike" in the sense that these people feel willing to explore issues and ideas for the sake of pure enjoyment, not just to accomplish a task.

One creativity expert, David Tanner, has tried to get his clients to focus on the importance of dreams as a problem-solving mechanism. In one curious incident, a DuPont scientist used dreams to conquer a problem he had been having: He could not determine why vacuum hoses that he had invented would suddenly collapse. Curiously, during this period, he found himself dreaming about the springlike toy Slinky, an object about which mature scientists would not dream, and if they did, they would probably dismiss as a nostalgic return to childhood. Under Tanner's encouragement, the scientist pondered the meaning of the dream. As it turned out, his subconscious was employing dreams to suggest the solution to the vacuum hose problem. The scientist realized that he should place springs inside these hoses to prevent their collapse.

Companies are also beginning to realize that humor has many uses in scaling the heights of creativity. The underlying reason for this relationship lies in brain theory. According to many, the right side of the brain, the side with which we think in a more creative and artistic fashion, is also the side from which humor emerges. According to the theory, the use of humor stimulates and wakes up the right side of the brain, so that the creative self is alerted and incorporated in any problem solving activity. Evidence also exists that laughing releases endorphins, the body's so-called pleasure drug. Thus, humor both enlists a person's creative faculties and simultaneously relaxes the person (and those people in his or her presence). Hence companies such as General Electric and IBM, as well as MIT, now attempt to infuse organizational meetings with humor.

These corporate forays into the world of creativity are encouraging and seem to be generating positive results in product and organizational innovations. From the point of view of the requirements of the Macroindustrial Era, the inclusion of the greatest number of people in the invention process will quickly move society forward.

Companies and other organizations must develop cultures that nurture and protect creativity. If not, the work organization, the vanguard of the Macroindustrial Era, will devolve into a lifeless and unimaginative collection of worker bees. Only a free atmosphere can set off the needed mental explosions. Roy Rowan in his book *The Intuitive Manager* expressed the hope that organizations could transform themselves into places in which innovation becomes the modus operandi. Intuition and rationality would operate hand in hand, a transcendental process applied to very pragmatic purposes.

Elementary and grade schools are being encouraged to help their students actualize their inner creativity. Stephen H. Schneider, winner of a MacArthur award and senior scientist at the National Center for Atmospheric Research in Boulder, Colorado, suggested in a recent *World Monitor* article that schools turn over 10 percent of class time to creativity exercises. During these periods students would openly question ideas, experiment with new concepts, and brainstorm. Schneider suggests that students be allowed to "challenge their teachers' premises —provided they take the next step, which is to back up their arguments with evidence." He feels that if the school system rewarded students for thinking independently, they would be better able to diagnose and solve long-term global problems.

This sentiment is echoed by Harold J. Raveche, president of New Jersey's Stevens Institute of Technology, who has stated that schools must encourage students' curiosity about the way the world works. He feels that primary and high schools should reinstitute debating exercises. According to Raveche, "Debating enables them to cope with ambiguous and complex topics."

Both Schneider and Raveche echo a guiding principle of the Macroindustrial Era, that progress in the next age is dependent on universal participation in the creation and production process. Therefore, both the schools and the work organizations must endeavor to help each of their members develop the creativity and individual genius critical in the next Era.

An Enlightened Minority

The sheer bulk of people involved in creativity expansion is large and growing—millions of grammar, high school, and college students, along with thousands of corporate members, spread throughout the globe. If we continue to train people in these expansionary techniques of brainstorming and guided fantasies, several results will occur.

First, this group will eventually compose an enlightened minority that will form a critical mass ready to act as a catalyst for widespread social change. Having been liberated to think their own thoughts, they will surely want to apply this newly discovered creative spark to a host of political and sociological problems. They may insist on transforming their own communities, for instance.

Second, they may insist that their own leaders—presidents, governors, and media personalities—apply a similar degree of inventiveness to world, state, and local problems.

Third, this enlightened minority may demand a restructuring of organizational hierarchies. After all, if they are contributing original profit-making concepts to the company, do they not merit more of a say in how the company is run?

Finally, this creative outburst may lead to not only new innovations, but the establishment of entrepreneurial enterprises to capture the possible benefits of such innovations.

Looking Inward/Controlling Outward

There are other techniques that are helping the species advance the frontiers of human potential. One such set of techniques helps the individual gain increased control over a plethora of physical, mental, and emotional faculties that were once thought to be beyond human mastery.

Many of these developed in non-Western traditions but have recently been adopted by Western practitioners. Although decidedly spiritual in origin and style, as we shall see these techniques are definitely well suited to the pragmatic needs of the Macroindustrial Era.

For centuries Eastern societies, including Japan and India, have featured religions that required their adherents to practice the contemplative arts, namely, meditation. Central to such religions is the search for inner truth, a journey that could require the spiritual pilgrim to assume often awkward body postures, learn complex breathing procedures, and master the mysterious arts of imaging and visualization. Not until the 1960s did the West become seriously interested in the contemplative arts. Even then, these practices were limited to a number of isolated countercultural movements and sects.

Why, then, at the dawn of the Macroindustrial Era, are American and European companies, schools, and individuals becoming increasingly enamored of such esoteric matters? The answer is simple: Individuals and institutions recognize that by controlling themselves, they can master the universe.

A leading light in this area is Jon Kabat-Zinn, director of the Stress Reduction Clinic at the University of Massachusetts. His clinic prescribes an eight-week program of meditation, yoga, breathing exercises, and what he calls mutual support to reduce stress in people suffering from cancer, anxiety, and hypertension. Program participants have been able to reduce chronic pain by more than 50 percent and in posttreatment studies have been able to maintain their improved status.

A recent Harvard Medical School study demonstrated how simple meditation techniques can relieve physical and emotional symptoms of premenstrual syndrome such as social withdrawal, lowered sense of well-being, discomfort, and suppressed appetite. After three months, the women who were taught meditation techniques had improved in a variety of areas. They showed physical responses such as drops in pulse, respiratory rate, and blood pressure. Not surprisingly, the meditation techniques helped the women decelerate brain wave patterns, an issue that we will address later on.

This mind–body connection has increasingly intrigued the public. In early 1993, awareness of this issue was heightened when Bill Moyers hosted a five-part PBS series entitled "Healing and the Mind with Bill Moyers." The series explored issues such as the general role that meditation, relaxation, biofeedback, and other mental technologies plays in healing and health.

People are also using these voyages into the interior self to reach a higher state of creativity. The methods of achieving such a goal vary. For instance, Japanese companies like Fujitsu use traditional Zen instructional methods to help their middle managers increase concentration and creativity. Zen is a form of Buddhism predicated on the use of meditation to achieve *satori*, a higher level of consciousness. It often requires sitting in uncomfortable positions for long hours concentrating on, in essence, consciousness itself.

The sessions that Japanese executives endure take forty minutes and are ensconced in a jam-packed program of management seminars, lectures, and other conventional conference topics. The Japanese chose Zen as the technique of choice for highly pragmatic reasons: It is more technique than religion, more goal oriented than ideological, and the results are at times impressive. One integrated-circuit designer believes that practicing Zen meditation sharpened his ability to concentrate on one matter at a time, a skill critical to success in his field.

The Pentagon has even experimented with these techniques. A Pentagon Meditation Club was started by Edward Winchester, a Pentagon financial analyst who feels that such meditation groups can help in a number of areas, including stress reduction and strategy-oriented problem solving. He even sent top admirals and generals meditation kits and is himself applying his deep-thought techniques to a knotty problem, defense acquisitions.

The U.S. prison system houses one of the more intriguing experiments in the application of meditation to social problems. In California, transcendental meditation adherents have been granted permission to instruct prisoners, many of them hardened murderers and violent crime offenders, in meditation techniques.

Several ex-convicts credit their nonrecidivist behavior to their adoption of transcendental meditation as a technique to explore themselves and their motivations for committing crime. At the risk of a bad pun, researchers would have to agree that the jury is still out on the ultimate application of transcendental meditation to solving society's crime problem, but even the limited results suggest that for some prisoners who are psychologically ready to reform, transcendental meditation may be a useful tool. If nothing else, the contemplative life makes prison life bearable for some prisoners.

Spurred on by a continual spate of articles and reports attesting to the interior arts' ability to enhance the mental and physical powers of its practitioners, commercial interest in this subject is expanding faster than the consciousness of the most practiced yogi. On late-night television, especially on the cable channels, we are deluged with advertisments by companies that specialize in mastery of the interior and the subconscious.

One individual at the forefront of the commercialization of the interior arts is Jonathan Parker, Ph.D. In 1979, he founded the Institute of Human Development in order to support work in the field of consciousness expansion carried on by a variety of university professors and psychologists. Now he is the president of Gateways Institute. His company, although interested in standard meditation techniques, takes the approach that self-improvement starts with "taking charge of the subconscious." He offers subliminal tapes that he claims will program the user's mind so that he or she can accomplish any desired goal, including becoming successful, increasing concentration, improving the memory, and unleashing creativity.

These tapes encourage the relaxed state as a prelude to receptivity to the specific message. In a remarkable cross-pollination between the fields of meditation and positive thinking, the Gateways Institute offers tapes in which guided meditations purport to help people reach their highest potential.

Why are so many people investing the time, money, and energy to meditate, practice transcendental meditation, and listen to subliminal tapes? The answer is more sociological than psychological: People suspect that to succeed in the coming era they will have to be creative, perceptive, and in control.

Regardless of the technique used, a person gaining knowledge of and mastery over the spiritual/transcendental interior seems better able to accomplish tangible goals and exercise control on the material plane. Mihaly Civszentmihalyi, in his book *Flow: The Psychology of Optimal Experience*, stresses that in order to become more creative and achieve higher actualization a person should become involved in solitary activities, such as thinking, working on creative projects, or solving puzzles. This leads to what the author calls "flow experiences," those that push the person to higher levels of performance.

This enraptured state of activity generates what he labels a "previously undreamed of state of consciousness," the proof of which lies in the fact that those who have reached the state of flow emit brain wave patterns resembling those of longtime practitioners of meditation.

The growing social trend to gain control of the interior, encompassing a larger commitment to meeting the challenges of the real world, bodes well for society's ability to meet the demands of the emerging Macroindustrial Era. As humankind learns to master the spiritual, it will gain dominance over the physical.

Putting Human Potential in a Whole New Light

There seems to be no limit to methods that the species devises to expand its ability to produce and create. One of these new methods incorporates light and illumination.

Exposure to large amounts of light can improve individuals' experiences in many different areas. For instance, it can increase productivity, change moods, and make transcontinental travel more tolerable. The amount of light used in most of these projects is about 10,000 lux of white fluorescent lights, which represents a sufficient amplitude to fool the brain into thinking that it is experiencing daylight.

The National Institute of Mental Health has just spent $15.5 million on research into light therapy experiments. For instance, we have documented proof that light therapy has been successful in treating a clinical form of depression known as SAD, or seasonal affective disorder. This depression affects about 6 percent of the people in northern areas of the country during the winter.

Possibly the most intriguing and potentially productive area of light research involves the use of intense illumination to change the biological clock that wakes us and puts us to sleep. Our internal rhythm follows a twenty-four-hour cycle. Sunrise and sunset affect such elements as body temperature, blood pressure, hormones, and nervous system chemistry, all of which combine to determine how alert or tired we feel at different times of the day.

A Harvard research team discovered that for most individuals the period between 4 and 5 A.M. determines a person's level of alertness or sleepiness. By exposing a person to bright light prior to 4 A.M., the team was able to shift subjects' biological clocks and reset them by up to twelve hours in just two to three days' time. Hence, exposure to light can quickly set a person's interior clock to that of another time zone, say, European time. We can thereby eliminate the dreadful time warps that occur during the first days of a European vacation.

Experimentation has revealed that we can similarly reprogram workers' inner time clocks by exposing these workers to large amounts of light. When working in these "sunlit" areas, night workers can perform as alertly and accurately in the dead of night as they would during daylight hours. Studies show that night workers exposed to such high degrees of luminosity become more productive. This breakthrough should revolutionize the workday.

Harvard University has recently formed a venture capital consulting group that advises companies on how to use light to help night-shift workers overcome drowsiness. Light Sciences, a fledgling new company, is selling light fixtures to be used in conjunction with software that regulates light amplitudes in offices. Through this software, the user can customize light regulation to individual needs. Light in each office or building sector can be modified to take into account the length of a company's shifts, how often the shifts rotate, and the age of its employees.

We are only at the earliest stages in applications of light to human behavior. New ideas emerge regularly. According to R. Curtis Graeber, manager of flight-deck research at the Boeing Commercial Airplane Group in Seattle, his company is planning an innovation called *light-class service*. Business travelers on their planes could request to sit in a section in which they would be bathed in bright light shining from high-intensity lamps situated above their seats. The light goes on for a few hours, off for a few more, and then back on. Although the traveler does not feel any different physically, her internal time clock is being reset for her destination's time zone—perhaps Pacific Coast time.

The way in which the species is using light to transform its mood and its own physical condition is quite consistent with other sociological trends in the Macroindustrial Era. It is almost as though we have decided that the rhythms of night and day, dictated by nature over the eons, are just too inconvenient and do not fit *our* needs. We have therefore proceeded to eliminate darkness from our environment when it no longer suits us.

Controlling the Uncontrollable

Biofeedback is perhaps the least understood of all the human frontiers technologies. However, this principle, first uncovered by psychologist Neal Miller in the 1940s, has been creating a quiet revolution in the species' ability to achieve mastery over its own destiny.

The principle behind biofeedback is simple and can be explained in terms of one of its more common applications. For instance, suppose a person who suffers from anxiety desires to control one of the more annoying symptoms of this problem, a fast-beating heart. He could employ biofeedback therapy to gain control of his heartbeat.

The person is hooked up to a machine that measures the heart rate. The machine also emits a constant low-volume hum. Every time the patient's heart beat slows down, the pitch of the hum lowers a half note or so; and of course, the higher-pitched sound is emitted whenever the heartbeat increases. In other words, the information about the heartbeat is "fed back" to the individual through this amplified tone. He actually begins to sense what the body does to make the heartbeat slow because he becomes aware, at a purely sensate level, of exactly what the body is doing at the time it experiences a reduction in heartbeat. Over time, the patient learns how to make the pitch of the hum decline a note or two. In effect, the amplified signal guides the user to increase or decrease his heart rate.

A variety of disciplines now apply this revolutionary technology to solving specific problems. Biofeedback techniques are being used to help people regulate aspects of their physical beings, including the autonomic nervous system, heartbeat, and brain waves, that were originally considered outside the domain of human control. Biofeedback is also used to reduce stress, increase memory, and achieve higher levels of consciousness.

A Medical Miracle

Since the 1970s and 1980s, biofeedback's successes in the area of medical improvements have grown. One of the most successful exponents of biofeedback is psychologist Bernard Brucker, Ph.D., director of a facility at the University of Miami/Jackson Memorial Medical Center. At the clinic, practitioners have developed revolutionary treatments for stroke and spinal cord damage using biofeedback as the central therapy.

One of the center's most dramatic cases involved a young woman, Tammy DeMichael, who became a quadriplegic as the result of a 1985 accident in which she suffered a broken neck and crushed spinal cord. Dr. Brucker felt that if he could get her brain to transmit some signals to the rest of the body, the other cells might regenerate and help her achieve full movement.

He used standard biofeedback procedure: He attached to her head electrodes emanating from an electromyograph and rigged the machine so that a horizontal blue line on its screen would react to her brain patterns. Brucker then instructed her to envision her arm moving upward. As she would imagine this action, she would generate signals from her brain to the arm. The more she successfully thought of this, the higher the horizontal line on the machine's screen would rise. Within eight sessions, Tammy was emitting close to 80 percent of the normal microvolt activity from brain to arm.

Unfortunately, even though her brain was performing the correct electrical operations, the muscles in her body would not cooperate. Because they had atrophied over the year since her accident, she was unable to move the arm. Brucker spent the next year working directly on the arm itself, administering massage, electrical stimulation, icing, and other external passive exercises to restore the arm. She maintained the biofeedback sessions throughout and eventually got her brain to repair the lost links between brain and arm.

The day finally came when she could move her arm. From therein, the relearning accelerated to the point where she could actually walk. As of 1991, Tammy DeMichael was on crutches, mobile, no longer a quadriplegic.

Since 1981, of the 2000 people the hospital has treated for paralysis and other motion disabilities, 90 percent have improved. Miraculously, a dozen who were as incapacitated as DeMichael—no limb use whatsoever—have been given back most of their mobility.

This stunning success has been replicated elsewhere. Stephen Walker, Ph.D., director of the Rocky Mountain Institute for Health and Performance in Boulder, Colorado, uses biofeedback to relieve many psychosomatic ailments. He helped one patient utilize biofeedback to relieve herself of her stress-related asthma attacks. He even induced a famous shot-putter to increase his performance level. Walker noticed that the athlete was clenching his teeth too strongly during each shot put, thereby draining energy from the shot-put activity. Walker decided to wire the athlete's jaw to an electromyograph anytime the athlete performed strenuous activity. Gradually Walker taught the athlete, through biofeedback, to relax his jaws. Biofeedback has been instrumental in teaching other athletes how to utilize only certain important muscles during their activities.

Even the most skeptical observer must admit that the positive results pouring forth from biofeedback laboratories are becoming curiouser and curiouser. Two London researchers, Chandra Patel and Michael Marmot, found that meditation induced by biofeedback can lower blood pressure and might even reduce the incidence of heart disease. In their research on 116 people who had taken part in a study on mild hypertension in 1985, they discovered that in many cases relaxation techniques that were mastered using biofeedback were as effective as drugs in lowering blood pressure. They documented long-lasting benefits even with people who had previously become dependent on blood pressure medication to regulate their condition.

In an equally startling experiment, Richard S. Surwit of Duke University Medical Center found that biofeedback-induced relaxation techniques can help in the fight against diabetes. Through biofeedback, diabetics can self-induce relaxation, thereby stabilizing their blood sugar levels. Again, the effects of these treatments have lasted for the year-plus testing period.

In the coming era, the combination of human will and advanced technology to achieve what was only recently considered impossible will become quite commonplace. As the species comes to realize what humanity can accomplish it will acquire the confidence to make even the aforementioned achievements seem mundane.

Mind/Brain Expansion

Through biofeedback people are now being taught how to change and control their brain wave patterns and mental functioning. Thousands have been trained to relax, concentrate, and even raise their own IQ. Even in brain wave modification the teaching technique generally remains the same: A person is attached to an electroencephalograph, and when the brain emits an alpha wave, a slight sound emerges from the electroencephalograph. The person learns to make the machine repeat the sound by creating more alpha waves. Eventually the person can enter this alpha state at will without the assistance of electronic devices.

One of the more successful applications of brain wave retraining occurred at the University of Tennessee. There, professor of psychology Joel F. Lubar has used biofeedback to treat children with attention deficit hyperactivity disorder. We know that some bright and creative children who become frustrated with academic material suffer from a change in brain wave activity that can lead to disruptive behavior. In most cases, psychologists have found that children suffering from attention deficit hyperactivity disorder produce higher theta waves and extremely low beta waves when doing tasks like reading or drawing.

Researchers like Lubar have helped such children to stay focused and alert by teaching them to change their brain wave functioning. Through the aid of biofeedback technology, the children have learned to produce higher beta waves when reading or studying. Follow-up studies since 1986 have shown dramatic results in those so trained: increases in IQ scores of as much as 20 points, reduction in hyperactivity (as their frustration with learning wanes), and better grades. It is not that biofeedback made these children "smarter"; rather, it helps the children focus on their schoolwork so that they can use their intelligence fully when studying or performing academic work. Lubar claims that, after training, his attention deficit hyperactivity disorder patients leap an average two-and-a-half-grade-year levels in academic achievement.

Companies have sprung up thoughout the United States and Europe to help people perform these mental miracles without the help of clinicians. These companies claim to help individuals control their brain waves through such gadgets as Relaxman and Dreammachine. One leading distributor of such products, Psych-Research, Inc., of Little Rock, Arkansas, features a line of electronic mind expanders under the trade name Inner Quest (IQ for short). The device, a computer-driven light and sound creator, transmits its signals to a user attached to the machine by headphones and goggles. The headphones emit sound that pulses and wafts through the listener's ear, and the lights gently pass before the goggle-encased eyes, causing some users to experience color changes.

The claims for this type of brain wave synchronizer are enormous: It can be used to stimulate centers of the mind that regulate creativity, memory, motivation, mental images, and problem solving. Such experiences can also make the mind susceptible to programming from other sources, say, a tape on smoking or stress reduction, thereby facilitating personal programming aimed at behavior change. Tapes are available to help the listener permanently lose weight, build confidence, enhance self-image, even gain the courage to end a personal relationship.

Of course, there are always available for purchase computers that will measure brain wave activity and aid the individual attempting to master transcendental meditation. We are even seeing the onset of what are labeled mind spas. As of 1992, there were about thirty such spas where people can experience sight and sound machine sessions at a nominal price. Such clubs as Altered States in West Hollywood and MindWorld outside Miami promise both spiritual enlightenment and the chance to meet new friends.

This is only the beginning. The applications of biofeedback technology to the needs of the emerging Macroindustrial Era are enormous. The society with a growing need for creative and inventive individuals can only benefit from a technology empowering individuals to achieve mental states in which creative thoughts can emerge and the mind can express itself free of self-censorship. The ability of biofeedback to enhance the species' mastery of its own physical being can only lead to healthier, more productive individuals.

The Computer: Pushing Us to New Levels

The expansionary culture is one in which humanity expands its ability to master itself and its environment. As we have already observed, the human does not hesitate to invent technologies to aid her in her quest.

As the species gradually became aware of the calculating and analytic abilities of the computer, in fields from finance to chess to data base management, it responded in predictable fashion. Many expressed the fear that the machines would eventually outperform human beings, take their jobs, even begin making decisions for them. The mutiny of the spaceship computer HAL in the movie 2001 has achieved the status of cultural archetype, representing the worst-case scenario of role reversal between human and intelligent machine.

Now, however, we are discovering that the computer, our own brainchild, is an excellent servant, a tool to be used by the human species to increase its capabilities exponentially and enhance the quality of its experience.

Is there any doubt that the computer is making the human species smarter? Chess grandmasters who once feared playing against supercomputers now use them to explore new end-game techniques. The ability of computers to do the human species' drudge work, like computation and memorization, is actually freeing up the individual to perform more abstract, scientific thinking. The computer's ability to mimic human thinking through artificial intelligence may ultimately help us perfect our own scientific formulations.

Theorists such as Roger Penrose invite us to make our peace with this marvelous device. He suggests that as we use the computer we in fact become smarter than the computer, even while it contributes to our ability to achieve greater feats.

At one time, scientists at such institutions as MIT hoped to develop robots who not only mimicked human thought, but actually replicated it. Over time, they realized that computer-based artificial intelligence systems worked best in well-defined and controlled environments. As we have seen, assembly-line robots and chess-playing programs work beautifully, but artificial intelligence programs that at one time were considered a match for the human mind are now seen to exhibit critical shortfalls when faced with real-life complexities.

However, even if it merely complements the human mind, the computer becomes a fantastic tool for expanding human ability. It helps us calculate, create, remember, analyze, and perhaps even evolve. In short, computers will serve as a trusty guide and faithful companion at the frontiers of human potential and will thus be the key to our transition into the Macroindustrial Era.

Computer Visualization: A New Way of Seeing

To attempt to understand a system—a society, an engine, the human body—the human being can examine data, create and explore a model, or look at the physical reality itself. However, there are limits to all such representations. Numbers are cumbersome and sometimes lead to information overload. Even physical reality can be known only to the limits of the human's spatial perspective—his position in relation to an object and his own physical limitations. Often he can at best examine the object's exterior. Much of what we know about reality, sad to say, is alarmingly superficial.

Computers are changing our ability to see. Margaret Geller, a Harvard astronomy professor, has devised a three-dimensional computerized map of the galaxies. Using this map, she can visit other parts of the universe. During her "flight," she made a vital discovery not revealed by numerical data and telescopic evidence, that galaxies cluster mysteriously along the edges of invisible bubbles. Her map now encompasses 15,000 known galaxies.

Her discoveries are matched by those in genetics, where scientists are beginning to map the human body with the aid of the tools of this new field, labeled scientific visualization. The computers are converting the numbers in the data into color, motion, and, in some cases, sound. For instance, computers can recreate simulated waves breaking on a simulated beach to help the user understand ocean behavior and tide patterns.

Some observers see these new computer visualization technologies as equivalents in their novelty and importance to the microscope and telescope. They start with a minimum of information, extrapolate from that data, and project images that might have earlier been considered impossible to construct or access.

For instance, researchers at NEC Corporation's Exploratory Research Lab in Japan predict that visualization technology may at some point eliminate the need for some lab experiments. With the help of computer visualization, a meteorology professor, Robert B. Wilhelmson, has deciphered the process by which storm clouds spawn tornadoes. The data from storm clouds are analyzed by a supercomputer that then translates these figures into images. The four satellites that the United States will begin launching in 1996 will be tracking changes in the Earth's atmosphere, oceans, and land, and will send back to the Earth Observing System billions of bits of data every day. According to Daniel Brady, manager at the National Center for Supercomputing Applications, without visualization the data could never be fully understood.

Arco Oil and Gas Company is using three-dimensional visualization to decide how to extract oil from its increasingly dry western Texas reservoirs. As mentioned earlier, computers are also helping in the analysis of bodily functions. In industry, CAD is helping engineers design appliances, cars, and spaceships and construct buildings. Computers were used to help in the architectural design process of such Macroindustrial projects as New York City's Worldwide Plaza.

Eventually, we will all be able to share in this new method of seeing. As PCs become more adept at processing information, the nonscientist and nonprofessional will be able to visualize almost any system. By democratizing the scientific enterprise, computer visualization will help unlock the creativity necessary for the species' movement into the Macroindustrial Era.

Expanding the Arts

For some reason, the use of the computer in fields such as industry, science, and mathematics seems natural. After all, the computer calculates, reasons, and, of course, computes—skills that are congruent with the underlying methodology of those fields. The computer seems innately suited to playing the game of chess, which possesses at least a superficial relationship to geometry and other spatially oriented sciences.

However, as the Macroindustrial Era looms on the horizon, the computer is being incorporated into a realm of activity that seems at first glance to be incompatible with the logical world of the computer: the world of the arts.

The work of composer Ted Machover and others at MIT's media lab demonstrate this technological marriage of convenience. They are developing *hyperinstruments*, collections of electronic components orchestrated to work with one or two computers. Machover can sit at a keyboard and compose, conduct, and perform, using standard instrument sounds created by musical synthesizers.

This technology for the most part is available to the average consumer. People can now connect music synthesizers, machines that create literally any sound or instrument conceivable, to computers, which can record, store, arrange, and play the music.

The computer is already becoming both a composing and a performing aid on the international concert stage. Machover's 1987 opera VALIS, with computers as featured artists, has received international acclaim. Ironically, it seems that computers can perhaps be even more unpredictable and temperamental than human musical accompanists; In one performance, one of his electronic instruments decided to take off on its own and play a solo!

This unique fusion of computers and synthesized sound with both performance and composing enhances the human ability to create. With access to a computer, the individual does not need years of training to play an instrument. The novice musician can play the instrument, make mistakes, incorporate a wrong tempo, lose his or her place in the piece, and later electronically modify the recorded results so that they sound correct.

The computer has literally liberated the composer from the drudgework aspects of writing music. He or she does not have to hire an orchestra to write the next great concerto: Musical samplers can reproduce the sound of any known instrument and store these sounds on computer disk for later incorporation into the next Beethoven's symphonic work.

The synthesizer has also led to much of the mentally stimulating and expansionary experimental music that bubbles under the current cultural surface of rock and rap music. Such composers as Vangelis, the movie-scoring genius Danny Elfman, and the German New Ager Andreas Vollenweider have expanded musical frontiers with the use of synthesizers and computers. Their admixture of inspiration and technology has created sounds and forms that the human species has never heard before.

One of the pioneers of the hyperinstrument revolution, Max Mathews of Stanford University, has developed a radio baton to help today's computer composer become next year's computer conductor. When the smallish radio baton is waved over an electronic array containing the conductor's or anyone else's preprogrammed composition, the music begins to play. Although the program will only play the notes and chords that the composer intended, the radio-baton-wielding conductor can influence how the piece is actually played by this electronic orchestra. With just a flick of the wrist the baton wielder can change the piece's phrasing, tempo, dynamics, pauses, and the duration of individual notes. With this baton, the conductor puts the element of human expression back into a prerecorded, computer-programmed musical composition.

We are now witnessing possibly the furthest extension of human/computer interface in the arts: Biomuse, a musical instrument that requires no instrument at all. The Biomuse uses biofeedback principles and technologies described earlier to help the human create sounds. Created by Hugh Lusted of Stanford and Ben Knapp of San Jose State, it operates on a principle that allows the human to use brain waves to create sound. The electrical sensors are wrapped around the musician's scalp and forearms to monitor brain and muscle waves. The machine then transforms waves into sound; users play the violin simply by moving their arms in space, even though they are holding no instrument. In one hypothetical scenario, the disabled may now be able to perform music.

This technology opens the possibility that at some point dancers covered in electrical sensors may dance and simultaneously create their own musical accompaniment. In fact, this region of the art world has already been influenced by technology. A special software program called Life Forms (devised at the Simon Fraser University in Vancouver) helps choreographers create and record dances. It allows them to input dance steps on a computer screen, manipulate these steps, and work out the dynamics of the movements. At age seventy-one, Merce Cunningham, a modern dance master, has introduced the use of this software to create a new work called Tracers at New York's City Center. According to Cunningham, "things can happen that you think are impossible, but if you try them out, they lead you into something else."

Mirroring the sentiments of so many people who have experienced the visual capabilities of the computer, he claims that "instead of thinking in time, you're looking visually and putting things in space." His dancers are performing acts and moves that he could not have thought possible without having experimented with the conceptual possibilities through the Life Forms software program.

Such advances have far-reaching implications. The fact that music can be created without instruments or performers and ballets choreographed without dancers suggests that we now have the capability of unlocking the hidden genius in the nonprofessional. We may transcend the concept of the creative artist as specialist, much like the modern corporation and school have overcome their belief that only the denizens of the top layers of an organization have original ideas or that only the researchers in the lab create and invent.

We may reach the point where the entire population creates and invents. Furthermore, the fact that so much creative product can be stored on the computer means that through modems and fiber-optic technology we may achieve instantaneous distribution patterns, from composer to audience, totally bypassing the old route of music studio to retail outlet to consumer. The music can be transmitted over phone lines and downloaded by the receiving computers.

We may be on the verge of the creative explosion in the arts that we already see in the sciences!

Reality and Virtual Reality

With all its advantages, computer visualization and other such techniques still imply a separation between the user and the technology. For instance, although a person may enhance her knowledge through such advances as three-dimensional imaging, she still is on the outside looking in. She is one step removed from the data in much the same way that a television viewer, no matter how involved in a given program, is ultimately only watching, not participating.

However, virtual reality (VR) is changing the very definition of the media experience. The term *virtual reality* refers to techniques that represent the ultimate application of computer technology. VR is so-called because it emplaces the participant right in the middle of a computer-created environment. To date, it represents the closest thing to a final merging of cybernetic techniques and human experience, involving the participant in a visual and tactile experience that borders on the real.

In 1986, science/science fiction writer William Gibson in a novel called *Neuromancer* introduced a concept called *cyberspace*, a region existing in the world of information that humans can visit but not touch —corporate data banks, computer conferencing systems, and books. In a sense, every time an individual calls into a data bank, turns on a computer to browse a file, or plays a videogame, he or she has entered into cyberspace. However, there is a vast difference between experiencing the information and images of cyberspace on a computer screen and doing so in VR. In VR, according to the cybernauts who use such systems, you are directly in the vision.

This near real experience is accomplished with the aid of highly sophisticated technology. The EyePhone is a bulky set of goggles that the cybernaut places on his head. These goggles project images directly onto the eye; the user looks through these goggles and watches lifelike images that seem to be part of his field of vision. The goggles are connected to the head with sensors, so that as the wearer turns his head, his field of visions changes; he imagines that he is spanning the horizon.

The second apparatus is the Dataglove, which is fitted to the hand and enables the hands to become part of the computer's simulated field of vision. With the aid of the Dataglove, the viewer can manipulate objects in VR—rearrange furniture, lift mountains, and so on. The early applications of VR to human expansionary activity have utilized this capacity.

One of the more famous VR programs is Kitchen World, already used in many countries to help newlyweds plan and design their first kitchen for their new houses. The user, clothed in standard VR garb such as the Dataglove and goggles, can "walk though" the artificial home in cyberspace and with little exertion change the room's decor, appliances, and furniture. Architects at the University of North Carolina have used VR models developed at the university's labs to design and build the lobby of a new computer science building. (The best VR apparatus allows one to "walk" down the hall of the simulated structure, peruse the environment, and "see" just where the designer went wrong even before the structure has ever been assembled.)

The effectiveness of this technology is beyond question. Chemists have used VR to play out a variety of experimental scenarios to enhance their understanding of the structure of proteins. (In the VR world, chemists can get to know the protein from the inside.) Some hospitals and medical schools are employing VR devices in the training of surgeons in the art of performing various types of surgery. The physician/trainee can operate on the virtual patient with the use of Datagloves and the EyePhone and make her surgical mistakes long before she ever finds herself in the real world of medical practice.

NASA has pioneered some of the more advanced VR technology. Their flight simulator, in which the pilot sits in a virtual plane and flies through cyberspace, has been known to cause tremendous anxiety in its users, including sweating and nausea. Some VR operators are surprised that more people have not intuited the obvious military applications of this new technology: hordes of empty tanks rolling over deserts and navigating city streets piloted by phantom drivers sitting in front of computer screens half a continent away.

This new technology may also revolutionize the arts. Projected as the ultimate linkage between the artist and the audience, VR allows the viewer to experience movies and television programs on both the visual and tactile dimensions. This possibility is already suggested in computer gaming; Nintendo already features a Power Glove, based on the Dataglove, to help spice up its computer games. Of course, it does not compare to the NASA level of simulation sophistication, but many think that this type of interactive entertainment, in which the viewer can somehow manipulate the reality, is the wave of the future. Some think that eventually computer-generated movies will provide the setting in which the goggle/glove wearer will participate in the action, influencing plot and activity.

In the summer of 1992, a gallery in Manhattan held a showing called Through the Looking Glass: Artists' First Encounters with Virtual Reality. Artists showed off the latest in a growing field of truly interactive media. West Coast artists Lynn Hershman and Sara Roberts produced an interactive videodisc called *Deep Contact*. In this artwork, viewers can touch different parts of a computer image of a blond woman with a German accent and set off a number of scenes dealing with connections between machines and the body. Later in the disc, viewers can summon up encounters with a Zen master or a charging tiger.

VR takes computer visualization to its conceptual limits. Visualization allows the participant to see reality, not just understand it quantitatively or mathematically. VR permits the individual to truly *experience* what is in fact a representation of reality.

This merging of the experimental with the real will lead to breakthroughs in the biological sciences we can barely imagine. For instance, the behavior of the AIDS virus, especially its tendency to mutate and expand, eludes human comprehension. It is only a matter of time before some biologist will enlist VR in his or her quest for a cure. Programmers will create a human body in cyberspace and allow the physician to become the AIDS virus, experiencing from the point of view of the virus the process of mutating, gestating, and attacking T cells while fending off prospective vaccines. Through VR, this researcher will finally understand why this virus acts the way it does and ultimately how to combat this deadly virus.

The best way to know and defeat an enemy is to walk in his or her shoes for a day. VR bestows this ability on the human species.

One intriguing application of virtual reality to the field of medicine is currently being tested at the University of North Carolina at Chapel Hill. Here, a physician wearing VR headgear can see ultrasound images as he looks at the uterus of a woman lying in front of him. Video cameras are placed on both sides of his headgear so that the ultrasound images of the fetus are superimposed on his external view. The physician virtually sees through the patient. According to Gary Bishop, a research associate professor at the university, the doctor can "see the three-dimensional position of the baby in the mother's body." A doctor performing a biopsy can with certainty hit the right place. Such precision may make VR a perfect tool for brain surgery. Bishop claims that a VR-assisted neurosurgeon "holds the probe, sees the tumor underneath, and knows the angle to go in."

The United States government now shows great interest in funding medical virtual reality projects. The National Competitiveness Act of 1993 cites health care as "showing particular promise for virtual reality," and would allot $210 million over the next five years to create what it terms "visualization technology" and develop "databases of remote-sensing images" that would be available over computer networks.

According to Jaron Lanier, archguru of VR and president of VPL Research, Inc., the next generation of machines will incorporate the sense of *touch* into the user's universe. It would require sensors built into the gloves and headsets. Journalists such as Howard Rheingold have already ruminated on the effects of touch in the world of VR.

Rheingold has predicted that sensor-based VR machinery may soon open up interesting new vistas in the world of sexual behavior; he has coined the term *teledildonics* to represent high-tech/high-touch sexual experience in cyberspace.

At Lanier's vanguard VR company, researchers perform experiments that portend the application of this new technology to the species' intellectual psychological growth. In some experiments, participants assume different shapes and personas in cyberspace and see how it feels to be, for instance, a lobster, an alien, or a famous historical figure. His research demonstrates how easily the human adapts to the constraints and challenges of alien environments and different body dimensions.

One interesting experiment involves the workers at VPL assuming in cyberspace the size and proportions of human children, allowing them to experience among other things walking through a room and dealing with life-size adults in the virtually real universe. These experiments in assuming different persona open up possibilities of enhancing any individual's ability to experience and hence understand the perspectives of other people. For instance, parents could learn to empathize more with their own offspring by literally experiencing the little people's physical and emotional worlds from the inside.

One of the most useful applications of VR may be in the field of psychological research. According to Lanier, "The field is crying out for more study of phenomena like this, which VPL is not set up to do." He jokingly claims that his company will publish a book of suggestions for research projects called *100 Dissertations for 50 Cents*.

People who spend part of the day in cyberspace lifting mountains, assuming the perspective of a child, and traveling through their own bodies seem to begin to develop a more expansionary perspective. The sociological implications are daunting; the greater the imagination of the cybernaut, eventually the more momentous will be his or her discoveries and inventions to the emerging society.

In fact, it could be said that those with regular access to VR apparatus may have a distinct advantage over those without—in research and development, the arts, and even in business. The executive in a large corporation crunching numbers and brainstorming to induce creativity may be at a distinct disadvantage compared to the West Coast VR whiz inventing the next means of transportation or the next wonder drug in the limitless world of cyberspace.

The implications of VR's role in the expansion of human potential may transcend even the above. It would seem that the linkage of VR with biofeedback should arrive shortly. A researcher at Wright-Paterson Air Force Base has developed an apparatus that allows the participant to play a flight simulation video game not by manipulating hand and finger, but by changing brain wave length. Captain David Tumey has set up a system in which the player sits in front of the video game, a flight simulator, and pilots a plane that pursues another aircraft—banking, dodging, and lifting the cab.

The subject sits in the cab and uses not a hand-held mouse or joystick but his own brain waves. Two fluorescent lights that sit at either side of the screen strobe thirteen times a second, which causes the subject's visual cortex to fire at the same frequency (a principle not unlike that of the commercial meditating devices). As his brain waves begin to fire in synch with the strobe lights, electrodes attached to the subject's head feed his brain waves into an amplifier, which picks out the waves, deduces how strong they are, and then displays this information on a bar scale situated right below the screen displaying the images of planes and sky.

The game is programmed so that as Tumey increases the strength and frequency of his brain waves, the "cab" banks to the right; if he reduces their strength, the cab banks left. In other words, Tumey is controlling the direction and speed of the simulated fighter plane not by hand, but by modifying brain wave strength.

This new technology is revolutionary, but not because it helps the individual change brain waves—that has already been accomplished by biofeedback. Unique here is the application. Tumey can control a cab in a simulator with his brain waves!

But why stop there! We can attach any machine, device, appliance, or technological gizmo to this brain/biofeedback apparatus. By simply wiring, say, your household appliances to a master monitor, you could turn off the heat, run a train set, turn on the television, or open the garage door simply by using your brain wave patterns as a master switch control. The applications are boundless!

When we consider VR's ability to jolt the human imagination suddenly, to, in essence, accelerate and change the thought patterns emanating from the mind, it seems quite clear that VR may be one of the catalysts in the transformation of every citizen into a potential inventor and creator.

Suprasensory Potential: What We Now Know

Out on the farthest frontiers of human potential can be heard such terms as ESP, psychokinesis, and other experimental concepts. Extrasensory perception, or ESP, has long held the fascination of millions. The ability to read someone's mind has served as the subject of countless parlor tricks, Las Vegas shows, and elaborate confidence games.

In the world of hard science, such concepts, although the subject of apprehensive curiosity, occupy tenuous terrain. We know that for years Russia performed experiments in the field of parapsychology, and we think that they have empirically examined the hypothesis that one human can read another's mind. Other suprasensory abilities have periodically been hinted at. Telepathy, the ability to project thoughts, has been the source of both scientific experimentation and Stephen King novels. Telekinesis, the purported ability to move, bend, or transform objects, has had its share of controversy. I classify all such activity under the heading of suprasensory potential.

Although we now have proof that through biofeedback machines and VR people can use mental powers to influence physical events, only a smattering of evidence supports the contention that the human species indeed possess suprasensory potential. Findings that do emerge from disparate sources are usually contradicted or refuted by a wide range of skeptics and doubters.

Nevertheless, the research findings, which hint at powers and abilities far exceeding normal human ability, although controversial, never fail to fascinate and mystify. That evidence is presented here as part of our discussion of human potential.

In the summer of 1990, two Princeton University researchers, an engineer and a psychologist, startled their colleagues with their claim that human subjects in a number of experiments were able to control external random events by using supranormal or mental power.

Roger Nelson and Dean Radin, both from Princeton's Engineering Anomalies Research laboratory (PEAR), presented results of over 800 experiments conducted by sixty-eight researchers examining whether humans can influence random events. These widely varying events include a computer that is set up to generate random numbers and an electronic circuit that generates random coin flips. According to Nelson and Radin, subjects instructed to concentrate on heads in a random experiment, for instance, could make the computer generate a more than expected number of heads coin flips.

What the psychological world heard that day is old hat at the Princeton Engineering Anomalies Research laboratory (PEAR), founded by noted engineering researcher Robert Jahn. Jahn, who until 1979 spent most of his time running aerospace research programs, started the lab when research performed by graduate students presented him with irrefutable statistical evidence that subjects sitting in front of a computer could make the computer generate slightly more than 50 percent heads results by telling it to "think high" and more than 50 percent tails by commanding it to "think low."

After receiving some research funding to continue such experiments, Jahn teamed up with Brenda Dunne, a developmental psychologist from Chicago. Together they set up the lab to study two different sets of phenomena: remote perception and psychokinesis. Remote perception is the ability to sense, for instance, someone's location at a given time just by concentrating on him or her. Psychokinesis is similar to the force experimenters described earlier with the coin flips.

The results of the remote perception experiments are perhaps the most eerie. Jahn and his researchers send one person out to the woods, to Illinois, to New York, and instruct this person to remain stationary in the area for at least 15 minutes. This person is told to relay his thoughts to another subject in Princeton, who in turn tries to perceive the other person's thoughts and thereby guess his location.

They have run 336 trials, and although some of the respondents' guesses were totally inaccurate, far more were completely correct. The researchers quantitatively tested the Princeton-based subjects' perceptions by asking him or her thirty true–false questions about the locale of the other participant, such as Is the person in a closed area? The information gathered from these questionnaires is on average 15 percent more on target than could be guessed if the subject was answering randomly. This accuracy is maintained no matter how great the distance between the perceiver and sender.

The psychokinesis experiments are equally revealing. Jahn feels that his experiments, which show that people can influence the way that machines generate heads and tails, provide irrefutable evidence that humans have abilities that we only imagined they have. Other such experiments have subjects attempting to influence the behavior of balls dropping into a number of slots in a pinball-like fashion. As the balls drop, they are supposed to fall mostly in the middle, with others arranging themselves evenly from the middle out, so that the final result looks like a bell curve. In fact, human subjects at the PEAR labs are able to make the balls distribute themselves slightly askew simply by concentrating on the balls as they drop and mentally directing them.

The critics of such research have been vociferous and unrelenting. The Committee for the Scientific Investigation of Claims of the Paranormal claims that the experiments are of dubious value, and many colleagues of Jahn's wonder why a respected Princeton professor would stake his reputation on proving the existence of paranormal powers in humans.

Jahn responds that "I can't allow the lack of support to control my life. We have incontrovertible evidence that these phenomena exist. We have asked the cosmos a question, and the cosmos has answered."

Even as humanity conquers, transforms, and enriches all that appears across its landscape, it realizes that its most formidable chore lies in first perfecting itself. There can be no material progress without a profound improvement of the individual, including the ability to learn, comprehend, and ultimately to create.

It is perhaps a tribute to American and Western common sense that it has been able to adapt much of what would otherwise be considered mystical and arcane—computer visualization, biofeedback, the other technologies reviewed here—to the pragmatically oriented goals of higher productivity and societal progress. Our journey to the frontiers of human potential involves a unique blend of humanism, spirituality, and materialism that will be necessary for our evolution into a Macroindustrial society.

The continual process of unlocking human potential will help forge an Expansionary innovation-oriented culture, in which everyone—janitor, administrative assistant, student—will think abstractly and scientifically and thus ultimately contribute to improving the human condition.

When all members of the population begin to experiment mentally, create independently, and attempt to transform their ideas into reality, they are ready to take their place in the forefront of the Macroindustrial Era!

9: Creating the Expansionary Culture We Need

As we have seen, the family and educational systems exert a profound influence on the individual's personality and values. Without strongly functioning family units and schools, the society cannot hope to develop individuals who can contribute to the next era's efforts in biology, space, and macromanufacturing. Nevertheless, these social units that nurture the human being are themselves shaped and influenced by the surrounding culture. Therefore, it is reasonable to suggest that the entire Macroindustrial effort must be supported by a culture that establishes the necessary conditions for meaningful material progress.

A culture includes a society's values, behavior patterns, customs, norms, beliefs, and most importantly its Weltanshauung. This last term, translated from the German, really means the worldview of a society. So pervasive is a society's Weltanshauung that it largely determines that society's overall direction and shapes the actions of its members.

In the Macroindustrial Era, society will require what I label the Expansionary Culture (Table 9.1). The society possessing this culture welcomes progress, fosters human potential, and encourages and celebrates growth. Its members envision the current state of affairs not as an end point, but as a launching pad to greater achievements. It does not look for a compromise between the species and the universe, but sees the growth of one intertwined with the progress of the other.

No country can hope to lead the way into the next century unless the culture supports growth and progress. A country that doubts its

Table 9.1   *The Expansionary Culture*

- A strong sense of purpose
- A positive national outlook
- Visionary leadership
- A respect for both material production and consumption
- A firm grounding in reality
- A propensity to risk
- Progressive attitudes toward immigration
- A well-integrated citizenry
- Individual freedom
- A vibrant artistic milieu

---

ability to create and produce or, worse, questions whether it should even commit itself to a pro-growth policy will soon lose the ability to innovate, expand, and seize the future.

In this chapter we will explore the Expansionary Culture trait by trait and examine the extent to which a variety of nations have begun to evolve into such a culture. Here then is a portrait of the Expansionary Culture.

A Strong Sense of Purpose

Of the many dimensions that comprise the Expansionary concept, none best conditions a country for a place of leadership and productivity in the coming Era than that which I label a strong sense of purpose.

During the 1980s and 1990s, the West has generally expressed an admixture of concern and fear over Japan's increasing domination of the global economic structure. One almost suspects that this apprehension does not stem from a belief that Japan possesses better scientists or superior technology or even a larger capital investment nest egg. What strikes fear in the hearts of many Westerners is the tenacity that Japan and now Hong Kong, Singapore, and Korea seem to exhibit in pursuing their economic goals.

Why are the Japanese and Koreans so persistent? Are they simply more diligent, intelligent, and avaricious than Westerners? Or is there some other quality spurring on these newly affluent societies?

As we probably intuit, countries such as Japan and their leaders, corporate heads, and the general population are motivated by a strong sense of purpose. Their ultimate objectives seemingly transcend the mere accumulation of wealth. A PBS special on the corporate conglomerate Matsushita chronicled the rise of this company from a small electronics company to the dominant player in the global VCR and television market. As the workers and their managers describe their company and their relationship to it, they seemingly refer to Matsushita and the entire country of Japan in the same breath. They make it clear that the company's success is important primarily because such success ultimately helps the country and its citizens.

Although everyone may not find such a nationalistic goal orientation desirable or even laudable, no one can doubt that a strong sense of purpose can propel a country or group to higher levels of achievement. Hong Kong's success is similarly conditioned by its purpose-driven culture. In a recent cross-national attitude survey, a large percentage of Hong Kongers described themselves as overly diligent and overly ambitious. Asked to comment on the findings, a vice president of a Hong Kong firm explained that such responses were congruent with the fact that Hong Kong is "on the cutting edge of the modern world."

Such a statement demonstrates a strong sense of purpose sadly absent in Western culture. How many Americans or French would describe their country as cutting edge? How many could even clearly articulate any sense of national purpose? Such a clear goal orientation has economic effects: Over the last twenty years, Hong Kong's GNP has grown at a rate of 6.1 percent per annum compared to the United States' meager 1.7 percent annual increase.

For several reasons, a strong sense of purpose is a key element of the Expansionary Culture. First, this overriding purpose becomes a principle or set of principles around which a society can organize. The society becomes focused and directed. Americans fondly remember World War II and the years directly afterward not only because of the country's military victory, but also because that era provided people with a totally unambiguous purpose upon which they could focus their energies.

Of course, war is an obvious organizing principle, but history provides us with other examples of large national undertakings, like international migration and exploration, that galvanized public sentiment and captured society's soul. It is hardly accidental that America's extension of its nation to the Pacific Coast was and is referred to as manifest destiny. During that period, most Americans were devoted either to exploring and settling the Western regions directly or to providing support services in the financial and industrial sectors to guarantee this mission's success.

Second, its power derives from the fact that this sense of purpose helps motivate the individual members of society. Once people understand ultimate societal goals, they have something to work for. The dynamics of this process are most obvious during times of war. A society fights to ensure its survival, to overcome some injustice, or to rescue others, and the members need little motivation other than this dominant purpose to power their actions and behaviors.

A third reason that a society needs a strong sense of purpose is that it imbues members with a tangible vision of the future and a sense of continuity over time. Such a goal orientation literally pulls society forward into the future. The head of Matsushita, a strongly purpose-driven firm, considered it consistent with his company's culture to involve himself and his employees in the development of a *250-year plan!* Many American executives consider it daring to peek beyond the next quarter's earnings report.

To be powerful and effective, societal goals must be transcendent, looming larger than the individual and extending across time. This expansiveness of vision explains the predominance religion has enjoyed over human action. To serve God, His dicta, and His Commandments provided the species with an overarching goal orientation that induced it to bow before popes, engage in turbulent crusades, and produce magnificent cathedrals. Political ideologies such as Marxism and democracy have had the same transcendent qualities, leading some to label these ideologies secular religions.

In addition, this goal or set of goals must be perceived by the individuals in the society as ultimately serving their needs. Religion provides salvation; Marxism provides equality; democracy promises political participation, personal power, and self-determination. Most important, this goal or set of goals must be consistent with popular sentiment and the society's history.

A leader with a particularly acute sense of vision can fathom a society's purpose long before its members do. Certainly, the founders of the American Republic, the Jeffersons, Franklins, and Adamses, could not impose the overriding sense of purpose—self-government and independence from the crown—on the population. Their vision was accepted because it embodied society's next logical step.

In the late-twentieth century, a number of leaders and factions have attempted and will continue to attempt to provide nations and global society with such a sense of purpose. In 1991, President Bush, fresh from his victory in the Persian Gulf War, proposed an overriding national and international goal, the New World Order. The purpose of such an order was the maintenance of world peace through a combination of international economic cooperation and a large UN peacekeeping force. Bush certainly expected the United States and the world to rally around such a goal in much the same way Americans rallied around John Kennedy's New Frontier concept. But George Bush, however, was mistaken.

The reason that such a concept failed lies in the fact that people perceived it to be just what Bush and others claimed it would be—a system of order. Order in and of itself promises individuals little; it merely offers the absence of war, conflict, and political agitation. Even if the New World Order would deliver as advertised, it ultimately promised a state of homeostasis. The New World Order as Bush presented it promised the absence of conflict, but people have difficulty becoming truly inspired by the absence of anything, no matter how odious that object is.

To be inspirational, the vision must be substantive and proactive. Manifest destiny presented a vision of expansion, as did the space program during the Kennedy administration. The New World Order as currently stated lacks the glitter even of old-time religions. It is difficult to envision a revival tent filled with adherents of the New World Order.

By the time the 1992 U.S. presidential elections rolled around, a scant twelve months after the announcement of this "vision," the concept of the New World Order was not invoked as a rallying cry. Although Bush desperately needed a message and a slogan to salvage his faltering campaign, even he realized that the concept of the New World Order was so vacuous as to be useless. George Bush's subsequent 1992 defeat became a referendum on his lack of vision.

Other visions and ideologies are periodically presented to the population for adoption as overarching societal purposes. Religions still attempt to capture the need for the transcendent, but the weakness of traditional religions in this area is evident in the growing interest Westerners have in counter-Judeo/Christian New Age practices and philosophies. For many, the New Age movement's vision of the immersion of the individual in the eternal cosmos offers a sense of purpose not found in many traditional religions.

I suspect that in the Macroindustrial Era society the goal orientation will speak to the need for the transcendent in each individual. The overall purpose will not be world order or national supremacy, but the very expansion of human capacity and power. Of course, at this point of historical development, this goal must be articulated with reference to specific national agendas. After all, we still live in a world of nation-states, and most citizens look first to the satisfaction of national and local needs. Nevertheless, in the late twentieth century, the more global approach has become increasingly relevant and legitimate to most nations' citizens. We are witnessing a growing tendency toward the internationalization of economic, military, and political activity, a trend that seems likely to only increase. This era seems most favorable for the inception of a goal orientation that involves the human species as a whole.

However, such a vision will not take hold until it concludes its ideological battle with countervisions such as hard-core environmentalism. These ideologies focus on saving the planet, not on enhancing the species. Although the human being senses that his species is meant for something better, a barrage of input from the zero-growth lobby suggests to him that he is nothing more than just another player in the cosmological panorama and should thus concentrate on achieving a balance with nature. The shrinkage of the human species back to the state of nature is now being promoted by Vice President Albert Gore and others as the ultimate raison d'être of nations and the species as a whole.

Any leader will first have to recognize and contend with the countervailing power of such ideologies if he or she hopes to instill in the nation or group a strong sense of its own purpose and destiny. A people must believe in its inherent legitimacy, as a nation and species, in order to muster and maintain the enthusiasm and willpower necessary to survive and thrive in the emerging Macroindustrial Era.

A Positive National Outlook

Although a strong sense of purpose will be indispensable for any nation hoping to achieve success in the Macroindustrial Era, it must be accompanied by other characteristics. Besides having a clear goal orientation, a society must possess a positive outlook regarding itself and its future. On an individual level, evidence overwhelmingly suggests that the more positively a person views his or her future, the greater his or her chances for career and personal success. The same principle holds true for large groups and society as a whole.

An Expansionary society possesses a positive attitude about itself and its ability to grow and achieve. Conversely, countries that see themselves as doomed and in fact celebrate their own demise on the world stage can hardly expect to successfully compete.

This cultural trait is composed of several subcomponents. One of these is pure and simple optimism, the belief that the future will improve and that the lot of a nation and its inhabitants will progress materially, intellectually, and economically. A second component is self-confidence. A confident nation believes that it can make things happen. Most countries marvel at—and incidentally also resent—this can-do attitude embedded deeply in the American psyche: Give us a problem and we can solve it. The ability to accomplish grandiose objectives—the taming of the West, the Moon landing, the achievement of a high standard of living—results from such self-confidence. A third component of a positive national outlook is the propensity to recognize opportunities for growth.

Future historians will realize that the American application of positive thinking to problem solving became a model of behavior adopted by a host of emerging countries throughout the twentieth century. America demonstrated to these countries how valuable self-confidence is to the achievement of success: Believe in yourself, and it will happen!

Why the Positive Outlook Works

The species' positive outlook has become an increasingly powerful force in its historical evolution, an underlying mechanism by which the species has extended its powers and capabilities. In the last chapter, we witnessed many examples of individuals changing their lives and their destinies through positive thinking. This dynamic manifests itself on the societal level also.

To understand why the power of positive thinking works, we must first accept that in absolute terms there are no limits to what the human species can accomplish. That is, we cannot say for sure that only 1 billion people as opposed to 10 billion people can survive and thrive on the planet; that the human species can travel no faster than 100 miles per hour or 4000 miles per hour; or that the species will extend itself only as far as the Moon, Mars, the Solar System, or the universe. What we conceive, we can accomplish.

Conversely, if humanity is so foolish as to choose not to continue to grow materially and expand economically, it should be willing to recognize that no invisible hand will save it from stagnation and extinction.

In fact, if the species had chosen not to expend the mental and physical energy to develop the technological and knowledge base we currently possess, the forces of nature, through famine and disease, would probably have terminated human existence centuries ago.

However, the species fathomed early that it possessed a unique quality, the ability to create the means for its own survival and advancement: the wheel, the steam engine, electricity, writing, the computer, and other marvels. However, the act of creation is an almost mystical process. Initially, an individual envisions a technology or event. Then, he pursues activities that will lead to the actualization of the idea that previously existed only in his mind or on a computer screen. As I demonstrated in the last chapter, critical to this process is positive thinking, an individual's faith in the power of his own creation. Positive thinking becomes the connection between a fantasy and its actualization. On a societal level, a positive outlook—optimism and self-confidence—becomes the mechanism by which society evolves. A society envisions its future, then proceeds to create it.

Without such a positive outlook—faith, if you will—the society becomes primarily reactive to events, the physical environment, other nations, or imaginary historical forces. Economic theory is rife with a myriad of theories that purport to describe economic cycles, usually stated in ironclad terms spiked with theorems, laws, and corollaries that operate beyond the reach of societal and individual action. In this view, an oscillating wave of feast and famine, boom and bust, asserts itself at regular intervals regardless of human intention and activity.

However, economists and other social scientists ignore the fact that all economic activity, be it growth or contraction, directly derives from human behavior. These cycles, although a measurement of human activity, do not cause such behavior. Such belief in the power of cycles as an influence on economic growth is an example of reactive, regressive thinking. In reality, humanity has induced megagrowth in the GNP and the economy in general by rejecting the belief that outside forces, be they the gods, the wind, or cycles, determine human events and instead using positive thinking and proactive behavior to seize control of its own economic development.

It is only through developing a national positive outlook that the species has been able to build the world as we know it. History demonstrates that a country can will itself into prosperity. An optimistic population will take control of its destiny and launch itself into a dynamic growth pattern. A society composed of depressed individuals will stagnate no matter how creative its policy agenda or how sophisticated its technology.

The World Today: Caught Between Moods

Although many nations demonstrate at least a superficial optimism at present, various polls detect a certain ambivalence about the future.

One gauge of national morale is the happiness indicator, a measure of a population's current level of positive feeling. These detailed studies, conducted throughout the world, ask respondents to describe on a ten-point scale how happy they actually are. These studies have identified several interesting factors that influence happiness. For one, there is a direct correlation between GNP per capita and reported happiness: the richer the average citizen, the higher the aggregate score on the happiness scale. Relatively affluent countries, such as Scandinavia, Canada, the United States, and Australia, score very high on such scales, whereas poorer nations in Asia score low on happiness. Also, the more internal peace that exists in a society, the higher the amount of happiness. African respondents, many of whom suffer through internal civil wars and domestic insurrections, scored lowest on happiness indicators.

However, even the countries scoring high on happiness indicators betray an evolving pessimistic national outlook. A 1991 study of Americans found that from January to June of that year an increasing number of respondents felt that the country was "seriously on the wrong path." This pessimism was remarkable, considering the fact that the country had just enjoyed its greatest military victory since World War II, the Cold War had ended, and the country was relatively prosperous.

Other surveys buttress these findings. Recent studies indicate that baby boomers in the United States are suffering clinical depression at earlier ages than did preceding generations. In fact, female baby boomers have a 65 percent greater chance than earlier cohorts of being depressed at some time in their lives. Suicide rates have also increased among fifteen to twenty-four-year-olds, tripling between 1950 and 1980. Similar indications of gloom show up in international studies—a twenty-five-year study in Iceland, for instance, found the same increase in depression rates among baby boomers. A study performed by the National Opinion Research Center, one of the most respected polling institutions in America, reported an alarming decline in the percentage of American women who are prepared to say that they are "very happy."

Statistics on consumer confidence reflect the decline of optimism in American culture. Such statistics directly measure the degree to which people feel confident that their own finances and the national economy will be better, worse, or the same over the next one to five years. The decades of the 1950s and 1960s saw U.S. consumers brimming with confidence, but in the 1970s the confidence indicators began to plummet. Although throughout the 1980s the United States enjoyed a recovery in consumer confidence, all measures now reflect a return to the pessimism of the mid to late 1970s.

Behavioral measures point to a pervasive pessimism. The most dramatic is the birth dearth that has swept through Western society, specifically Western Europe. Although lauded by many population control advocates, the baby bust is causing alarm in a variety of academic and policy circles. The decline in European fertility rates is so precipitous that many of these countries' populations will soon begin to shrink. For example, Austria reproduces 30 percent below the rate required to maintain its current population size. Other countries, such as France and Great Britain, are also grossly underproducing the next generation. In other words, at these levels, within fifty years, countries such as Germany will have half the number of citizens they currently possess.

Commentators usually explain these low rates in terms of such factors as the increased number of women working, a poor economy, abortion-on-demand, and high divorce rates. Few, however, have zeroed in on what may be an unmeasured, unforeseen reason for low fertility—lack of faith in the future. A society with a positive outlook regarding the future would be motivated to bring more people into the world to share the wealth and to help build a new society. A pessimistic society, fearing the future, slowly eradicates itself.

Pessimism has a tendency to feed on itself. Yale University professor Paul Kennedy has turned despair into a cottage industry. His 1987 book, *The Rise and Fall of Great Powers*, described how the United States would join the ranks of nations that had become overwhelmed by their military commitments and collapsed. Although within two years, it was not America, but its greatest enemy, the Soviet Empire, that collapsed economically, Kennedy never admitted his error. In fact, he wrote an even more pessimistic tome in 1993, *Preparing for the Twenty-First Century*, in which he carefully catalogs the catastrophes awaiting various countries throughout the next century—ecological holocausts, starvation, war, and the like.

Kennedy's pessimism is so pervasive that he adamantly refuses to admit that biotech and macromanufacturing can usher in a whole new era of material progress. From his perspective, any gains that we make will ruin the environment and/or "expand the gap between the rich and poor."

One suspects that Kennedy's sense of despair is shared by a sizable minority of Westerners. Can such despair ruin an economy? Certainly, it is a truism that a population that thinks that the economy will get worse rather than better in the near future will restrict its spending, forcing businesses to lay off workers, who in turn have less to spend. A whole population that restricts its spending in anticipation of a recession will very likely create one. If pessimism halves the birth rate, eventually the hands and minds to solve society's problems will exist in decreasing numbers. Again, pessimism becomes a self-fulfilling prophecy.

In his review of Kennedy's book, progrowth advocate George Gilder aptly summarizes the weaknesses in Kennedy's and others' pessimistic Weltanshauung: "The prospects of humanity always seem dire to people who cannot imagine the exponential bounties of technological advance. Human creativity always comes as a surprise to us; if it didn't, we could plan it and it wouldn't be needed."

Pessimism can be cynically exploited. Bill Clinton and his staff recognized long before the election that the American population was increasingly manifesting feelings of despair and anomie on opinion surveys. Surely, two years of economic stagnation had taken its toll on the American psyche. Instead of replacing the public's pessimism with a substantive vision of hope (as required by the Expansionary Culture), Clinton and handlers such as James Carville, playing for political advantage, used these feelings of hopelessness as building blocks for a total reconstitution of the memories Americans had of the prosperous 1980s.

The period 1983–1989 represented the longest economic boom in post-World War II America; it was so successful that many have labeled this period "the seven fat years." Clinton skillfully manipulated American pessimism circa 1992 so that people began to remember the seven years of prosperity as "the worst economic period since the Depression." George Bush's personal inability to shape a vision beyond the uninspiring New World Order led to a series of disjointed, impotent responses to Clinton's recasting of historical memory.

To succeed in major socioeconomic transitions such as the emergence of the Macroindustrial Era, the population must recognize those periods when it veers dangerously close to the darker feelings of depression and hopelessness and must consciously combat such tendencies and replace them with creative positive action and energy.

The population must exhibit a positive outlook, an enthusiasm for the new, a joy in discovery, and a sense of wonder. The people must invent, create, and literally seize the future.

Visionary Leadership

A strong sense of purpose and a positive national outlook may emanate either directly from the nation's spirit or simply from a long-standing tradition. In times of change, however, society depends at least partially for direction from those in positions of power and authority.

Leaders and opinion molders—the media, government, corporations, and educators—can provide the country with an agenda of new possibilities for growth and progress. They, more than any other group, can revitalize a stagnant culture so that the country can begin to move forward. As mentioned earlier, leaders can play a critical role in providing the population with a sense of the future. They may sense the natural direction of the society even before the citizens do or may create an entire new agenda based on unique personal insight into changing historical forces.

In a seminal article on the subject, management expert Albert Zaleznik drew a sharp distinction between leaders and managers. Managers take over a concern, be it a school, business, or government, and help it fulfill established agendas. Such managers work well as heads of established corporations in mature industries, overseeing the administration of a going concern.

Leaders are different: They provide a vision of the future, transmit this vision to the organization, and then convince others to support these new ideas. Leaders understand how to articulate this new vision in such a way that others perceive the change as positive. Sometimes they must stand against the crowd: Churchill had to labor for years to convince the British government and public that Germany was serious about rearming and militarily dominating the European continent. Chamberlain, a true manager, told the British what they wanted to hear, Churchill told them what they had to know.

A 1992 poll conducted for the Chrysler Corporation revealed what Americans desire as the focus of the nation's future agenda. Some of their suggestions, like improving the education system and lowering the tax rate, would help the society grow, but most of their stated priorities reflected years of exposure to leaders and molders of opinion totally bereft of a cogent and original perspective on the future. Suggestions included compulsory national service at age eighteen, harsher prison terms, and a jobs program. Furthermore, responding to years of bombardment by a media that has sought to convince them that the human species' productive activity threatens the planet, a majority said that we should be willing to sacrifice jobs to save the environment. The number one priority for scientific research cited was research to save the planet.

Leadership that hopes to direct its country into the Macroindustrial Era ought to study such a survey first and then decide how to convince the population that the number one priority is economic growth. In the 1992 U.S. election campaign, no candidate seemed to consider it important to inform the electorate that within the decade the country will be confronting energy shortfalls and a concomitant reduced standard of living!

A leader must also be a good motivator. He or she must rally a society, build morale, and help create a positive national outlook. In order to cheerlead a society and revive its spirit, the leader must be charismatic and inspiring. Do we presently have such leaders? At the 1992 Group of Seven (G7) meetings, it would have been excusable if a passerby confused the presidents and prime ministers of the United Kingdom, Italy, and Germany for loan officers at the local commmercial bank.

Try as he may, Bill Clinton will have great difficulty making the transition from policy wonk to charismatic visionary. His early calls for tax increases, sacrifice, and national service smack of a reformulation of 1930s-style New Dealism with a bit of JFK idealism. Indications of Clinton's leadership potential can be gleaned from his actions immediately before his inauguration. In late 1992, he quickly gathered 300 business and academic leaders in Little Rock, Arkansas, to help him understand the economy and consider policy options. Whereas on one level such a meeting can be applauded as an attempt to build consensus, on another level, it betrays a deep need on Clinton's part to discover a guiding ideology (other than his own political survival). True leaders build consensus around *their* vision, not others'.

A leadership vacuum at the top of the political structure does not mean that other institutions cannot provide inspiration and direction. For all the criticism heaped upon the media of late for their glorification of violence and glamorization of nihilism, for much of this century, television and the cinema served the world quite well as both cheer-leader and morale booster.

We will examine the role of the arts in the Expansionary Culture more fully when we discuss the importance of a vibrant artistic milieu. Here, however, we will focus on the media as opinion leaders and cultural cheerleaders.

In the United States, certainly the media have historically been un-abashed purveyors of patriotism and cultural pride. During World War II, the mass of the public drew inspiration from the movies. Cinematic portrayals of heroic valor on the battlefield and in the air boosted mo-rale on the homefront and provided recognition and honor for those confronting the horror of armed combat.

Hollywood has been criticized for its tendency during World War II to sugarcoat portrayals of battle, maximizing the glory and eliminating the blood. The cinematic version of World War II is so romanticized that many people's memory of that war has most certainly been fash-ioned by Hollywood's presentation of the great conflagration. For those who never experienced the war, it is hard to understand how so many retain happy memories of a period that saw the death of tens of millions of young men and women in battle, the dropping of the atomic bomb on civilians, and the mass extermination of peoples and populations in Nazi concentration camps.

The rejoinder is that the real horror of such events required that the movies present the war to the homefront in a more romantic mode. A nation that truly understood the horror awaiting it in the period 1941 to 1945 could have become critically demoralized. If a country ever needed a positive national outlook to accomplish its goals, it was the United States during the early years of the war. Hollywood provided the country with a fantasy: It could beat Germany and Japan. This fantasy sustained a positive national outlook that generated the energy and will needed to transform fantasy into reality.

The role of the media in establishing and sustaining a national mood cannot be underestimated. Hollywood has often been criticized for the classic "happy ending," which the movie industry has unabashedly purveyed throughout the entire century. Critics have wailed for de-cades that "life is not like that." In their demand for more realism, social critics have lambasted the movies for continuing the myths that good triumphs over evil, the hero always gets the girl, and people live happily ever after.

Ironically, the propensity of American moviemakers and television writers to always search out the happy ending may serve a greater cultural function than anyone has ever imagined. A constant barrage of happy endings may smack of creating a fantasy world. However, after all, novels, mysteries, and adventure stories are fantasy. That is why they are labeled fiction. The question is, What kind of fantasy ought people to receive from their mythmakers and storytellers?

Sociologists constantly worry that such myths provide the citizenry a false impression of the world, shielding from them the real world of poverty, war, homelessness, and other misfortunes. Yet intellectuals give the public too little credit. People worldwide gravitate to such movies not because the cinema presents the world the way it is, but because it presents a vision of how it could be. Certainly, the case can be made that while an individual is enveloped in Hollywood's dream-world, he or she suspends judgment about reality. However, Hollywood's cinematic dreams, including those of wealth and personal fulfillment, have instilled in millions a vision of what the individual can accomplish. The cinema presents the masses with a concept of the possible.

Such messages, however unrealistic, have real implications for behavior. Studies have shown that positive attitudes are a precursor to positive action. It seems logical that the myths of Hollywood have contributed to the positive national outlook necessary for economic and personal growth, a vision now taking hold in Hong Kong, Japan, and Europe. The dream conditions the reality!

The world of optimism and the happy ending is still maintained somewhat on TV sitcoms and dramas. However, increasingly the message from the cinema is cynical and depressing. Government is evil and conspiratorial, technology will enslave us, business will pollute, and parents are incompetent. The most destructive message slipping through the cinematic cracks is the attack on industrial development and economic growth. A subtle pattern of antigrowth messages has developed in the media. This emerging antigrowth ideology has a number of dimensions.

One such dimension is the continual diatribe against nuclear power and, by implication, all exotic and potentially dangerous energy sources. In the movie *Police Squad 2 1/2*, the builders of a local nuclear power plant were portrayed as mobsters willing to jeopardize the population's safety for the sake of profits. Even murder was not beneath them. The popular sitcom "The Simpsons" features the bumbling anti-hero Homer Simpson running key reactor controls as a senior technician. Again, the owner of the plant is a greedy egomaniac who encourages his workers to overlook safety procedures.

Another part of the emerging message is the attack on the concept of growth itself. *Batman Returns*, the sequel to *Batman*, opens with a three-way debate between the neurotic blueblood Bruce Wayne (a.k.a. Batman), a local Trump-like billionaire, and the hapless mayor of Gotham (New York) about the building of a new power plant. The debate eventually evolves into the real issue, the acceptable rate of economic growth. The mogul, who wants to build the plant, argues that such a plant will allow the economy to grow at a 3-plus percent rate. Bruce Wayne defends a moderate 1 percent growth rate. The mogul replies that such a slow growth rate will not allow Gotham to shine brightly, keep its lights on, and increase industrial production.

This debate was deftly slipped into the movie past an unsuspecting public. Of course, the progrowth mogul becomes the heavy. His other companies create toxic waste; he murders his secretary, cuts deals with the underworld, and, we discover, intends to divert the plant's energy to his own private use. On the other hand, Bruce Wayne, the low-growth advocate, the humanist, well, he is Batman.

The other dimension involves the rights of the human species vis-à-vis animals, plants, insects and the Earth itself. A plethora of antispecies messages are routinely slipped into movies and television without notice. *E.T.*, the favorite of kids and their parents, contained remarkably antihuman overtones. The belief that other species have rights equal to humanity's permeated the movie. Spielberg established this theme in an early scene in which a young boy rebels against an inclass biology assignment to dissect a frog, dramatically opening the cages and liberating all the class frogs. The analogy is, of course, extended into the main theme, E.T. against an overwhelmingly intolerant, though inferior, human species.

Nineteen ninety-one's *Here Come the Applegates* called for establishing peace and understanding between humans and, of all things, insects. TV's "Star Trek: The Next Generation" periodically tests the bounds of antispecies thinking by equating androids and robots with humans. Picard, the captain of the *Enterprise*, even once made a dramatic speech defending the rights of "life crystals," asking why rocks should not have the same rights as human beings!

It is certainly within the realm of possibility that messages from the media may undermine support for political sector plans for economic growth and energy development. If a national leader suggests building nuclear power plants, how many voters considering a bond issue for such construction will perhaps unconsciously imagine a Homer Simpson at the controls? Most disturbing is the fact that a population bombarded by cynical and pessimistic messages from the media and subjected to uninspired leadership from its politicians will eventually lose the will to succeed and the energy to grow. In the emerging Macroindustrial Era, such an eventuality would prove deadly for a society's prospects.

The Expansionary Culture is one in which those in power provide visionary leadership and inspiration. The political elite and the media owe their societies creative solutions to problems and fresh agendas for the future. They must help the population to dream! If they do anything less, they have failed in their mission.

A Respect for Both Material Production and Consumption

Although acknowledging the spiritual and having a strong sense of the transcendent, the Expansionary Culture maintains and nurtures a profound respect for both material production and consumption. A society wishing to succeed in the Macroindustrial Era must possess such a sentiment.

We are, to a great extent, what we create—art, music, along with the technology to produce buildings, food, and automobiles. The production of goods is one proof of the species' uniqueness; no other species is able to achieve the technological wonders and scientific breakthroughs that humanity has. To disparage material goods is tantamount to scorning the species itself.

A society that respects material goods will work that much harder to produce and acquire them. Americans' constant dwelling on the good life, couched as it is in material terms, is constantly criticized by both foreign and home-grown social analysts, but there is a functionality to such an obsession: The desire for material possessions motivates the individual and the society as a whole to expend the energy needed to produce them. A society that repudiates its desire for the material is well on its way to economic ruin.

The materialistic sentiment has even more subtle influences on societal growth. Historically, sociologists have expressed the fear that the emphasis on material consumption establishes expectations that cannot be met. Their argument claims that the media lead them to believe that they have within their grasp the material good life that they actually cannot afford. In essence, they have been somehow deceived into establishing unrealistic material demands.

However, these expectations actually pressure industry to produce both a greater quantity and quality of goods. Industry understands that once the society comes to expect goods and services, such demands must be met. The public demands cars that operate efficiently, a power supply that can light its houses, and an agricultural system that produces food in abundance. If a company cannot meet such demands, the public will buy from another company.

Hence, these sets of increasing expectations form a ground swell of constant social and economic pressure on industry and institutions in general to become more and more productive. Ultimately, these heightened material expectations become a force by which nations and the species itself progress. Countries like India languished in squalor for centuries while the West flourished. India was ethereal; the West, materialistic. The cultural values determined the level of economic progress.

Actually, the United States pioneered avid materialism as a cultural trait. Even in the 1800s, Alexis de Tocqueville noted the "feverish ardor [with which] the Americans pursue their own welfare." De Tocqueville saw an America that "clutches everything . . . but soon loosens this grasp to pursue fresh gratifications," an apt description of a species awakening to its potential for ever-greater material production.

Material goods provide society and its members a sense of temporal continuity impossible to imagine without them. Societies cherish their buildings and monuments as a symbol of the immortality of the nation, race, religious, or ethnic group. Families hold dear their precious heirlooms because these objects—the family clock, grandmother's jewelry, a parent's childhood toys—provide a sense of permanence and timelessness impossible to achieve without such material goods.

In the 1980s, the United States enjoyed a rebirth of prosperity. For most, this economic success revealed the more noble side of materialism. People produced more, earned more, and therefore purchased more—a perfect balance that led to even greater economic growth. A chorus of naysayers have restated the facts to present a very different case: They point to this decade as proof positive of the underlying dysfunctionality of the materialist ethic. According to this scenario, in the 1980s, the United States and the West were seduced by the materialistic urge to engage in a buying binge on credit for which it is paying mightily in the slow-growth 1990s. The hidden message—change your ways, repent, or your days are numbered.

Such thinking smacks of ideological bias and faulty logic. Materialism was alive and well during that period, but it served to motivate people not only to consume, but to produce. Factory output jumped a full 30 percent in the 1980s; 18 million jobs were created. By the latter part of the decade, GNP growth began to approach a 3 percent annual average, the highest in twenty years. During the period of 1983–1990, people did buy—homes, cars, luxuries—yet they also worked hard. We began to hear complaints about people becoming workaholics, overly competitive, too career-minded. Although materialism was the overriding ethic, it made them not only play hard, but work hard as well.

In an Expansionary society, since both material consumption and production are the objects of respect, members are encouraged to take seriously the role they play in economic growth and material production. Their jobs, careers, and education are of paramount concern. Excellence is venerated; mediocrity, discouraged.

It is only logical that the Expansionary culture recognizes and celebrates the accomplishments of entrepreneurs, inventors, and people of science. By celebrating their achievements, society reaffirms its belief that the individual is at least partially defined in terms of what he or she creates and produces. Such recognition also serves as motivator to others, who perceive that their own social standing will be enhanced by producing goods and services of value to the society.

The Rise of Antimaterialism

Considering that the emphasis on material production and consumption can generate such positive results, it would seem logical to expect society to gravitate toward such a sentiment. Yet at least for the last two or three decades, a countersentiment has arisen, a bald-faced antimaterialism that threatens to upend economic growth and technological progress.

Antimaterialism has emerged from several different ideological and political corners. The most potent attacks on material consumption come from self-labeled environmentalists. The basic scenario is as follows: The per capita consumption of energy and raw materials among the United States, Western Europe, and Japan has increased precipitously since 1950, and these countries are setting a poor example for developing countries and Third World nations. Our global materialism will eventually deplete all resources and leave the Earth barren.

This message has been trumpeted by the mainstream media in such publications as *Time* and *USA Today*, by the World Futures Society, and by Vice President Albert Gore in his best-selling 1992 book, *Earth in the Balance*. The World Futures Society's occasional support for this position is particularly distressing: This organization purports to speak for the future and represents a major conduit of information between professional futurologists and corporate and governmental policy bodies.

Nowhere do we find in such critiques a hint that material growth is desirous simply because it enhances the quality and quantity of life, that the materialist urge motivates individuals to work harder and produce more, or that material comfort allows individuals to become more creative and more productive. Rather, the environmental critique generally assumes that individuals have been duped by advertising into buying and using goods and services that they do not need.

Closely allied to environmentalism is the "voluntary simplicity" lobby. They attack materialism more on sociological and psychological grounds than on issues such as resource depletion and endangered species extinction. The point of view that the simple life is the source of joy, that a life with few material possessions leads to personal fulfillment, has a long history in the West. The hippie communes of the 1960s and 1970s and the like have existed in striking contrast to the acquisitive, productivity-oriented culture of abundance that has reigned supreme in the West at least since the Renaissance.

The media has accorded much attention to such experimentation in current years. In 1991, *Time* ran a cover story extolling the simple life. The article informed us that Americans are tired of trendiness and materialism and celebrated Americans' rediscovery of the joys of home life, low-pressure living, "basic values," and freedom from material possessions. The media simultaneously portrays individuals who desire material gain for self, family, and the species as "greedy" and avaricious. Such people are "uncaring" and selfish and somehow harmful to the body social.

This extensive coverage is highly suspect. The pressure for so-called voluntary simplicity seems to conveniently support life-styles that the environmental groups want us to adopt, albeit for slightly different reasons. A more cynical observer could intuit that as a nation's economy sags, a method for assuaging the population's anger and frustration over recession and concomitant reduction in living standards is to convince the citizenry that doing without is more fulfilling than material growth. In short, promoting the simple life as a basic virtue camouflages the real purpose, the selling of austerity.

Those who critique materialism seem consistently blinded to the powerful role materialism plays in economic growth and human progress. If we harbor any doubt about the inner worth of material production and consumption, we have only to witness the human misery extant in any society that possesses few goods or luxuries or the means to procure or produce them.

Through the various revolutions that have occurred in the West—the scientific, agriculture, and industrial—the human population has been able to free itself from the yokes of starvation and scarcity that the species endured for many centuries. The standing legacy of these revolutions, material progress itself, now extends throughout the globe.

In the coming Macroindustrial Era, the species must continue to nurture all the traits of the Expansionary Culture outlined in this chapter. A respect for materialism, both in terms of consumption and production, must receive particular attention. Breaking biological constraints, reaching space, and producing food are inherently material objectives. Without the same materialistic ethos that has guided the West at least since the Renaissance, the species will never reach such goals.

A Firm Grounding in Reality

In the emerging Macroindustrial Era, a society that wishes to progress must have a firm grounding in reality. The more connected to reality a society is, the more it is able to articulate its goals and determine how it will achieve them.

A society that is grounded in reality exhibits several characteristics. It has a profound belief that human action is the primary determinant of its future. Although external events, such as geological shifts and environmental catastrophes, can contravene some human activity, it is humanity itself that significantly determines outcomes. Such a grounded society also has a limited amount of patience with concepts such as luck; in such a society any person who continually refers to luck as an explanation of his or her own or others' success or failure finds his or her judgment questioned. The grounded society also holds in disfavor superstitious beliefs and serious dabbling in superstitious practices. The use of signs and rituals to influence human events is considered outside the realm of reasonable behavior. Also, this society can quickly differentiate superstition from other types of beliefs and behaviors.

Of course, this society favors the material over the ethereal. It accepts that the human species has established its presence and will continue its existence in the material world and therefore endeavors to build and embellish that world.

This is not to say that the Expansionary society does not believe in divinities, the afterlife, and the spiritual, but it also understands the difference between the material and the spiritual and knows where one stops and the other begins.

Such a firm grounding in reality stands as one of the most important cultural traits in the emerging Macroindustrial Era. This orientation compels societies to assume responsibility for their own fortunes and become proactive in building their futures. By contrast, societies that wait for the intervention of deities to feed their populations and utilize Ouija boards and astrological charts to divine the future instead of shaping it themselves will find themselves stagnating.

So obvious is the importance of a country maintaining its grip on reality that it should not require more than a mention here. Unfortunately, we have many examples in history in which an obsession with the occult and the ethereal has sabotaged a society's culture and caused human misery. As societies have reached their nadir, many have sunk into the morass of occultism. Hitler was at least in part driven by cabalistic insights, and the final years of the Russian monarchy saw the rise of the mystic Rasputin, a monk who advised, if not controlled, the Romanov dynasty.

The West has witnessed a growing interest in the occult and the rise of superstition in general in the last thirty years. The phenomenon is so pervasive that it would not be feasible to catalog it here. However, a mere sampling will serve to remind us that our world is increasingly coming under the influence of the occult, the ethereal, and the superstitious.

Astrology has been with us for almost the length of recorded history. Egyptian pharaohs and Roman emperors consulted seers and astrologers to determine political maneuverings and military game plans. In the West, consulting astrological charts was a hobby for some, a game for others. Until recently. During the late 1980s, the media reported that Nancy Reagan consulted astrologers for advice on a variety of issues, including when to hold social events and where to travel. Some White House insiders later suggested that Nancy might have been basing her political advice to her husband, the president, on astrological predictions. The public squirmed just a little at the thought that a necessary military action might have been postponed or a treaty not signed because Nancy Reagan's astrologer warned that these events were not currently in the stars.

Since those days, reports continue to emerge about financiers and stock brokerage firms clandestinely retaining the services of "financial astrologers." These "specialists" chart company fortunes in much the same way they would those of individuals, using the corporation's exact date of birth as a starting point for their analysis. Word even leaked that former Treasury Secretary William Simon retained a private astrologer. Such disclosures actually serve to provide this pseudoscience with more, not less, legitimacy. How many more thousands are attracted to this superstition because they believe Wall Street brokers use it as a tool for stock market analysis?

One of the more disturbing aspects of the ascendency of astrology is the fact that its practitioners and users seem so willing to relinquish control over their actions. They as much as admit that the stars and planets control their futures, not themselves. Such a belief leads to tentativeness of action and eventual self-doubt. The large-scale adoption of such beliefs will have ominous implications for any nation. A society whose members are convinced that their futures have been predetermined at birth will never develop the national will to seize the future.

However, the belief in astrology is the more benign face of etherealism and superstition in comparison to the alarming rise in Satanism and witchcraft. Certainly, Satanism, the practice of attempting to contact the spiritual dark underworld and enlist its influence, has a marked presence in certain types of rock music. Satanic imagery in this music affects many troubled teenagers in the United States and Europe. We occasionally hear of ritual killings, and many child molestation accounts reveal a disturbing pattern of parents incorporating their own children in satanic rituals.

Witchcraft has certainly received its fair share of publicity since the mid-1980s. Chronologers of the ethereal claim that the rise of witchcraft owes much to the pervasiveness of feminism in the late twentieth century. The United States and Europe have witnessed a gradual increase in goddess worship, which adherents claim was the major form of religion until 6000 B.C. This prepatriarchal utopia was egalitarian, peace loving, and in harmony with Mother Earth. (This religion was supposedly eradicated by patriarchal invaders.) Goddess worship has solid roots in worship of the earth and the elements. Although the modern version of the goddess descends from such ancient goddesses as Isis and Astarte, her followers most frequently depict her as Mother Earth or Gaia. In fact, many current practitioners of Wicca (witchcraft) embrace beliefs that stress harmony with nature.

This belief in the primacy of nature over humanity often links the occult and the pagan with environmentalism. Such festivals as the Healing Mother Earth exposition feature a mixture of environmentalism and New Age theology, including witchcraft.

The onset of the New Age movement typifies more than any other the growth of the ethereal in the West. The 1992 fall catalog of the Pyramid Book Company (founded in, of all places, Salem, Massachusettes) reveals the breadth and depth of this movement. The company features books on astrology, dreams and divination, chakras, witchcraft, the Druid tradition, and the casting of spells. There is a whole section in the catalog of books dealing with prophecy, UFO experiences, and tarot card readings. It also features a variety of rocks and crystals guaranteed to provide the holder with power and energy, natural quartz crystal balls, and "fairy gems," described as self-charged good luck pieces. Surprisingly, the catalog now includes candles and statues depicting angels, ironically imbuing the catalog with the role of traditional religion. However, New Agers' interest in angels has little to do with Christianity; angels clearly serve as surrogates for the goddess. New Age now encourages adherents to use meditation to establish contact with these species.

The New Age movement has its roots in Madame Blavatsky's turn-of-the-century Theosophical Society. Blavatsky's disciple, Alice Bailey, was already referring to the New Age in her writings in the 1920s. At that time, such notables as Arthur Conan Doyle and W. B. Yeats, ardent adherents of spritualism and other beliefs, popularized the New Age philosophy. Celebrities have always been a fruitful source of publicity for the New Age movement; even today Shirley MacLaine spreads the belief in reincarnation and in UFOs through best-selling books and TV miniseries.

New Age philosophy has a profound international influence and is supported worldwide by the work of such organizations as the Esalen Institute, the personal awareness center founded in 1962 at Big Sur, California. Esalen more than any other organization was responsible for introducing to major corporations and government agencies Gestalt therapy, encounter groups, rolfing, and est.

They also support Russian-American peace tours. Unbeknownst to most Americans, Boris Yeltsin's 1989 U.S. tour was sponsored and financed through the Esalen Institute. Although the New Age movement promotes such tours in support of one of their guiding principles, world peace, many have wondered whether this political connection will be used to spread New Age philosophy and practices into the international political arena. Are the penetration of these networks into official circles the first step in a world government informed not by science and technology but by sorcery and witchcraft?

For some time, Esalen has been establishing connections between American and Russian New Agers. These interfaces actually predate the thawing of the Cold War between Russia and the United States. In the early 1980s, even as est was losing popularity among Americans, Werner Erhard, the founder of the psychological technique, was under contract to the Soviet Union to run est sessions for government bureaucrats in Moscow and elsewhere.

Observers have been amazed at the size and the organizational sophistication of the huge network of American and Russian New Agers. The network features groups with names like the Network of Light, the Institute for Security and Cooperation in Outer Space, the Center for U.S.–USSR Initiatives, and Bridges World Wide. It seems that even before the world had caught on to Glasnost, the New Age was already in the USSR promoting global networking and interpersonal connections.

How widespread is the influence of the ideologies and beliefs on the general public? According to survey data and anecdotal information, over the last decade, the popularity of astrology, the belief in reincarnation, and even Satanism has risen dramatically. Yet this trend seems to contradict another trend in which the species seems to be employing logic, creativity, and scientific principle to solve its problems. How is it that both science and superstition seem to be simultaneously increasing their dominance over the Western mind?

The answer is that, in truth, Western society suffers from a profound social dichotomy, rooted in differences in education and occupation. On one hand, we have the scientific and technical elite enjoined by the managerial classes. On the other, we have a large mass of individuals connected to the scientific enterprise as users but not as consumers.

Sad to say, many in this second group have a knowledge and appreciation of science equivalent to that of the average medieval farmer. Science may have progressed, but it failed to bring everyone up to speed. This lower group, purchasers of tabloids and viewers of "shock" television programming, exists in a netherworld easily penetrated by superstition and the occult.

Even members of the so-called educated classes have little appreciation of the scientific method and in fact may even fear science. This group can also be seduced by the ethereal promise of a better, simpler life free of the risks of technology. In many ways, even this educated group is subject to the siren call of the New Age.

So now, the modern mind finds itself confused, vulnerable to concepts it might once have rejected out of hand and ironically dismissing that which lies within the realm of possibility. Many in our society now consider it a sheer fantasy that humanity may develop the capability to populate distant planets but will assign a measure of validity to accounts of small gray creatures that periodically drop onto Earth to abduct, rape, and medically examine human beings. In fact, so convinced are they of the latter's truth that they may even perceive critics of such contentions as part of the cover-up.

Society ought to oppose this increased focus on etherealization. Those in positions of leadership must recognize that a nation steeped in superstition and valuing the ethereal over the real is in no position to develop and execute an agenda for the future. More importantly, real efforts must be made to increase the technological and scientific educational level and knowledge base of the general population. Superstition can only be eradicated if it is replaced by a fundamental understanding of how the physical world actually works.

A society with an Expansionary Culture has a firm grounding in reality, a characteristic that will serve it well throughout the Macroindustrial Era. Such a society will believe in its ability to influence events and will not wait for mystic intervention to correct its mistakes. This society does not believe in a predetermined future, only in one that can be created by human action. It perceives science, not pseudosciences such as astrology, as the pathway to the fulfillment of human potential. The Expansionary society always has its eyes on the stars, but remembers to keep its feet on the ground.

A Propensity to Risk

In order to participate fully in the Macroindustrial Era, a society must possess a propensity to risk. In fact, its willingness to take risks will determine whether it will achieve a leadership position in the Macroindustrial Era or simply be another country reacting to the initiatives and bold actions of the innovators and pioneers.

The growth of Western society is inextricably wedded to the concept of risk. The age of exploration that began in fifteenth-century Italy, Spain, England, and Portugal and continues to this day would not have occurred without this propensity to risk. Christopher Columbus, regularly excoriated by the late twentieth-century antigrowth and entropist intellectual establishment, actually represents the prototypical risk taker. Motivated by both his vision of a round Earth and the need to establish a trading route to the Indies, Columbus spent the better part of his life convincing the world that his vision was correct. The Weltanshauung of the age supported his efforts; others were willing to risk their capital and their lives to fulfill his vision.

The propensity to risk underwrote the entire scientific enterprise in the eighteenth and nineteenth centuries. People risked lives, reputation, and, more importantly, the psychological comfort that accompanies the retention of old beliefs to venture into unknown intellectual and scientific areas of discovery. We see this spirit of risk continuing among genetic engineers and quantum physicists who challenge accepted ideas of the role of the species in the universe.

In fact, the entire industrial enterprise of the last two centuries would not have transpired without the propensity to risk of entrepreneurs, financiers, and workers. Entrepreneurs especially succeeded because they were able to interest others in their enterprises and convince them to take the same risks the entrepreneur was willing to assume. Such visionaries inherently understood society's needs and had the courage to act on premonitory impulses.

For a society to succeed in the current era, it must possess a shared propensity to take chances. Although visionaries introduce ideas and establish the agenda, the culture of the society must support these ventures. In fact, it can be stated that the Expansionary Culture not only supports such ideas, but provides the wellspring from which such ideas emanate.

A society with a mature attitude toward risk displays several distinctive characteristics. For one thing, this type of society does not fear challenging the unknown. If anything, it relishes encounters with the unknown and the unusual. The members of such a society consider the risks well worth taking in exploring outer space, extending the frontiers of science, and even experimenting with new forms of social and economic organization.

Such a society is also characterized by an inner self-confidence that it can accomplish its goals no matter what the risk. It is unfortunate that during the 1990s, as Western society celebrates the 500th anniversary of the inception of the age of discovery, we have not more deeply examined the level of risk involved in the early explorer's journey. We would then realize the extent to which self-confidence facilitates risk-taking behavior. The Renaissance explorer sailed into what we would now have to describe objectively as the total unknown. The navigators had no idea where they were going, how long it would take to get there, and whether they had the means to return. Remember that most ship travel up to that time took place within sight of land; sailors and navigators followed coastlines to prevent being lost at sea.

New technologies, innovative biologies, even novel psychologies—the stuff of the Macroindustrial Era—all involve traveling into areas in which we as a species can no longer see familiar terrain and touch comforting coastlines. A society without such self-confidence will fear all forays into the unknown.

In addition, a mature attitude toward risk includes two other separate but related sentiments. First, the Expansionary society perceives risk as a normal part of the life process. Second, that society knows that risk taking forms the foundation for societal, economic, even personal, growth. Hence, both social policy and everyday life are conducted with the belief that risk taking may be necessary in order to achieve success.

Economist George Gilder makes the point that Western society has progressed by achieving a counterbalance between risk and stability. The mass of people found a safe haven for money in banks, savings, and insurance policies, whereas the business elite, the prime movers and shakers, invested their economic resources in relatively risky endeavors. Most investment generally represents positioning resources in what is essentially unknown, the future.

Gilder and others have rightly designated the entire monetary system and its prime representation, money, as the ultimate form of risk. The fact that someone would accept paper or credit in his or her account for a week's work or a car demonstrates that people are willing to engage in a great amount of risk taking.

Because risk taking has played such a key role in social and technological development and therefore has proven itself a useful cultural trait, legitimate questions do arise about why Western society has become increasingly overcautious in its response to science and technology. Both social scientists and policymakers have attempted to identify the key influences that began to erode the West's propensity to risk.

Starting in the 1970s, citizens of Western nations, especially America, began to experience a loss of faith in technology. Some link this to the U.S.'s inability to win the Vietnam War in spite of its massive strategic and material advantage. If machinery could not defeat a poorly equipped enemy, what else could science not do?

The aversion to risk was caused as much by science's power as by its supposed impotence, however. Science creates the weapons of war, pesticides, pollution, toxic wastes, and unpredictable new strands of DNA. This belief that science has the potential to betray the human race ultimately has enjoyed a sub rosa existence in the Western psyche for at least two centuries. In Mary Shelley's tome *Frankenstein*, we are warned that humanity's incursions into hitherto restricted domains are fraught with risks and will inevitably spell humanity's doom. Shelley's myth continues to have a powerful influence in the arguments against taking risks in scientific and technological endeavors.

By the 1990s, the public had become so risk averse that alarmists and fearmongers needed only to raise the specter of risk in order to frighten the public into demanding governmental and, increasingly, international action on the problem. A risk-averse public is more likely to develop a constellation of antigrowth and antitechnology attitudes. Thus, the 1986 *Challenger* disaster forced the entire American shuttle program to cease operations for several years. The 1979 incident at the Three Mile Island nuclear power plant led to a political stance preventing the approval of any new nuclear power plants. The scientifically questionable theory that the trapping of airborne toxins such as carbon dioxide inside the Earth's atmosphere will lead to global warming now motivates the public to call for the dismantling of whole industries.

Such a climate of fear allows almost any claim to flourish unchallenged. In late 1992, the *New York Times Magazine* section trumpeted on its front page a contention by a biologist that "historically hardy frog species" are becoming extinct. The article suggested that the disappearance of frogs is a harbinger of a worldwide ecological holocaust. It quotes one biologist, "We don't know how many species can be lost before the system ceases to function . . . but eliminate enough species and sooner or later it will cease to function." Edward O. Wilson contributes that we are "in the midst of a cataclysm," caused by many factors, that will upset evolution. The evidence for all these claims is sketchy; it needn't be more conclusive, though, when the public is only looking for reasons to reject technology and the concept of risk.

In May 1993, Wilson himself extended the alarmist argument in a front-page article in *The New York Times Magazine* section entitled "Is Humanity Suicidal?" Here the biologist compared the fate of the human species to that of the dinosaur and other long-lost species. In chronicling our demise, Wilson repeats the familiar claim that through its propensity to overpopulate, pollute the atmosphere, and misuse natural resources, humanity is causing its own extinction. Throughout the article, Wilson demonstrates a complete lack of faith in the human species' ability to survive and thrive through its own ingenuity. In fact, Wilson betrays a decidedly anti-species bias when he summarily rejects any theory that contends that "humankind is transcendent in intelligence and spirit."

A constant barrage of such articles induce the public to believe that the world is a frightening, unpredictable place in which human action can only make matters worse, and to finally come to agree with Wilson that "human and spiritual health depends on sustaining the planet in a relatively unaltered state." Eventually, the alarmist message serves to erode the national will to engage in risk-taking behaviors that lead to human growth and progress.

Without a willingness to accept some level of risk, a society will falter in the coming Macroindustrial Era. Fortunately, polling data demonstrate that a sizable minority is willing to accept some level of risk in order to pursue growth, especially in the areas of energy, health, and biological science. An enlightened national leadership can help a society regain this valuable cultural trait. The public will not abandon its risk-averse mind-set unless the benefits of new technologies are carefully and thoroughly explained. Also, and this most impacts the current energy situation, leadership must convince the public that there are risks involved in choosing *not* to pursue growth-oriented programs and technologies.

Also, knowledge can overcome fear. The more people are brought into the scientific process, as amateurs, professional practitioners, or as informed observers, the less likely they are to fear the unknown. In the final analysis, society will most likely regain its propensity to risk through education.

Progressive Attitudes Toward Immigration

Because immigrants bring with them new energy, fresh ideas, and high commitment, the society with an Expansionary Culture tolerates, if not encourages, a healthy influx of these newcomers.

The continuous infusion of new blood is perhaps one of the real strengths of a select group of countries, including the United States and Canada, and helps them maintain a competitive edge. Whereas most countries are issuing guest worker passes to foreigners, preventing or restricting immigration, and treating with suspicion those foreigners who do attempt to settle, the United States continues to encourage an annual influx of a half-million plus immigrants.

As demographer Julian Simon points out, whereas other countries give lip service to an open society, the United States has incorporated this expansionary sentiment into its very cultural framework. This cultural trait profoundly helps a society compete in the Macroindustrial Era. The United States has long recognized the critical role that fresh talent has played in helping the country flourish throughout history. In an age when knowledge is power, the United States simply does not produce as many knowledge workers—scientists, mathematicians, and engineers—as it needs to retain its position as a first-class technological power.

In 1989, over half of the doctorates in engineering went to foreigners, as did almost half of those granted in math and computer science. At Carnegie-Mellon University, for instance, about 60 percent of the graduate students in science and engineering are foreign, mostly of Indian and Chinese origin. In 1987, foreigners in U.S. universities garnered 32 percent of the business Ph.D.'s and 29 percent of those in the physical sciences.

In our increasingly global society, a myriad of countries contribute to the talent pool. Industry has now become so dependent on foreign graduates of American and other universities that if this foreign supply suddenly dried up, companies would confront a dramatic talent crisis. At Texas Instruments, 25 percent of the Ph.D.'s in its research labs are foreign born. Incredibly, of the 1000 resumes in R&D that Texas Instruments receives every year, only 42 percent are from U.S. citizens. At IBM, 35 percent of the Ph.D.'s hired in R&D in recent years required help with visa conversions. At AT&T's Bell Labs, of all the Ph.D.'s in research, 40 percent are foreign born.

In short, the United States must either begin to produce its knowledge workers here or increase its current immigration level of 12,000 knowledge workers annually to satisfy the demand of academia and business. The State Department is now examining methods to reduce the bureaucratic red tape that immigrants, including newly minted Ph.D.'s, must survive to achieve permanent resident status. The U.S. Chamber of Commerce and the National Association of Manufacturers, whose member companies heavily employ skilled workers, lobbied strongly to produce the first major changes in immigration since 1965. The new immigration law, which went into effect in October 1991, increased the number of employment-related visas from 54,000 to 140,000. This will certainly help companies recruit skilled foreign workers.

Some believe, though, that the new law does not go far enough in ensuring the retention of valued scientists and engineers. Demographer Julian Simon suggests simply giving permanent residence visas to foreign students whose skills are needed here instead of forcing these future contributors to jump bureaucratic hurdles in order to stay in the country.

As the Macroindustrial Era evolves, in the United States and elsewhere, the demand will increase for scientists of all types. Such a demand will emanate not just from the Western developed countries but from the scientists' countries of origin. Countries such as Korea and Taiwan that produce these Ph.D. students obviously would like their citizens to return to build their own industries. For many, their decision to stay in the host country or return home largely depends on how welcome they feel politically, culturally, and occupationally. For instance, some Taiwanese engineering Ph.D.'s return home because they can more quickly take command of several major research projects at such employers as the Industrial Technology Research Institute in Taiwan.

The United States has an advantage here, having essentially pioneered the art of recruiting and retaining immigrants with needed skills. This progressive attitude toward immigration stands as a crucial characteristic of the Expansionary Culture, and the countries without such an expansionary constellation of attitudes will encounter difficulty competing against countries with them.

In Europe, we may observe the most schizophrenic reaction to skilled foreigners: The countries want the labor, they just do not want the workers. Switzerland's guest worker strategy calls for systematically uninviting workers after the workers have labored in the country for a stipulated period of time, and countries like Germany and France have experienced grass roots political backlashes against non-native immigrants. At least in Germany's favor is its commitment to accepting thousands of German-speaking people from Russia, Poland, and other East European countries. Intergroup tension in Europe will be exacerbated by European Community rules that allow foreigners who enter one European Community country to move freely into the other member countries.

Japan's enormous language and cultural barriers and its notorious commitment to preserving its racial homogeneity make permanent immigration to Japan a formidable task for foreigners. Even veteran Japan watchers cannot predict whether that country, needing to draw workers from a culturally and ethnically diverse international labor market, will suddenly throw open its arms to foreign workers. As an alternative to immigration, Japan may simply export its own industry to countries that possess a large pool of skilled labor. Japan can then employ on non-Japanese territory foreign engineers and scientists without having these skilled workers move to Japan. Honda's billboard advertisements heralding its Accord automobile as 100 percent "homegrown" is not that far from the truth: It is built by American labor in American-based plants.

The problem with such "outsourcing" to foreign soil is that the country of origin may eventually lose its manufacturing base. It no longer maintains its own factories, and its native workers lose critical manufacturing skills. In essence, it increasingly depends for its economic growth on foreigners working in distant lands. Japan's decline, if it ever should occur, will be inextricably linked to its inability to get its culture past its bias against the *ginseng*, the foreigner.

In reality, critics of progressive immigration policies do not comprehend the finer points of an Expansionary Culture. Ultimate societal objectives must include progress and growth, and society must do whatever is necessary to achieve such goals. The United States has been tinkering with its immigration policy for most of the twentieth century. It now realizes that changing international economic conditions require some enhancement of the immigration policy to ensure that fresh perspectives and renewed energy found its way to its shore.

A progressive attitude toward immigration ensures that the national talent pool increases. The willingness of the United States to accept all talented individuals who agree to be Americanized may prove its redemption.

Now it is projected that the U.S. population will grow dramatically from 1993 to 2050, from its current 250 million to a mid-twenty-first-century level of about 383 million, a full 50 percent increase. Although American women are reproducing at barely the replacement rate, the influx of close to 1 million immigrants per year will send the population numbers zooming, because most immigrants, optimistic over the improved economic and life chances in their new home country, reproduce at significantly higher rates than the native American population. Already California must build on average one new school per day to educate the burgeoning school-age population, mostly the children of those immigrating to the United States in the 1970s and 1980s. We can only hope that these children will help shepherd the United States into a leadership position in the Macroindustrial Era.

A Well-Integrated Citizenry

An integrated society is one in which the large majority of the population, even if comprised of a diverse set of ethnic and racial groups, draw their identity from the culture and are likewise recognized as members of that society by other members.

If the majority or large minority of a society's inhabitants draw their primary identity from their ethnic origins, sex, social class, occupation, or any geographic subunit of the larger unit, we can deduce that such a society has yet to achieve integration. In addition, in the integrated system members largely share the same cultural and values systems. That is not to say that the members do not disagree, sometimes vehemently, on policy and philosophical issues, but the people share the same worldview.

In the Macroindustrial Era, the society that can fully integrate both new and old members will have a distinct advantage over more fragmented societies. The reasons for this are varied, and their subtlety eludes many social observers. The issue, however, is well worth exploring.

Integration and the Macroindustrial Mission

There are several reasons why this specific trait of the Expansionary Culture, a well-integrated citizenry, is necessary for a nation to compete in the Macroindustrial Era and, conversely, why lack of such integration could actually serve as a hindrance to a nation's economic and technological success.

Consensus over Societal Goals

In the Macroindustrial Era, a society will succeed when its members agree with the nation's goals and objectives. The more well integrated a society is, the more easily it can arrive at a group consensus over major goals and projects. Because the value system is already shared by the vast majority of individuals, such a society can unabashedly speak in terms of "we" when articulating nationwide programs and goals. It already understands that the members' sentiments are reflected in such goals.

Societies whose occupants are fractious, warring, even tribal, will distrust every dictum that descends from the political councils. Conspiratorial views of the political process usually develop among groups who suffer a tenuous integration into the larger society.

Integration and Self-Esteem

Individuals who are accepted as members of a society will tend to have higher self-esteem than those who are not, and the person who has high regard for him- or herself will naturally translate such high self-esteem into high performance. For this reason, any country hoping to succeed in the Macroindustrial Era must signal to its citizens that society values them as individuals. Indications to any group that they are less a member tends to depress the value that such groups place on themselves, which can directly affect job and academic performance.

Integration and Occupational Opportunity

Again, integration exists on two levels: the extent to which individuals feel affiliation to the group and the extent to which the group accepts them.

This second aspect of integration has special meaning in the emerging Macroindustrial Era. As I have mentioned throughout this book, societies thrive to the extent that the best and the brightest, regardless of their racial and ethnic background, are allowed to rise to the top and perform to the best of their abilities. Although such sentiments are usually defended on moral grounds, they are less frequently supported in terms of national self-interest. Certainly, in the economic arena full integration helps a society.

In the early part of the twentieth century, Jews began to knock at the doors of the American economic and academic establishment. Although they were unmistakably talented, they had the misfortune of being cultural outsiders, a fact that lead Harvard and other major institutions to place quotas on the admission of Jews. Hitler and the Nazis deemed Jews outsiders at a time when a sizable minority of German Jews already felt fully integrated into German society.

In all such cases, the society deprives itself of the talents of these groups' best and brightest and suffers declining productivity and economic stagnation. The German case is most ironic, because key physicists and natural scientists were Jewish. Some believe that when Hitler forced this group into exile, he deprived himself of achieving true technological superiority in both the economic and military realms.

Little doubt exists that, even in the United States, key government, financial, and corporate positions are subtly placed off-limits to certain groups. Women's caucuses have made the point for years that there are few women on the corporate boards or in the ranks of senior management of Fortune 1000 companies. This critique begs the question, as neither are there many blacks, Jews, Hispanics, or Americans of non-WASP background in the upper echelons of corporate America. Although social analyst Robert. C. Christopher claims that there is a "DeWASPING of America's Power Elite," very little empirical or anecdotal evidence supports such a contention, at least in regard to the key areas of American policy and practice.

This state of affairs stems from the fact that certain groups are considered less than full members of the society and thus unworthy of assuming key positions of responsibility. But in the process of exclusion, the society incurs as much damage as does the excluded individuals, though, because such exclusion automatically limits the size of the talent pool from which key positions are filled.

Such a state of affairs may explain why Indians, Taiwanese, and Filipinos, whether born in America or elsewhere, enter the sciences and the computer fields in such large numbers. They may already sense that Western society considers them to an extent outsiders and would exclude them from positions in management and government. Not so in the hard sciences, where companies and universities make such biased judgments at their own peril. It is amazing how little race and ethnicity matter to high-tech firms starving for computer professionals, physicists, and genetic biologists.

In the Expansionary Culture, people achieve membership not through ethnicity, religion, or race, but through a willingness to be a member of the society, ascribe to its values, and contribute to its success. Talent then becomes the primary criterion for selection for even the key power positions. Hence, full integration expands the available talent pool, allowing a society to utilize all members' skills to the maximum.

America: Test Case for the Macroindustrial Era

In many ways the demographic changes that the United States has begun to experience and will continue to encounter for the next half century at least portend variations in population composition that a good part of the globe, especially the West, may expect. Therefore, the success or failure of the United States in assimilating the new groups into its overall value structure and economic mission carry implications for the evolution of global society.

The U.S. population mix is undergoing significant change. In 1970, 4.7 percent of the country was foreign born. In 1990, 8.6 percent came from elsewhere. At current rates of immigation, America in 2040 will be composed of 14.2 percent foreign-born.

As mentioned earlier, the U.S. population will rise significantly. Because native birth rates have been falling since 1964, however, immigration will account for a fair share of the population growth. Until recently, the ethnic makeup of immigrants was largely European, but 88 percent of the immigration today is from Latin America and Asia.

This means that the number of Asian-Americans may jump fivefold, from 7 million in 1990 to 35 million in 2040. Hispanics may triple to 64 million to become the nation's largest minority. Non-Hispanic whites will still make up the majority of the U.S. population but may grow only to 211 million in 2040, from 187 million in 1990.

In short, the United States will become increasingly populated by people from groups who are of non-European stock. Various predictions have been made whether the United States will successfully integrate these peoples as members of American society.

Before we deal with this issue, let us understand why countries in the Macroindustrial Era will be required to increase immigration and thus be confronted with the integration issue. Although humanitarian concerns certainly guide immigration policy, the overriding reasons will be the absorption of new talent, increase of the skilled labor supply, recruitment of entrepreneurs, and simply the need for new blood and fresh ideas.

Societies that stymie immigration will find themselves isolated from the talent pool and eventually will be driven by international economic competition to recruit from outside their borders.

The United States recognized long ago that it would have to depend on immigration to meet its skill needs and populate the country. Each major change, including the Industrial Revolution, the building of the huge infrastructure in the late nineteenth century, and the extension of its border to the Pacific Coast, led the United States to encourage immigration from Europe and elsewhere. The Macroindustrial Era has already forced changes in America's immigration laws to permit the influx of entrepreneurs and high-tech workers.

The coming American experiment will succeed if on the one hand the country accepts the new members not only as citizens but as members, and on the other hand the new citizens and their descendants assume an identity as Americans. In other words, what must transpire is integration of the new immigrants into the social fabric.

For the United States to acquire a well-integrated citizenry, several conditions must be met, which will be contingent on actions of both the existing society and the new members. For one, certain values must be preserved. The predominant values of Western society must be maintained and learned by all members, regardless of their race. The United States, regardless of its ever-changing ethnic composition, is an embodiment of several centuries of Western values, including the faith in progress, materialism, optimism, and freedom. We can truly say that the American identity is fused in such a value system. Any attempt to replace or destroy these values could quickly lead to cultural and social disintegration.

Second, the United States may soon discover that integration may be better achieved if all its citizens downplay their national, racial, and ethnic origins. Although this suggestion may sound radical, many now agree that an over-emphasis on race and national origins can lead to fragmentation and chaos. People who adhere to their ethnic and racial identities are only forestalling acceptance of their new identity as Americans.

I believe that Americans in the 1990s will receive an invaluable education on the negative consequences of the overemphasis on racial and ethnic differences. Lesson 1 may be the turmoil in what was previously Yugoslavia. We nightly see the horror, bloodshed, and social disruption caused by the Yugoslav fixation on the establishment of Bosnian and Serbian ethnic purity! How quickly diversity devolves into rigid and rabid tribalism.

However, questions arise. Even if we agree that an overemphasis on racial and ethnic roots may lead to divisiveness, how do we overcome what seems to be a natural tendency to notice differences? Part of the answer may lie in the development of an overall Expansionary culture as described in this chapter. People living in such a culture look to the future and have a vested interest in progress. As people become more concerned about the future, they may realize that an overemphasis on race undermines the societal solidarity needed to achieve the goals and projects they all consider worthy. If they are truly goal oriented, they will avoid whatever would tend to create conflict and deflect from the achievement of the goal.

There is a third condition that must be met if a society hopes to achieve full integration. This condition is related to a factor that, though rarely discussed, has a tremendous influence on both the extent to which a society considers a person a member and the extent to which a person perceives him- or herself to be a member. When people do discuss this factor, they usually do so in whispers.

In the United States, one of the clandestine battles that has been waged for decades concerns what we mean by "looking American." A country whose population hails from all over the globe should feature a myriad of representations of its people. However, many would argue that the acceptable face, the right nose, the correct facial angle and body height, have been predefined. It is more than the image of beauty at issue here. No, what concerns us is who does and does not "look" American and the effect such impressions will have on any individual's ability to be considered a true member of society. The United States will wrestle mightily with this image over the next half century. The battles will take place on billboards, on magazine covers, in movies, in *Playboy* magazine, and certainly in soap operas and TV sitcoms.

When the hero gets the girl, will an increasingly brown America accept a blond-haired maiden? Will advertisements for cars and colas still feature models seemingly transported from the American West? Does a country increasingly made up of Indians and Hispanics want its seven o'clock news read by a Canadian WASP? Will these new ethnic groups consider a Miss America contest in which most of the semifinalists are young Southern debutantes a rigged election? Will a population with a shrinking white European component insist their image portrayed in ads and movies remain essentially white?

The physical image America will project of itself has and will continue to have a profound effect on its citizens. In a society, to feel like a member and to be integrated into it a person must feel welcome. Open educational, occupational, and housing systems, along with laws protecting all citizens from discrimination, help a person feel like a member of that society.

If a person, however, finds that people who look like her are largely absent from the advertisements and billboards, that no characters of her ethnic or racial background appear in sitcoms or soaps, she may receive certain signals about how the culture really operates. One is that the society has a certain persona that it wishes to portray in regard to itself, and that persona is not hers. Second, society does not consider her a full member of the group. Third, society may be suggesting a ranking of races and ethnicity, in which lower ranks have less chance of achieving visibility in the media. This third signal could influence the individual's self-esteem in ways discussed earlier in this section.

The ability of America to achieve full integration will be contingent on the willingness of the media to represent the entire spectrum of the population in commercials, dramas, and news programs. Hopefully, the rest of the world will be taking notes.

Individual Freedom

The human spirit, free and unfettered by the constraint of government and society, has been the mechanism by which the West has gotten to the material plateau we currently inhabit. As we enter the Macroindustrial Era, that human spirit, left unbridled, will elevate civilization to even greater heights.

Freedom has become a cultural constant because it liberates the mind of each individual to dream and create without fear of censorship or criticisim. In effect, this freedom forms a protective psychological boundary around the individual.

In spite of the modern contention that teamwork and group brainstorming techniques form the nexus of all creative work, in reality all ideas originate with the individual. He or she may read others' work or collaborate on research, but the major scientific breakthroughs, the great works of music and literature, and the unique inventions are generated by individual thought and concentration. Rarely do we apply the word *inspiration* to group processes.

The Expansionary Culture, by definition, is one in which the individual has the freedom and receives the encouragement to actualize his or her creations. The culture also places great emphasis on personal experimentation. Such freedom, which presumes openness of expression and communication, is a trademark of Western society. Totalitarian and authoritarian countries that want to achieve real progress—such as the CIS (Commonwealth of Independent States), and China—realize that they must sooner or later begin to emulate the West.

This individual freedom depends greatly on one particular condition: The individuals must be afforded a great deal of privacy. The right to be left alone is a cornerstone of individual personal development. Some theorists and judicial experts have posited that privacy is the basis of all human freedom.

Nothing threatens the development of an Expansionary Culture more than the intrusion of government and corporation into the privacy of individuals and families. The assault on privacy has developed on several fronts.

One area of potential violation of individual privacy is drugs and drug testing. Companies and government agencies consider employees' drug use so detrimental to safety and productivity that many have decided to engage in on-site drug testing. Several states, responding to civil rights violations lawsuits, have banned involuntary testing, but companies still insist that what their employees do on their own time can affect company welfare. Companies continue the pressure to test employees and applicants for drugs.

By 1993, drug arrests had clogged courts, jammed jails, and diverted law enforcement funds and judicial time from a host of other crimes and concerns. Worse, the drug laws were becoming a method the government was using to enlarge its powers over individuals and families. One operation, known as DARE, sponsored police officer visits to schools to encourage students to share any information they had about parental drug use with the authorities. The United States experienced its first spate of child informants sending parents to jail.

Social critic Stanton Peele railed against the entire rehabilitation industry. Peele termed this process the "diseasing of America," in which all citizens are suspected of suffering from some mental disease or addiction. He claimed that addiction treatment has gotten out of control.

In the future, some argue, individuals will lose their freedoms not through armed coup d'état or foreign invasion. They will gradually lose control of their rights through a process whereby the state redefines more and more actions (e.g., high-cholesterol diets) as deviant. The fear is that such redefinition of behavior may subject increasing numbers of citizens to enforced rehabilitation. In California, in the late 1970s, a feminist group seriously suggested that the state should forcibly enter into treatment those workers found to suffer from male chauvinist attitudes.

As Peele has demonstrated, the excessive use of rehabilitation and wars on drugs and other addictions, while rarely solving the targeted problem, often undermines citizens' civil liberties.

Individual freedom can also be threatened by advances in computer and electronic surveillance. Employers are claiming the right to monitor employee telephone calls to and from the workplace, and they are also monitoring electronic mail, which serves as a conduit for the employees sharing of ideas and opinions. Such monitoring of private information threatens the creative spirit companies need to increase productivity.

The violation of individual privacy through the computer occurs in other ways. We are all by now familiar with how a range of interested parties, including credit bureaus, market research companies, nosey lovers, and private investigators can commit gross intrusions into our private lives by gaining access to computer data banks. Such banks contain a myriad of facts and myths about us—our credit rating, purchasing habits, travel plans, work history, school records, and court battles. Such data can be accessed through a variety of means, many of which are vaguely legal.

This loss of privacy again threatens citizens' autonomy and freedom, as do the use of lie detector tests on the job, genetic screening of potential employees, and unnecessary AIDS tests.

Although we become sensitized to the more egregious intrusions, we underestimate the potential of seemingly benign practices to rip apart our private lives. For instance, television programs seem to be making a habit of intruding on ordinary people's lives and broadcasting footage on local and national TV. This type of journalism is a direct descendant of "eyewitness reports" style in which the news is reported on the scene as it happens. Unfortunately, what the media considers news has expanded to the point wherein almost any occurrence outside of private homes is considered fair game for public exposure.

This constant intrusion may have long-term harmful effects. People need space, privacy, and room to breathe in order to create and express themselves. The constant feeling that someone is lurking in the background, hand on VCR, can eventually deaden the population's creative edge. People require the psychological room to make mistakes, express themselves at their worst, if necessary. Rob people of their privacy and you sabotage their creativity!

In the Macroindustrial Era, personal freedom must be a paramount cultural trait. Any attempts to shrink individual autonomy or obstruct interpersonal communication must be countered by judicial and political action. The body social must maintain vigilance especially against the more benign forms of government and organizational intrusion that may eventually result in loss of liberty.

A Vibrant Artistic Milieu

The society that possesses an Expansionary Culture is the beneficiary of lively and vibrant developments in art, music, and other media.

A definite connection exists between a society's artistic development and its overall progress on the technological and material levels. Artists —and that includes everyone from sitcom writers to rock musicians— can play a critical role in a nation's growth. It is hardly an accident that great periods of exploration and societal growth are accompanied by an explosion of artistic fervor and creative activity. During the Renaissance, the same curiosity and optimism fueled scientific discovery, artistic breakthroughs, and geographical exploration. We can speak in one sentence of Columbus, Michelangelo, Galileo, and Shakespeare, because they all breathed the same air of freedom and human creativity.

Breakthroughs in the arts, science, and space exploration were all generated by the same cultural dynamic. In the Macroindustrial Era, a vibrant artistic milieu will be an important crucible for the further development of science and exploration, and signs abound that the species is about to break out of its artistic lethargy.

For instance, a musical subculture thrives outside the bounds of MTV and FM radio stations. Composers like Philip Glass challenge the bounds of sound and common taste and fill concert halls all over the world. Laurie Anderson represents the apotheosis of new music, presenting truly multimedia performances. Anderson uses electronic violin and filtered voices, even singing duets with herself through a gizmo called the vocoder. Her performances combine social criticism, dance, video, original musical creations, along with what at times seems to be a cryptic form of stand-up comedy.

Danny Elfman writes movie scores for the *Batman* series and a host of other films, music so grandiose that he might be the Macroindustrial Era's Wagner. Vangelis, known for his scoring of the movie *Chariots of Fire,* has been charting totally new areas of musical expression since the late 1970s. Yanni, hailing from Greece like Vangelis, is a proponent of what has been loosely labeled New Age music. Enya, a female composer/singer/producer from Ireland, mixes modern technology with Gaelic and Irish folk tunes to develop totally new sounds.

The experimenters on the musical frontier are not heard through the usual commercial media. However, each influences the culture and forms an artistic vanguard critical to scientific and technological growth.

These artists are creating at a level of artistic accomplishment that in a certain sense has no roots and is without precedent. Philip Glass, a graduate of Juilliard, created his music simply because he did not hear the music in his head being created by anyone else. He wrote primarily to bring these innovative melodies and structures into existence. (He paid the price, driving a cab until age forty-two.)

According to a very loose estimate, this new music recorded sales in 1990 in the area of of $70 million, paltry in comparison to rock music's annual revenues. However, the effort may well be worth it. According to one critic, the experimental music endeavor "has captured the pioneering character of influential new music and adult listeners have responded dramatically."

Increasingly, we will see the nonprofessional drawn into the arts. With the aid of modern technology, a person can sit at a music synthesizer and reprogram any piece of music to a different key or different instrumentation. We can now with the flick of a wrist hear Beethoven's Pastoral Symphony as it would sound played by guitars and saxophone or add our own additional themes. Through computer animation and a video camcorder we can add our own images to film to star in *Gone With the Wind* or *The Wizard of Oz* or change the plot line of these films.

Thus, in the coming era, the artistic milieu will include a greater number of people. Technology will be a key catalyst in such an expansion of the artistic milieu. In fact, it can be said that there may be as close a relationship between art and science as in earlier periods of inventive explosions. Artists are now forced to master fiber optics, computer interfaces, sound wave theory, and laser technology to practice in their field competently.

Artists, through their own search for perfection, will serve as an example to the rest of the population. They ought not to shy away from the complex and the difficult. After all, much of the material each of us will have to master to survive in this next era will require intelligence and concentration.

The artists, musicians, and writers of the emerging era must be intense and passionate and most importantly provide the path into the future. Instead of reflecting the reality of the current age, they ought to envision the next one.

Naturally, although I have described the Expansionary culture in terms of its individual dimensions, these subcomponents are ultimately interdependent. A nation with an open attitude toward immigration has probably already accepted the need to integrate these new citizens. A country that senses that it has a purpose, a destiny, will most likely display a positive national outlook and be willing to take risks to achieve its destiny. The respect for material production and consumption inhibits the tendency to glorify the ethereal.

The Expansionary Culture is a unified concept, something a country experiences in its totality. Is any country at this point the proud possessor of an Expansionary Culture? The United States exhibits some of the fundamental traits, such as individuality and open attitudes toward immigration, but simultaneously seems to be flirting with the ethereal. Japan has become solidly progrowth and has a strong sense of purpose but seems hesitant to open up the society to outsiders.

Once they realize that the Expansionary Culture is a critical component of national growth, countries and their citizens may try consciously to change the nature and direction of their cultures toward the Expansionary model. This will put them well on the road to excellence in the Macroindustrial Era.

10: Seize the Future!

Crossing the Threshold to the Macroindustrial Era

To colonize space, extend the life span, and feed an ever growing population, the species must develop a well-defined strategy and a precise plan of action. In this chapter I present several steps that must be taken by governments, private groups and organizations, and, most importantly, the individual in order to ensure society's smooth transition into the next era (Table 10.1).

Some of these items are more global in scope and would probably require national action and/or international cooperation. However, the transition into the Macroindustrial Era will only occur if the majority of the world's citizens desire it. Therefore, national and corporate leaders must act together to develop a global and national movement that will propel the species into the Macroindustrial Era.

To seize the future, humanity must dedicate its brains, its hands, and certainly its spirit and will.

Stepping-stones to the Macroindustrial Era

Aggressively Pursue 5 to 7 Percent Hypergrowth per Annum

As the Macroindustrial Era represents a whole new level of invention and expansion of human ability, it is clear that such breakthroughs call for a total reconceptualization of our expectations about economic growth.

This 5 to 7 percent range seems large only because the West's citizenry has been induced by circumstances and ideology to maintain a lowered sense of expectations about future growth. Major periods of

Stepping-stones to the Macroindustrial Era

- Aggressively pursue 5 to 7 percent hypergrowth per annum
- Foster international growth and prosperity
- Establish an international mentor system
- Enhance international communication
- Support self-determination in population issues
- Refocus our attention on early childhood development
- Redefine the life cycle
- Restructure educational priorities
- Enhance technological involvement
- Emancipate the power structure
- The culture must include expansionary thinking
- Make growth and progress part of the political dialogue

economic expansion, such as the nineteenth-century Industrial Revolution in the United States and Europe, featured growth rates much higher than present levels. Seemingly erased from our national consciousness is the memory that as recently as the 1960–1972 period the United States prospered, expanding at an average 3.8 percent per year with minimal inflation. In some of those years, GNP growth actually approached the baseline of my hypergrowth projections.

During the post-oil embargo years of 1973–1985, the growth rate dropped to 2.3 percent per annum, and in some of those years the U.S. economy actually contracted. Except for the late 1980s, during the period in which the Reagan tax cuts had their greatest positive effects, the growth rate over the last twenty years has been below that of the 1960s. By 1990, the rate returned to a sluggish 1.7 percent per annum return, and in 1991, the economy slowed down to recessionary levels.

These low-growth rates are not a worldwide phenomenon. Until very recently, Japan has comfortably sustained 5+ percent GNP annual increments. Over the last twenty years, Singapore has experienced a GNP per annum increment of 7.6 percent, Taiwan, one of 7.2 percent, and Hong Kong, 6.1 percent. South Korea experiences similar rates. Is it any wonder that the world now refers to the Southeast Asia countries as the Five Dragons? Chile has overcome its economic and political problems to become so prosperous as to be labeled "Latin America's tiger." Its growing businesses, including the production and exportation of canned goods, furniture, wine, and food, has sent its GNP soaring to a 9.7 percent rate. Latin American countries such as Argentina and Venezuela are not far behind.

If we are ever to approximate such high growth rates on a worldwide basis, we must dispense with the idea of the business cycle. It has taken civilization centuries to exorcise from its culture the illusion of cyclical thinking and replace it with a meaningful concept of social and economic progress. Still, economists continue to talk about and think in terms of "business cycles," when any objective observer knows that on a material basis alone over the last ten years, fifty years, and one hundred years the species has experienced steady growth. If cyclical theory had any basis in reality, after each period of prosperity, society would regress to its earlier material state. Yet history proves that real progress does really occur: Our material state improves, building on each new peak, to reach higher levels of productive achievements: better products, longer lives, the capacity to move faster and live healthier. Progress is a reality!

We must also divest ourselves of cyclical theory's second cousin, the mechanistic image of the economy. Orthodox views perceive economic systems as mechanical engines that will "overheat" if they run too quickly or work too fast. In this view, a 3 percent increase in GNP must invariably be followed by a recession, a resting place. In fact, economists adhering to this model defend the need for recessions on the basis that somehow the system will permanently malfunction if it operates full tilt for extended periods of time. This particular configuration of cyclical growth theory has economists already anticipating the next economic downturn even during the boom periods.

By ignoring the Imperative of Growth and embracing the doctrine of the economic cycle, modern economists have built stop lights and yield signs into the system. When linked with cultural predispositions toward simplicity and the ethereal, the conditions are established for a downward spiral in spending and industrial growth.

Countries like Japan are succeeding not because they are smarter or work harder than Western nations. They have merely recognized the cyclical as essentially an exercise in self-delusion. In his book *Why Japan Will Be the First Among Equals*, Ishihara, author and head of Japan's Liberal Democratic party, berates the U.S. citizenry, academics, and policymakers for considering zero or low GNP growth acceptable. He warns the West that such rates may lead to economic stagnation.

With a 5 to 7 percent annual GNP increase, we can expect a doubling in the standard of living within ten to fourteen years or, with minor adjustments for unforseen factors, twenty years on the outside. These numbers translate into tangible improvements in the quality and quantity of life for a nation's population. Hong Kong, a city-state that does enjoy such growth rates, has a growing per capita income, a real estate boom, and, not coincidentally, the highest density of Mercedes in the world. Such annual growth rates would buy us the time to enjoy our lives, to raise families that can live well on one income, and ultimately to afford us the leisure to invent our next growth period. Such conditions are, after all, the most fertile for the sprouting of a renaissance in the arts and sciences.

Such economic hypergrowth depends on the abundant supply of cheap energy. New energy supplies and technologies must continually be developed in order to meet the demands of the Macroindustrial growth rates. The species is already responding to such needs. For instance, Westinghouse Corporation is busy building new nuclear power plants all over the world (except in the United States). Japan is importing plutonium from the Commonwealth of Independent States and France to fuel its new fast reactors. The United States, if it hopes to increase its growth rate, must build an estimated 250 power plants before 2010.

We may witness the development of a world energy grid in which countries agree to supply energy to other nations. This already happens on a regional basis: France supplies electricity to Germany and other countries, Canada provides the United States' hydropower, and nations provide uranium and oil to other countries. The next step may be a U.N.-style agency that monitors and facilitates such energy transfers to ensure economic hypergrowth.

Because of the critical role cheap and available energy plays in economic growth, both the citizenry and industry rightfully grow nervous at any suggestions that we increase taxes on energy consumption and production. As many critics are beginning to realize, such a tax, like the one President Clinton proposed in the hope of reducing the U.S. budget deficit, will stifle economic growth. Because energy comprises 40 percent or more of the cost of manufacturing a product, any significant increase in the price of energy could make manufacturing on U.S. soil a prohibitive venture.

In the Macroindustrial Era, all efforts must be made to not only make energy as cheap and abundant as possible, but also to develop a plethora of new forms of energy. Only then can we be reasonably certain of sustaining economic hypergrowth rates of 7 percent or better.

Foster International Growth and Prosperity

In the Macroindustrial Era, each country's prosperity will greatly depend on the growth and productivity of other nations. This means that all countries must be both consumers and producers of goods and services as well as inventors of the next generation of technology. How much more prosperity we would all enjoy if we had all 5 billion minds creating and building the macroindustrial world.

Certainly, we are rapidly moving in the direction of a global macroindustrial system. This century has already seen the inclusion of countries such as India, Japan, the aforementioned Five Dragons of the Far East, and a host of other non-Western countries in the global economic system as consumers and producers of goods. And a few Latin American countries such as Chile and Venezuela are making remarkable economic strides. Nevertheless, a sizable portion of the world population is excluded not only from the current prosperity enjoyed by the developed and developing countries, but from the production system as well.

The developed countries, representing roughly one-fifth of the world's population, must quickly take steps to bring the remaining four-fifths up to speed economically and technologically. As daunting as it may seem, global macroindustrialization can take place within two generations. However, this will happen only if several events transpire.

First, the developed countries must become convinced that global prosperity will benefit them. To a degree, they have already accepted the basic premise of cross-national interdependency. Most economists understand that the economies of Japan and the United States, for instance, have become sufficiently intertwined so that prosperity and boom in one country generates growth in the other. For some reason, though, the reality eludes most analysts that enhanced per capita productivity of a half-billion Africans can exert a similar positive effect on the U.S. or Japanese economy.

Second, the West must begin to shift its focus from merely maintaining world order to becoming a catalyst for global prosperity and growth. In order to help countries achieve economic growth, the West must adopt new attitudes toward Third World technological development, especially in the area of energy and biotechnology. Although Western leaders proclaim a dedication to global prosperity, they seem to harbor a profound apprehension about Third World countries acquiring the technology necessary to become truly wealthy.

The nuclear power issue exemplifies this contradiction. Although no Westerner openly denies any country's right to energy independence, many Western policymakers consider the spread of nuclear technologies to the Third World a security risk. They defend this position by contending that nuclear power plant technology could be diverted to weapons research and development.

As the French paper *Le Monde* has stated, taken to extremes this restrictive policy "would be tantamount to reserving nuclear energy for the rich, forcing poorer countries to content themselves with simpler forms of energy." Ironically, such policies would force Third World countries to revert to the use of such known pollutants as coal.

The West has exhibited similar opposition to Third World development of a viable space program. In mid-1993 Russia bowed to intense pressure from the Clinton administration to renege on a $350 million contract to supply India with sophisticated rocket engines and related aeronautic technology. The United States claimed that it feared that such rockets could be used as part of a delivery system for nuclear warheads. But the Indians responded that they needed the Russian rocket engines to develop their own program to manufacture and launch commercial rockets. India suspected that the United States was really trying to prevent India from offering cut-rate deals on private space launches that Western companies could not match.

Environmental groups would also restrict global prosperity, but for reasons different than the more conservative governmental policy elite. As enviromentalists made clear at the 1992 ecology conference held in Rio de Janeiro, Third World countries must not go down the dangerous path of fossil fuel and nuclear energy technologies. They must seriously consider utilizing more benign energy sources (such as windmills and biomass). If this choice forces these countries to develop a simpler life-style, so be it.

Although emerging from two totally divergent ideologies, the solution to these problems lead to the same result: restricted economic growth for the Third World. A danger is that environmentalists and political leaders allow such concerns about the ultimate use of advanced technologies in the Third World to undermine our commitment to the inclusion of these countries in the evolving Macroindustrial production system.

Third, to foster international growth, countries must develop a system of open trade and free movement of labor and material. We already see the proliferation of agreements supporting such principles, including the European Community's various treaties and the recently adopted North American Free Trade Agreement between the United States, Canada, and Mexico. Such agreements should guarantee that the signing countries can exchange goods without fear of restrictive tariffs and that the citizens of such countries can immigrate to and work in the other countries.

Encouraged by its current economic successes, Chile wants to become the next beneficiary of a free trade agreement with the United States. According to Jose Antonio Guzman, president of Chile's Confederation of Production and Commerce, "If Chile is acceptable as a partner to the U.S., it will draw the attention of investors. A free-trade agreement can bring in investment from third countries seeking access to the U.S. market."

Yes, the West must cease merely mouthing homilies about the need for world economic growth and become a catalyst in the development of global prosperity.

Establish an International Mentor System

The United States and other leading societies should establish a formal network of advice and aid to help the developing countries fully participate in the Macroindustrial Era. Because the West has spent the better part of the last several centuries mastering the art of adaptation and growth, it is in an optimum position to serve as a guide, tutor, coach, in fact mentor, to many of the developing countries. Western countries can show the emerging nations how to adapt and progress, providing counsel in the economic, political, and social areas.

Changing demographics mandate this. Quite simply, the industrial democracies, countries such as the United States, Canada, Japan, Italy, Spain, and the United Kingdom, represent a shrinking proportion of the world's population. In 1950, fully 22 percent, or one out of five, individuals on the globe lived in the industrial democracies. By 1985, only 15 percent of the world's population resided there. By the year 2030, only 9 percent of the world's population will live in the countries mentioned above. By the end of the twenty-first century, a mere handful, 5 percent, of the world's population will be living in the geographical space that the industrial democracies currently occupy.

Because it is unlikely that only 5 percent of the world will perform the major share of the world's production and invention, the major productive and creative work of the Macroindustrial Era will be performed by countries other than the current Western democracies. In the next era, there must be a global system in which all nations produce and consume at peak performance levels, fulfilling the productive and economic functions that the West had until recently.

The West must pass its brilliantly burning torch to those who will help continue the work of the human species, spreading its knowledge and, importantly, the "habit of progress," to other countries. The Western media is already teaching the world to be good consumers; the West must now extend to the world the tools to unlock the creativity and innovative powers of the billions.

A formal international mentor system, in which the developed countries can systematically transmit their knowledge, cultural ideals, and values to the emerging countries, should therefore be established posthaste. Such a program would include several components. The industrialized countries could establish universities inside the borders of their protégé nations that would impart scientific, technical, and business skills necessary for the next era. Such an education would also provide students with a sense of the West's historical development and examine with them the role of the Expansionary Culture as a necessary foundation of hyperprogress.

The mentor program would also involve policymakers and academics of the mentor country working directly with the business, political, and scientific leaders of the protégé country, providing a wealth of information on how to succeed in the emerging era. This could include leadership conferences, seminars, and more interpersonal mentoring between key personnel of each country.

Such a program could be formalized to the point that specific two-way relationships could be established between Canada and Peru or the United States and Nigeria, for example, for a set period of five or ten years. By formalizing this relationship, each country can determine the key players in such a program. Universities, businesses, and citizens of the mentor and protégé nations would be invited to submit proposals describing the services or training they would provide the protégé country. Importantly, the countries could establish a central bureau or agency to evaluate the proposals, oversee and monitor the diverse activities, and even provide training for potential mentors.

In short, this program would represent a national effort in both mentor and protégé nations. The mentor country would also reap benefits from such a program. Such close two-way relationships would enable the mentor country to gain an in-depth knowledge of the protégé nation's culture and history. Such a program also could potentially lead to trade agreements and cooperation in scientific and business projects.

Enhance International Communication

In the Macroindustrial Era, information and knowledge will become the lifeblood of global society. The more individuals and organizations know, the easier it is to advance their technologies, enhance their skills, and improve their lives and their societies. Although the international mentor system will already serve as a structured conduit for information and knowledge in a structured manner, there should also exist an open system of informal information transfer, including satellite transmissions, radio broadcasts, and print media distribution.

Because information is so crucial to the achievement of material progress, its flow must not be impeded by government or business, unless national security is at stake, and even in that case such restriction ought not to be abused. Communication between nations must be two-way—West–East, East–West, North–South, South–North.

Today, the flow of information between countries varies tremendously. For years European countries attempted to prevent CNN from broadcasting to the average Belgian or French, even while American hotels situated in these cities could receive this American news channel. Reasons for this restriction varied: CNN competed against European news channels for viewership; its advertisements promoted American products; and Europeans simply wanted to control signals that descended from the skies on their country. A more troubling contention is that European governments, realizing the propaganda potential of the mass media, did not want an American TV network influencing their citizens' view of the world and current events.

Third World countries in the 1980s tried to convince the U.N. to establish a so-called global information order, which called for, among other things, all foreign journalists working in their countries to clear news stories through these countries' governments before wiring the story to their home newspaper.

Both the government and the citizens must resist such restrictions. As the Macroindustrial Era evolves, the species will understand that it has more to lose by restricting information than by sharing it. As the distance colleges and universities proliferate, we will witness more and more of these institutions providing instruction across national borders through satellite and cable technologies. Such innovations will enhance international learning and increase global productivity.

At some point, governments will just have to relinquish their control over information. International fiber-optic systems, along with sophisticated encryption technologies, will make the transmission of images and data untrackable, undecodable, and unstoppable. We will all be the better for it!

Support Self-Determination in Population Issues

Based on our knowledge of the causes and effects of population growth, societies ought to take a laissez-faire approach to this issue and concentrate more on improving global economic conditions.

Many in the West demonstrate an unsettling tendency to regard population growth in developing and Third World countries with a mixture of suspicion and fear. In light of the poverty and hunger that plague certain regions, such reactions are understandable. However, as we have seen, there is no reason to assume that a large population "causes" poverty and hunger any more than a small population does. A barren agricultural system or a poorly operating economy will impoverish a nation whose population stands at a thousand, a million, or a billion people.

On the other hand, large populations present opportunities for growth: Quickly growing populations tend to draw investment; dense populations tend to make better use of their land and infrastructure; large populations are associated with economic growth; and they also enlarge the human genetic pool from which we draw our talented and creative individuals. As the research of Julian Simon and others concludes, although we cannot speak of an ideal demographic growth rate, in economic terms, growing populations tend to do better than contracting populations. Fears that such populations will live in overcrowded conditions and outstrip the storehouse of available food, materials, and energy are grossly overstated. In the Macroindustrial Era, societal growth will require a growing population consisting of creative and productive individuals. We cannot aggressively pursue 5 to 7 percent economic growth if we simultaneously restrict the size of our populations.

The international mentor system we just examined should provide an excellent forum for developed and emerging countries to discuss at length the role population can play in economic progress.

Refocus Attention on Early Childhood Development

The research examined in this book strongly suggests that any society that wants to improve its adaptive capacity, that desires to progress and grow in the emerging Macroindustrial Era, must be concerned with the cognitive and emotional development of its children. Its citizens' abilities to produce and create throughout their lives are strongly determined by their early childhood learning experiences,

Society must refocus its attention on early childhood development. Families, schools, government, and business together must tackle this problem through programs that seek to increase children's basic level of intelligence and enhance the quality of their education.

One such program, Missouri's Parents as Teachers (PAT) program, provides parents with special educators who make visits to the home of each child in the district, starting at birth, to give parents individualized information about child development, learning, constructive play, and effective discipline. Early research indicates that this program improves children's intellectual abilities in such areas as language, development, and problem solving. As a side benefit, the children learn to get along with adults earlier. The PAT program is voluntary and open to all families, not just the poor and disadvantaged.

Of the millions allocated to education in county, state, and federal budgets, only a small percentage finds its way into such early childhood education. If research is correct, however, we need to divert more of the education budget to the early childhood years.

Although such programs perform wonders, the attention and care parents afford their children ultimately determine their development. After all, even if these learning enhancement programs are available, only the parents' love for the child will induce them to enroll their child and themselves in such a program. Only the parents' commitment to their child's development will motivate them to devote the time and energy such programs require. In addition, although a program can instruct parents in the importance of paying their children compliments, disciplining them when needed, and providing them with a nurturing environment, the parents themselves must perform such activities.

No government or legal system can mandate that parents provide their children the perfect learning environment, a secure and happy home. Parents alone decide to separate, divorce, or stay married. Regardless of the sophistication of programs promulgated by business, government, and schools, it is a society's parents who ultimately must refocus attention on their children's early development.

Redefine the Life Cycle

In the Macroindustrial Era, people will live longer and healthier lives than any generation before them. These two simple changes will require society to reconstitute completely its notion of the life cycle, that social construct which assigns people their appropriate roles and functions at different ages. In the next Era we must radically rethink such concepts as retirement, childbearing, leisure, and especially career.

Current projections suggest that society ought to articulate a new image of the human life cycle and replace it with that of the *human growth process*. Because people will be living longer and more healthy lives, their ability to contribute and produce will actually increase with the years, not decrease.

In accordance with this new concept, we should first phase out the concept of retirement. This archaic notion assumes that people have a set period of productivity, after which point their knowledge becomes obsolete, their energy wanes, and their commitment to work disappears. In fact, as we explore the frontiers of advanced age, we find that many people, while appreciating the opportunity to retire, resent the concomitant lack of activity, commitment, and connectedness to the productive sphere.

When we assume that the basic motivating force of human behavior is leisure, or the absence of work, we misread fundamental human needs. Although they value their free time, people get their primary satisfaction from participating in and contributing to the common good.

Corporations and other employers must rethink the role of retirement in human resource planning. Are there no new functions that seasoned citizens can fulfill? Does the older worker's wisdom, accumulated knowledge, and perspective have no value for his or her employer? Organizations such as the American Association of Retired Persons ought to initiate a dialogue with corporations and government exploring the idea of continuing work into the later years at least on a voluntary basis.

Second, *recareering* should be considered a normal part of the human growth cycle. Workers displaced by technological improvement and economic change ought not to be considered obsolete. Rather, they should be part of a permanent work force that merely has to be recareered, that is, retrained for a new career. Workers and executives should be allowed to change careers as they would jobs.

Although politicians and educators agree that retraining is important, they have taken very little serious action to institutionalize the process. Governments can deal with this social problem by establishing a recareering fund that would operate along principles similar to those of an unemployment insurance fund. All workers and their employers would make contributions to this fund. In the event that the person is laid off, he or she could opt to look for another job or take a second option heretofore unavailable in most countries. The unemployed worker could choose, within perhaps two years of his or her firing, to receive a voucher that could be applied to tuition or other such payments for reeducation or training. The worker could make choices about a school and a new occupation under the guidance of a program counselor.

Such a program could solve a host of problems. For one, this program would make retraining available to the large number of baby boomers about to retire over the next few decades. The social system cannot easily withstand the withdrawal of tens of millions of people; the loss of skill alone could cripple some industries. Second, and most importantly, this retraining may ease society's transition into the Macroindustrial Era. Millions of managers, marketing specialists, and salespeople—well educated, intelligent, and talented—are losing their jobs because we are shifting into a more technologically oriented era. Why not use a recareering fund program to help retrain the forty- and fifty-year-old manager to be a newly minted engineer, scientist, or computer specialist? For a relatively small investment society can upgrade its entire work force.

The human growth process concept also upends our traditional notion of the timing of childbearing and childrearing. In current Western practice, women attend school and college and begin a career, putting off the childbearing decision until a later date. The woman must then make this decision in relation to a myriad of other factors, including disruption of her career, use of day care, and her husband's career demands.

This becomes problematic because women now have children after they start their career. Ironically, childbearing and -rearing can be much more easily performed not during the occupational period, but during the education/training period. As radical as it sounds, it would be easier for a woman to rear toddlers during either the college years or the recareering period as outlined above (possibly in her thirties), especially considering the breakthroughs in distance learning and the trend toward digitized education.

In a truly Expansionary culture, such choices would be available to all women. Voluntary lifetime employment and regular recareering will be accessible to all.

Restructure Educational Priorities

In order to complete the transition into the Macroindustrial Era successfully, nations must determine the extent to which their educational systems are preparing the next generations for successful participation in this exciting enterprise. In many cases, the system will have to be fine-tuned, in others, it will require deeper restructuring.

In general, schools must enhance their emphasis on science and math in their curricula. This does not mean that every student must become an engineer or biologist but that all should have an understanding of science and its relationship to their world. Also, the system must emphasize in all courses issues like logic, creativity, and critical thinking.

The education system's primary concern must be advancing human progress. Although science and technology areas ought to be emphasized, something else may be needed in the Macroindustrial Era.

What universities and high schools seem to be lacking is any curriculum that can serve as both a repository for and wellspring of expansionary thinking. Therefore, universities should contemplate instituting schools or departments of Expansionary Studies, a new field that would essentially provide a knowledge of the ideological and technical underpinnings of growth and progress. Courses would deal with such subjects as the history of the idea of progress, technological underpinnings of society, futurology, creative thinking, and social and institutional foundations of growth. Hopefully, in all countries, these subjects will be presented from a global perspective, with an international exchange of students and professors integrated into the learning experience.

Expansionary Studies could either be a major, minor, and/or part of the core requirements for graduation. Because of its emphasis on creative thinking, it could serve as a perfect minor for those majoring in sciences and business. On the graduate level, a School of Expansionary Studies could become a permanent site for professionals and students from such fields as government, science, business, and academia to discuss philosophical and technological issues related to social and material progress.

From the expansionary perspective, the prime purpose of education is to prepare people for roles in the emerging Macroindustrial Era, as scientists, engineers, business people, social scientists, even creative artists. Schools would be advised to stick to the knitting and not mandate that their students complete human service volunteer programs such as those we discussed in Chapter 7 in order to graduate. These severely reduce the time students can use for invention, play (which can lead to invention and discovery), and the leisure and relaxation that allow people to work at their best.

Education will be key in the Macroindustrial Era. Therefore, a nation must restructure its educational priorities so they are focused on maximizing the chance that its students and workers develop the knowledge and skills to succeed in this era.

Enhance Technological Involvement

To improve technological literacy and proficiency, formal education is not enough. Real technological advancement will occur only when the mass of the people transform themselves from technological consumers to technological producers. They must not only understand, appreciate, and know science and technology, they must also participate in its creation.

Ironically, although the general population has been faulted for its lack of scientific knowledge and expertise, a surprising number of laypeople have become involved in amateur science, mostly through personal and job-related computer use and exposure to electronic gizmos in the entertainment area.

The early breakthroughs in personal computer technology were forged by amateurs such as Stephen Jobs. Many were high school and college graduates who envisioned their creations and realized that they could accomplish their goals without professional guidance, credentials, or peer approval. Now, because of the progress made in such areas as computer graphics, computer-based training, VR, and other technological tools, we may see more nonscientists, average people with little formal technical training, making their mark in the world of technological and scientific invention and discovery.

The fact of the matter is, as we transform research and exploratory activity to a manipulation of the computer or cyberspace, we reduce the need for access to formal training and expensive equipment. The computer makes knowledge of systems, like the blueprint of a home, the structure of a molecule, or the composition of the universe, available to a greater number of people. Even advanced scientific concepts such as chaos theory, which at one time would have been the exclusive playthings of the scientific establishment, have been adapted to software programs for the home computer. Now the mystery of how unpredictable random numbers reveal an inner order will be revealed in all its glory to the nonscientist sitting at his or her home computer.

The day may come soon when amateur scientists again will be storming the gates of professional society meetings to present their findings regarding chemistry, pharmaceuticals, and astronomy and challenging sciences dicta about the origins of the universe!

Science and educational institutions as well as manufacturers of computer technology should be encouraging the idea of "everyman as scientist." Dean Kamen, a self-made millionaire, entrepreneur, and electromechanical wizard, has pioneered methods of encouraging participation in the scientific enterprise. He has founded USFirst, a nonprofit organization dedicated to building interest in science, engineering, and math careers. This foundation oversees an annual creative engineering competition in Nashua, New Hampshire, which showcases robotic devices designed and built by high school students who are paired with engineers from universities and corporations such as AT&T, Xerox, and Boeing. Kamen is trying to convince cable sports network ESPN to cover the various "athletic" contests between students' robots.

According to Kamen, "We need to make the right heroes and role models. We need to show kids that the 200 best inventors in the world make enough money to own their own N.F.L. team, that no one will ever make as much money with their muscles as with their mind." Kamen believes that such events as his engineering competition will draw the mass of young people into a love of science and technology. He may be right: The 1993 competition, held in a high school auditorium, drew so many participants that he will have to move future events to much larger quarters, such as a stadium. He even has plans for a science hall of fame, with a special wing dedicated to the unique contributions of science fiction writers.

Other groups have similar plans to reinvigorate scientific activity among American youth. Engineers from around the United States have formed the California Engineering Foundation, which has as its overarching goal the reindustrialization of America. One method will be to establish a movement called Mission America, which will send speakers to high schools around the United States to encourage students to pursue scientific careers.

In reality, the younger generation circa 1994 may be already wresting control of the technological foundation from the formal control of universities and scientific academies. The growing cybernautic movement (mislabeled by major media outlets as "cyberpunk") is a perfect example of this trend. Young fourteen- and fifteen-year-olds sit at their computers and perform any number of complex operations in cyberspace, that gray area in which computers and people meet. They communicate; "flame" (write long, uninhibited messages emboldened by computer anonymity); perform scientific experiments utilizing enhanced graphics software; and even illegally tap into computer banks of credit card companies, governments, even the Defense Department and the CIA.

In new "zines" (trans. magazines) such as *Mondo 2000*, the emerging generation of technoids and cybernauts rant enthusiastically about advances in science and technology. While baby boomer social critics wait for this next generation to define itself in terms boomers comprehend, such as music or politics, young people are already forging an identity based on breakthroughs in science, biotechnology, computers, VR, and space travel.

As individuals experience this enhanced technological involvement, they become more integrated into society's productive framework. This involvement in science will have a profound positive impact on an individual's sense of the world and his or her place in it. He or she will be less likely to experience the unrest, malaise, and anomie that has haunted some members of the Western community.

Having the ability to connect to the real world and the emerging society and contributing in a meaningful way to societal growth and prosperity counters feelings of alienation. As techniques are developed to enhance people's technological involvement, make everyone a potential scientist, and hence increase his or her potential contribution to the emerging Macroindustrial endeavor, alienation will rapidly wane.

Emancipate the Power Structure

Any society that hopes to compete in the Macroindustrial Era must devise methods and develop structures that ensure that it will fully utilize its skill base. The only way to accomplish such a goal is to make power/prestige positions and jobs available to qualified members of all races, and ethnic and class groups. In Western countries, corporations have done a fairly good job at ending discrimination against women, minorities, and others in many areas. Certainly, the middle management ranks of a large corporation typically include a fair cross-section of the population.

However, at the very top of private and public organizations, a different pattern emerges. The senior management group or operating committee of most companies is still overwhelmingly male and white, replicating the standard concept of a WASP power elite. In the United States and elsewhere, such a state of affairs is due to the fact that large companies primarily select for top management positions the graduates of elite universities. Although such universities draw many bright students, quite frankly they accept others simply because of their ability to pay or the fact that their parents or close relatives are alumni of the university. (Some estimate that each year 20 percent or more of the students admitted to Ivy League colleges are relatives of alumni.)

So we can assume that by recruiting only from these top schools corporations are overlooking bright people from the state universities and colleges, as well as those from the nonelite private schools.

In the Macroindustrial Era, any society that wishes to successfully compete must ensure that the very best people occupy its business leadership positions. Americans have become deeply disturbed over the failure of major U.S. corporations to adopt innovations and changes necessary to compete in the emerging Era. They witness other countries' corporations adapting to new economic conditions while American companies seem to stagnate. People point an accusing finger increasingly at the leadership of these organizations, questioning the skills and competence of those at the top. Increasingly, the public wonders how mediocre performers are able to commandeer the top corporate positions.

Clearly, the power structure must be emancipated so that access to it becomes completely open to not just the elite, but the broad middle class, historically a repository of great talent and skill. If the corporate elite is not willing to open their networks to high achievers, other interested parties can certainly make their voices heard in this matter. These companies are, after all, publicly held corporations, not personal fiefdoms. Stockholders must challenge the entrenched corporate elite's grasp on their organizations. This happened in the case of General Motors stockholders, tired of losing money while senior management rewarded themselves with large bonuses, insisted on a voice in choosing its leadership. Pension funds and other institutional investors are clamoring for more of a say in company policies and practice. Some even want seats on the board of directors of many of these companies.

The political apparatus must respond constructively to the leadership selection process. In truth, very often the Securities and Exchange Commission rules allow top management to establish a lock on internal power. However, if the Securities and Exchange Commission would make it easier for institutional investors such as pension and mutual funds to acquire seats on corporate boards, companies would be less likely to retain nonproductive members of the "old boy network" in senior management positions.

In order to make certain that the best talent gets every consideration for top positions, companies must not only establish a new set of criteria for recruitment into the company, but must reconsider who gets selected into their high-potential programs." Because these programs usually serve as the predominant pathway to positions in higher corporate strata, companies should ensure that all employees have a chance to be selected. A typical high-potential program should be composed of graduates from elite schools, state universities, and state colleges.

The political system must also be made more accessible. In the United States, the Ross Perot phenomenon signaled the beginning of the American people's battle for inclusion in the national decision-making process. After turning out an incumbent president in the 1992 election, many Americans expected a waning of elitism in government. Unfortunately, the new Clinton administration, which pledged itself to extend the reach of opportunity to ordinary Americans, quickly filled its key positions with members of the economic and academic upper strata. As the *Wall Street Journal* claimed, "The contrast is part of a striking gulf between the common people to whom the Clinton campaign made its appeal and the well-educated, well-off group who will be governing them."

As Bush did before him, Clinton staffed his cabinet with multimillionaires who attended Harvard, Yale, or Georgetown. Many of these people are connected to top law firms or own stakes in major investment banks such as Goldman Sachs. One can only wonder whether these people developed and approved many of the seemingly foolish economic policy proposals, such as a tax on gasoline and other forms of energy, because they have occupied too long an economic strata that simply will not feel the deleterious effects of their own policies. Would a staunch member of the middle class, for example, so capriciously levy taxes on the gasoline his or her fellow class members need to drive to work? (And which was opposed by two-thirds of all Americans?)

In the Macroindustrial Era, elitism in government and business must be swept away. Society needs the talent of the best and the brightest from all social classes at the top rungs of business and government. By emancipating the power structure, companies help their nations progress from mediocracies to meritocracies, and governments make policy with its citizens' best interests in mind.

The Culture Must Include Expansionary Thinking

For any country to succeed in the coming years, the citizenry must be involved in the basic productive process. Certainly, by increasing the public's technological involvement we increase the chance that it will be substantively integrated into the Macroindustrial Era.

To effect such integration, however, the citizenry must receive cues from the culture—the arts in general, TV, music, and literature—that themselves reflect expansionary thinking. We already described how schools might effect such a change, through establishment of Expansionary Studies departments, but it is the mass media that fashions the atmosphere in which the average person lives, thinks, and forms his or her value structure.

In the chapter on culture, we explored how breakthroughs in art, music, and literature can accompany and possibly condition innovations in the sciences. In the Macroindustrial Era, it will be incumbent on all artists to examine and determine to what extent their work helps create an atmosphere of societal and personal growth and development.

Although a creative artistic milieu conditions growth in other societal sectors, artists need not become cheerleaders of the new Macroindustrial Era. In fact, in an era as complex as this, their most important contributions may be criticism and satire.

However, extensive negativity, common in current movies and music, can certainly affect performance in other sectors. An Expansionary Culture is one in which the artists think through problems and apply solutions. An artist's production of quality moves a society forward and sets a standard of excellence for others, artists and nonartist alike. Conversely, a society can be undermined as much by a population that cannot produce challenging music, plays, and art as by a citizenry unable to read, write, and add.

Of course, in the coming era the definition of art and the very format which art itself takes will change dramatically. Theme parks may help advance expansionary thinking in the general population. The Hyperion Project's City of Mars, the Japanese theme park we visited briefly in our discussion of space in Chapter 3, will feature many exhibits that ought to inspire the public. They plan Miracle 10,000, a ride through the centuries; ZooDNA, in which visitors are introduced to tomorrow's genetic possibilities in a "zoo without cages"; and a Dreamsphere, a living encyclopedia of human dreams, where individuals may add their own dreams and compare symbolism in their dreams with the dreams of individuals of other cultures. Visitors will be encouraged to participate in creating the ideal image of future humanity, or *Miraijinrui*, starting with their own images and recreating and enhancing them with the aid of computer graphics.

A culture that transmits strong cues about society's overall purpose and goal orientation produces people more certain of how their own lives fit into the greater cosmic matrix. In the Macroindustrial Era, the artist, regardless of the medium in which he or she works (including theme parks), must understand that he or she paints, writes, and creates not in a vacuum, but in a wider cultural and social milieu.

Make Growth and Progress Part of the Political Dialogue

In order to survive, humanity must adapt to changing conditions. We must discover new sources of energy, increase the productivity of our agricultural resources, and improve the health and durability of the human species. The many breakthroughs we have explored in this book represent the species' adaptation to these new challenges.

In a perfect world, societies would recognize these challenges, accept them, and get on with the business of rebuilding their world. Humanity certainly has the technological proficiency to move into the Macroindustrial Era. As a species, we have the ability to explore space, extend the life span, and expand our reach throughout the universe. We can transform this planet and others, reprogram our genes, commandeer the atom. In fact, there is more technology on the shelf than the species knows what to do with.

In the latter decade of the twentieth century, many seem totally oblivious to the changes necessary for the species to progress. They operate under the illusion that the species can survive without achieving hyperprogress in the areas of biology, energy, travel, agriculture, and macromanufacturing.

Even if they accept the need for growth, most seem unaware of the obligations such progress will make on the individual, that each of us will have to become smarter, more ambitious, more industrious, and more willing to take risks. Unless all members of society agree we need such a transition and also are willing to contribute to its success, the Macroindustrial Era will not emerge. The average citizen, not back room corporate moguls and faceless policymakers, must build the next era.

Here political leadership must assert itself. Before society can move forward into the Macroindustrial Era, strong political leadership must construct a political consensus around growth and progress. Key political leaders in all countries must convince the electorate to accept these new challenges and mobilize the people to expend the energy and time necessary to make this transition.

Presidents and prime ministers will have to provide that vibrant leadership at the top we discussed earlier. They must become educators and cheerleaders, involving the electorate in their quest. In the United States, both political parties will have to add growth and progress specifically to the political dialogue as issues in and of themselves, marshaling sentiment in favor of hyperprogress. In the sixties, John F. Kennedy was able to build support for such issues as the space program and civil rights. Leadership in the nineties has to be willing to support and debate publicly issues around the development of nuclear power, biotechnology, nanotechnology, and other aspects of the Macroindustrial Era.

Establishing such a political agenda may be the most critical stepping-stone to the Macroindustrial Era. However, all presidents, senators, and public figures must be forewarned. Any political leader attempting to shepherd his country into the next era will find to his surprise that the political battle in which he will be embroiled will be unlike any other he has ever experienced.

Upon advancing such concepts he will find himself enjoined in an ideological conflict that has been brewing for some time right below our culture's surface. Ironically, although few people outside of the direct combatants even know such a war exists, the outcome of this secret conflict will ultimately determine whether nations, or perhaps humanity itself, ever completes the transition into the Macroindustrial Era.

This is the battle over progress, technology, and ultimately the very role of the species on the planet and in the universe. It is to this war that we now turn our attention.

The Coming Battle for Humanity's Future

There are two opposing forces attempting to define the future of the human species. One side, composed of an amalgam of self-styled environmentalists and zero-growth advocates, will call for massive cutbacks in factories, production of chlorofluorocarbons, automobile usage, and most activities that we would have considered progressive in the last five centuries. The other side, composed of some industry groups, trade associations, and loose-knit citizens' action groups, continues to lobby for material growth and an enhanced standard of living.

The zero-growth, antiprogress faction seems to exert a strong influence in the media, the social sciences, and some parts of the political spectrum. They even have a prominent voice in the home of futurology, the World Future Society itself. The antigrowth and antiprogress ideology has only taken root in the West in the last twenty to thirty years. In 1962, Rachel Carson's *Silent Spring* informed the public of the problems of pollution, and 1970 saw the first Earth Day. What started as a movement over commonsense issues like pollution and impure water, about which everyone should be concerned, was soon transformed into something quite different, becoming an all out assault on industrialization, population growth, the eating of meat, and the development of natural resources. The movement we see today has as its ultimate target progress itself. At its most extreme, it questions the right of humanity to assert itself on the planet and cosmos and contends that the species must live in total balance with nature.

What bills itself as environmentalism has developed into a bizarre, but internally consistent, philosophical outlook on humanity and nature, which by the 1990s had crossed over from political ideology to quasi-religion. In fact, many of its major proponents speak in religious terms of the "fall of man." Dave Foreman, founder of the radical Earth First, dates that fall to about 10,000 years ago, when what he labels the "nascency of agriculture" started humanity on the road from the natural world to the evils of the city, war, patriarchy, and technology. Paul Watson, founder of Greenpeace, claims that man is innately good, but because he drifted away from the garden (of Eden), he has lost touch with natural reality. Watson thus feels justified to claim that "we, the human species, have become a viral epidemic to the earth" and "the AIDS of the earth."

This new environmental theology teaches that human greed has infected the world with sin—pollution and toxic wastes. Of course, by following this new religion, we can rid ourselves of this evil in ourselves and our products, enter a state of grace, and achieve heaven on earth.

To dupe an unwitting public into accepting concepts it most certainly would reject on principle, the antigrowth movement camouflages the real effects of their programs. It serves the public the ultimate anodyne, the belief that we can continue to enjoy our standard of living while living in balance with nature, without asserting ourselves on the planet and throughout the universe, and without taking risks.

In 1992, the United Nations Conference on Environment and Development held in Rio de Janeiro, Brazil, provided a startling example of the extent to which the environmental movement had penetrated the world's political, economic, and cultural institutions. The conference had many objectives. The main concern was the so-called worldwide environmental crisis caused by global warming. The conference members were to sign a treaty under which nations would agree to try to limit emissions of greenhouse gases such as carbon dioxide, methane, and nitrous oxide, all believed to cause global warming, to 1990 levels. The conference also hoped to gain a consensus on issues such as forest protection and a global commitment to something called Agenda 21, a forty-chapter anthology of the ills affecting the planet, replete with an action plan for the twenty-first century that included a commitment to mass transit and energy conservation.

The impetus for holding the conference came out of agitation by such environmental groups as Greenpeace and the World Wildlife Fund. These groups, working through their national arms, created a political climate within countries that literally forced national leaders to attend these conferences. For instance, Germany's Helmut Kohl was pressured into attending by home-based environmentalist political forces, especially the highly organized Green Party. Once most Western leaders made the commitment to go to the conference, the U.S. president, George Bush, could not avoid attending a conference with which he had fundamental ideological disagreements.

Environmental groups like Greenpeace, which has an annual operating budget of around $50 million, lured Third World representatives to this conference with promises of economic gain. They implied that the conference would produce a treaty wherein developed countries would agree to pay "reparations" to the Third World for all the pollution they were sending South. The environmental groups hinted that this treaty would mandate that the West pay the Third World countries hundreds of billions of dollars over several years.

A quick review of the organizers and chief players illustrates the depth and breadth of this movement. One Mr. Strong, the secretary-general for the Rio summit, is a Canadian with a long history in the environmental movement. He is past president of PetroCanada, the Canadian national oil company. A Mr. Schmidheiny is the head of the Swiss Eternity Group, a large Swiss multinational manufacturing and trading business. He is also the founder of the Business Council for Sustainable Development. A Ms. Robertson is a pollution-policy officer for the World Wildlife Fund, whose particular specialty is building bridges between the environmental movement and government.

With the election of the Clinton–Gore ticket, it remains to be seen whether the American government will move closer to this global environmental movement. Certainly, the presence of Albert Gore as vice president in 1992 brought such a state of affairs closer to reality. In his apocalyptic book *Earth in the Balance*, Gore presents his pessimistic views of humanity and the environment, sharing with his readers his deeply felt view that "we have lost our feeling of connectedness to the rest of nature."

Gore betrays a deep distrust of humanity when he asks sarcastically, "When giving us dominion over the Earth, did God choose an appropriate technology?" Contrast this with the expansionary view, which essentially sees the planet improved by the presence of the human species. Not surprisingly, one writer came away from a luncheon interview with Gore with the impression that Gore was a person with more than a hint of the Malthusian in him, "as if the world is going to hell in an internal-combustion engine." Is it any wonder that gasoline was one of the first items the Clinton administration decided to tax in 1993?

Some critics think that Gore crosses the line separating true environmentalism, which wants to make the world safe for humanity, and those who want to make the world safe from humanity. Gore seems to desire the latter, and he plans to save us through a huge national bureaucracy that will oversee internal business action and cede large amounts of national power to international bureaucracies that will decide whether the U.S. economic policy falls within environmental guidelines.

Gore would like Third World countries to come under the jurisdiction of such bureaucracies. Instead of adopting protechnology, pro-growth practices like irrigation, biotech, and genetic engineering, these countries would pursue a future in which they measure all actions in terms of their effect on the Earth, forests, and other species. These countries could also forget participating in the emerging growth era.

An early indication of the new administration's ideological stance on the issue of technology and the environment came in January 1993 in the controversial Von Roll case. Swiss company Von Roll, a world leader in antipollution technology, designed and built a state-of-the-art hazardous waste incinerator in East Liverpool, Ohio. The plant was about to start operating when Vice President-elect Albert Gore publicly stated that once in office he would block Environmental Protection Agency approval of this plant by denying Von Roll a license to operate. Gore was acting on the counsel of Greenpeace, who informed him that the plant itself, because it burned such items as drugs, paint, and dry-cleaning fluids, would itself emit some impurities.

Greenpeace was resurrecting charges that Von Roll had successfully refuted in court twenty-one times over the last several years. The amount of "impurities" emitted were so minuscule that no court or public agency could find reason to deny Von Roll a license. However, Greenpeace guessed correctly that Gore would ignore legal precedent and deny Von Roll the right to start operating the antipollution plant.

What some critics find perplexing about such cases is that they seem to contradict the administration's claims to be a champion of high technology. When confronted with the application of high technology to pollution control, Clinton/Gore seemed to be less than enthusiastic! Could it be that Al Gore is fundamentally antigrowth and realizes that antipollution technologies like the Von Roll incinerator and bioremediation are such efficient waste eliminators that they open the doors to greater Macroindustrialization. Certainly, Greenpeace's continued opposition to efficient waste management serves well its campaign for global deindustrialization.

Greenpeace's impact on the Clinton administration continued unabated throughout 1993. In May of that year, responding to pressure from this organization, EPA chief Carol Browner pushed to create further obstacles to any increase in new incinerator capacity. In fact, Browner, given carte-blanche on environmental policy from her mentor Al Gore, stated that the EPA would, over the next eighteen months, review permits issued to "already operating hazardous-waste incinerators and industrial furnaces."

Gore spent much of 1993 reshaping the executive branch of the United States government to serve his ecological agenda. Besides hiring

358 Seizing the Future

like-minded friends such as Browner, who actually helped write "Earth in the Balance," he also began purging government agencies of any officials not in step with his ideology. One early victim was the Department of Energy's director of research, William Happer, Jr., who has publicly stated, along with a majority in the academic and scientific committee, that current data do not support such hypotheses as global warming and the greenhouse effect. In fact, Happer has been submitting to Congress reports which show that of late there has actually been a slight decline in the ultraviolet radiation hitting the Earth's surface. Although Happer is only sticking to the facts, he was found "philosophically out of tune" with the Vice-President, according to one staffer, and was fired!

It seems that for several years before Gore assumed his new lofty position, he had been badgering scientists in full view of press and public to either profess their belief in Gore's greenhouse effect or recant their stated opposition to it. Sherwood Idso, a Department of Agriculture research physicist, had circulated evidence that rising levels of carbon dioxide (the main greenhouse gas) would actually serve as a catalyst to the growth and reproduction of vegetation on the planet. In 1991, Gore dragged Idso before a Senate subcommittee and publicly accused him of being a shill of the earth-raping coal companies.

It would seem that in order to ram through the various elements of such legislation as the Clean Air Act, and to head off any national campaign for its repeal or modification, Gore and his allies must discredit the pro-growth view. And one method is to utilize intimidation to neutralize scientists and other experts whose research supports the position that industrialization does not harm the planet's air and upper atmosphere.

A concerted thrust from Washington in the direction of environmental extremism could at least temporarily deprive the United States of a leadership role in the Macroindustrial Era.

Even celebrities have entered the fray over technology and growth. Actors such as Ted Danson and Meryl Streep have lent their names to a variety of organizations purporting to save the Earth, endangered species, forests, and so on. One of the more famous supporters of zero growth bridges the gap between government power and tabloid celebrity—Prince Charles. This member of royalty has become a staunch opponent of population growth. In April 1992, Prince Charles claimed that he could not imagine how "any society can hope to improve its lot when population growth regularly exceeds economic growth." He added: "Is it really wise to call for such rapid growth, until we can be certain that growth which emerges will serve the people most in need?"

Charles, who fancies himself an architectural savant/critic, once cheered the citizens of Pittsburgh with the news that they ought not be upset with the decline of the city's industrial base. Their steel mills, he informed them, would be surely replaced with shopping malls and boutiques. Is it any wonder that the *Wall Street Journal* dubbed Charles "Prince Malthus"?

One can only admire the tireless efforts of this billionaire/monarch to teach the rest of us how to survive with less. In 1993, Prince Charles began urging hoteliers to become more environmentally conscious "step by step, flush by flush." In May of that year, Charles cajoled eleven major hotel chains, including Hilton, Holiday Inn, Marriott, and Sheraton, to sign a new International Hotel Environment Initiative in which they agree to take efforts to become more "green." Although the specific details have not yet been finalized, Charles would like the hotels to offer guests fewer sheets and towels in their rooms, and to place soap dispensers in all bathrooms. The hotels will also feature low-flow showers and toilets, as well as recycling buckets. As a first step in meeting the goals of the Prince's Initiative, many hotels will now begin to offer a certain number of "environmentally correct" green rooms, replete with reminders to the guests to conserve energy.

Nowhere is there a more striking example of the inroads the zero-growth movement has made than its increasing influence over the energy industry itself. It would seem that business would be decidedly antagonistic to environmentalism and its antigrowth message. After all, the restrictions on energy use and technology proposed by zero growthers would seem to make it very difficult for the average business to turn a profit, but zero growthers have discovered a way to sell their wares to business by making nonproduction a profitable enterprise.

A perfect example of this is how environmentalists have managed to make a reduction in service profitable to electric utilities. A CNN interview in November 1990 featured a member of California's Pacific Gas and Electric (PG&E) company proudly announcing how it would still turn a profit even as the company would cut back on energy production and discontinue construction of power plants.

The power company announced that it would not build large power plants of any sort but instead would force customers to comply with a number of conservation techniques. These techniques are based on those developed by Amory Lovins, an ardent advocate of zero growth.

Lovins believes that if utilities educate the customer in conservation and introduce a series of draconian measures such as monitoring individual energy use, utilities will not have to worry about increasing production of electricity. As Californians are forced to use less energy and drastically change their life-style, PG&E would be reimbursed for the lost revenue from state coffers. Of course, the state will have to recoup this payout through its only available source of income: taxes on the very people whose energy supply is being reduced. Thus, through an increase in their tax bill, Californians will enjoy the dubious honor of paying more to receive less energy.

The PG&E case is only the beginning of a nationwide movement that goes under the label "demand side management." There are now at least 1500 such projects in the United States. Con Edison of New York State has initiated its enlightened energy use program, which encourages the public to consume less. Others will surely follow.

It is fairly obvious that the only way that energy consumption can decrease is if industries either dramatically shrink or disappear entirely. The environmental groups know this. It is safe to say that many in the zero-growth movement are utilizing demand side management as a first step in their plan to deindustrialize the United States.

The list goes on. Jeremy Rifkin, president of the Washington-based Foundation on Economic Trends, will use his group's million-dollar "war chest" to whip up a public frenzy over biotechnologically produced food products. One suspects that Luddites like Rifkin fear that hypergrowth in the food industry will threaten to upset their doomsday predictions such as poverty and famine and prove that large populations can be supported. Better to sabotage biotech now than risk cornucopia later.

As we learned, the media are laced with writers and commentators antagonistic to technology and progress and quite willing to support an antigrowth position. In 1993, MTV, the cable rock network, announced plans to run what its executives labeled socially conscious public service announcements. Of course, their concept of responsibility will skew the content of these commercials in the direction of, among other issues, environmentalism. Considering the ideological predisposition of the current administration on this matter and the sympathetic ear MTV has given Clinton/Gore, we may be witnessing an unprecedented and highly unlikely merger: a cultural/political alliance between the counterculture and the White House.

The Emerging Consensus on Human Progress

In spite of the powerful forces amassed to block further real material progress, their influence will not maintain its dominance. Several forces will eventually overwhelm those groups' attempts to reverse the 500-year trend toward greater material growth and higher standards of living.

The emerging consensus will demand growth, more technology, and a greater ability to live comfortably. In other words, this consensus will insist that nations successfully transition into the Macroindustrial Era.

A Growing Coalition

There are signs throughout the nation and world of a resounding demand for growth and progress. In the United States, at present, the political culture shows signs of awakening to the fact that without industrial growth a country will never be able to compete. Federal courts are currently dominated by Reagan and Bush appointees sympathetic to the idea that environmentalism often uses questionable quasi-scientific studies to gut industries and block development. In 1991 and 1992, the federal district and appellate courts threw out a number of environmental regulations, including those that restricted hazardous wastes and directed the government to set higher automobile mileage standards.

Even the U.S. Congress, often sympathetic to extreme environmentalism, had formed a coalition with the Bush administration and business groups to block attempts to strengthen the Clean Water Act and the Endangered Species Act. Democrats from western states had worked with the Bush administration to open land and resources to development. Senator Max Baucus, a Democrat from Montana, has proposed legislation that would allow 4 million acres of wilderness in Montana to be logged and mined.

This side of the political spectrum seems to be correctly reading the public's attitude, which is gradually weighing in on the side of economic and technological development. One poll revealed that more than half the United States' citizens think that environmentalist groups go too far in their demands on business and government, outnumbering those who think that the United States should go full speed ahead in enacting environmental protection plans.

It is clear that the 1992 American elections served as a repudiation of the so-called environmentalist movement. Although voters supported a presidential ticket that included environmentalist Albert Gore, it is obvious that when electing a president the voters had more on their minds than saving the planet. However, a close inspection of the state-by-state votes on environmental initiatives demonstrated that Americans were in no way swayed by ecological arguments.

For instance, in Ohio voters rejected an attempt to expand on the toxic warning concept for consumer products. The initiative would have mandated a Naderite-style law that would have required a strict notification label on any items that had even a hint of carcinogenic content. This was based on the notorious California Proposition 65, which sent businesses and jobs scurrying out of the state in droves. When scientists along with the AFL–CIO stepped forward to point out that this rule would have disastrous repercussions for the state, it was soundly defeated.

In Massachusetts, PIRG (Public Interest Research Group) sponsored a recycling requirement that would have forced companies to utilize reusable packaging. It lost 59 percent to 41 percent, mainly because the voters discovered that such packaging would cost each household in the state an extra $230 a year. Oregon defeated two measures that attempted to close down the Trojan nuclear power plant prematurely.

Activists for growth and progress are emboldened by such poll and election results. For instance, "wise-use" groups are emerging who want to roll back a host of environmental regulations that they feel hurt the economy more than help the environment. The Alliance for America represents cattle owners who are losing access to land that has come under environmental protection. They lobby Congress and hold public demonstrations to get their message heard. They even managed to get General Electric to pull its sponsorship of the "World of Audubon" TV series when it ran a show attacking the cattle industry.

Another such group, the Washington State-based Center for the Defense of Free Enterprise, put together and is promoting a wise-use agenda that listed twenty-five specific goals for the future. The agenda included opening up the Arctic National Wildlife Refuge for oil drilling and a powerful statement that would require the U.S. government to attach an economic impact statement to proposed environmental regulations.

Some of these groups are suing environmental groups such as the Natural Resources Defense Council on the basis that these groups have caused businesses economic hardship with phony statements about the risks attached to some products. One such suit involves the economic loss some farmers sustained when environmentalists raised the now-discredited scare about the dangers of Alar, a ripening agent sprayed on fruit.

Science is certainly joining in the fray. The bloated claims about global warming and the depletion of the ozone layer eventually backfired. By the summer of 1992, books and articles refuting global warming were proliferating. Already, a growing number of prominent scientists nationwide have signed a declaration that says the environmental movement is an irrational ideology that has exaggerated environmental problems and threatens that ability of scientists and business executives to advance technology. This may be one of the first statements by established scientists that link no-growth policies and economic decline. Such a statement moves the agenda from concerns about the environment to the issue of economic growth.

This emerging consensus over the importance of growth will be as much forged by grass roots agitation as by government or business activism. Ironically, a major catalyst for such a consciousness-raising may be the draconian environmental laws that are only now taking effect.

Businesses in states like New Jersey are already feeling the effects of this act. The bill mandates that businesses in states that fall outside of environmental standards must cooperate in the quest to reduce pollution. Because New Jersey is one of the many states whose air quality and ozone levels fall outside of the Clean Air Act parameters of environmental acceptability, businesses there are already drawing up plans to induce employees to restrict automobile travel. Whether companies like it or not, they may have to invest in van services for their employees or allow many employees to work at home a few days a week regardless of whether such measures are economically efficient.

Businesses are beginning to realize the costs involved in funding the global campaign to phase out chlorofluorocarbons, or CFCs, by 1995. Even as science becomes increasingly skeptical about the role of CFCs in ozone depletion, government fiat will force industry to adopt a new generation of air conditioners free of CFCs. The problem of meeting such demands is rooted in both economics and technology. The cost of adapting to the CFC-free world envisaged by legislators will run into the tens of billions of dollars, for new air conditioners in supermarkets, restaurants, and automobiles. But even if we could afford such a transition, we are not sure whether the chemicals that will replace CFCs are totally safe. So these new chemicals could also face future bans, in which case society again would have to retool its cooling infrastructure at a cost of many more billions.

And legislators ignored technological realities when issuing their decrees regarding the elimination of CFCs. By 1995 or 1996, millions of office workers around the United States could face almost intolerably hot working environments unless their companies shift to CFC-free cooling units. But only about 6,000 new cooling units, called chillers, are produced every year, far fewer than those needed.

By mid-1993, consumers were already registering their distaste for the new austerity programs instituted in response to environmental rules. Consider the growing consumer resistance to the utilities' "negawatt" programs. In keeping with the new "demand-side" energy paradigm, local and state governments are now measuring the efficiency of utilities in terms of "negawatts," units of energy that consumers do not use that they ordinarily would. To produce these phantom energy units, utilities such as Central Maine Power and the New England Electrical System have embarked on programs to convince the public to reduce its energy consumption.

To the dismay of the power companies and rate commissions, consumers are already learning that this new age of the energy negawatt requires that they live in a darker, less vibrant physical environment, and they are rebelling. For instance, one method that utilities suggest for reducing energy use (or "increasing negawatts") is switching to power-saving compact fluorescent light bulbs. However, consumers quickly discover such bulbs to be much dimmer than originally advertised and remove all the lights the utility representatives install and replace them with their old brighter bulbs.

As we learned in Chapter 8, people exposed to bright light, such as that produced by high-intensity halogens, tend to be more alert, and therefore more productive, at work and at school. I envision the home of the future as not simply living quarters but a fully digitized learning environment, replete with electronic computers, modems, and faxes. In order to work, play, and thrive in such an environment, the individual must be surrounded by the proper ergonomic tools, including bright lighting. But such a goal will be frustrated by utility companies that would rather turn off the lights than build new power plants.

As yet, very few private citizens know just how radically the Clean Air Act will change their life-style. They are unaware that they will be restricted in their use of creature comforts such as air conditioners and automobiles. And few realize that the act will indirectly force them to move closer to their jobs.

The prediction here is that by 1996, the inconveniences and health hazards of such laws, plus their negative impact on the standard of living, will push the debate over the rights of the public versus those of the environment into the political arena. It is not unlikely that when industry and workers realize the implications of such requirements as the shift to a non-CFC world and a limit on automobile use, they will demand the repeal of the Clean Air Act or at the very least sharp curtailment of its applications. And they may demand adoption of myriad pro-growth policies.

Some Third World countries attending the Rio environmental summit had their consciousness similarly raised over the real effects of zero-growth policies. Although many were attracted to this conference by the lure of a major North to South transfer of billions of dollars, they suddenly realized that the new environmental order proposed by the U.N. and the Worldwatch Institute would impose restrictions on their economic growth. For example, Brazil discovered that its economically lucrative timber-cutting practices in the rainforest could be severely curtailed. India and China found how different the environmentalists view of third world population growth was from theirs: The countries saw such growth as a way to increase its labor supply. To environmentalists, extra people represent a drain on the planet Earth and its valuable natural resources.

Certainly the myriad of classes, countries, and castes at the convention hardly registered a heterogeneous perspective on the meaning of environmentalism. When the citizens of India, Africa, and South America finally discover how a U.N.-run world environmental order will stifle their economies, they will join with the average Westerner in the growing consensus on the need for human progress.

Strategy and Tactics

In all countries, the battle for humanity's future will be fought on several fronts: the political, cultural, and educational realms. Nevertheless, although a nascent progrowth movement has begun to assert itself, it has yet to crystallize into the force that will overcome the remaining political and cultural obstacles to the species' transition into the Macroindustrial Era. Several actions will accelerate this process.

First, the proprogress political, business, and citizen groups must recognize their commonality and find each other in the ideological landscape. Once disparate groups understand their commonality, they are in a better position to establish a working coalition.

Second, they must organize around their basic principles, such as economic growth and the role and rights of humanity. And they must recognize that in the battles over issues such as the Clean Air Act of 1990 and the Endangered Species Act, it is these principles that they are ultimately defending.

Certainly, by the early 1990s the pro-growth message was coming through clearer than it had in several decades. In 1993, such books appeared as Ronald Bailey's *Eco-Scam*, Dixy Lee Ray's *Environmental Overkill*, and Michael Fumento's *Science Under Siege*, which challenged numerous theories of environmental doom and gloom. Since journalists are now exposing many false claims of environmentalists and others, Congress and citizens should be less prone to allow alarmism and pseudo-science to create science-and-technology policy.

Third, the proprogress group must attempt to establish a degree of organizational sophistication comparable to zero-growthers'. In the last section, I discussed the wide-ranging presence of environmentalists within the media, governments, the U.N., even royalty. Perhaps an organized pressure group will evolve that will lobby for expansionary principles. Certainly, such an umbrella organization could serve as a needed counterbalance to the organized environmental/zero-growth lobby that manages not only to make its views felt but understands how to use legal measures, including lawsuits and hearings, to attain their goals. These legal maneuvers have been known to make new plant production so expensive that utilities have in desperation stopped building them in many states.

This new force must stand as a bulwark to the seemingly ubiquitous zero-growth forces that permeate every aspect of the legislative, political, and cultural process. It is certainly conceivable that the expansionary ethos will find its voice as a wing or position group within one or both of the major parties in the United States.

A tangible first effort might be to lobby for the passing of an economic impact law. This law would simply state that any bill, statute, or mandate must include an economic impact statement which describes how it will affect economic growth and the species' development. Before a bill is passed we would have to know the extent to which the law in question would contribute to economic growth or cause financial hardship to businesses and individuals? I believe that if an economic impact law had existed throughout the 1970s and 1980s, the Endangered Species Act and Clean Air Act would have looked radically different.

Fourth, centralized intellectual and political leadership must develop for such a movement to succeed. Such leadership must articulate the positions and provide a vision to the newly organized expansionary groups. This leadership must also serve as the lobby's human face to politicians as well as the public.

Fifth, this movement must consider the media a natural conduit for its expansionary message. A media campaign could present to the public a series of arguments for progress. The public has to be helped to confront such issues as the need for energy, the argument for material progress, and the balance between risk and societal benefits in technological growth. Such a media campaign could also help to create a positive outlook, the cornerstone of the Expansionary Culture. The populace could begin to think in terms of possibilities, not limits, a mind-set that is the necessary precondition for individual and national achievement.

Through the media, the expansionary coalition could encourage individuals to learn more about technology, become more entrepreneurial, demand greater training and responsibility at work, involve themselves in creative activities, participate in children's learning, and motivate their local and national politicians to create more growth. Importantly, such a media campaign would encourage the individual to question environmental claims such as global warming and ozone depletion. For instance, the Expansionary movement ought to demand the chance to present its own viewpoint on MTV as part of that channel's new emphasis on socially conscious public service advertising.

Sixth, this movement must ensure that the Western intellectual tradition of growth and progress continues to be taught in the schools and universities and maintained in the arts and sciences. Progress must be defended in the classrooms and the academic journals.

Currently, progress has come under attack in the educational institutions. For example, the purpose of the current trend in American universities toward teaching all courses from a multicultural perspective is supposedly to give equal time to the history and customs of diverse countries and nationalities. In reality, the banning of the study of Western civilization and culture has the effect of excising from students' consciousness any notion of the Western idea of progress. Once the intellectual tradition of progress disappears, the path clears for the introduction and final victory of cyclical thinking and zero-growth theology throughout the culture.

Academics and professionals concerned about such issues can combat such trends through activism in schools, professional associations, and the media. It may involve consciousness-raising of colleagues and students. Without such activity, the well-organized antiprogress minority will continue to proselytize in textbooks, curricula, and the classroom.

Through such methods the expansionary forces will smooth the cultural and political path for nations and society itself to enter into the Macroindustrial Era.

We Will Seize the Future!

Progress, survival, and growth are ultimately accomplished by an act of will, both collective and individual. The desire must precede action regardless of the skills, talents, and resources present in a particular society, and that desire will burst upon the scene throughout the 1990s. In reality, all attempts to decelerate progress and obstruct material, intellectual, and artistic growth will prove ultimately fruitless. Clintonite zero growthers, German Greens, and international environmental organizations can slow progress, but society's inexorable momentum forward will eventually neutralize such groups' power. The Macroindustrial Era will emerge because it represents global society's next logical step. Humanity will either progress or disappear, and it will never willingly choose its own demise.

Humanity has an almost innate desire for progress and improvement. Certainly, over the last 500 years in the West the idea of human and material progress has become so established that we can speak of this value as not just a cultural trait, but almost as a genetic disposition. The globalization of Western values has generated a universal desire for material improvement.

These values establish the necessary conditions for progress. They include the belief that humanity, not nature, has ultimate domain over the planet; that the world is generally better off with the presence of *Homo sapiens*; and that humankind has an innate responsibility to develop, direct, and improve nature and the universe.

Once humanity comprehends the true nature and scope of its abilities, it will demand that those abilities be actualized. At that point, the entire globe will contribute its creative and productive energies to the emerging Macroindustrial Era. The species will extend the life span, increase its industrial output, dominate and improve the planet, and begin to stretch its influence throughout the Solar System, the galaxy, and eventually the universe.

As technology eliminates pollution and toxicity from the air, water, and the soil, humankind will realize that material progress and technological sophistication are the best environmental policies of all.

We stand at the most critical juncture in the history of humanity. We blanket the globe with our technology and ourselves, conquer our ancient limits, transform the Earth, and rewrite nature's laws. Yet, at the very threshold of the Macroindustrial Era, with success almost within our grasp, we pause, quaking with apprehension, wondering whether we tempt the fates when we test the frontiers of time and space.

We cannot let such self-doubt impede our progress. The species must be willing to accept the responsibility that its unique abilities and superior intelligence thrust upon it to improve itself, enrich the planet, and ultimately perfect the universe.

History beckons, the cosmos awaits. Our destiny demands that we seize the future!

Notes

CHAPTER ONE

Page

17 Consider for a moment: Kitta MacPherson, "Radical Changes Arriving in New Era of Discovery," *Newark Star-Ledger*, July 14, 1991. Andrew Pollack, John Holusha, Matthew Wald, "Transforming the Decade: 10 Critical Technologies," *New York Times*, January 1, 1991, Science Times section, p. 1.

20 Nothing typifies: John L. McLucas, *Space Commerce* (Cambridge, MA: Harvard University Press, 1991). William E. Burrows, *Exploring Space: Voyages in the Solar System and Beyond*. "Underground Cities: Japan's Answers to Overcrowding," *The Futurist*, March–April 1990. Eric K. Drexler, *Engines of Creation: The Coming Era of Nanotechnology* (New York: Doubleday Anchor, 1987).

21 This transmutation: David Stipp, "Science Is Pushing Heart Disease Farther into Old Age," *Wall Street Journal*, November 19, 1990, p. 1.

21 We also measure: Michael Rogers, "Marvels of the Future," *Newsweek*, December 25, 1990, pp. 77–78.

22 Humanity will introduce: Geoffrey Sheldon, "They Can Control a Steel Plant from Just One P.C.," *Achievement*, December 1990, p. 7.

22 The production of: "Fast Reactors—The Logical Successors to Present Nuclear Power Stations," *Achievement*, March 1990.

22 Food will also: "The World Could Be Fed," *Scientific American*, February 1990, p. 106.

23 The next step: "The New Alchemy: How Science Is Molding Molecules into Miracle Materials," *Business Week*, July 19, 1991, p. 48.

24 They are well: William B. Johnston, "Global Work Force 2000: The New World Labor Market," *Harvard Business Review*, February 1991, pp. 115–27. John W. Mellor and Frank Reilly, "Expanding the Green Revolution to Reduce Third World Poverty," *Issues in Science and Technology*, Fall 1989.

24 There has been a change from: "Tapping Foreign Talent Pool Can Yield Lush Growth," *Wall Street Journal*, March 1992, p. B1.

24 One other factor: Damien Lewis and Frank Nowikowski, "Saving Earth, Dividing Earthlings, "Gemini News Service, London, August 1991, cited in

Page

World Press Review, p. 52. Marvin Cetron and Owen Davies, "50 Trends Shaping the World," *The Futurist*, September–October 1991, p. 11. Dr. Norman Myers, ed., *Gaia: An Atlas of Planet Management* (New York: Anchor Doubleday, 1984).

25 Enlarging the size: "Going Height Crazy," *The Futurist*, November–December 1986, p. 114.

25 While skyscrapers: Jeffrey Kluger, "Tokyo Takes to the Sea," *Discover*, November 1988, p. 88.

26 The Macroindustrial obsession: McKinley Conway, "Tomorrow's Supercities for Land, Sea, and Air," *The Futurist*, May–June 1993, p. 27.

27 The onset of the Macroindustrial Era: Alvin Toffler, *The Third Wave* (New York: Bantam Books, 1980). John Naisbit, *Megatrends* (New York: Warner Books, 1982) and *Megatrends 2000* (New York: Warner Books, 1990). Mark Satin, *New Options for America: The Second American Experiment Has Begun* (Fresno: California State University Press, 1991).

28 Lester Thurow, in his recent: Lester Thurow, *Head to Head: Japan, Europe, America—Who Will Prevail?* (New York: Morrow, 1992).

29 In the United States and elsewhere: "Has Our Standard of Living Stalled?" *Consumer Reports*, June 1992, p. 392. Louis Uchitelle, "Stanching the Loss of Good Jobs," *New York Times*, January 31, 1993, Business section, p. 1.

29 Fortunately, signs abound: Stephen S. Cohen and John Zysman, *Manufacturing Matters: The Myth of the Post-Industrial Economy*. "It Ain't a Recovery Till the Factories Hum," *Business Week*, August 31, 1922. Norman Jonas, "The Hollow Corporation," *Business Week*, March 3, 1986, p. 57.

31 Robert Nisbet, a leading theorist: Robert Nisbet, *History of the Idea of Progress* (New York: Basic Books, 1980).

31 In the 1400s, the West: William R. Hawkings, "The Sun Never Sets," *Chronicles*, June 1991, p. 44. Daniel Boorstin, *The Discoverers: A History of Man's Search to Know His World and Himself* (New York: Random House, 1983). Nathan Rosenberg and L. E. Birdzell, *How the West Grew Rich* (New York: Basic Books, 1986).

32 It is understanding that cyclical: Mircea Eliade, *Cosmos and History: The Myth of the Eternal Return* (New York: Harper Torchbooks, 1959).

37 Although economic growth: Sylvia Nasar, "Cooling the World Would Be Nice, But Saving Lives Now May Cost Less," *New York Times*, May 31, 1992, Week in Review, p. 5. "Saving Ourselves with Progress," *Le Figaro*, cited in *World Press Review*, December 1992, p. 23.

37 According to Norio Yamamoto: Douglas C. McGill, "Scour Technology's Stain with Technology," *New York Times Magazine*, October 4, 1992, p. 32.

38 Companies now use such bacteria: Dawn Stover, "Toxic Avengers," *Popular Science*, July 1992, pp. 70–93. Robert Kunzig, "Earth on Ice: A Bold Attack on Global Warning," *Discover*, April 1991, p. 54.

38 According to the American Academy: Reed Abelson, "Bugs Clean up Their Act," *Forbes*, September 28, 1992. "Microbe Can Break Down Ozone-Destroying HCFC's," *Wall Street Journal*, September 1992. Kitta MacPherson, "Bioremediation Battles to Counter Forces of Nature," *Newark Star-Ledger*, January 11, 1993.

38 The human imagination: "Environmental Research," *R&D Magazine*, September 28, 1992, p. 83.

Page
40 The Clean Air Act of 1990: Jay Romano, "Getting to Work Will Never Be the Same," *New York Times*, February 23, 1992, Sec. 12, p. 1.
42 Much of the sustainable development theory: Donella H. Meadows, Dennis L. Meadows, and Jorgen Randers, *Beyond the Limits: Confronting Global Collapse, Envisioning a Sustainable Future* (Post Mills, VT: Chelsea Green Publishing Co., 1992).
44 Perhaps we should consider: Clive Ponting, *A Green History of the World: The Environment and the Collapse of Great Civilizations* (New York: St. Martin's Press, 1992).
44 Regardless of the protestations: "Growth vs. the Environment: The Push for Sustainable Development," *Business Week*, May 11, 1992.
45 The breakthroughs that will enable: "Why the U.S. Is Losing Its Lead," in *Innovation '90*, special edition of *Business Week*, 1990, p. 35. Ralph E. Gomory and Harold T. Shapiro, "A Dialogue on Competitiveness," *Issues in Science and Technology*, September 1988, p. 36. "How Congress 'Competes' " (editorial), *Wall Street Journal*, January 15, 1990. "For All Its Difficulties, U.S. Stands to Retain Its Global Leadership," *Wall Street Journal*, January 23, 1989, p. 1.

CHAPTER TWO
Page
48 Although the year 1914 is usually remembered: "1914: The Focus Was Transportation: Imaginative Bridges, Interocean Canals, and Better Roads Were the Main Projects," *ENR*, January 5, 1989.
48 This year also saw: Ronald E. Shaw, *Canals for a Nation: A History of the Canal Era in the United States, 1790–1860* (Lexington, KY: University of Kentucky Press, 1990).
48 There is no greater evidence: "Underground Cities: Japan's Answers to Overcrowding," *The Futurist*, March–April 1990.
49 Businesspeople and visionaries for centuries: Fred Guterl and Russel Ruthen, "Chunnel Vision: An Undersea Link Between Great Britain and France," *Scientific American*, January 1991.
50 Although principally meant to: Joel Sleed, "Chunneling to France," *Newark Star-Ledger*, January 7, 1992, Section 8, p. 9.
51 Ocean City's formulator: Jeffrey Kluger, "Tokyo Takes to the Sea," *Discover*, November 1988, p. 88. Dwight Holing, "Surf and Turf," *Omni*, December 1988.
51 Although the stuff of: "Build Island in the Bay, Tokyo Architect Urges," *Wall Street Journal*, January 5, 1988, p. 1.
51 Then, prefabricated pontoons containing: "Tiny Monaco Plans Expansion by Building 'Floating Suburb.' " Reuters press release, April 20, 1992.
52 Also, the building of artificial islands: Frank P. Davidson and John Stuart Cox, *Macro: A Clear Vision of How Science and Technology Will Shape Our Future* (New York: Morrow, 1983), p. 146.
52 Dozens of communities: Bruce Weber, "Greening the Desert," *New York Times Magazine*, September 9, 1990, p. 122.
52 The midcontinent of North America: Frank Davidson, "Macro-engineering: Some Next Steps," *The Futurist*, March–April 1990, pp. 16–20. Davidson and Cox, *Macro*.
53 The Russians have their own: Davidson and Cox, *Macro*, pp. 197–98.
53 The Japanese will not be excluded: Douglas C. McGill, "Scour Technolo-

Page
gy's Stain with Technology," *New York Times Magazine*, October 4, 1992, p. 54.

54 Over the years, America and other countries: Joseph Vranich, *Supertrains: Solutions to America's Transportation Gridlock* (New York: St. Martin's Press, 1991). "Levitating Trains," *The Futurist*, March–April 1990.

56 Unfortunately, this may be: "U.S. Lags in Developing High-Speed Rail Systems," AP wire story, June 10, 1992.

57 The supertrain will play: Joel Garreau, *Edge Cities* (New York: Doubleday/ Anchor, 1991).

57 Most developed countries are planning: McKinley Conway, "Super Projects: New Wonders of the World," *The Futurist*, March–April 1993, p. 25.

58 NASA's National Aero-Space Plane: John Holusha, "Needed by Space Plane: Space-Age Composites," *New York Times*, July 1, 1992, p. D7. *Science News*, October 26, 1990, p. 3.

59 It would be an ironic twist: Davidson and Cox, *Macro*, pp. 63–67.

59 The Palleted Automated Transportation (PAT) system: "Computer Aids Steering," *USA Today*, The World of Science, June 1989, p. 19. "Smart Highways," *Scientific American*, July 1990, p. 286.

59 Driving will be made smarter: Vernon M. Church, "Technology Takes the Toll," *Popular Science*, March 1992, pp. 78–81. Samia El-Badry and Peter K. Nance, "Driving into the 21st Century," *American Demographics*, September 1992, p. 46.

60 Unfortunately, these cars at present: Jerry E. Bishop, "New Generation of Electric-Car Batteries to Be Unveiled," *Wall Street Journal*, February 1992.

61 Efforts are being made: David Stipp, "GM and Utility Mount Charge on Electric Cars," *Wall Street Journal*, May 19, 1993.

62 One example of CIM: John H. Sheridan, "Toward the CIM Solution," *Industry Week*, October 16, 1989. John J. Xenakis, "A Revolution in the Workplace," *Information Week*, July 22, 1991, p. 38. "Rebuilding America: Start at the Factory" (Outlook column). *Wall Street Journal*, March 1988.

64 This becomes more obvious: "Reinventing the Robot," *The Economist*, October 27, 1990, pp. 91–92. Tom Dworetzky, "Mech Animals," *Omni*, pp. 50–52. John Rossant, "Will These Robots Conquer the World," in *Innovation '90*, special edition of *Business Week*, 1990, p. 144.

66 Many analysts agree that: David J. Jefferson, "Floating on Air," *Wall Street Journal*, April 6, 1992, p. R19.

67 This sea change in our perspective: Tom Dworetzky, "Perpetual Power: Can We Develop a Sane Energy Strategy for the Future?" *Omni*, March 1991, pp. 36–38. Phil Scott, "Good to the Last Drop," *Omni*, March 1991, pp. 41.

68 As an example of the: USCEA 1991 International Nuclear Wrap-Up. News Release of the U.S. Council for Energy Awareness, May 26, 1992.

69 In spite of the monumental effort: "The Electricity/GNP Connection: Recent Trend Reinforces Need for New Generating Capacity," *USCEA Energy Analysis*, June 1991. Author interview with Rep. Dick Zimmer, member of House Subcommittee on Space, Energy, Technology, regarding U.S. plans and possibilities in the Macroindustrial Era, February 11, 1993.

71 These plants will be standardized: Nuclear Power Oversight Committee, "Strategic Plan for Building New Nuclear Power Plants," November 1991.

71 The European Community will not: John Greenwald, "Time to Choose," *Time*, April 29, 1991, p. 54. Charles Krauthammer, "Pulling the Plug on Nu-

Page

clear Power Is No Victory," Washington Post Writers Group syndication, June 19, 1988. Joan Beck, "The Real Danger Is Writing Off Nuclear Power," Chicago Tribune syndication, August 8, 1988. Françoise Vaysse, *Le Monde*, excerpted in *World Press Review*, January 1991.

71 Japan is also building: David Sanger, "Japan's Nuclear Fiasco," *New York Times*, December 20, 1992, Business section, p. 1.

72 Some fears about disposing: Dawn Stover, "Toxic Avengers," *Popular Science*, July 1992, p. 70.

73 I interviewed Congressman Dick Zimmer in early 1993: Interview with Zimmer, February 11, 1993.

74 Of course, DuPont and other: Interview with Marvin S. Fertel, vice president, Technical Programs, U.S. Council for Energy Awareness, June 15, 1992.

75 At the JET: "Optimism for Future Electricity from Sun and Stars Power Source," *Achievement*, March 1990, pp. 21–23.

76 However, many believe that: "Scientists Claim Nuclear Fusion Breakthrough," AP wire story, November 11, 1991.

76 By 1994, the Princeton Tokamak: Robert Cohen, "Fusion at Princeton," *Newark Star-Ledger*, May 6, 1993, p. 1.

76 Of course, the race for: Joelle Godfrey, "Tight Aid Threatens Research on Fusion," Medill News Service, November 11, 1991. "U.S. Falling Behind in Fusion Tests," AP wire story, dateline Trenton, November 11, 1991.

77 Of course, you can: "Navy's Cold Fusion Research Claims Results Like Utah's," AP wire story, March 1991. Ron Dagani, "New Evidence Claimed for Nuclear Process in Cold Fusion," *Chemical and Engineering News*, April 1, 1991.

78 In spite of such skepticism: William J. Brand, "Two Teams Put New Life in 'Cold' Fusion Theory of Energy," *New York Times*, April 26, 1991, p. A7. Jerry E. Bishop, "Utah Funds for Cold Fusion Run Low Just as Concept Gets Boost from Navy," *Wall Street Journal*, April 8, 1991, p. B4.

78 In 1991, Eugene Mallove: "Cold Fusion Tempest at MIT," *Nature*, September 12, 1991.

79 The skeptics openly describe: Denis L. Rousseau, "Case Studies in Pathological Science," *American Scientist*, Vol. 80, January–February 1992, pp. 54–63.

79 In the summer of 1992: Jerry G. Bishop and Jacob M. Schlesinger, "U.S. Researcher Claims to Replicate Japanese Experiment in Cold Fusion," *Wall Street Journal*, July 27, 1992, p. B4.

80 Although the quest for: Jerry E. Bishop, "Electric Power Research Institute to Pay $12 Million More to Study 'Cold Fusion.' " *Wall Street Journal*, March 18, 1992.

80 By 1993, more and more: Jerry G. Bishop, "Cold Fusion: It Ain't Over till It's Over," *Popular Science*, August 1993, p. 47.

81 According to George Hazelrigg: "Welcome to Lilliput," *Newsweek*, April 15, 1991, pp. 60–61.

82 Nanotechnology hopes to: Eric K. Drexler, *Engines of Creation: The Coming Era of Nanotechnology* (New York: Anchor Books, 1987).

83 One of the physical obstacles confronting: J. Madeleine Nash, "Adventures in Lilliput," *Time*, December 30, 1991, pp. 60–61.

83 IBM's Research Division has developed: "Atom Mover Opens Era of Nanoelectronics," *New Scientist*, July 20, 1991, p. 20.

Page
83 Prognosticators now believe: "Tiny Machines, Major Benefits," *USA Today*, June 1991, p. 3.
83 Eric Drexler, nanotechnology guru: Robert Langreth, "Molecular Marvels," *Popular Science*, May 1993, p. 91. "Why Scientists Are Thinking Small," *Popular Science*, April 1993. "Japan's Big Push to Build Chips Atom by Atom," *Business Week*, December 21, 1992, p. 58.

CHAPTER THREE
Page
86 As soon as humanity began: "Can Space Still Sing?: A Former Astronaut Urges America to Rediscover the Romance of Space Exploration," *Omni*, March 1991. "Bush Targets Distant Date for Mars Landing," AP wire story, June 1991.
87 He couched this mission: "Bush: 'The Inescapable Challenge' " (Viewpoint), *Aviation Week and Space Technology*, July 31, 1989, p. 13. "Manned Lunar Base, Mars Initiative, Raised in Secret White House Review," *Aviation Week and Space Technology*, July 17, 1989, p. 89.
90 Recent studies of the Pyramids: Daniel Boorstin, *The Creators* (New York: Random House, 1992), pp. 88–89.
92 Early successes have spawned: Elizabeth Corcoran and Tim Beardsley, "The New Space Race," *Scientific American*, July 1990, p. 72. Craig Covault, "Commercial Space Ventures Face Harsh Market Realities," *Aviation Week and Space Technology*, December 19, 1988, p. 34. Nicholas C. Kernstock, "Most Investors Shun High-Risk Commercial Space Ventures, *Aviation Week and Space Technology*, December 19, 1988, p. 45. Ben Bova et al., "Spaceward Ho," *Omni*, July 1991. "Is NASA Overcautious When It Comes to Safety?" AP wire service, March 11, 1991. "We Have Liftoff," *Omni*, June 1991.
93 Nineteen ninety-three will see the launching: Ron Cowen, "Space '93," *Science News*, January 9, 1993, pp. 24–26.
93 One of the most successful applications: "Space-Grown Protein Crystals Will Aid in Drug Research," *Aviation Week and Space Technology*, December 19, 1988. "New Products Benefit Earth," *USA Today*, The World of Science, 1989.
94 "Under NASA's Auspices": Warren E. Leary, "Shuttle Begins 13-Day Trip to Study the Uses of Gravity," *New York Times*, June 26, 1992.
94 Experimentation continues: Cowen, "Space '93." Jeffrey M. Lenorovitz, "Alenia Spazio Begins Development of Manned Modules for Space Station," *Aviation Week and Space Technology*, March 2, 1992, p. 47.
95 Like many other low: Dick Zimmer, "Space Station Under Fire," *Washington Post*, June 5, 1991, p. A79. James J. Kilpatrick, "Suddenly, the Moon Seems Affordable" (column), Universal press syndicate, July 1991.
96 Future proposals: Michael Mautner, "Engineering Earth's Climate from Space," *The Futurist*, March–April 1993, p. 33.
98 One of the most ambitious robotic spacecraft probes: Carl Sagan, "Titan: Key to the Origins of Life," *Parade Magazine*, December 1, 1991, p. 6.
98 In NASA's plans is a craft: Cowen, "Space '93."
99 The moon is a prize coveted: James Asker, "Synthesis Group to Add Asteroids to Moon/Mars Exploration Plans," *Aviation Week and Space Technology*, June 10, 1991. "To Boldly Go," *The Economist*, June 15, 1991.
100 According to this scenario: "Manned Lunar Base, Mars Initiative, Raised

Page

in Secret White House Review," *Aviation Week and Space Technology*, July 17, 1989, p. 26.

100   In other areas: "Japan Goes to the Moon," *Time*, February 5, 1990, p. 58. Constance Holden, "Japan Reaches for the Moon, *Science*, February 2, 1990.

101   Mars and the Earth share: John Wilford Nobel, *Mars Beckons* (New York: Knopf, 1990). The Quest for Planet Mars, segment of 1991 PBS special, "The Space Age."

102   According to Michael Griffin: Leonard David, "Michael Griffin: NASA's Moon-Mars Man," *Final Frontier*, May–June 1992.

103   To most observers, Mars appears intimidating: "Mars," *Life*, March 1991. "Panel Offers Plan for Reaching Mars," *New York Times*, June 12, 1991.

105   "There are many, many barriers": Dr. Mel Averner, "Can Mars Be Made Hospitable to Humans," *New York Times*, October 1, 1991, p. C1.

105   The "greening" of Mars: Leonard David, "Exploring Mars with Ants, Crabs, and Snakes," *Ad Astra*, January 1991. "Slithering Across Mars," *Sky and Telescope*, March 1991. Robert Buderi, "Will 'Gnat Robots' Take Wing?" in *Innovation '90*, special edition of *Business Week*, 1990, p. 56.

106   Some feel that the: "Outlook '91 and Beyond," *World Future Society*, 1991. Dorion Sagan, *Biospheres: The Metamorphosis of Planet Earth* (New York: McGraw Hill, 1990). "Visitors to Mars by 2011," *Machine Design*, January 25, 1990. Joan Beck, "The Biosphere Hideaway" (column), Chicago Tribune syndication service, January 1991.

106   Many scientists strongly support: Bruce Murray, "Destination Mars—A Manifesto," *Nature*, May 1990, pp. 199–200. Bob Davis, "Nuclear Craft Recommended to Explore Mars," *Wall Street Journal*, June 12, 1991. A. J. Austin, "Space Writer Robert M. Powers: Dreaming of Mankind's Life on Mars," *Astronomy*, April 1988.

106   In the future: Donald F. Robertson, "Have Laser Will Travel," Final Frontier, January–February 1992, p. 19.

108   Physicist Eugene Saenger: Helmut Muller, "We Can Reach the Stars," *Final Frontier*, May–June 1990, pp. 44–45.

108   As Paul Davies and others: Paul Davies, "Wormholes and Time Machines," *Sky and Telescope*, January 1992, p. 20. Chip Walker, "Space Base," *Final Frontier*, May–June 1990.

109   Regardless of the: Frank White, *The Overview Effect: Space Exploration and Human Evolution* (New York: Atheneum, 1990).

110   As I will make clear in later chapters: "Designing a City for Mars," *The Futurist*, March–April 1993, p. 29.

112   Yuri Semenov: "Russians Offer Use of *Mir* Space Station as a Prelude to Mars," AP Wire story, February 22, 1992, p. 37.

113   Mars is a critical focus: Warren E. Leary, "Space-Race Rivals Agree to Fly on Joint Missions," *New York Times*, June 17, 1992.

113   Although nothing like a global space program: "Space Race Becomes a Joint Venture," *Wall Street Journal*, November 11, 1992.

115   Unless the space establishment: Adam Dworetsky, "Rim Shots: The Pacific Could Be the Next Gateway to the Moon and Beyond," *Omni*, July 1991, p. 36.

116   As John Logsdon: Carl Sagan, "Why Send Humans to Mars?" *Issues in Science and Technology*, Spring 1991, p. 80.

116   It has been postulated: George A. Seielstad, *At the Heart of the Web: The*

Page
Inevitable Genesis of Intelligent Life (New York: Harcourt, Brace, Jovanovich, 1989).
116 The literal extension of: Teilhard de Chardin, *The Phenomenon of Man* (New York: Harper Torchbooks, 1961), originally published in French in 1955.
117 In a challenging: German Arciniegas, *America in Europe* (New York: Harcourt, Brace, Jovanovich, 1986).

CHAPTER FOUR
Page
118 Within less than a century: "Life Expectancy" (Newsbrief), *AFP*, Vol. 36, No. 2.
119 In the United States: Amy Schuylman Eskind, "Is This You in the Year 2045?" *USA Weekend*, August 30–September 1, 1991.
119 Antibiotics also have contributed: Theodore J. Gordon, "Medical Breakthrough: Cutting the Toll of Killer Diseases," *The Futurist*, January–February 1987, p. 60.
120 In this chapter we will: Phillip Elmer-DeWitt, "You Should Live So Long," *Time*, November 12, 1990. "Why Do Women Live Longer Than Men?" *Science*, October 1987. Leonard Hayflick, "Why Do We Live So Long?" *Geriatrics*, October 1988, p. 77. Leigh Dayton, "The Perils of Living in a Right-handed World," *New Scientist*, October 1989, p. 32. "So Long, Lefty: Slightly Sinister Statistics for Left-Handed People," *Scientific American*, August 1988, p. 26.
121 French geneticist Daniel Cohen: Christine Gorman, "The Race to Map Our Genes," *Time*, February 8, 1993, p. 57.
123 To the nonscientist: "The Genetic Age," *Business Week*, May 28, 1990.
123 Ironically, our enhanced knowledge of: "Stalking a Killer: Scientists Near the End of Race to Discover a Breast-Cancer Gene," *Wall Street Journal*, December 11, 1992, p. 1.
124 In 1990, an NIH team: Leon Jaroff, "Brave New Babies," *Time*, May 31, 1993, pp. 56–57.
124 We may see such a breakthrough: "Scientists Splice Genes into HIV to Derail It" (Lab Notes section), *Wall Street Journal*, May 14, 1992, p. B1.
125 This is only the beginning: Tom Fennell, "Nearing the Final Frontier," *Maclean's*, July 15, 1991, p. 37.
125 Joan Rothschild, of the: Joan Beck, "Gene Therapy: The Coming Revolution" (column), Chicago Tribune syndication, January 12, 1991.
126 One method transforming: Marilyn Chase, "Using PCR Gene Technology, Physician Can Diagnose Elusive Diseases Earlier," *Wall Street Journal*, October 30, 1991, p. B1.
127 The diagnostic revolution is further: Abraham Katzir, "Optical Fibers in Medicine," *Scientific American*, May 1989, p. 120. "Move Over Mr. Spock," *Scientific American*, June 1990. J. Madeleine Nash, "Ultimate Gene Machine," *Time*, August 12, 1991, p. 54.
128 The application of: "Do You See What I See? Pathologists Lead the Way for Long-Distance Diagnosis," *Scientific American*, July 1990, p. 88.
129 Other superdrug designers: "The Search for Superdrugs: A Union of Biotech and Chemistry May Conquer the Great Killers," *Business Week*, May 13, 1991. Harold M. Weintraub, "Antisense RNA and DNA," *Scientific American*,

Page

January 1990, p. 40. Joan O'C. Hamilton, "One Day, There May Be Balm from Gilead," in *Innovation '90*, special edition of *Business Week*, 1990, p. 6. "New Drug Makes Cancer Cells Grow and Behave Normally," AP wire story, August 29, 1991. Andre Ulmann, Georges Teutsch, and Daniel Philibert, "RU 486," *Scientific American*, June 1990, p. 42. Richard Edelson, "Light Activated Drugs," *Scientific American*, August 1988, p. 68. "Rational Drugs: Transforming Drug Research from an Art into a Science," *Scientific American*, January 1990, p. 100.

130 At the University of Bradford: Michael Wladholz, "Altered States: Brain Explorers Use Chemical Messengers to Design New Drugs," *Wall Street Journal*, October 25, 1991, p. 1.

130 A new drug, clozapine: Claudia Wallis and James Willwerth, "Schizophrenia: A New Drug Brings Patients Back to Life," *Time*, July 6, 1992.

131 Reported breakthroughs: Diane Brady, "Designer Genes: New Genetic Weapons Fight Disease," *Maclean's*, July 15, 1991, p. 36. John Barton, "Patenting Life," *Scientific American*, March 1991, p. 40. Charles Kingon and Sean Newcombe, "Engineers Have Designs on Biology," *New Scientist*, April 1987. J. Madeleine Nash, "Cracking Cancer's Code," *Time*, November 12, 1990, p. 97. John Carey, "Tracking Down the Gene for Cystic Fibrosis," in *Innovation '90*, special edition of *Business Week*, 1990, p. 52. "Can You Choose Your Baby's Sex?" *USA Today*, World of Science, June 1989.

132 The assault on aging: Brad Darrach, "The War on Aging," *Life*, September 1992, pp. 33–41.

132 According to researcher David Clemons: Marilyn Chase, "Scientists Work to Slow Human Aging," *Wall Street Journal*, March 12, 1992, p. B1.

133 A host of other companies: "Nerve Growth Factors Brighten the Medical Horizon," *Wall Street Journal*, March 12, 1992, p. B1.

133 Several companies believe: Barnaby J. Feder, "The Pharmers Who Breed Cows That Can Make Drugs," *New York Times*, February 1992. Tabitha M. Powledge, "Gene Pharming." *Technology Review*, August–September 1992, p. 61.

135 How useful will: Beth Howard, "Ape Apothecary," *Omni*, March 1991, p. 25.

136 Every day new advances make dissection: J. Madeleine Nash, "The Kindest Cuts of All," *Time*, March 23, 1992, p. 53.

136 Fiber optics: Vic Comello, "Lasers and Electro-Optics," *R&D Magazine*, September 28, 1992, p. 87.

137 Further challenges will involve: Abraham Katzir, "Optical Fibers in Medicine," *Scientific American*, May 1989, p. 120.

137 In 1990, Dr. Ralph Clayman: J. Madeleine Nash, "The Kindest Cuts of All."

137 The introduction of technology: Elizabeth Corcoran, "Robots for the Operating Room," *New York Times*, July 19, 1992, p. 9.

138 In 1990, doctors: "Dramatic Fetal Surgery Corrects Birth Defects in Womb," AP wire story, May 31, 1990. Pat Ohlendorf-Moffat, "Surgery Before Birth," *Discover*, February 1991.

141 Genetic tests will: David Stipp, "Altered Fates: Science Pushing Heart Disease's Toll Farther into Old Age," *Wall Street Journal*, June 1991, p. 1.

142 In 1993, two separate studies: Christine Gorman, "E Is for Eluding Heart Disease," *Time*, May 31, 1993, p. 57.

Page
142   The likelihood is that: Anastasia Toufexis, "The New Scoop on Vitamins," *Time*, April 6, 1991, p. 34.
142   According to a study: Judith Hooper, *Health*, October 1989, p. 35. "The Power to Heal," *Newsweek*, September 24, 1990, p. 38.
143   The public is gradually: Gina Kolata, "Confronting New Ideas, Doctors Often Hold on to the Old," *New York Times*, May 10, 1992, p. 37.
144   The AIDS experience: John Platt, "The Future of AIDS," *The Futurist*, November–December 1987, p. 53.
145   Again, nano- and microtechnologies: "Tiny Machines, Major Benefits," *USA Today*, The World of Science, June 1991, p. 3.
146   In fact, medical researchers: "Welcome to Lilliput," *Newsweek*, April 15, 1992, pp. 60–61.
146   Expert K. Eric Drexler: K. Eric Drexler and Chris Peterson, *Unbounding the Future: The Nanotechnology Revolution* (New York: Morrow, 1991), p. 195.
148   Once we realize that: K. Eric Drexler, "Engines of Healing," Chapter 7 in *Engines of Creation: The Coming Era of Nanotechnology* (New York: Anchor Books, 1990).
149   The battle against cystic fibrosis: Andrew Purvis, "Laying Siege to a Deadly Gene," *Time*, February 24, 1992.
150   In late 1992: C. Ezzell, "Gene Therapy for Cystic Fibrosis Patients," *Science News*, December 12, 1992, p. 405.
150   This full-pronged approach: James Glanz, "The Mars Landing of Biotech," *Across the Board*, March 1993, p. 40.
154   In 1990, demographer S. Jay Olshansky: Phillip Elmer-DeWitt, "You Should Live So Long."
154   It is predicted that: "Gaining an Edge on Age," *Omni*, November 1989.
155   Researchers at the University of Texas: Brad Darrach, "The War on Aging."
156   Let us suppose that: Jeremy Rifkin and Ted Howard, *Who Shall Play God* (New York: Delacorte, 1977).
156   This convoluted logic: Joan Beck, "The Rising Cost of Living Longer" (column), Chicago Tribune syndication, March 12, 1991.
156   According to Kenneth Manton: David Stipp, "Altered Fates."
158   The danger inherent in such: Dick Thompson, "The Most Hated Man in Science," *Time*, December 4, 1989, pp. 102–4.

CHAPTER FIVE

Page
159   As the Macroindustrial Era unfolds: Eugene Linden, "Will We Run Low on Food?" *Time*, August 19, 1991, pp. 48–50. Jacqueline Kasun, *The War Against Population* (San Francisco: Ignatius Press, 1988), especially Chapter 4, "Scarcity or Lifeboat Economics."
160   By 1993 the continuing increase: Scott Kilman, "Amber Waves: U.S. Is Steadily Losing Share of World Trade in Grain and Soybeans," *Wall Street Journal*, December 3, 1992, p. 1.
161   The population of the world: Jacqueline Kasun, *The War Against Population*.
161   Roger Revelle, former director: Roger Revelle, "The World Supply of Agricultural Land," in *The Resourceful Earth* (New York: Basil Blackwell, 1984).

Page

162 Examples abound of how human imagination: "Greening the Desert," *New York Times.*

162 The price is well: Jacqueline Kasun, *The War Against Population.* John M. Krochta, "Innovation for Tomorrow's Foods," *USA Today*, January 1991.

162 The species is developing: Ann Gibbons, "Growing Crops in Saltwater," *Research News*, May 1990.

163 According to a Food and Agriculture: Ray Percival, "Malthus and His Ghost: When He Formulated His Theory, Malthus Ignored the Ingenuity of Many," *National Review*, August 1989, p. 38.

163 The biologist Francis P. Felice: D. Gale Johnson, "World Food and Agriculture," in *The Resourceful Earth: A Response to Global 2000*, eds. Julian L. Simon and Herman Kahn (Oxford: Basil Blackwell, 1984).

164 As we have seen: Richard P. Brennan, *Levitating Trains and Kamikaze Genes* (New York: Wiley, 1990).

165 Gene implantation occurs: Alex Korkov, "High Tech Hits the Dirt," *Discover*, November 2, 1988, p. 58.

165 The impact of biotechnology: Susan Harlander, "Introduction to Biotechnology," *Food Technology*, July 1989, p. 44. Susan Harlander, "Food Biotechnology: Yesterday, Today, and Tomorrow," *Food Technology*, September 1989, p. 196.

166 For many companies the 1990s: Scott McMurray, "New Clagene Tomato Might Have Tasted Just as Good Without Genetic Alteration," *Wall Street Journal*, January 12, 1993, p. B1.

166 According to Winston Brill: Alex Korkov, "High Tech Hits the Dirt." "Biotechnology Charges Ahead into the Crop Fields," *New Scientist*, January 1989, p. 34.

167 This change was expected to spur: Elizabeth Whelan, "Make Mine Bacon, Lettuce, and (Bioengineered) Tomato," *Wall Street Journal*, May 29, 1992, p. 24.

168 This will have the effect: Kitta MacPherson, "Science's Cold Feet: Genetic Lab's Chilling Discovery Confounds 'Freezer Burn,' " *Newark Star-Ledger*, June 9, 1992, p. 3. Bruce P. Wasserman, "Expectations and Role of Biotechnology in Improving Fruit and Vegetable Quality," *Food Technology*, February 1990.

168 If this policy holds: Bruce Ingersoll, "New Policy Eases Market Path for Bioengineered Foods," *Wall Street Journal*, May 26, 1992, p. B1. Edward L. Korwek, "Food Biotechnology Regulation: Overview and Selected Issues," *Food Technology*, March 1990, p. 76.

169 The market for pesticides: John Hoffman, "Natural Pesticides Growing: Biotechnology Comes of Age," *Chemical Age*, January 21, 1991, p. 5.

169 These clusters are: "Cell 'Factories' Churn Out Goods," *USA Today*, The World of Science, June 1989.

169 One of the more amazing: Judie Dziezak, "Epcot Center Adds New Exhibit: A Plant Biotechnology Laboratory," *Food Technology*, December 1988, p. 110. Alan Boyd, "Plant Switches on Genes in Response to Touch," *Science*, April 1990. Ivan Amato, "Lab-Made Proteins Stretch like Life," *Science News*, December 16, 1989. David Eppley and Kristen Muller, "Biotech's Promise— Panacea or Pie in the Sky?" *Agrichemical Age*, April 1989.

170 Breakthroughs in tissue culture: Walter Truett Anderson, "Food Without

Page
Farms: The Biotech Revolution in Agriculture," *The Futurist*, January–February 1990, p. 16.
171   Because of these breakthroughs: John Webster, "Sense and Sensibility down on the Farm: Biotechnology Seems to Provide Us with New Ways of Producing Bigger and Better Livestock," *New Scientist*, July 21, 1988.
171   We have any number of sources: "Scientists Inject Foreign Genes in Tree in Feat That Could Speed Up Growth," *Wall Street Journal*, December 18, 1992.
173   The beef and dairy industries: Richard P. Brennan, *Levitating Trains and Kamikaze Genes.*
173   They want to invest: "Biotechnology Takes Root in the Third World," *Science*, May 1990, p. 962. John W. Mellor and Frank Reilly, "Expanding the Green Revolution to Reduce Third World Poverty," *Issues in Science and Technology*, Fall 1989. Alan Goldhammer, "What Does It Take to Do Biotechnology?" *Chemtech*, March 1990.
175   This advanced material revolution: "New Materials by Design," *USA Today*, The World of Science, June 1989, pp. 8–10. John Carey and Neil Gross, "The Hottest Research Is Still Near Absolute Zero," *Business Week*, November 26, 1990, p. 88.
175   Most of us already: "Superconducting Ceramics," *USA Today*, The World of Science, June 1989, p. 9.
176   Breakthroughs in the development: John Holusha, "Layer by Layer to the Perfect Blend of Metals," *New York Times*, December 1, 1991, p. 9.
176   Of course, such breakthroughs: "The New Alchemy: How Science Is Molding Molecules into Miracle Materials," *Business Week*, July 29, 1991, p. 48.
177   These new material sciences: Tim Studt, "The Genius of R&D: Materials," p. 90G.
177   Many of these breakthroughs: "The New Alchemy."
178   Some engineers: Ibid.
179   Expert K. Eric Drexler imagines: K. Eric Drexler, "Engines of Abundance," Chapter 4 in *Engines of Creation: The Coming Era of Nanotechnology* (New York: Anchor Books, 1990).
179   Other machines in this: K. Eric Drexler, Chris Peterson, with Gayle Pergamit, *Unbounding the Future: The Nanotechnology Revolution* (New York: Morrow, 1991).
180   The country that moves: Tom Forester, "The Materials Revolution," *The Futurist*, July–August 1988, p. 63.
181   According to Lonnie Ingram: "Turning Plants into Auto Fuel," *USA Today*, June 1991, p. 3.
182   The Imperative of Growth states: Jacqueline Kasun, *The War Against Population*. Ray Percival, "Malthus and His Ghost: When He Formulated His Theory, Malthus Ignored the Ingenuity of Many." Jacqueline Kasun, "A Nation of Davids," *Chronicles*, October 1991, pp. 23–24.
185   Reacting to such figures: William B. Johnston, "Global Work Force 2000: The New World Labor Market," *Harvard Business Review*, March–April 1991, p. 115.
187   In other words: Mark R. Rosenzweig, "Population Growth and Human Capital: Theory and Evidence," The Problem of Development: A Conference of the Institute for the Study of Free Enterprise Systems, *Journal of Political*

Page

Economy, October 1990. Mark Perlman, "The Role of Population Projections for the Year 2000," in *The Resourceful Earth*. Nafis Sadik, "The World's Population Continues to Rise," *The Futurist*, March–April 1991, p. 9.

187   From the above: Dennis Avery, *Global Food Progress 1991* (Indianapolis: Hudson Institute, 1991).

188   However, the goal justifies: Elizabeth Whelan, "Make Mine Bacon, Lettuce, and (Bioengineered) Tomato." Joseph Palca, "Changes Ahead for U.S. Policy on Biotechnology Regulations," *Nature*, October 1987.

188   Orville Freeman: Orville L. Freeman, "Meeting the Food Needs of the Coming Decade," *The Futurist*, November–December 1990, p. 15.

189   Obviously, the Third World: Eugene Linden, "Will We Run Low on Food?" *Time*, August 19, 1991, pp. 48–50.

CHAPTER SIX

Page

195   In a study of several: Miles D. Storfer, *Intelligence and Giftedness: The Contributions of Heredity and Early Environment* (San Francisco: Jossey Bass, 1990).

196   In a 1991 survey of 27,000 elementary: "Principals Say Few Parents Prepare Children for School," AP wire service, August 15, 1991.

196   One study carried out: Ronald Rutti, "BW Study Says More Preschoolers Lagging," *Cleveland Plain Dealer*, February 10, 1992.

196   "A recent national study": Deborah Dawson, "Family Structure and Children's Health: United States, 1988, *Vital and Health Statistics of the National Center for Health Statistics*, Series 10, No. 178, June 1991, pp. 3–9.

197   Studies consistently demonstrate: Jim Stevenson and Glenda Friedman, "The Social Correlates of Reading Ability," *Journal of Child Psychology and Psychiatry*, Vol. 31, 1990, pp. 689–90.

197   Another study dealing: Nicholas Zill and Charlotte Schoenborn, "Developmental Learning and Emotional Problems: Health of Our Nation's Children, United States, 1988," *Vital and Health Statistics of the National Center for Health Statistics*, November 16, 1990.

197   We have found that the: Marianne D. Parsons, "Lone Parent Canadian Families and the Socioeconomic Achievements of Children as Adults," *Journal of Comparative Family Studies*, Vol. 21, 1990, pp. 353–65.

198   Studies show that a: Beverly Raphael et al., "The Impact of Parental Loss on Adolescents' Psychological Characteristics," *Adolescence*, Vol. 25, 1990, pp. 689–700.

198   In a recent study of: Alan C. Acock and K. Hill Kiecolt, "Is It Family Structure or Socioeconomic Status?" Family Structure During Adolescence and Adult Adjustment," *Social Forces*, Vol. 68, 1989, pp. 553–71.

199   The emotional effects of: Deborah Dawson, "Family Structure and Children's Health: United States, 1988," *Vital and Health Statistics*.

199   The effect of divorce: Lise M. C. Bisnairs, Philip Fireston, and David Rynard, "Factors Associated with Academic Achievement in Children Following Parental Separation," *American Journal of Orthopsychiatry*, 1990, pp. 67–76.

200   Recently an Eisenhower Army Medical Center: Lynne A. Hoyt, "Anxiety and Depression in Young Children of Divorce," *Journal of Clinical Child Psychology*, Vol. 19, 1990, pp. 26–32.

Page
200 After investigating 400 white fifteen-year-olds: Abbie K. Frost and Bilge Pakiz, "The Effects of Marital Disruption on Adolescents: Time as a Dynamic," *American Journal of Orthopsychiatry*, 1990, pp. 544–55.
200 The behavioral patterns of divorced fathers: Frank F. Furstenberg, Jr., and Kathleen M. Harris, "The Disappearing American Father? Divorce and the Waning Significance of Biological Parenthood," unpublished paper, University of Pennsylvania, March 1990. Peter S. Jensen et al., "Children at Risk I: Risk Factors and Child Symptomology," *Journal of the American Academy of Child and Adolescent Psychiatry* 29, 1990, pp. 51–59. Abbie K. Frost and Bilge Pakiz, "The Effects of Marital Disruption on Adolescents: Time as a Dynamic." William J. Doherty and Richard H. Needle, "Psychological Adjustment and Substance Use Among Adolescents Before and After a Parental Divorce," *Child Development*, Vol. 62, pp. 328–37. Gary D. Sadefur, Sara McLanahan, and Roger A. Wojtkiewicz, "Race and Ethnicity, Family Structure, and High School Graduation," Institute for Research on Poverty Discussion Paper No. 893–89, University of Wisconsin, Madison, August 1989. Bryan Rodgers, "Adult Affective Disorder and Early Environment," *British Journal of Psychiatry*, Vol. 57, pp. 539–50. Ian M. Goodyear, "Family Relationships, Life Events, and Childhood Psychopathology," *Journal of Child Psychology and Psychiatry*, Vol. 31, 1990, pp. 161–81. Birgitte R. Mednick, Robert L. Baker, and Linn E. Carothers, "Patterns of Family Instability and Crime: The Association of Timing of the Family's Disruption with Subsequent Adolescent and Young Adult Criminality," *Journal of Youth and Adolescence*, Vol. 19, 1990, p. 201. Richard H. Needle, S. Susan Su, and William Doherty, "Divorce, Remarriage and Adolescent Substance Use," *Journal of Marriage and the Family*, Vol. 52, 1990, pp. 157–59. Steven Stack, "New Microlevel Data on the Impact of Divorce and Suicide, 1959–1980: A Test of Two Theories," *Journal of Marriage and the Family*, Vol. 52, 1990, pp. 119–27. Dan Brubeck and John Beer, "Depression, Self-Esteem, Suicide Ideation, Death Anxiety, and GPA in High School Students of Divorced and Nondivorced Parents," *Psychological Reports*, Vol. 71, 1992, pp. 755–63.
201 The relationship between family stability: U.S. Bureau of the Census, "Poverty in the United States: 1991," *Current Population Reports*, Series P-60, No. 181, August 1992, pp. xiii, 6–9.
201 Marriage, especially when: Allan C. Carlson, "The New Poverty and the Crisis in Contemporary Family Life," *The Family in America*, special report, Vol. 5, No. 10, October 1991. Allan Tapper, *The Family in the Welfare State* (North Sydney: Allen and Unwin/Australian Institute for Public Policy, 1990).
201 What do these statistics indicate?: Sylvia Ann Hewlett, *When the Bough Breaks: The Cost of Neglecting Our Children* (New York: Basic Books, 1991). "Watching a Generation Waste Away," *Time*, August 26, 1991.
202 We depend on social units: Susan Caminiti, "Who's Minding America's Kids?" *Fortune*, August 10, 1992, p. 50.
203 In a study of eight-year-olds: Bryce Christensen, ed., *Day Care: Child Psychology and Adult Economics* (Rockford, The Rockford Institute, 1989), especially Jack Westman, "The Risk of Day Care for Children, Parents, and Society, pp. 1–41.
204 Most worrisome is: J. Craig Peery, "Children at Risk: The Case Against Day Care," *Family in America*, special report, February 1991.

Page

205 A University of London study found: E. C. Melhuish et al., "Types of Childcare at 18 Months—I. Differences in Interactional Experience," *Journal of Child Psychology and Psychiatry*, Vol. 31, 1990, pp. 849–57.

205 Other studies support: David Caruso, "Quality of Day Care and Home-Reared Infants' Interaction Patterns with Mothers and Day Care Providers," *Child and Youth Care Quarterly*, Vol. 18, Fall 1989, pp. 177–91.

205 A recent newspaper article: Janet Beigale French, "New Dawn of Day Care," *Cleveland Plain Dealer*, September 2, 1991.

206 The American family has: Roberto Suro, "The New American Family: Reality Is Wearing the Pants," *New York Times*, December 29, 1991. Sue Shellenbarger, "Leaving Infants for Work: Child-Care Costs," *Wall Street Journal*, April 1991. Larry Bumpass et al., "Changing Patterns of Remarriage," *Journal of Marriage and the Family*, Vol. 52, 1990, pp. 747–56.

206 Another contributing factor: Katherine Trent and Eve Posell-Griner, "Differences in Race, Marital Status, and Education Among Women Obtaining Abortions," *Social Forces*, Vol. 69, 1991, pp. 1121–41. "American Families: As They Are and Were," *Sociology and Social Research*, Vol. 74, 1990, pp. 139–45. "By the Decades: The Troubled Course of the Family, 1945–1990 . . . and Beyond," *The Family in America*, special report of the Rockford Institute Center, May 1990. Roger A. Wojtkiewicz et al., "The Growth of Families Headed by Women: 1950–1980," *Demography*, Vol. 27, 1990, pp. 19–30. Kathryn A. London, "Cohabitation, Marriage, Marital Dissolution, and Remarriage: United States, 1988," U.S. Department of Health and Human Services, National Center for Health Statistics, *Monthly Vital Statistics Report*, No. 194, January 1991, pp. 1–7. Myron Magnet, "The American Family, 1992," *Fortune*, August 10, 1992, p. 42.

207 Sad to say, children: Larry L. Bumpass and James A. Sweet, "Children's Experience in Single-Parent Families: Implications of Cohabitation and Marital Transitions," *Family Planning Perspectives*, Vol. 21, November/December 1989, pp. 256–60.

207 Critics and policy analysts: David Blankenhorn, Steven Bayme, and Jean Bethke Elshtain, eds., *Rebuilding the Next: A New Commitment to the American Family* (Milwaukee: Family Service America, 1990).

208 Proponents justify such proposals: Susan Caminiti, "Who's Minding America's Kids?"

209 Proponents of: Allan C. Carlson, "The New Poverty and the Crisis in Contemporary Family Life," *The Family in America*, special report, Vol. 5, No. 10, October 1991.

210 A study by Robert Plotnick: Robert D. Plotnick, "Welfare and Out-of-Wedlock Childbearing: Evidence from the 1980s," *Journal of Marriage and the Family*, Vol. 52, 1990, pp. 735–46.

210 The draconian alternative: Monroe and Garland, "On the Relationship Between Divorce Rates and Welfare Spending in the American States: A Comment on Zimmerman, *Family Relationships*, Vol. 40, 1991, pp. 148–51. David Blankenhorn, Steven Bayme, and Jean Bethke Elshtain, eds., *Rebuilding the Next: A New Commitment to the American Family*. Allan C. Carlson, "The New Poverty and the Crisis in Contemporary Family Life."

211 In a recent RAND Corporation: Linda J. Waite, Arleen Leibowitz, and Christina Witsberger, "What Parents Pay For: Childcare Characteristics, Quality, and Costs," *Journal of Social Issues*, Vol. 47, No. 2, 1991, pp. 3–48.

Page
212 Corporations, acting in: J. Craig Peery, "Children at Risk: The Case Against Day Care." Norman Horton, "Children and the Corporation," *Management Review*, January 1989, p. 6. Melvin Oliver and Thomas Shapiro, "Wealth of a Nation: A Reassessment of Asset Inequality in America Shows at Least One Third of Households Are Asset-Poor," *The American Journal of Economics and Sociology*, Vol. 49, 1990. Richard Louv, *Childhoods Future* (New York: Houghton Mifflin, 1990). Allan Carlson, "Leviathan's Children: The Family Policy of Sweden . . . and the U.S. Army," *Chronicles*, May 1990, p. 25.
213 According to social historian: Edward Hoffman, "Pop Psychology and the Rise of Anti-Child Ideology: 1966–1974," *The Family in America*, special report, August 1991.
214 These figures for the: "Rate of Marriage Continuous Decline," *New York Times*, July 17, 1992, p. A20.
215 Scholars who publicize research: "Books Say Supermom a Myth," *Los Angeles Daily News* wire story, August 26, 1991.
216 Other cultural institutions have a major: Diane Medved, *The Case Against Divorce* (New York: Donald I. Fine, 1989).
217 A Massachusetts Mutual American Value study: Norval D. Glenn, "What Does Family Mean?" *American Demographics*, June 1992, p. 34.
218 The parents assume a proactive: "Principals Say Few Parents Prepare Children for School," AP wire story, August 15, 1991.
218 The media, the schools: Kristen A. Moore and Thomas M. Stief, "Changes in Marriage and Fertility Behavior: Behavior Versus Attitudes of Young Adults," unpublished study, Child Trends, Inc., July 1989. Aimee Dorr, Peter Kovaric, and Catherine Doubleday, "Age and Content Influence on Children's Perceptions of the Realism of Television Families," *Journal of Broadcasting and Electronic Media*, Vol. 34, 1990, pp. 377–97. American Academy of Pediatrics, Committee on Communication, "Children, Adolescents, and Television," *Pediatrics*, Vol. 85, 1990. Paul Pearsall, *The Power of the Family: Strength, Comfort, and Healing* (New York: Doubleday, 1990). Edward Hoffman, *Against All Odds: The Story of Lubavitch* (New York: Simon & Schuster, 1990). Pat McNeill, "The Changing Generation Gap," *New Statesman and Society*, September 23, 1988.
219 The impact of family: Bryce Christensen, "Boardroom Blunder: American Business and the Family," *The Family in America*, special report, March 1990.
220 Family instability: "Marital Problems, Not Drugs, Seen as the Biggest Burden on Business Productivity," Ohio Psychological Association news release based on 1989 survey.

CHAPTER SEVEN
Page
222 The Macroindustrial Era will witness: "Solving the Problem at the Source," *Working Woman*, January 1990. Alecia Swasy and Carol Hymowitz, "The Workplace Revolution," *Wall Street Journal*, February 1990, p. R6.
224 In the Macroindustrial Era, the greater: Anthony Carnevale, "America and the New Economy," Part 6 of *Skill and the New Economy*, American Society of Training and Development and the U.S. Department of Labor, Washington, 1991. "Even the Most Basic Jobs Now Require Basic Skills," *Insight*, May 23, 1988, p. 38. Dale Feuer, "The Skill Gap: America's Crisis of Competence," *Training*, December 1987, p. 27. "Skills Lacking for Tomorrow's

Page

Jobs," *USA Today*, December 8, 1990, p. 11. Timothy Evans, Raymond Cossini, and George M. Gazda, "Individual Education and the 4 R's," *Educational Leadership*, September 1990. Julie Johnson and Ratu Kamlani, "Do We Have Too Many Lawyers?" *Time*, August 26, 1991, p. 54. Harold G. Shane, "Educated Foresight for the 1990s," *Educational Leadership*, September 1989, p. 4. James A. Mecklenburger, "The New Revolution," *Business Week*, December 1990, p. 22.

228   The computer's unique ability: "Computerized Children Learning Music on Mac," *New Brunswick Home News*, November 1991, p. B1.

228   Another suggestion is for: Albert Gore, "The Digitization of Schools," *Business Week*, December 1990, p. 28.

229   Of course, the digitizing: Glenn Rifkin, "Can Technology Effectively Replace Human Teachers?" *Computerworld*, October 8, 1990.

229   Ironically, the private sector: "Yale President Quitting for Private Teaching Venture," *New York Times*, May 26, 1992, p. 1.

229   A pertinent issue: Ellen Graham, "High Tech Training, *Wall Street Journal*, February 3, 1990, p. R16.

230   To survive and thrive: "Learning in America," 2-hour PBS documentary, narrated by Roger Mudd, August 1991. Anne Dees, "Basic Skills Go High Tech," *Vocational Education Journal*, January/February 1990, p. 31. John Carey, "Plato at the Keyboard: Telecommunications for Technology and Education Policy," *The Annals of the American Academy of Political and Social Science*, March 1991. Jane Schielack, "Reaching Young Pupils with Technology," *Arithmetic Teacher*, February 1991, p. 51. Christopher J. Ded, "Emerging Technologies: Impacts on Distance Learning," *The Annals of the American Academy of Political and Social Science*, March 1991, p. 146.

230   In an *Omni* magazine article: Keith Ferrell, "They Roll Their Eyes and Groan," *Omni*, April 1990, p. 14.

231   One teacher in Louisiana: Bobby Erisminger, "Television Lesson," *Letter to the Science Teacher*, September 1990, p. 47.

231   One researcher has developed: Betsy Carpenter, "On the Trail of Nintendo's Magic," *U.S. News and World Report*, July 18, 1990, p. 58.

232   Other approaches can be utilized: "All over State, Latin Redux," *New York Times*, November 15, 1992, New Jersey section, p. 1.

233   The association is attempting: Kevin G. Salwen, "Their Question Doesn't Factor in Elvis Sightings on the Mississippi," *Wall Street Journal*, May 15, 1992, p. B1.

233   We do know that; Dana Milbank, "Shortage of Scientists Approaches a Crisis as More Students Drop Out of the Field," *Wall Street Journal*, February 1990, p. B1.

234   If we do not begin: Susan Mernit, "Get with the Program: Teach with TV," *Instructor*, April 1991, p. 42. Gerald Haight, "The Age of TV," *New York Times Educational Supplement*, October 26, 1990, p. R10. Dale A. Johnson, "Training by Television," *Training and Development Journal*, August 1989, p. 4. Susan Tifft, "Beam Me Up, Students: Satellite TV Brings Live Teachers to Far Flung Schools," *Time*, May 22, 1989, p. 107.

234   The university recognizes: John Elson, "The Campus of the Future," *Time*, April 13, 1992, pp. 54–59.

236   Through Mind Extension University: Mark Robichaux, "Giving College Degrees for Watching TV," *Wall Street Journal*, May 3, 1992, p. B1.

Page

237 According to recent surveys: Helene Cooper, "Carpet Firm Sets Up an In-House School to Stay Competitive," *Wall Street Journal*, January 1993, p. A1.

238 Polaroid has always tried: Marj Charlier, "Back to Basics," *Wall Street Journal*, February 9, 1990, p. R14.

239 Corporations understood that: Ellen Graham, "High Tech Training."

240 Companies like AMP: Joseph P. Giustin, David R. Baker, and Peter J. Graybash, "Satellites Dish Out Global Training," *Personnel Journal*, June 1991, p. 80.

240 Thus, corporations are expanding: Thomas R. Horton, "Children and the Corporation," *Management Review*, January 1989, p. 5.

240 For example, corporations are involved: Hilary Stout, "Teams Vie to Redesign U.S. Education," *Wall Street Journal*, February 17, 1992, p. B1.

242 The results have been inspiring: Kendra Enson, "N.J. Bell Employees Working to Bolster Workforce of Future," *New Brunswick Home News*, March 1991.

242 In 1988, Fannie Mae: Sandra Salmans, "Nurturing the Next Work Force," *New York Times*, May 27, 1990, p. 23.

243 Businesses also look to mentor: "Mentor Program Stresses Fieldwork," AP wire story, August 22, 1991.

243 Second, individualized teaching: Michael Zey, *The Mentor Connection: Strategic Alliances in Corporate Life* (New Brunswick: Transaction Press, 1991), especially Introduction.

243 The program's results: Jerald L. Wilbur, "Mentoring Achievement Motivation, and the Literacy Challenge," *Mentoring International*, Summer 1989. "N.Y. Tutor-Mentors Target Would-Be Dropouts," AP wire story, August 22, 1991.

244 Business is also helping: Alex Molnar, "Are Schools the Business of Business?" *Wall Street Journal*, February 9, 1990. Hilary Stout, "Firms Help Set Up, Run Public Schools," *Wall Street Journal*, April 19, 1991. Diana Feldman, "Public Schools and the Business Community: An Uneasy Marriage," *Management Review*, January 1989, p. 31.

245 The growth of youth apprenticeship: Rick Wartzman, "Learning by Doing: Apprenticeship Plans Spring Up for High School Students Not Headed for College," *Wall Street Journal*, May 19, 1992.

247 As mentioned, plans are afoot: George Kaplan, "Pushing and Shoving in Videoland USA: TV's Version of Education," *Phi Delta Kappan*, January 1990, p. K1.

247 Many diverse formats: Phillip Elmer-Dewitt, "The World on a Screen," *Time*, October 21, 1992, p. 78.

248 Entrepreneurs use a variety: William M. Bulkeley, "With New Planning Software, Entrepreneurs Act like M.B.A.'s," *Wall Street Journal*, May 29, 1992, p. B1.

249 Rollins will next target: Ellen Graham, "Tapes Take Top Teachers into Homes," *Wall Street Journal*, April 18, 1991, p. B1.

250 In a national survey: "Study Finds TV Keeps U.S. Kids from Books," *Newark Star-Ledger* wire service, May 12, 1992.

251 Although studies seem to indicate: "Distractions of Modern Life at Key Ages Are Cited for Drop in Student Literacy," *Wall Street Journal*, October 1, 1990, p. B1.

Page
251 The parents, of course: Susan Chira, "Made in America: Asia's School Success," *New York Times*, April 26, 1992, News in Review section, p. 5.
252 For many young adolescent students: "The Dead End Kids," *Wall Street Journal*, February 9, 1990, p. R36.
253 Because the culture can exert: Scott D. Thomson, "How Much Do Americans Value Schooling?" *NASSP Bulletin*, October 1989, p. 51.

CHAPTER EIGHT

Page
255 For instance, Dr. Charles R. Snyder: Daniel Goleman, "Hope Emerges as Key to Success in Life," *New York Times*, December 25, 1991, p. C1.
257 The relationship between: Michael O'Donnell, "The Healing Powers of positive Thinking," *International Management*, April 1990, p. 72.
257 Positive thinking establishes: Carol Tavris, "Affirmative Reaction: The Power of Positive Thinking," *Vogue*, June 1988, p. 128.
257 With the onset of: Andrew J. Lothian, "Unlocking Your Full Potential," *Industrial Management and Data Systems Annual '90*, p. 16.
258 An experimental program: Fred Sedgwick, "Accentuate the Positive If You Want Results," *New York Times Educational Supplement*, January 25, 1990.
258 Children are encouraged: Cynthia Chandler and Cheryle A. Kolander, "Helping Students Accentuate Positive Thought," *Education Digest*, January 1988, p. 52.
259 Positive thinking has quietly: Paul Hellman, "Almost Heaven, Tennessee . . . ," *Management Review*, February 1991, p. 61. Richard Poe, "The Motivation Generation," *Success*, October 1990, p. 80. Seymour Epstein and Petra Meier, "Constructive Thinking: A Broad Coping Variable with Specific Components," *Journal of Personality and Social Psychology*, August 1989, p. 332.
259 The bedrock of this: Jennifer M. George, "State or Trait: Effects of Positive Mood on Prosocial Behaviors at Work," *Journal of Applied Psychology*, April 1991, p. 299.
259 The enthusiasm with which business: Ray Wise, "The Boom in Creativity Training," *Across the Board*, June 1991. Tudor Richards, "Innovation and Creativity: Woods, Trees, and Pathways," *R&D Management*, Vol. 21, No. 2, 1991. Jack Byrd, Jr., and Julie M. Smith, "Innovation Revolution: Getting Better Ideas," *Training and Development Journal*, January 1989, p. 69. Lesley Dormen, Peter Edilin, and Marjory Roberts, "Original Spin: Creativity Is NOT Just for Geniuses and Artists," *Psychology Today*, July–August 1988, p. 45. Sam Crowell, "A New Way of Thinking: A Challenge of the Future," *Educational Leadership*, September 1989, p. 60. "Last of the Great Tinkerers," *Times*, August 12, 1991, p. 55.
262 Companies are also beginning: Sue Birchmore, "Lying in Wait for an Idea," *New Scientist*, March 2, 1991, p. 60. Terry McDaniel Masters, "The Critical Thinking Workout," *Instructor*, February 1991, p. 64. Charles Brashers, "Creative Logic: The Best Route Through a Problem May Be Around It," *Executive Female*, January–February 1988. Lea Hall, "Can You Picture That?" *Training and Development Journal*, September 1990. John Cleese, "And Now for Something Completely Different," *Personnel*, April 1991, p. 13. James Bandrowski, "Taking Creative Leaps," *Planning Review*, January–February 1990. Ray Wise, "The Boom in Creativity Training," *Across the Board*, June 1991,

Page

p. 38. Dina Chancellor, "Higher Order Thinking: A Basic Skill for Everyone," *Arithmetic Teacher*, February 1991, p. 48.

262   "Companies and other organizations . . .": Roy Rowan, *The Intuitive Manager* (Boston: Little Brown, 1986).

262   Elementary and grade schools: Stephen Schneider, "A Better Way to Learn," *World Monitor*, April 1993, p. 31.

263   This sentiment is echoed: Harold J. Raveche, "21st Century Will Require Higher Level of Thinking," *Newark Star-Ledger*, April 4, 1993, p. 51.

264   A leading light: James S. Gordon: "The Inner Life," *The Atlantic*, May 1991, p. 115.

264   A recent Harvard Medical School: Priscilla Scherer, "Meditation Relieves PMS (Premenstrual Syndrome)," *American Journal of Nursing*, December 1990.

265   This mind-body connection has increasingly: "Healing and the Mind with Bill Moyers," PBS special originally shown February 22–24, 1993.

265   The sessions that Japanese: Neil Gross, "Zen and the Art of Middle Management," *Business Week*, October 15, 1990, p. 20B. Joan Connell, "Zen Finds New Path in the Silicon Valley," *Sunday Star-Ledger*, January 10, 1993, Section 3, p. 1.

265   The Pentagon has even: "Peace Shield: At the Pentagon, a New SDI," *Time*, April 25, 1988, p. 42. Alan Boyd, "Can Transcendental Meditation Make You Live Long and Prosper?" *Science*, April 30, 1990, p. 40.

265   Several ex-convicts: Jim Carlton, "For $1500 a Head, Maharishi Promises Mellower Inmates," *Wall Street Journal*, March 20, 1991, p. 1.

267   Exposure to large amounts of light: Susan Gilbert, "Harnessing the Power of Light," *The Good Health Magazine* in *New York Times*, April 26, 1992, p. 16.

269   The principle behind biofeedback: Bruce Masek, "Biofeedback," *Harvard Medical School Health Letter*, August 1990, p. 1. Laurence Miller, "What Biofeedback Does (and Doesn't) Do," *Psychology Today*, November 1989, p. 22.

270   Since 1981, of the 2000: J. Morrow and Rick Wolff, "Wired for a Miracle," *Health*, May 1991, p. 64.

271   Even the most skeptical observer: "Doctors Tell Stress Patients to Relax," *New Scientist*, January 21, 1988, p. 38. Tom O'Sullivan, "Stress and Biofeedback," *Canadian Manager*, Summer 1988, p. 16. Edward Blanchard et al., "Two Studies of the Long-Term Follow-up of Minimal Therapist Contact Treatments of Vascular and Tension Headache," *Journal of Consulting and Clinical Psychology*, June 1988. An encyclopedic recounting of the mind-body relationship can be found in Michael Murphy's *The Future of the Body* (Los Angeles: J.D. Tarcher, 1992); Murphy explores not only biofeedback but a plethora of "transformative" technologies, including hypnosis, ESP, and telekinesis.

271   In an equally startling: Eleanor Grant, "A Delicate Balance," *Psychology Today*, July–August 1988.

271   One of the more successful: J. Morrow and Rick Wolff, "Wired for a Miracle."

272   Companies have sprung: "Mind Games for the '90s," *USA Weekend*, October 1990.

273   Theorists such as Roger Penrose: "Nova" program on chess and artificial intelligence, PBS, 1990.

274   At one time, scientists; Paul M. Churchland and Patricia Smith Church-

Page

land, "Could a Machine Think?" January 1990, p. 32. David Stipp, "MIT Scientist Rethink Artificial Intelligence," *Wall Street Journal*, June 1991, p. B1. John Searle, "Is the Brain's Mind a Computer Program?" *Scientific American*, January 1990, p. 26. Robin P. Bergstrom, "Robots: What Wasn't, What Is, What Will Be," *Production*, March 1990, p. 38. Tom Steinert-Threlkeld, "Coming: A Computer That You'll Be Able to Wear," *Dallas Morning News*, September 1, 1991.

274 Computers are changing our ability: "A Whole New Way of Looking at the World," *Business Week*, November 12, 1990, p. 77. Tracy Nathan, "Computer Visualization: Changing the Way We Think," *The Futurist*, May–June 1990, p. 29.

275 Eventually, we will all: "Where Brain and Electronics Meet," *Omni*, February 1991. Edward Rothstein, "Just Some Games? Yes, But These Are Too Real," *New York Times*, April 4, 1991, p. B4. David Thornburg, "Simulations Make You Wonder What's Real Anymore," *Compute!*, November 1989, p. 71.

276 This technology for the most: John Markoff, "Art Invents a Jarring New World from Technology," *New York Times*, March 7, 1991. Andrew Pollack, "Where Electronics and Art Converge," *New York Times*, September 15, 1991, section 3, p. 1.

276 The computer is already becoming: Gurney Williams III, "Bach to the Future," *Omni*, April 1991, p. 43.

277 One of the pioneers; "All in the Wrist," *The Economist*, February 23, 1991, p. 88.

277 We are now witnessing: Michael Rogers, "Sound Bytes, Neon Dreams," *Newsweek*, November 5, 1990, p. 58.

278 Mirroring the sentiments of: Jennifer Dunning, "Dance by the Light of the Tube," *New York Times Magazine*, February 10, 1991, p. 26.

278 We may be on the verge: Bruce Masek, "Biofeedback," *Harvard Medical School Health Letter*, August 1990, p. 1.

279 The second apparatus is the Dataglove: "The Unreal Thing" (Science and Technology), *The Economist*, September 15, 1991, p. 107.

279 One of the more famous: "Virtual Reality Takes Its Place in the Real World," *New York Times*, January 1991, p. 1.

279 The effectiveness of this technology: Teresa Carpenter, "Slouching Toward Cyberspace," *Village Voice*, March 12, 1991. Phillip Elmer-Dewitt, *Time*, February 8, 1933, p. 59.

280 NASA has pioneered: Woody Hochswender, "Battles So Real They Almost Hurt," *New York Times*, March 8, 1991, p. C1.

280 In the summer of 1992, a gallery: Charles Hagen, "Virtual Reality: Is It Art Yet," *New York Times*, Arts and Leisure, July 5, 1992, p. 1.

281 One intriguing application: Michael Antonoff, "Living in a Virtual World," *Popular Science*, June 1993, p. 83.

281 According to Jaron Lanier: Howard Rheingold, *Virtual Reality* (New York: Summit Books, 1991).

282 One of the most useful: "Interview with Jaron Lanier on Virtual Reality," *Omni*, June 1991, p. 45.

282 The implications of VR's role: "Mind over Matter," *Discovery*, August 1990, p. 16.

284 Roger Nelson and Dean Radin: Dick Pothier, "Scientific Evidence of ESP Documented," Knight Ridder wire service, June 5, 1990.

Page
285 The psychokinesis experiments: Steve Fishman, "The Dean of Psi," *Omni*, February 1991, p. 42.

CHAPTER NINE
Page
288 As we probably intuit: "Frontline," program on the growth of Matsushita, PBS, February 1992.
289 Such a statement demonstrates: "A Thousand Imperfections," *The Economist*, November 11, 1988.
291 I suspect that: Teilhard de Chardin, *The Phenomenon of Man* (New York: Harper Torchbooks, 1961), originally published in French in 1955, p. 226.
294 It is only through developing: Willard Gaylin, *Adam and Eve and Pinocchio: On Being and Becoming Human* (New York: Viking, 1990).
295 One gauge of national morale: Lorne Tepperman and Hilja Laasen, "The Future of Happiness," *Paradigms of Human Development*, Special edition of *Futures*, December 1990, p. 1059. Donald L. Kanter and Philip H. Mirvis, "Cynicism: The New American Malaise," *Business and Society Review*, June 1991, p. 57.
295 However, even the countries: David S. Broder, "A Popular President, A Pessimistic Populace," Washington Post Writers Group syndication, July 14, 1991.
295 Other surveys buttress: Lance Morrow et al., "What's Happening to the American Character?" *Time*, August 2, 1991. Malcolm Ritter, "High Depression Rates Among Baby Boomers Mystify Researchers," *Health and Fitness News Service*, July 5, 1988.
295 A study performed by: Andrew Greeley, "The Declining Morale of Women," *Sociology and Social Research*, January 1989, p. 53.
296 Statistics on consumer confidence: Louis Uchitelle, "Three Decades of Dwindling Hope for Prosperity," *New York Times*, Week in Review, May 10, 1993, p. 1.
296 Commentators usually explain: "Parental Leave: Domestic Opportunity or Foreign Failure?" *The Family in America*, special report, Rockford Institute Center, June 1991. Ben Wattenburg, *The Birth Dearth: What Happens When People in Free Countries Don't Have Enough Babies?* (New York: Pharos Books, 1987). François Geinox et al., *Europe: L'Hiver Démographique* (Lausanne: L'Institut Suisse de Démographie et de Developpement aux Editions l'Age d'Homme, 1987).
296 Pessimism has a tendency: Paul Kennedy, *The Rise and Fall of Great Powers: Economic Change and Military Conflict from 1500 to 2000* (New York: Random House, 1988). Paul Kennedy, *Preparing for the Twenty-first Century* (New York: Random House, 1993). Ralph Hyatt, "Self-Esteem: The Keystone to Happiness," *USA Today*, March 10, 1991.
297 Pessimism can be: George Gilder, "Yale's Dr. Doom Looks into the Impoverished Future" (book review), *Wall Street Journal*, February 25, 1933, p. A12.
298 In a seminal article: Abraham Zaleznick, "Management Leaders: Are They Different?" *Harvard Business Review*, Vol. 55, 1977, pp. 67–78.
298 A 1992 poll: "Americans Tell Us What the Nation Needs," *Money Magazine*, August 1992, special advertising section.

Page

302   It is certainly within the realm: "Public in the Dark on Energy Issues," *The Oil Daily*, November 14, 1990, p. 1.

304   Hence, these sets of: Russell W. Belk, "My Possession, Myself: Our Sense of Self Depends Heavily on What We Possess," *Psychology Today*, July/August 1988, p. 50. Jon Lafayette, "Backer Predicts Material World," *Advertising Age*, July 24, 1989, p. 79. Stanley J. Baran et al., "You Are What You Buy: Mass-Mediated Judgments of People's Worth," *Journal of Communication*, Spring 1989, p. 46. "A Thousand Imperfections," *The Economist*, November 11, 1989, p. 40.

304   Avid materialism: Alexis de Tocqueville, *Democracy in America* (New York: Harper & Row, 1988).

305   Such thinking smacks: Robert J. Samuelson, "A Frivolous Decade? Don't Buy All the Instant History: The 1980's Were Far More Complex Than That," *Newsweek*, January 8, 1990, p. 48.

306   Nowhere do we find: Alan Durning, "Limiting Consumption: Toward a Sustainable Culture," *The Futurist*, July–August 1991, p. 11. Andrew Bard Schmookler, "The Insatiable Society: Materialistic Values and Human Needs," *The Futurist*, July–August 1991, p. 17, Charles P. Covino, "Global Materialism Threatens the Planet," *USA Today*, January 10, 1991, p. 46.

306   The media has accorded: Ronald J. Faber and Thomas C. O'Guinn, "Compulsive Consumption and Credit Abuse," *Journal of Consumer Policy*, March 1988, p. 97. Arthur Levine, "What Charlie Peters Can Learn from Jerry Brown: The Small Is Beautiful Economy," *Washington Monthly*, March 1989, p. 46. Robert Bellah, *Habits of the Heart* (Berkeley: University of California Press, 1986).

306   This extensive coverage: George Leonard, "The Case for Pleasure: More Than an End in Itself. . . ." *Esquire*, May 1989, p. 153. Janet Castro, "The Simple Life: Goodbye to Having It All," *Time*, April 8, 1991, p. 58. Duane Elgin, *Voluntary Simplicity: Toward a Way of Life That Is Outwardly Simple* (New York: Morrow, 1981). Gregory McNamee, "The Preservation of the World," *Chronicles*, July 1990, pp. 32–34.

307   In the emerging Macroindustrial Era: N. R. Kleinfield, "Seeing Dollar Signs in Searching the Stars," *New York Times*, Business section, May 15, 1988. John Wauck, "Paganism: American Style (New Age Movement)," *National Review*, March 19, 1990, p. 43. Alex Heard, "Rolfing with Yeltsin: The Society Opposition and the California Cult," *The New Republic*, October 9, 1989, p. 11. Jay Kinney, "Déja Vu: The Hidden History of the New Age," *Utne Reader*, September/October 1989, p. 109. Marilyn Ferguson, *The Aquarian Conspiracy* (Beverly Hills: Tarcher, 1980). Sophia Tarila, "A Global Outreach: Countries Around the World Have Their Different Approach to New Age, but the Appeal Is Universal," *Publishers Weekly*, December 7, 1990, p. 33.

310   This belief in the primacy: Richard N. Ostling, "When God Was Woman," *Time*, May 6, 1991, p. 73.

314   Economist George Gilder: George Gilder, *Wealth and Poverty* New York: Basic Books, 1980).

315   By the 1990s: Various articles in *Daedalus*, Fall 1990, including articles on the politics of risk, justifying risk, theories of risk perception, especially American Exceptionalism.

315   Such a climate of fear allows: Emily Yoffe, "Silence of the Frogs," *New York Times Magazine*, December 13, 1992, p. 36.

Page
316   In May 1993: Edward O. Wilson, "Is Humanity Suicidal?" *New York Times Magazine*, May 30, 1993.

317   As demographer Julian Simon: Julian Simon, *Population Matters: People, Resources, Environment, and Immigration* (New Brunswick: Transaction Books, 1990).

317   In 1989, over half of the doctorates: Susan Lee, "Train 'Em Here, Keep 'Em Here," *Forbes*, May 27, 1991, p. 110.

318   In Europe, we may observe: Alan Riding, "In Europe, Immigrants Are Needed, Not Wanted," *New York Times*, February 11, 1990.

319   The problem with such: William B. Johnston, "Global Work Force 2000: The New World Labor Market," *Harvard Business Review*, March–April 1991, p. 124.

319   A progressive attitude toward: Samuel Francis, "The Middle Class Moment," *Chronicles*, March 1992, pp. 12–13. Donna Harrington Lueker, "Demography as Destiny: Immigration and Schools" (from the *American School Board Journal*), *Educational Digest*, January 1991, p. 3. "Transnational America (Multiculture and Education in the American Society)," *The New York Review of Books*, November 22, 1990, p. 18. Bruce W. Nelan, "Racism," *Time*, August 12, 1991. Ira H. Mehlman, "Mixing Oil and Water: The Common Problems of Assimilating Immigrants in Israel and the United States," *Chronicles*, March 1990, p. 80. Thomas Fleming, "The Real American Dilemma," *Chronicles*, March 1990, pp. 8–11. "The Pros and Cons of Immigration: A Debate," *Chronicles*, July 1990, pp. 14–19.

320   Now it is projected: "Census Bureau Lifts Population Forecast, Citing Fertility, Immigration, Longevity," *Wall Street Journal*, December 20, 1992, p. B1.

322   Little doubt exists: Richard Brookhiser, *The Way of the Wasp* (New York: Free Press, 1991). Robert C. Christopher, *Crashing the Gates: The DeWASPing of America's Power Elite* (New York: Simon & Schuster, 1990). William Henry III, "Beyond the Melting Pot," *Time*, April 9, 1990, p. 28. Arifin Bey, "Multiculturalism in a Global Village: What Japan Can Learn from the American Experience," *Futures*, August 1989, p. 366.

323   This means that: Diane Crane, "Immigration Impact Grow on U.S. Population," *Wall Street Journal*, p. B1, extracted from *American Demographics*, March 20, 1992.

327   Social critic Stanton Peele: Stanton Peele, *The Diseasing of America: Addiction Treatment Out of Control* (Lexington, MA: Lexington Books, 1989).

328   Individual freedom can also: David Bellin, "Is Big Brother Watching Your Computer?" (letter to the editor), *New York Times*, April 8, 1992.

328   This loss of privacy again: Katie Haffner and Susan Garland, "Privacy," *Business Week*, March 28, 1988.

329   For instance, a musical subculture: "Laurie Anderson Sings the Body Electric," *New York Times*, October 1, 1989, p. 1.

330   According to a very: Terry Wood, "More Than Just Another Musical Genre, New Age Has Affected Baby Boomers," *Billboard*, October 29, 1990, p. 11.

330   Increasingly, we will see: "Yamaha Music Sequencer" (Innovation), *Fortune*, May 25, 1991. Also, "Making Your Own Music," *The Futurist*, September–October 1991, p. 5

Page

CHAPTER TEN

Page

333 These low-growth rates: Thomas Kamm, "Chile's Economy Roars as Exports Take Off in a Post-Pinochet Era," *Wall Street Journal*, January 5, 1993, p. 1.

337 The West has exhibited: "India angry the U.S. pressured Russia into canceling rocket deal," *Washington Post* Wire Service, July 18, 1993.

338 The U.S. and other leading societies: Thomas Fleming, "Peace on Earth Among Men of Good Will," *Chronicles*, February 1990, p. 17.

339 In short, this program would: R. Cort Kirkwood, "Missionaries for Democracy," *Chronicles*, March 1990, pp. 22–25. Jim Fisher-Thompson, "Sociologist Runs Capital Market Workshops for Poles," United States Information Agency staff writer, February 1990.

341 On the other hand: Jacqueline Kasun, *The War Against Population* (San Francisco: Ignatius Press, 1988). Phillip Elmer-DeWitt, "Why Isn't Our Birth Control Better?" *Time*, August 12, 1991, p. 52.

342 One such program: Joan Beck, "Feeding Hungry, Young Minds," Chicago Tribune syndicated column.

343 Corporations and other employers: Pamela Weintraub, "Challenge and Response: Business Management in the 21st Century," *Omni*, January 1991. Marvin Cetron, "Retiring Baby Boomers: Technological Marvels Will Enhance Life for Tomorrow's Aged," *Omni*, January 1991, p. 8. Peter A. Morrison, "Applied Demography," *The Futurist*, March–April 1990.

345 What universities and high schools: Philip G. Altback, "Needed: An International Perspective," *Phi Delta Kappan*, November 1989, p. 243. Victor J. Mayer, "Teaching from the Global Point of View," *The Science Teacher*, January 1990, p. 247.

347 Science and educational institutions: Glenn Rifkin, "Inventing Heroes for the 21st Century," *New York Times*, February 14, 1993, Business section, p. 10.

347 Other groups have similar plans: Kitta MacPherson, "Action Plan Aims to Reinvigorate U.S. Industry," *Newark Star-Ledger*, October 12, 1992.

350 The political system must: David Rogers and Rick Wartzman, "Clinton's People: President's Team Is Elite Crew Addressing Common Many's Woes," *Wall Street Journal*, January 21, 1993, p. 1.

351 However, extensive negativity: Georgia Anne Geyer, "American 'Culture' Is a Disease, Not a Liberator" (column), March 17, 1992.

354 What bills itself as environmentalism: Robert H. Nelson, "Tom Hayden, Meet Adam Smith and Thomas Aquinas," *Forbes*, October 29, 1990, pp. 94–95.

355 In 1992, the United Nations Conference: "Rio Eco-Fest: Big Problems Await Leaders at Summit," *Wall Street Journal*, May 29, 1992, p. 1.

355 The impetus for holding: Damien Lewis and Frank Nowikowski, "Saving Earth, Dividing Earthlings," Gemini News Service, London, August 1991.

356 A quick review of the organizers: Frank Edward Allen, "Earth Movers: Five Who Will Shape the Course of the Rio Conference," *Wall Street Journal*, June 1992, p. 23.

356 Gore betrays a deep distrust: Fred L. Smith, "Al Gore, Reactionary Environmentalist," *Wall Street Journal*, July 17, 1992, p. A23.

357 An early indication: Review of Von Roll controversy from several *Wall Street Journal* editorials, including "Environmental Preview?" December 30,

Page
1992; "Gore on a Von Roll," January 19, 1993. Michael Fumento, "Clinton's Cabinet Gets Greener," *Investor's Business Daily*, December 28, 1992.

357   Greenpeace's impact: Timothy Noah, "EPA Unveils Plans to Curb Incinerators of Hazardous Waste by Blocking Growth," *Wall Street Journal*, May 19, 1993.

357   Gore spent much of 1993: Holman Jenkins, Jr., "Al Gore Leads a Purge," *Wall Street Journal*, May 25, 1993.

359   Charles, who fancies himself: Statement by Prince Charles, *New York Times*, Special advertising section, "To Save the Planet," June 7, 1992.

359   One can only admire: Laura Bly, "For hotels, it's not easy being green," *Newark Star-Ledger*, July 18, 1993, section 8, p. 7.

359   The power company announced: Art Kleiner, "Two Times a Hero," *Popular Science*, July 1992, p. 76.

360   The list goes on: Robert H. Hogner, "Environmentalists Lock Up Canal Development," *Corporations and the Environment: Greening or Preening?*, special issue of *Business and Society Review*, Fall 1990, pp. 74–77. Woody Hochswender, "The Green Movement in the Fashion World," *New York Times*, March 25, 1990.

360   As we learned, the media: Keith Schneider, "Environmental Fight in Prime Time," *New York Times*, August 15, 1992, News in Review section, p. 1.

361   This side of the: Yankelovich survey of 500 adults in United States, January 1992. Charles P. Alexander, "Gunning for the Greens," *Times*, February 3, 1992, p. 50.

361   It is clear that: "Gore's Tattered Green Flag" (editorial), *Wall Street Journal*, November 10, 1992.

363   Science is certainly: Keith Schneider, "Environmental Fight in Prime Time." Gregg Easterbrook, "A House of Cards," *Newsweek*, June 1, 1992. In that issue, other rejoinders to the doom and gloom arguments regarding global warming: "Is It Apocalypse Now?" by Sharon Begley; "The End Is Not at Hand" by Robert Samuelson.

363   Businesses in states: Scott J. Parker, "Trenton Must Help on Clean Air Rules" (letter to the editor), *Newark Star-Ledger*, August 1, 1992.

363   Businesses are beginning: Scott McMurray, "Air-Conditioner Firms Put Chill on Plans to Phase Out Use of Chlorofluorocarbons," *Wall Street Journal*, May 10, 1993, p. B1.

364   By mid-1993: David Stipp, "Some Utilities' Plans to Cut Energy Use Cost More and Save Less than Projected," *Wall Street Journal*, May 27, 1993, p. B1.

366   Certainly, by the early 1990s: Ronald Bailey, *Eco-Scam: The False Prophets of Ecological Apocalypse* (New York: St. Martin's, 1993). Michael Fumento, *Science Under Siege* (New York: Morrow, 1993).

Index

About the Author

Sociologist Michael G. Zey is an internationally recognized expert on the economy, society, and management, and author of several books including *The Mentor Connection* and *Winning with People*. He consults to such major corporations as NCR, Inc., Hoechst-Celanese Inc., and the Legent Corporation. Dr. Zey appears frequently on radio and television programs and makes regular public presentations before corporate groups and university audiences.

His ideas and articles on societal trends and management have appeared in such diverse publications as *Computer Decisions, Success, The Wall Street Journal, Forbes, Training and Development,* and *Investor's Daily*.

Zey holds a Ph.D. in sociology from Rutgers University, and is a management professor in the School of Business Administration at Montclair State, Upper Montclair, New Jersey. He is executive director of the Expansionary Institute, Morristown, New Jersey.